BEHAVIOR SCIENCE BIBLIOGRAPHIES

WEST MALAYSIA AND SINGAPORE: A SELECTED BIBLIOGRAPHY

by

Karl J. Pelzer

HUMAN RELATIONS AREA FILES PRESS

New Haven

1971

243158

Library of Congress Catalog Card Number: 72-87853
ISBN   0-87536-235-4

Printed in the United States of America

CONTENTS

CONTENTS (Continued)

PREFACE

This bibliography is intended to serve as reference and reading list for students of the Behavioral Sciences (Anthropology, Economics, Geography, Political Science and Sociology) as well as History and the Natural Sciences (Biology, Climatology, Geology, Geomorphology, and Soil Science) of West Malaysia and the Republic of Singapore.

This is a revised and greatly expanded edition of a volume originally entitled _Selected Bibliography on the Geography of Southeast Asia: Part III, Malaya._ The new title is due to changes in the structure of the Federation of Malaya which became Western Malaysia with the incorporation of Sarawak and Sabah in 1963, but separated from Singapore in 1965. Sarawak and Sabah form Eastern Malaysia.

The author wishes to acknowledge the invaluable aid of Mr. Beda Lim, Librarian of the University of Malaya, and of Miss S. Devey, Librarian of the Economic Planning Unit, Prime Minister's Department, Kuala Lumpur.

Karl J. Pelzer
New Haven, Conn.

KARL J. PELZER is Professor of Geography and Director, Southeast Asia Studies, at Yale University. He received his Ph.D. in Geography at the University of Bonn (1935) and is the author of: _Pioneer Settlement in the Asiatic Tropics_ (1945) and _Population and Land Utilization_ (1941). He was a Fulbright research professor in the Philippines in 1950 and a Ford fellow in Indonesia, 1955-1956. His present book, a complete revision of the 1956 _Selected Bibliography on the Geography of Southeast Asia: Part III, Malaya_, was prepared during the course of his recent year of research in Malaysia.

PUBLISHER'S NOTE

    This bibliography has been produced by an application of the HRAF Automated Bibliographic System (HABS). The bibliographic entries have been keypunched, and page copies printed on an IBM 870 Document Writing System. The bibliography has been edited and organized to conform to the HABS standardized, machine-readable format.

CHAPTER 1

PERIODICALS AND CONFERENCE PROCEEDINGS CITED

Periodicals and conference proceedings cited in the
bibliography are listed below. The abbreviations used are
given in the left-hand column.

	Age (Melbourne)
	Agricultura e Pecuaria (Rio de Janeiro)
	Agricultural Bulletin of the Straits and Federated Malay States (Singapore)
Akademische M	Akademische Mitteilungen (Heidelberg)
	Alpine Journal (London)
	Amerasia (New York)
Am Anthr	American Anthropologist (Washington, D.C., etc.)
	American Geophysical Union, Transactions (Washington, D.C.)
Am Jl Sci	American Journal of Science (New Haven, Conn.)
Am Jl Sociol	American Journal of Sociology (Chicago)
AUFS-SEA	American Universities Field Staff, Reports Service, Southeast Asia Series (New York)
Ann Propag Foi	Annales de la Propagation de la Foi (Lyons)
Ann Am Ac Pol Soc Sc	Annals of the American Academy of Political and Social Science (Philadelphia)
Annals	Annals of the Association of American Geographers (Albany, N.Y./Lancaster, Pa.)

1

PERIODICALS AND CONFERENCE PROCEEDINGS CITED

Annual Bib Ind Arch

Annual Bibliography of
Indian Archaeology (Leyden)

Annual Report of the Institute
for Medical Research
(Kuala Lumpur)

Anthr Pap Am Mus
Nat Hist

Anthropological Papers of
the American Museum of
Natural History (New York)

Anthropological Society
(Bombay)

L'Anthr

L'Anthropologie (Paris)

Anthr Praha

Anthropologie (Prague)

Anthropos (St. Gabriel-Moedling,
Vienna, etc.)

Ar Rubbercult Ned en
Ned Ind

Archief voor de Rubbercultuur
in Nederland en Nederlandsch
Indië (Buitenzorg)

Ar Anthr

Archiv für Anthropologie
und Völkerforschung (Brunswick)

Archiv für Eisenbahnwesen
(Berlin)

Ar Rassenbilder

Archiv für Rassenbilder
(München)

Ar Relig

Archiv für Religionswissenschaft
(Leipzig)

Ar Disease Childhood

Archives of Disease in
Childhood (London)

Ar Miss Sc Lit

Archives des Missions Scientifiques
et Litteraires (Paris)

Archives de Sociologie
des Religions (Paris)

PERIODICALS AND CONFERENCE PROCEEDINGS CITED

Army Quarterly (London)

Asia (New York)

Asia and the Americas (New York)

Asian Horizon (London)

AP   Asian Perspectives (Hong Kong)

AR   Asian Review (London)

Asian Studies (Manila)

AS   Asian Survey (Berkeley)

As Col Q Jl   Asiatic and Colonial Quarterly Journal (London)

Asiatic Researches (Calcutta)

Asiatic Review (London)

Atlantis: Länder, Völker, Reisen

Aussenpolitik (Stuttgart)

Austral-Asiatic Bulletin (Melbourne)

Australian Geographer (Sydney)

Australian Journal of Politics and History (Brisbane)

Australian Outlook (Melbourne)

Australian Planning Institute Journal (Sydney)

Australian Quarterly (Sydney)

Behavior Science Notes (New Haven, Conn.)

3

	Beihefte Tropenpflanzer (Berlin)
	Benih (Singapore)
	Berita Mara (Kuala Lumpur)
BTLV	Bijdragen tot de Taal- Land- en Volken-kunde van Nederlandsch Indie (The Hague)
	Blackwood's Magazine (Edinburgh)
	Blumea (Leyden)
	Board of Trade Journal (London)
Br Mal	British Malaya (London)
	British Medical Association, Malayan Branch, Journal (Singapore)
B Assoc Fran Amis Or	Bulletin de l'Association Française des Amis de l'Orient (Paris)
Bull Colonisation Comparée	Bulletin de Colonisation Comparée, published by Ministry of Colonies, Belgium (Brussels)
B Comm Arch Indoch	Bulletin de la Commission Archéologique de l'Indochine (Paris)
BEFEO	Bulletin de l'Ecole Française d'Extrême-Orient (Hanoi)
	Bulletin Economique de l'Indochine (Saigon)
B Imperial Inst	Bulletin of the Imperial Institute (London)

PERIODICALS AND CONFERENCE PROCEEDINGS CITED

B Inter News	Bulletin of International News (London)
	Bulletin of the National Museum, State of Singapore (Singapore)
BRM	Bulletin of the Raffles Museum (Singapore)
BRM Ser B	Bulletin of the Raffles Museum, Series B (Singapore)
B Rubber Growers' Assoc	Bulletin of the Rubber Growers' Association (London)
BSOAS	Bulletin of the School of Oriental and African Studies (London)
Bull Sc Soc Malay	Bulletin of the Science Society of Malaya (Singapore)
B Soc d'Anthr	Bulletin de la Société d'Anthropologie de Bordeaux et du Sud-Ouest (Bordeaux)
BSEI	Bulletin de la Société des Etudes Indochinoises de Saigon (Saigon)
B Soc G Paris	Bulletin de la Société de Géographie de Paris (Paris)
B Soc Normande G	Bulletin de la Société Normande de Géographie (Rouen)
	Cambridge Journal (Cambridge, England)
Can G Jl	Canadian Geographical Journal (Ottowa)

PERIODICALS AND CONFERENCE PROCEEDINGS CITED

Ceylon R Bot Gdns	Ceylon Royal Botanical Gardens, Annals (Peradeniya)
	Chambers's Journal (Edinburgh/London)
CQ	China Quarterly (Shanghai)
	China Weekly Review (Shanghai)
	Chinese Repository (Canton/Hong Kong)
	Ciba Symposia (Summit, N.J.)
Ciba Z	Ciba Zeitschrift (Basel)
	Civilisations (Brussels)
Col Rev	Colonial Review (London)
	Commerce (Singapore)
	Commonwealth Survey (London)
	Community Development Bulletin (London)
	Comparative Studies in Society and History (The Hague)
CR Cong Int G	Comptes Rendus du Congrès International de Géographie
	Contemporary Review (London)
	Corona (London)
	Correspondenz-Blatt der Deutschen Gesellschaft für Anthropologie, Ethnologie und Urgeschichte (Braunschweig, etc.)
	Crown Colonist (London)

	Cultureel Indië (Leyden)
	Current History (New York)
	Current Sociology (Oxford)
	Dalhousie Review (Halifax)
	Deutsche Aussenpolitik (Berlin)
	Developing Economies (Tokyo)
	Dublin Review (London)
	East Asian Cultural Studies (Tokyo)
	Eastern Economist (New Delhi)
	Eastern Horizon (Hong Kong)
	Eastern World (London)
	Economic Bulletin for Asia and the Far East (New York)
EDCC	Economic Development and Cultural Change (Chicago)
Ec G	Economic Geography (Worcester, Mass.)
Ec Jl	Economic Journal (London/New York)
	Economic Record (Melbourne)
	Economic Survey (London)
	Economica (London)
Ec Weekbl Ned Ind	Economisch Weekblad voor Nederlandsch-Indie (Batavia)
	Economist (London)
	Editorial Research Reports (Washington, D.C.)

Ekistics (Athens)

Ekonomi (Kuala Lumpur)

Empire Forestry Journal (London)

Empire Forestry Review (London)

Empire Journal of Experimental Agriculture (Oxford)

Empire Review (London)

Endeavour (London)

Engineering Assoc of Malaya Jl — Engineering Association of Malaya, Journal (Kuala Lumpur)

Erdball (Berlin)

Erde — Erde: Zeitschrift der Gesellschaft für Erdkunde zu Berlin

Erdkunde (Bonn)

Ethn Anzgr — Ethnologischer Anzeiger (Stuttgart)

Ethnos (Stockholm)

Etudes (Paris)

Export (London)

Far Eastern Association of Tropical Medicine, Transactions (Singapore/Wettevreden)

FEER — Far Eastern Economic Review (Hongkong)

FEQ — Far Eastern Quarterly (Lancaster, Pa.)

Far Eastern Review (Shanghai)

PERIODICALS AND CONFERENCE PROCEEDINGS CITED

FES	Far Eastern Survey (New York)
	Farm Management Notes, Asia Far East (Bangkok)
	Federal Publications (Kuala Lumpur)
FMJ	Federation Museums Journal (Kuala Lumpur)
	Folklore (London)
	Food (San Francisco)
FA	Foreign Affairs (New York)
	Foreign Affairs Reports (New Delhi)
For Ag	Foreign Agriculture (Washington, D.C.)
For Policy Bul	Foreign Policy Bulletin (New York)
For Policy Reports	Foreign Policy Reports (New York)
	Foreign Trade (Ottawa)
Fortnightly Rev	Fortnightly Review (London)
	Fraser's Magazine (London)
	Garden Cities and Town Planning (London)
	Gardens' Bulletin (Singapore)
G Tid	Geografisk Tidsskrift (Copenhagen)
	Geographia (St. Ouen, France)
	Geographica (Geographical Society, University of Malaya, Kuala Lumpur)

9

PERIODICALS AND CONFERENCE PROCEEDINGS CITED

G Jl	Geographical Journal (London)
GM	Geographical Magazine (London)
GR	Geographical Review (New York)
La G	La Geographie (Paris)
	Geographische Rundschau (Braunschweig)
	Geographisches Jahrbuch (Gotha)
G	Geography (London)
Geol Mag	Geological Magazine (London)
	Geologie en Mijnbouw (The Hague)
Geol Jber	Geologische Jahresberichte (Berlin)
	De Gids (Amsterdam)
	Globus (Hildburghausen)
	Gordian (Hamburg)
	Great Britain and the East (London)
	Harper's Monthly Magazine (New York)
	Health and Empire (London)
	Hemisphere (Sydney)
	Historical Journal (Singapore)
	History (London)
	History Today (London)
	Home Geographic Monthly (Worcester, Mass.)

L'Homme: Journal Illustré
des Sciences Anthropologiques
(Paris)

Hydroelectric Technical
Memorandum (Kuala Lumpur)

Illus Lond News   Illustrated London News
(London)

Imago Mundi (Leiden)

India Q   India Quarterly (New Delhi)

Indian Antiquary (Bombay)

Indian Archives (New Delhi)

Indian Art and Letters
(London)

Indian Forester (Allahabad/Calcutta)

Indian Journal of Public
Administration (New Delhi)

Ind Rev   Indian Review (Madras)

Indo-Asian Culture (New Delhi)

Indo-Chinese Gleaner (Malacca)

Indonesië (The Hague)

Industrial and Labor Relations
Review (Ithaca)

Industrial and Labour Information
(Geneva)

Industry and Labour (Geneva)

Information (New York)

Institute for Medical Research,
Annual Report (Kuala Lumpur)

	Institute for Medical Research, Bulletin (Kuala Lumpur)
	Institute for Medical Research, Studies (Kuala Lumpur/Singapore)
	Institute of Mining and Metallurgy, Transactions (London)
Inter Aff	International Affairs (London)
Int Comp Law Q	International and Comparative Law Quarterly (London)
Int Cong Trop Ag	International Congress of Tropical Agriculture, Proceedings (London)
Int Jl	International Journal (Toronto)
	International Journal of Adult and Youth Education (Paris)
Int Labour Rev	International Labour Review (Geneva)
Int Rev Ag	International Review of Agriculture (Rome)
Int Rev Missions	International Review of Missions (Edinburgh)
Int Rice Comm News Letter	International Rice Commission News Letter (London)
	Inter-ocean (Weltevreden)
	Intisari (Singapore, Malaysian Sociological Research Institute)
	Islamic Review (Woking, Surrey)
	Jorden Runt (Stockholm)

	Journal of Abnormal and Social Psychology (Washington, D.C.)
Jl Af Ad	Journal of African Administration (London)
Jl Anthr Inst	Journal of the Anthropological Institute (London)
Jl Applied Soc	Journal of Applied Sociology (Los Angeles)
	Journal of Asian and African Studies (Tokyo)
JAS	Journal of Asian Studies (Ann Arbor)
Jl Burma Research Soc	Journal of the Burma Research Society (Rangoon)
	Journal of Commonwealth Political Studies (Leicester)
	Journal of Comparative Legislation and International Law (London)
Jl Ecology	Journal of Ecology (London/Cambridge)
Jl Ethn Soc	Journal of the Ethnological Society (London)
JFMSM	Journal of the Federated Malay States Museums (Singapore)
Jl G	Journal of Geography (Lancaster, Pa.)
Jl G, Tokyo G Soc	Journal of Geography, Tokyo Geographical Society
Jl Geol	Journal of Geology (Chicago)
Jl Greater India Soc	Journal of the Greater India Society (Calcutta)

JHS	Journal of the Historical Society, University of Malaya (Kuala Lumpur)
Jl Ind Archip	Journal of the Indian Archipelago and Eastern Asia (Singapore)
	Journal of the Indian Geographical Association (Madras)
	Journal of Local Administration Overseas (London)
Jl Malayan Branch British Medical Ass	Journal of the Malayan Branch of the British Medical Association (Singapore)
Jl Manchester G Soc	Journal of the Manchester Geographical Society (Manchester)
JPHS	Journal of the Pakistan Historical Society (Karachi)
Jl Politics	Journal of Politics (Gainesville, Fla.)
Jl Polyn Soc	Journal of the Polynesian Society (Wellington)
Jl Proc As Soc Bengal	Journal and Proceedings of the Royal Asiatic Society of Bengal (Calcutta)
Jl R Anthr Inst	Journal of the Royal Anthropological Institute of Great Britain and Ireland (London)
Jl R Anthr Soc Bombay	Journal of the Royal Anthropological Society of Bombay
JRAS (or JRAS Gr B and I)	Journal of the Royal Asiatic Society of Great Britain and Ireland (London)
JRASMB	Journal of the Royal Asiatic Society of Great Britain and Ireland, Malayan Branch (Singapore)

PERIODICALS AND CONFERENCE PROCEEDINGS CITED

JRASNCB	Journal of the Royal Asiatic Society of Great Britain and Ireland, North-China Branch (Shanghai)
JRASSB	Journal of the Royal Asiatic Society of Great Britain and Ireland, Straits Branch (Singapore)
JRCAS	Journal of the Royal Central Asian Society (London)
Jl R G Soc	Journal of the Royal Geographical Society (London)
Jl R Inst Int Affairs	Journal of the Royal Institute of International Affairs (London)
Jl R Soc Arts	Journal of the Royal Society of Arts (London)
Jl R United Service Inst	Journal of the Royal United Service Institute (London)
JRRIM	Journal of the Rubber Research Institute of Malaya (Kuala Lumpur)
Jl Soil Sc	Journal of Soil Science (New Brunswick, N.J.)
JSAH	Journal of Southeast Asian History (Singapore)
	Journal of Southeast Asian Researches (Singapore)
SSS	Journal of the South Seas Society (Singapore)
JTAM	Journal of the Technical Association of Malaya/Malaysia (Kuala Lumpur)
	Journal of Town Planning Institute (Singapore)

JTG   Journal of Tropical Geography
                             (Singapore/Kuala Lumpur)

                             Journal of Tropical Pediatrics
                             and African Child Health
                             (London)

KEM   Kajian Ekonomi Malaysia
                             (Kuala Lumpur)

                             Kedah dari Segi Sejarah--Kedah
                             in History (Alor Star)

Kol St   Koloniale Studien (Weltevreden)

                             Kolonialforstliche Mitteilungen
                             (Tharandt - Dresden)

Labor Ind Brit   Labor and Industry in Britain
                             (New York)

                             Landbouw (Buitenzorg)

                             Library Association of
                             Malaya and Singapore,
                             Newsletter (Singapore)

                             Library Association Record
                             (London)

                             Lloyd Bank Review (London)

                             Majallah Perpustakaan
                             Singapura/Singapore Library
                             Journal (Singapore)

                             Majilis Amanah Ra'ayat
                             Malaysia (Kuala Lumpur)

                             Malaya (London)

                             Malaya. See also Federated
                             Museums Journal, Journal
                             of the Federated Malay
                             States Museums

                             Malaya, Forest Department.
                             Annual Reports (Kuala Lumpur)

Malaya, Forest Department.
Malayan Forest Records
(Kuala Lumpur/Singapore)

MH   Malaya in History (Kuala Lumpur)

Malaya, Information Department.
Fortnightly Press Digest
(Kuala Lumpur)

Malaya, Information Department.
Weekly News Summary (Kuala Lumpur)

Malaya Law Review (Singapore)

Mal Ag Jl   Malayan Agricultural Journal
(Singapore); also Malaysian
Agricultural Journal
(Kuala Lumpur)

Mal Ag   Malayan Agriculturalist
(Kuala Lumpur)

MER   Malayan Economic Review
(Singapore)

Mal For   Malayan Forester (Kuala Lumpur)

MHJ   Malayan Historical Journal
(Kuala Lumpur)

MJTG   Malayan Journal of Tropical
Geography (Singapore)

Malayan Law Journal (Singapore)

Malayan Library Group Newsletter
(Singapore)

Malayan Library Journal
(Kuala Lumpur)

Malayan Management Review
(Kuala Lumpur)

Mal Med Jl   Malayan Medical Journal
(Singapore)

Malayan Naturalist (Singapore)

Mal Nature Jl   Malayan Nature Journal
(Kuala Lumpur)

Malayan Review (Singapore)

Malayan Shell (Singapore)

Malaysia in History (Kuala Lumpur)

Mal Ag Jl   Malaysian Agricultural
Journal (Kuala Lumpur);
also Malayan Agricultural
Journal (Singapore)

Malaysian Journal of Education
(Singapore)

Malaysian Management Review
(Kuala Lumpur)

Man (London)

Medical Journal of Malaya
(Singapore)

Memoirs Mal Met   Memoirs of the Malayan
Service   Meteorological Service
(Singapore)

Mens en Maatschappij (Amsterdam)

Metallhüttenbetriebe (Halle)

Met Abst Bibliog   Meteorological Abstracts
and Bibliography (Lancaster, Pa.)

Met Mag   Meteorological Magazine
(London)

Michigan Ac Sc, Arts   Michigan Academy of Science,
Arts and Letters
(New York/Ann Arbor)

Middle East Journal
(Washington, D.C.)

Military Review (London)

Mineral Trade Notes
(Washington, D.C.)

Minerals (Kuala Lumpur)

Mining Engineering (London)

Mining Journal (London)

Missionary Research Library,
Occasional Bulletin (New York)

Missionary Review of the
World (Sydney)

Mitt Anthr Ges in Wien	Mitteilungen, Anthropologische Gesellschaft in Wien
Mitt G Ges Hamburg	Mitteilungen, Geographische Gesellschaft in Hamburg
Mitt G Ges München	Mitteilungen, Geographische Gesellschaft in München
Mitt G Ges Wien	Mitteilungen, Geographische Gesellschaft in Wien (Vienna)
Mitt Ö G Ges	Mitteilungen der Österreichischen Geographischen Gesellschaft (Wien)
MAS	Modern Asian Studies (London)

Modern Review (Calcutta)

Il Mondo (Rome)

Monodo (Stockholm)

Monthly Labor Rev	Monthly Labor Review (Washington, D.C.)

Moslem World (New York/London)

National Electricity Board
of the States of Malaya.
Annual Report (Kuala Lumpur)

Nat G Mag   National Geographic Magazine
(Washington, D.C.)

National Museum, Singapore.
Bulletin (Singapore)

National Museum, Singapore.
Memoirs (Singapore)

National Review (London)

NRN   Natural Rubber News
(Washington, D.C.)

Nature (London)

NTNI   Natuurkundig Tijdschrift
voor Nederlandsch-Indie
(Batavia)

Neue Ordnung (Vienna)

Neue Pflug

Neue Zeitschrift für
Missionswissenschaft (Beckenried)

New Commonwealth (London)

New Leader (London)

New Republic (New York)

New Statesman (London)

NY Times Mag   New York Times Magazine
(New York)

New Zealand Geographer
(Christchurch)

Newsweek (Dayton, Ohio)

	Nineteenth Century and After (London)
	Nouvelles Annales des Voyages (Paris)
	Oceania (Melbourne)
	Opinion (Montreal)
OG	Oriental Geographer (Dacca, E. Pakistan)
Overseas Ed	Overseas Education (London)
PA	Pacific Affairs (New York)
Pacific Historical Rev	Pacific Historical Review (Los Angeles)
PV	Pacific Viewpoint (Wellington)
	Pahang Planters' Association. Year Book (Kuala Lumpur)
	Papua and New Guinea Agricultural Journal (Port Moresby)
PS	Peninjau Sejarah (Kuala Lumpur)
	Perak Museum Notes (Taiping)
	Perpustakaan Malaysia (Singapore)
PM	Petermanns Geographische Mitteilungen (Gotha)
	Philippine Economic Journal (Manila)
	Philippine Journal of Education (Manila)
	Planning Outlook (Newscastle on Tyne)
	Planter (Kuala Lumpur)

Planters' Association of Malaya.
Annual Report (Kuala Lumpur)

Planters' Bulletin. See Rubber
Research Institute of Malaya,
Planters' Bulletin.

Political Quarterly (Edinburgh)

Politique Etrangère (Paris)

Population (Paris)

Population Review (Madras)

Population Studies (Cambridge)

Preussische Jahrbücher
(Berlin)

Prim Man	Primitive Man (Washington, D.C.)
Proc Br Emp For Conf	Proceedings of the British Empire Forestry Conference
Proc Conf World Land Tenure Prob	Proceedings of the Conference on World Tenure Problems
PCPE	Proceedings of the Congress of Prehistorians of the Far East
PPSC	Proceedings of the Pacific Science Congress
Proc Prehist Soc	Proceedings of the Prehistoric Society (London)
Proc R Col Inst	Proceedings of the Royal Colonial Institute (London)
Proc R Entom Soc	Proceedings of the Royal Entomological Society (London)
Proc R G Soc	Proceedings of the Royal Geographical Society (London)

Q Jl Geol Soc London	Quarterly Journal of the Geological Society of London (London)
Q Jl R Met Soc	Quarterly Journal of the Royal Meteorological Society (London)
	Quarterly Review (London)
Queen's Q	Queen's Quarterly (Kingston)
	Raffles Museum. See also Bulletin of the Raffles Museum.
	Raffles Museum, Singapore. Memoirs (Singapore)
	Railway Magazine (London)
	Religions (London)
Rep Br Assoc Sc	Report of the British Association for the Advancement of Science (London)
	Reporter (New York)
	Review of Agricultural Economics, Malaysia (Kuala Lumpur)
Rev Int Co-op	Review of International Co-operation (London)
Rev Bot Appl et Ag Trop	Revue de Botanique Appliquée et d'Agriculture Tropicale (Paris)
	Revue des Deux Mondes (Paris)
Rev d'Ethn	Revue d'Ethnographie (Paris)
Rev Gen du Caoutchouc	Revue Generale du Caoutchouc (Paris)
Rev G	Revue de Géographie (Paris)

PERIODICALS AND CONFERENCE PROCEEDINGS CITED

Rev Monde Musul   Revue du Monde Musulman
(Paris)

Rev Pacifique   Revue du Pacifique (Paris)

Revue du Sud-est Asiatique
(Brussels)

Round Table (London)

Royal Asiatic Society of Great
Britain and Ireland, Malayan
Branch (Singapore). See also
Journal of the Royal Asiatic
Society of Great Britain
and Ireland.

R Engineers Jl   Royal Engineers Journal
(London)

Royal Sanitary Institute
Journal (London)

Royal Society of Tropical
Medicine and Hygiene
(London)

R United Service   Royal United Service Institute
Inst Jl   Journal (London)

Rubber and Agriculture
Series Bulletin (London)

Rubber India (Bombay)

Rubber Industry Bulletin
(New York)

RRIM   Rubber Research Institute of
Malaya. See also Journal of the
Rubber Research Institute of Malaya

RRIMB   Rubber Research Institute of
Malaya, Bulletin (Kuala Lumpur)

Rubber Research Institute of
Malaya, Journal (Kuala Lumpur)

PERIODICALS AND CONFERENCE PROCEEDINGS CITED

RRIMPB   Rubber Research Institute
of Malaya, Planters'
Bulletin (Kuala Lumpur)

SMJ   Sarawak Museum Journal
(Kuching)

Sat Even Post   Saturday Evening Post
(Philadelphia)

SGM   Scottish Geographical Magazine
(Edinburgh)

                           Seed (Singapore)

Selangor Jl   Selangor Journal (Kuala Lumpur)

                           Selangor Planters' Association.
Annual Report (Kuala Lumpur)

                           Semaine d'Ethnologie Religieuse
(Enghiem)

                           Servant of India (Poona)

                           Singapore Library Journal
(Singapore)

                           Singapore Library Journal.
See Majallah Perpustakaan
Singapura.

Sinica Mitt   Sinica Mitteilungen (Frankfurt)

                           Sociology and Social Research
(Los Angeles)

                           Society of Comparative
Legislation (London)

                           Soil Science (New Brunswick, N.J.)

                           South Atlantic Quarterly
(Durham, N.C.)

SSS   South Seas Society, Journal
(Singapore)

PERIODICALS AND CONFERENCE PROCEEDINGS CITED

SE Asia Rev   Southeast Asia Review (Bangkok)

SAS   Southeast Asian Studies (Kyoto)

Southern Economic Journal (Chapel Hill, N.C.)

SWJA   Southwestern Journal of Anthropology (Santa Fe, N.M.)

Soviet Press Translations (Seattle, Wash.)

Spectator (London)

Star Weekly (Toronto)

Strasse (Berlin)

Studies on Asia (Lincoln, Neb.)

Suara Mahasiswa PBMUN (Kuala Lumpur)

Synd Exp Franc Indochine Bul   Syndicat des Exporteurs Français d'Indochine, Bulletin (Paris)

Tamil Culture (Madras)

Tanah Melayu dari segi Sejarah/Malaya in History (Kuala Lumpur)

Technical Association of Malaysia, Journal (Singapore)

Tectona (Buitenzorg)

TESG   Tijdschrift voor Economische en Sociale Geografie (The Hague/Rotterdam)

Times Rev Br Colonies   The Times: Review of British Colonies (London)

Tin News (Washington, D.C.)

Tōnan Ajia Kenkyū (Kyoto)

[Toronto] Star Weekly

Tour du Monde (Paris)

Town Planning Institute
Journal (London)

Town Planning Institute
Newsletter (Singapore)

Town Planning Review (Liverpool)

Trans Ethn Soc	Transactions of the Ethnological Society (London)
Trans Int Cong History Religions	Transactions of the International Congress of History of Religions
Trans R Soc Edinburgh	Transactions of the Royal Society of Edinburgh (Edinburgh)
Trans R Soc Med Hyg	Transactions of the Royal Society of Tropical Medicine and Hygiene (London)

Travaux et Memoires de l'Institut
d'Ethnologie (Paris)

Trinity Theological College
Annual (Singapore)

Trop Agriculturalist	Tropical Agriculturalist (Colombo)
Trop Ag	Tropical Agriculture (Port-of-Spain)

Tropical Science (London)

Tubercle (London)

20th Century (London)

Unasylva (Rome)

UA	United Asia (Bombay)

United Empire (London)

UMBCER   United Malaysian Banking
Corporation Economic Review
(Kuala Lumpur)

UNB   United Nations Bulletin
(Lake Success, N.Y.)

UNESCO Bulletin for Libraries
(New York)

U N Sci Conf Conserv   United Nations Scientific
and Util Resources   Conference on the Conservation
Proc   and Utilization of Resources,
Lake Success, N.Y., 1949.
Proceedings

United Nations Water Resources
Series (Bangkok/New York)

United Planting Association
of Malaya. Annual Reports
(Kuala Lumpur)

US Dept State Bul   United States Department
of State Bulletin
(Washington, D.C.)

USNIP   United States Naval Institute
Proceedings (Annapolis)

US News and World Report
(Washington, D.C.)

Univ Ceylon Rev   University Ceylon Review
(Colombo)

UMLR   University of Malaya Law
Review (Singapore)

Univ Q   University Quarterly
(New Haven, Conn.)

Verh Batav Gen   Verhandelingen van het Bataviaasch
Kunsten Wet   Genootschap van Kunsten en
Wetenschappen (Batavia)

PERIODICALS AND CONFERENCE PROCEEDINGS CITED

Verh Berl Ges Anthr	Verhandlungen der Berliner Gesellschaft für Anthropologie, Ethnologie und Urgeschichte (Berlin)
Veröf Kön Mus Völk	Veröffentlichungen aus dem Königlichen Museum für Völkerkunde (Berlin)
	Western Canner and Packer (San Francisco)
	Western Political Quarterly (Salt Lake City)
	World Affairs (London)
World Aff Interp	World Affairs Interpreter (Los Angeles)
	World Crops (London)
	World Muslims League Monthly Magazine (Singapore)
	World Today (London)
	Yale Review (New Haven, Conn.)
Z Ges E	Zeitschrift der Gesellschaft für Erdkunde zu Berlin (Berlin)
Z Erdk	Zeitschrift für Erdkunde (Frankfurt)
Z Ethn	Zeitschrift für Ethnologie (Berlin)
Z Geom	Zeitschrift für Geomorphologie (Berlin)
Z Geopol	Zeitschrift für Geopolitik (Berlin)
Z Indukt Abst Vererb	Zeitschrift für Induktive Abstammungs- und Vererbungslehre (Berlin)

PERIODICALS AND CONFERENCE PROCEEDINGS CITED

Z Kol -politik, -recht, -wirtschaft	Zeitschrift für Kolonialpolitik, Kolonialrecht, und Kolonialwirtschaft (Berlin)
Z Morph Anthr	Zeitschrift für Morphologie und Anthropologie (Stuttgart)
Z Rassenk	Zeitschrift für Rassenkunde (Stuttgart)
Z Weltforst	Zeitschrift für Weltforstwirtschaft (Berlin)

CHAPTER 2

BIBLIOGRAPHIES

Alfred, Eric R. An annotated bibliography of Malayan
fresh-water fisheries. JRASMB, 39, 1 (1966):
145-165.

Andrews, Isobel. Post-war bibliographies containing
Malayan material, with a note on current national
bibliography. Majallah Perpustakaan Singapura/Singapore
Library Journal, 2 (1962): 2-16.

Anuar, Hedwig. A guide to current government publications
of the Federation of Malaya. Library Association
of Malaya and Singapore, Newsletter 3, 3 (1959):
2-9.

Bastin, John. Sir Richard Winstedt and his writings.
In John Bastin and R. Roolvink, eds. Malayan
and Indonesian Studies. Oxford, 1964: 1-23.
A complete bibliography of the writings of
the "last and greatest of the British 'colonial'
scholars of Malaya."

Bibliography of Asian Studies. An annual bibliography
published in JAS since 1956.

Bibliography on Malaysia. Missionary Research Library,
Occasional Bulletin 15, 3 (1964): 1-31.

Bottoms, J. C. Malay historical works: a bibliographical
note on Malay histories as possible sources
for the history of Malaya. SSS, 15, 2 (1959):
69-98.
Reprinted in K. G. Tregonning, ed. Malaysian
Historical Sources. Singapore, 1962.

Bottoms, J. C. Some Malay historical sources: a
bibliographical note. In Soedjatmoko et al.,
eds. An Introduction to Indonesian Historiography.
Ithaca, 1965: 156-193.

Bouterwek, Konrad. Hinterindien und Indonesien,
1913-1925. Geographisches Jahrbuch, 42 (1927):
22-86.
See p. 26-28 for Malaya.

Catalogue of the Raffles Library, Singapore, 1901-1910.
Singapore, 1911. 363 p.

31

BIBLIOGRAPHIES

Challis, J. Annotated bibliography of economic
and social material in Singapore. Part I: Government
publications. 2nd ed. 1969. (Research Bibliography
Series, no. 1)

Challis, J. Annotated bibliography of economic
and social material in Singapore and West Malaysia:
non-government publications. 1969. (Research
Bibliography Series, no. 3)

Challis, Joyce, comp. Annotated bibliography of
economic and social material in Singapore. Part
I, Government publications. Economic Research
Centre, University of Singapore, 1967. 78 p.
(Research Bibliography Series, no. 1) Mimeo.

Challis, Joyce, comp. Annotated bibliography of
economic and social material in West Malaysia.
Part I, Government publications. Economic Research
Centre, University of Singapore, 1968. 151 p.
(Research Bibliography Series, no. 2) Mimeo.

Cheeseman, H. R. Bibliography of Malaya. New York,
1959. 234 p.

Chicago University. Bibliography of Malaya. Prepared
by HRAF Research Project at the University of
Chicago. New Haven, 1956. 55 p.

Conver, Helen F. Non self-governing areas, with
special emphasis on mandates and trusteeships:
a selected list of references. Washington, D.C.,
1947. 2 v.

Cordier, Henri. Bibliotheca Sinica: dictionnaire
bibliographique des ouvrages relatifs à l'Empire
Chinois. Paris, 1904-1908. 4 v.
   V. 3, p. 1,894-1,900, deals particularly with
Chinese secret societies and v. 4, p. 2,693-2,694,
with Chinese emigration to Malaya.

Daniel, Padma, comp. A descriptive catalogue of
the books relating to Malaysia in the Raffles
Museum and Library, Singapore. JRASMB, 19, 3
(1941): 1-125.

BIBLIOGRAPHIES

Dennys, N. B. A contribution to Malayan bibliography. JRASSB, 5 (1880): 59-124; 6 (1880): 225-272.

Embree, John F. A selected bibliography on Southeast Asia. 2d ed. Revised and expanded by Bruno Lasker. New York, 1952. 27 p. Mimeo.

Embree, John F., and Lillian O. Dotson. Bibliography of the peoples and cultures of mainland Southeast Asia. New Haven, 1950. 821 p. Material on Malaya found in chapter "Southeast Asia General," p. 1-98.

Far Eastern Bibliography. In FEQ, 1941. Quarterly until 1949, annually since 1950.

Federated Malay States, Department of Agriculture. Classified list of the principal original articles published in the Agricultural Bulletin of the Federated Malay States and Straits Settlements and the Malayan Agricultural Journal for the period 1913 to 1930 (v. 1-18). Kuala Lumpur, 1931. 35 p.

Gibson-Hill, C. A. An index to the papers in v. 1-20 (1923-1947) of the Malayan Branch, Royal Asiatic Society. JRASMB, 21, 3 (1948): 66 p.

Hanitsch, K. R. Catalogue of the Raffles Library, Singapore, 1900. Singapore, 1905. 636 p.

Harris, L. J. Guide to current Malaysian serials. Kuala Lumpur, University of Malaya Library, 1967. 73 p.

Hart, Donn Vorhis. Preliminary check list of novels with a Malayan background. Syracuse, N.Y. [196-?]. 25 p.

Hazra, Niranjan K. Malaysian serials: a check list of current official serials of the Malaysian Governments. By Niranjan K. Hazra and Edwin Lee Siew Cheng. Singapore, 1963. 18 p. Issued by Department of History, Centre for South-East Asian Studies in the Social Sciences, University of Singapore.

BIBLIOGRAPHIES

Helbig, Karl. Hinter- und Insel-Indien, 1926-39/40.
Geographisches Jahrbuch, 57 (1942): 138-343.
See p. 197-214 for Malaya.

Hellman, Florence, comp. British Malaya and British
North Borneo: a bibliographical list. Washington,
D.C., 1943. 103 p.

Hobbs, Cecil. Southeast Asia 1935-1945: a selected
list of reference books. Washington, D.C., 1946.
86 p.

Hobbs, Cecil. Southeast Asia: an annotated bibliography
of selected reference sources. Washington, D.C.,
1952. 163 p.
See p. 76-94 for Malaya.

Howard, Joseph H. Malay manuscripts: a bibliographic
guide. Kuala Lumpur, University of Malaya, 1966.
96 p.

Hussein, Ismail. Bibliography of works and articles
on traditional Malay literature. Kuala Lumpur
[n.d.]. 27 p. Mimeo.

Jackson, James C. Recent higher degree theses on
social, political and economic aspects of South
East Asia presented in the universities of the
United Kingdom and in the universities of Malaya
and Singapore. Hull, 1966. (Department of Geography,
Miscellaneous Series, no. 6) Mimeo.

Joint Standing Committee on Library Cooperation
and Bibliographical Services. Index to current
Malaysian Singapore and Brunei periodicals.
Kuala Lumpur, Singapura, 1969.

Journal of the Rubber Research Institute of Malaya.
Subject index, v. 1-12, 1928-1950. Kuala Lumpur,
1951.

Keeth, Kent H. A directory of libraries in Malaysia.
Kuala Lumpur, University of Malaya Library,
1965. 163 p.
Gives address, size of collection, and policies
of all libraries in Malaysia and Singapore.

Leong, Peng-chong. Nutrition bibliography of Malaya.
Honolulu, 1952. 23 p.

Lewin, Evans. Subject catalogue of the library
of the Royal Empire Society, formerly Royal
Colonial Society. V. 4: the Mediterranean colonies,
the Middle East, Indian Empire, Burma, Ceylon,
British Malaya, East Indian Islands, and the
Far East. London, 1937. 812 p.
See p. 585-623 for Malaya.

Leyh, S. G. H. Early records of the Government
of the Straits Settlements in the Colonial Secretary's
Library, Singapore. Singapore, 1928.
An index to manuscripts of the Straits Settlements
government up to 1867.

Lim, Beda, comp. Malaya, a background bibliography.
JRASMB, 35, 2-3 (1962): 199.

Lim, Huck-tee. Books and libraries in Malaya before
the coming of the West. Library Association
Record, 66 (1964): 241-247.

Lim, Patricia. An annotated list of books on Malaya
published in 1958. Library Association of Malaya
and Singapore, Newsletter, 3, 3 (1959): 22-26.

Lim, Pui-huen. Malaysian newspapers currently published.
Perpustakaan Malaysia, 1 (June 1965): 56-61.

Lim, Pui-huen. A survey of newspapers published
in the Malaysian areas; with a union list of
local holdings. 1968. 35 p. Unpublished paper
no. 65 presented at the International Conference
on Asian History, Kuala Lumpur, August 1968.
Mimeo.

Lim, Wong-pui-huen. Current Malayan serials. Majallah
Perpustakaan Singapura/Singapore Library Journal,
2, 2 (1962): 75-94.

London, University, School of Oriental and African
Studies. The Far East and Southeast Asia: a
cumulated list of periodical articles. May 1954-April
1955, +

BIBLIOGRAPHIES

Malaya. Government Gazette. Federal Government:
register under Section 6 of the Preservation
of Books Ordinance. 195- . Kuala Lumpur. Quarterly.

Malaya, Department of Agriculture. The Agricultural
Bulletin of Federated Malay States and the Malayan
Agricultural Journal; classified list of the
principal original articles, 1912 to 1954 (v. 1-37).
Kuala Lumpur [1955?].

Malaya, Government Printing Department. Current
list of publications. 19- . Kuala Lumpur. Quarterly.

Malaya, Ministry of Agriculture and Co-operatives.
(i) Index to the Agricultural Bulletin of the
Straits and Federated Malay States. (ii) Classified
list of principal original articles in the Agricultural
Bulletin of the Federated Malay States and the
Malayan Agricultural Journal. (iii) List of
publications of the Department of Agriculture,
Federation of Malaya. Kuala Lumpur, 1962. 139 p.

Nallal, B. A. Malayan legal bibliography. Majallah
Perpustakaan Singapura/Singapore Library Journal,
1 (1961): 55-75.

Pelzer, Karl J. Selected bibliography on the geography
of Southeast Asia. Pt. I: Southeast Asia - General.
New Haven, 1949. 45 p. Mimeo.
References to Malaya found in books and articles
dealing with Southeast Asia.

Peritz, Rene. A selected bibliography of recent
works in English on political processes in Malaysia
and Singapore (1963-1968). Providence, Rhode
Island, 1969. 32 p. (University of Rhode Island
Occasional Papers in Political Science, no. 14)

Plumbe, Wilfred J. Libraries and librarianship
in Malaya. Malayan Library Journal, 1 (Oct.
1960): 2-8.

Plumbe, Wilfred J. Libraries in Malaya and Singapore.
Malayan Library Journal, 3, 4 (1964): 140-151.

BIBLIOGRAPHIES

Robson, J. H. M., comp. A bibliography of Malaya,
also a short list of books relating to North
Borneo and Sarawak. 6th ed. Kuala Lumpur, 1938.
49 p.

Roff, William R. Guide to Malay periodicals, 1876-1941,
with details of known holdings in Malaya. Kuala
Lumpur, 1961. 46 p. (University of Malaya, Department
of History. Papers on Southeast Asian Subjects,
no. 4)

Sherborn, C. Davies. A bibliography of Malaya from
January 1888-June 1890. JRASSB, 22 (1890): 349-428.
Continuation for July 1890-June 1894. 24 (1891):
121-164; 26 (1894): 219-266; 27 (1894): 135-175;
29 (1896): 33-74.

Singapore, National Library. Books about Malaysia.
Singapore, 1964. 29 p.

Singapore, University, Economic Research Centre,
Library. Economic Research Centre holdings;
a list of published materials held in the documentation
library of the Economic Research Centre, University
of Singapore, including items acquired by end
December 1965. [Singapore, 1966?]. 44 p.

Singapore, University, Library, Reference Department.
Education in Malaysia: a bibliography. Compiled
by Wang Chen-hsiu-chin. Singapore, 1964. 35 p.

Soosai, J. S., and Kow Hun-woon, comps. A bibliography
of contributions to natural rubber research
from the Rubber Research Institute of Malaya:
1927-1967. Kuala Lumpur, 1968. 140 p.

Southern Asia publications in Western languages.
A quarterly accessions list. Division of Orientalia,
Library of Congress. V. 1- , 1952- .
Washington, D.C.

Srinivasagam, Elizabeth. Guide to Singapore government
departments and serials as of 30th August 1963.
Majallah Perpustakaan Singapura/Singapore Library
Journal, 3, 2 (1964): 79-90.

Suntharalingam, R. A survey of source materials
in Singapore relating to modern Malaya. Indian
Archives, 14 (1961/1962): 55-65.

BIBLIOGRAPHIES

Tan, Soo-chye. Straits Settlements records: a brief
outline of the records, in Raffles Library,
Singapore. JRASMB, 23, 1 (1949).

Taylor, A. P. The National Library today. Perpustakaan
Malaysia, 1 (June 1965): 19-28.

Tibbetts, G. R. Arabic works relating to South-East
Asia. Malayan Library Group Newsletter, 1, 4
(1956): 79-86.

Tilman, Robert O. A guide to British library holdings
of government publications relating to Malaysia
in the field of social sciences. By Robert O.
Tilman and Peter L. Burns. [n.p., 1963]. 67 p.

Turnbull, C. M. Bibliography of writings in English
on British Malaya, 1786-1867. In L. A. Mills.
British Malaya 1824-67. Kuala Lumpur, 1966:
287-361.

Wheatley, P. Ancient books containing references
to Malaya. Malayan Library Group Newsletter,
1, 2 (1955): 18-24.

Williams-Hunt, P. D. R., and E. F. S. Buxton. Early
Malayan books and maps in the archives section
of the National Museum, Kuala Lumpur. MHJ, 1
(Dec. 1954): 128-135.

Wurtzburg, C. E., comp. An index to all the journals
(1-86) (1878-1922) of the Straits Branch from
the foundation until its change of title to
the Malayan Branch of the Royal Asiatic Society:
and to notes and queries I to IV. JRASMB, 5,
4 (1927): 101 p.

Yale University Library. Checklist of Southeast
Asian Serials. Southeast Asia Collection. Boston,
Mass., 1968. 320 p.

CHAPTER 3

SERIALS DEVOTED EXCLUSIVELY TO WEST MALAYSIA/SINGAPORE

Agricultural Bulletin. See Gardens' Bulletin.

Berita Mara. Majilis Amanah Ra'ayat Malaysia. 1- ,
1967- . Kuala Lumpur.

British Malaya. Published by the Association of
British Malaya, London, 1926-1951. Renamed Malaya,
published by the British Association of Malaya,
London, 1952-1963.

Ekonomi. Journal of the Economics Society. University
of Malaya. V. 1- , 1960- . Kuala Lumpur.

Gardens' Bulletin. Botanic Gardens, Singapore. Published
under this title since 1949. Was preceded by
the Agricultural Bulletin of the Malay Peninsula,
v. 1-9, 1819-1900. Second ser., v. 1-10, 1901-1911,
Agricultural Bulletin of the Straits Settlements
and the Federated Malay States. Third ser., v. 1-11,
1912-1947, Gardens' Bulletin of the Straits Settlements.

Geographica. Geographical Society, University of
Malaya. V. 1- , 1965- . Kuala Lumpur.

Government Gazette.
A separate gazette published for each state
and settlement of Malaya. Each series published
in the respective capital.

Institute for Medical Research. Annual Report. 1900- .
Kuala Lumpur.

Institute for Medical Research. Bulletin. 1924-1941;
n.s., no. 1- , 1949- . Kuala Lumpur.

Institute for Medical Research. Studies. No. 1- ,
1901- . Singapore, Kuala Lumpur. Irregular.
Monograph series.

Intisari. Malaysian Sociological Research Institute.
V. 1- , 1962- . Singapore.

Journal of the Historical Society. University of
Malaya. V. 1, 1960/1963; v. 2, 1963/1964. Kuala
Lumpur. Since then, one issue a year.

Journal of the Indian Archipelago and Eastern Asia.
1847-1855; n.s., v. 1-4, 1856/1858-1859/1862.
Singapore. Quarterly.

Journal of the South Seas Society. V. 1- , 1940- .
Singapore. Index v. 1-5 (1940-1948) in v. 5;
v. 6-10 (1949-1954) in v. 10.

Journal of Southeast Asian History. 1- , 1960- .
Department of History, University of Singapore.
Singapore.

Journal of Southeast Asian Researches. V. 1- , 1965- .
Singapore.

Journal of Tropical Geography. Geography Department,
University of Singapore/Geography Department
of University of Malaya, Kuala Lumpur. V. 11- ,
1958- . Successor to Malayan Journal of Tropical
Geography.

Kajian Ekonomi Malaysia. Department of Economics,
University of Malaya. V. 1- , 1964- . Kuala Lumpur.

Kedah Dari Segi Sejarah--Kedah in History. 1, 1
(June 1966)- . Alor Star.

Lembaga Pemasaran Pertanian Persekutuan. Federal
Agricultural Marketing Authority. Annual Report
and Statement of Accounts. 1967- . Kuala Lumpur.

Majallah Perpustakaan Singapura/Singapore Library
Journal. V. 1- , 1961- . Library Association
of Singapore.

Malaya. 1952-1963. London. Replaced British Malaya.
London, 1926-1951. Became Malaysia, London, 1964- .

Malaya. Journal of the Federated Malay States Museums.
V. 1-19, 1905/1906-1936/1939. Singapore. Replaced
Perak Museum Notes. Succeeded by Federation Museums
Journal, starting in 1954/1955.

Malaya. Federation Museums Journal. N.s., v. 1/2- ,
1954/1955- . Kuala Lumpur.

Malaya, Department of Agriculture. Agricultural
Bulletin of the Straits and Federated Malay States.
O.s., 1891-1900; n.s., 1900-1910. Continued as
the Agricultural Bulletin of the Federated Malay
States, Kuala Lumpur, v. 1-9, 1912-1921. Became
Malayan Agricultural Journal, v. 10-44, 1922-1964.
Continued as Malaysian Agricultural Journal,
v. 45- , 1965- .

Malaya, Department of Agriculture. Agricultural
Leaflets.
Each leaflet covers a particular agricultural
product.

Malaya, Department of Agriculture. Circulars.

Malaya, Department of Mines. Bulletin of Statistics
Relating to the Mining Industry. 1956- . Kuala
Lumpur. Published annually.

Malaya, Forest Department. Annual Reports. Kuala Lumpur.

Malaya, Forest Department. Malayan Forester. V.
1- , 1931- . Kuala Lumpur.

Malaya, Forest Department. Malayan Forest Records.
No. 1- , 1921- . Singapore/Kuala Lumpur.
Monograph series.

Malaya, Forest Department. Forest Research Institute,
Kepong. Research Pamphlets. No. 1- , 1953- .
Irregular.
"For restricted distribution only. Issued from
time to time to record research programmes, research
techniques, preliminary reports and results,
or studies of too specialized nature to be of
general interest."

Malaya in History. See Malayan Historical Journal;
Tanah Melayu Dari Segi Sejarah.

Malaya, Information Department. Fortnightly Press
Digest. Kuala Lumpur.

Malaya, Information Department. Weekly News Summary.
Kuala Lumpur.

SERIALS - WEST MALAYSIA/SINGAPORE

Malayan Agriculturalist. University of Malaya, Agricultural
    Society. V. 1- , 1960/1961- . Kuala Lumpur.

Malayan Economic Review. Malayan Economic Society,
    University of Singapore. V. 1- , 1956- .

Malayan Historical Journal. Published by the Malayan
    Historical Society. V. 1-3, 1953-1956. Became
    Malaya in History. Kuala Lumpur. 1957- .
    (See also Tanah Melayu Dari Segi Sejarah, the
    Malay edition).

Malayan Journal of Tropical Geography. 1953-1957.
    Singapore. Two issues yearly. Succeeded by Journal
    of Tropical Geography.

Malayan Naturalist: official organ of the Singapore
    Natural History Society. 1922-1928. Singapore.

Malayan Nature Journal. V. 1- , 1940/1941- . Kuala Lumpur.

Malayan Trade Annual. 1952- . London.

Malaysia. See Malaya.

Malaysian Management Review. The Journal of the
    Malaysian Institute of Management. V. 1- , 1966- .

Medical Journal of Malaya. Malayan Medical Association.
    N.s., v. 1- , 1946- . Singapore. This journal
    was started in 1904 as the British Medical Association,
    Malayan Branch, Journal. From 1926-1937, it was
    issued as the Malayan Medical Journal, v. 1-12;
    after which it resumed its earlier name and issued
    v. 1-5, 1937-1941. After v. 14, 1959, it was
    published by the Malayan Medical Association.

Minerals. 1935- . Kuala Lumpur. Quarterly. Statistics
    of the mining industry.

National Museum, Singapore, Bulletin. See Raffles Museum.

National Museum, Singapore. Memoirs. No. 1- , 1960- .
    Prior to 1960, issued under its earlier name:
    Raffles Museum, Singapore. Memoirs.
        Monograph series.

Natural Rubber News. Natural Rubber Bureau, Washington, D.C.

Pahang Planters' Association. Year Book. Kuala Lumpur.

Papers on Malay Subjects--Series I. 1907-1929. Kuala
Lumpur. R. J. Wilkinson and R. O. Winstedt. "Malay
literature I, II, III." R. J. Wilkinson and J.
Rigby. "Law I, II, III." R. J. Wilkinson and
C. W. Harrison. "History I, II, III." R. J. Wilkinson
and R. O. Winstedt. "Life and customs I, II,
III." R. O. Winstedt and G. E. Shaw. "Industries:
I--Arts and crafts, II--Fishing, hunting and
trapping, III--Rice cultivation."

Papers on Malay Subjects--Series II. 1912-1920.
Kuala Lumpur. A. Caldecott. "Jelebu: its history
and constitution." R. J. Wilkinson. "Sri Menanti."
R. J. Wilkinson. "Vocabulary of central Sakai."
J. E. Nathan and R. O. Winstedt. "Johol."

Papers on Southeast Asian Subjects. No. 1- , 1960- .
Department of History, University of Malaya.
Kuala Lumpur.
    Monograph series.

Peninjau Sejarah/Journal of the History Teachers'
Association of Malaya. V. 1- , 1966- . Two issues
a year.

The Planter: Journal of the Incorporated Society
of Planters. 1920- . Kuala Lumpur. Monthly.

Planters' Association of Malaya. Annual Report and
Year-book. Kuala Lumpur.

Planters' Bulletin. See Rubber Research Institute of Malaya.

Raffles Museum. Bulletin of the Raffles Museum.
1-29, 1928-1961. Singapore. Continued as the
Bulletin of the National Museum, Singapore.

Raffles Museum. Bulletin of the Raffles Museum,
ser. B. 1-4, 1936-1949. Singapore.

Raffles Museum, Singapore. Memoirs. No. 1- , 1954-1959.
Became National Museum, Singapore. Memoirs. 1960- .

Review of Agricultural Economics, Malaysia. Issued
    by the Federal Agricultural Marketing Authority.
    V. 1- , 1967- . Kuala Lumpur. Two issues a year.

Royal Asiatic Society of Great Britain and Ireland.
    Malayan Branch. Journal. V. 1- , 1923- . Singapore.
    Quarterly. Nos. 1-86, 1878-1922, issued by the
    Society under its earlier name: Royal Asiatic
    Society of Great Britain and Ireland. Straits
    Branch. Index: nos. 1-86, 1878-1922, in v. 5;
    v. 1-20, 1923-1947, in v. 21.

Royal Asiatic Society of Great Britain and Ireland.
    Straits Branch. Journal. 1878-1922. Singapore.
    Twice yearly.

Rubber and Agriculture Series Bulletins. 1936- .
    London. Nos. 1-8 by Rubber Growers' Association.
    No. 9 by British Rubber Publicity Association.

Rubber Research Institute of Malaya. Bulletin. Nos.
    1-5, 1929-1934. Kuala Lumpur.

Rubber Research Institute of Malaya. Journal. V. 1- ,
    1929- . Kuala Lumpur. Quarterly.

Rubber Research Institute of Malaya. Planters' Bulletin.
    No. 1-18, 1939-1941. N.s. no. 1- , 1952- . Kuala Lumpur.

Rubber Research Institute of Malaya. Planting Manual.
    1928- . Kuala Lumpur.

Seed. Malaysian Sociological Research Institute.
    V. 1- , 1960- . Singapore.

Selangor Planters' Association. Annual Report. 1956- .
    Kuala Lumpur.

Singapore Chamber of Commerce. Annual Report.

Tanah Melayu Dari Segi Sejarah. Malayan Historical
    Society and Dewan Bahasa dan Pustaka. V. 1- ,
    1961- . Kuala Lumpur.
    Malay edition of Malaya in History.

Technical Association of Malaysia. Journal. Singapore.

Tin News. Malayan Tin Bureau. Washington, D.C. Monthly.

UMBC Economic Review published by the United Malaysian
  Banking Corporation. V. 1- , 1965- . Kuala Lumpur.

United Planting Association of Malaya. Annual Reports.
  Kuala Lumpur. Founded 1897. 1897-1906, United
  Planters' Association of the Federated Malay
  States; 1907, United Planters' Association of
  the Malay Peninsula; 1907-1934, Planters' Association
  of Malaya; in 1955 the Association assumed its
  current name.

CHAPTER 4

DESCRIPTION - POPULAR AND SCIENTIFIC

Ahpa, T. (pseud. for J. Nield). By jungle track and paddy field to rubber plantation and palm grove. Liverpool, 1913. 179 p. Plates.

Ainsworth, Leopold. The confessions of a planter in Malaya. London, 1933. 224 p.

Anderson, P. Snake wine: a Singapore episode. London, 1955. 288 p. Front., plates.

Ballentine, Frances Griswold. Tiger at the door. New York [1958]. 87 p.

Banner, H. S. A tropical tapestry. London, 1929. 319 p. Illus., map.

Bartlett, Vernon. Report from Malaya. London, 1954.

Bastian, Adolf. Die Völker des östlichen Asien. V. 5, Reisen im Indischen Archipel. Jena, 1869. 552 p. Includes Singapore, Batavia, Manila and Japan.

Belcher, Edward. Narrative of the voyage of the H.M.S. Samarang during the years 1843-46; employed surveying the islands of the eastern Archipelago; accompanied by a brief vocabulary of the principle languages . . . With notes on the natural history of the islands, by Arthur Adams. London, 1848. 2 v. Maps, plates.

Beu, Frank. Abenteuer eines Ausreissers. Alle Maschinen klar. Mein Urwald-Paradies. Berlin, 1938. 313 p.

Bickmore, A. S. Travels in the East Indian Archipelago. New York, 1869. 553 p.

Bilainkin, George. Hail, Penang: being the narrative of comedies and tragedies in a tropical outpost, among Europeans, Chinese, Malays and Indians. London, 1932. 242 p.

Bird, Isabella L. (afterward Mrs. Bishop). The golden Chersonese and the way thither. London, 1883. 379 p.

Bishop, Isabella Lucy (Bird). The golden Chersonese and the way thither. With an introduction by Wang Gung-wu. Kuala Lumpur, 1967. 384 p. (Oxford in Asia historical reprints) Illus., col. map.

DESCRIPTION - POPULAR AND SCIENTIFIC

Bitsch, Jørgen. Ulu: the world's end. Translated from
the Danish by Reginald Spink. London, 1961. 142 p.
Plates (part col.).

Bleackley, H. A tour of southern Asia: Indo-China,
Malaya, Java, Sumatra and Ceylon, 1925-1926. London,
1928. 297 p. Illus.

Boulle, Pierre. Sacrilege in Malaya. Translated from
the French by Xan Fielding. London, 1959. 321 p.

Braddell, R. The lights of Singapore. London, 1934.
218 p. Also other editions.

Braddell, T. Notes of a trip to the interior. from Malacca.
Jl Ind Archip, 7 (1853): 73-104.

Brandstetter, R. Mata Hari oder Wanderungen eines
indonesischen Sprachforschers durch drei Reiche
der Natur. Luzern, 1908.

Bredin, Alexander Edward Craven. The happy warriors.
Gillingham, Dorset, England, 1961. 356 p. Plates.

Britton, N. P. East of the sun. Edinburgh, London,
1956. 238 p.

Brown, Cecil B. Suez to Singapore. New York, 1942.
545 p. Map.
Journalist's account of period 1941-1942 before
and just after outbreak of the war.

Burbridge, F. W. The gardens of the sun. London, 1880.
364 p.

Burgess, Anthony (pseud. for John Wilson). Malayan
trilogy. London [1964]. 512 p.
Includes: Time for a tiger; The enemy in the blanket;
and Beds in the east.

Bush, Willard C. Pahang: the saga of a rubber planter.
New York, 1938. 284 p.

Bush, Willard C. Pahang: quatre années d'aventures
dans la jungle de Malaisie. Paris, 1950. 272 p.
(Collection de documents et de temoignages pour
servir à l'histoire de notre temps) Map.

DESCRIPTION - POPULAR AND SCIENTIFIC

Cameron, Charlotte. Wanderings in south-eastern seas. London, 1924. 269 p.

Campbell, Arthur. Jungle green. London, 1953. 216 p. Maps. Authentic story of the jungle campaign in Malaya.

Carpenter, Frank G. Java and the East Indies: Java, Sumatra, Celebes, the Moluccas, New Guinea, Borneo and the Malay Peninsula. New York, 1923. 278 p.

Carpenter, Kathleen. The password is love. London, 1955.

Chapman, F. Spencer. Travels in Japanese occupied Malaya. G Jl, 55 (1947): 17-37.

Chapman, F. Spencer. The jungle is neutral. New York, 1949. 384 p.

Chettur, S. K. Malayan adventure. Mangalore, 1948. 260 p.

Chidsey, Donald B. Singapore passage. New York, 1956. 191 p.

Claine, Jules. Un an en Malaisie. Tour du Monde (1892): 369-400.

[Clark, F. S.]. Men of Malaya. By Clive Dalton [pseud.]. London, 1942. 165 p. Map.
    Contents: Francis Light, Thomas Stamford Raffles, James Brooke, Andrew Clarke, Hugh Low, Frank A. Swettenham.

Clifford, Hugh. Journey through Trengganu and Kelantan. London, 1896.

Clifford, Hugh. Life in the Malay Peninsula: as it was and is. Proc R Col Inst, 30 (1898/1899): 369-401.

Clifford, Hugh. In a corner of Asia: being tales and impressions of man and things in the Malay Peninsula. London, 1899. 279 p.; 1926, 258 p.

Clifford, Hugh. British and Siamese Malaya. Proc R Col Inst, 34 (1902/1903): 45-75.

DESCRIPTION - POPULAR AND SCIENTIFIC

Clifford, Hugh. Malayan monochromes. New York, 1913.
321 p.

Clifford, Hugh. Studies in brown humanity: being scrawls
and smudges in sepia, white and yellow. London,
1927. 264 p.

Clifford, Hugh. In court and kampong: being tales and
sketches of native life in the Malay Peninsula.
London, 1928. 255 p. Other editions.

Clifford, Hugh. Bush-whacking and other Asiatic tales
and memories. London, 1929. 386 p.

Cook, J. A. Bethune. Sunny Singapore: an account of
the place and its people, with a sketch of the results
of missionary work. London, 1907. 183 p.

Crawford, Oliver. The door marked Malaya. London, 1958.
27 p. Illus.

Crockett, Anthony. Green beret, red star. With a foreword
by Sir John Harding. London, 1954. 221 p.

Cross, John. Red jungle. London [1957]. 244 p.

Curle, Richard. Into the East. Notes on Burma and Malaya.
London, 1923. 224 p.

Dalton, H. G. A visit to some islands off the east
coast of Johore and Pahang. JRASMB, 6, 3 (1928):
78-96. Illus.

Deistel, H. Bericht über eine Reise nach Britisch- und
Niederländisch-Indien. Beihefte Tropenpflanzer,
9 (1908): 63-131.

Denis, J. Impressions of life in Malaya today. JRCAS,
38 (1952): 56-60.

Douglas, William O. North from Malaya: adventure on
five fronts. Part I. Malayan jungle guerrillas,
19-99. New York, 1953. 352 p. Illus., index.

Duncanson, J. D. Impressions of life in Malaya today.
JRCAS, 38 (Jan. 1951): 56-70.

Earl, G. W. The eastern seas: or voyages and adventures
in the Indian Archipelago. Also an account of the
present state of Singapore. London, 1837. 461 p.

49

DESCRIPTION - POPULAR AND SCIENTIFIC

Ellinger, Suzette (Telenga). Agency house, Malaya;
the girl in the cheongsam. [By] Susan Yorke [pseud.].
New York [1962]. 242 p.

Enriquez, C. M. Malaya: an account of its people, flora
and fauna. London, 1927. 303 p. Illus., maps, plates.

Fauconnier, Henri. Malaisie. Paris, 1930. 271 p.

Fauconnier, Henri. Malaisie. Translated by Eric Sutton.
New York, 1931. 271 p.

Fauconnier, Henri. The soul of Malaya. Translated by
Eric Sutton. Kuala Lumpur, 1965. 247 p.

Foran, W. R. Malayan symphony: being the impressions
gathered during a six months journey through the
Straits Settlements, Federated Malay States, Siam,
Sumatra, Java and Bali. London, 1935. 302 p.

Forbes, Duncan Charles. The heart of Malaya. London,
1966. 221 p. Map, plates.

Forbes, Henry Ogg. A naturalist's wanderings in the
eastern archipelago: 1878-1883. London, 1885. 536 p.

Frank, Peter R. Wolken über Malaya; Roman. Zürich [1959].
269 p. Illus.

Gibson, Ashley. The Malay Peninsula and Archipelago.
London, 1928. 236 p. Illus., plates.

Gibson, Ashley. Malaya, land of "perpetual afternoons".
Can G Jl, 31 (1945): 169-175. Map.

Gibson-Hill, C. A. The Malayan landscape. Seventy camera
studies. With an introduction by Malcolm MacDonald.
Singapore, 1949. 143 p. Plates.

Glover, E. M. In 70 days: the story of the Japanese
campaign in British Malaya. London, 1946. 244 p.

Graham, W. A. Kelantan, a state of the Malay Peninsula.
Glasgow, 1908. 139 p. Plates.

Greenfell, R. Main fleet to Singapore. New York, 1952.
238 p.

DESCRIPTION - POPULAR AND SCIENTIFIC

Guillemard, Laurence N. Trivial fond records. London, 1937. 187 p. Plates.
See p. 80-148 for Malaya.

Haeckel, Ernst H. P. A. Aus Insulinde; malayische Reisebriefe. Bonn, 1901. 206 p. Illus., maps.

Han Su-yin (pseud.). . . . and the rain my drink. Boston, 1956.

Harrison, C. R. The last of the creepers. Memoirs of a Malayan rubber planter 1907-1917. MH, 7, 1 (1961): 18-27.

Harrison, Cuthbert W. The magic of Malaya. London, 1916. 240 p.

Hastain, R. White coolie. London, 1947. 302 p.

Helfritz, Hans. Im Urwald von Malaya. Land und Leute allgemein; eingehender das Völkergemisch und seine Auswirkungen. Berlin, 1936. 139 p. Illus., maps.

Henniker, M. C. A. Red shadow over Malaya. Foreword by Field-Marshal Sir John Harding. London (1955). 303 p. Diagrs., maps, plates.

Hodder, B. W. Man in Malaya. London, 1959.

Hubback, Theodore R. Three months in Pahang in search of big game. Singapore, 1912. 67 p.

Hummel, C. Malaya kreuz und quer. Mit Parang und Kompass in tropischen Wäldern. München, 1935. 167 p. Illus., maps.

Innes, E. The Chersonese with the gilding off. London, 1885. 2 v.

Jagor, F. Singapore, Malacca, Java: Reiseskizzen. Berlin, 1866. 252 p.

James, D. H. The rise and fall of the Japanese empire. London, New York, 1951. 409 p.
Contains an eyewitness account of the fall of Singapore.

Jeffrey, A. B. White coolies. London, Sydney, 1954. 204 p.

DESCRIPTION - POPULAR AND SCIENTIFIC

Keith, A. Account of journey across Malay Peninsula
from Koh Lak to Mergui. JRASSB, 24 (1891): 31-41.

Keon, Michael. The durian tree. New York, 1960. 309 p.
A novel.

Kin, D. G. Rage in Singapore: the cauldron of Asia
boils over. New York, 1942. 315 p.

Kirby, Stanley Woodburn. Johore in 1926. G Jl, 71 (1928):
240-260. Illus., map, plates.

Kirkup, James. Tropic temper; a memoir of Malaya. London,
1963. 287 p.

Knocker, Frederic William. A Malayan miscellany. Edited
by the Palia Dorai. Notes and jottings, reminiscences
and anecdotes, stories and essays from the scrap-books
of an Englishman resident in British Malaya: illustrated
by photographs from the same source and sketches
from elsewhere. Kuala Lumpur, 1924. 250 p. Illus.

Kranz, Herbert. Befehl des Radscha. Abenteuer in Malaya.
Freiburg, 1955. 218 p.

Leyh, S. G. H. Versified glimpses of Malaya. Penang,
1936.

Lockhart, R. H. Bruce. Malayan novitiate. In his, Memoirs
of a British Agent. London, New York, Putnam, 1932:
3-50. 355 p.

Lockhart, R. H. Bruce. Return to Malaya. New York,
1936. 376 p. Index.

Malcolm, Howard. Travels in South-eastern Asia; embracing
Hindustan, Malaya, Siam and China; with notices
of numerous mission stations, and a full account
of the Burman Empire. London, 1839. 2 v. (1) 324 p.
(2) 264 p. Various editions, including Travels in
the Burman Empire. Edinburgh, 1840. 82 p.

Marryat, Francis Samuel. Borneo and the Indian Archipelago.
With drawings of costume and scenery. London, 1848.
232 p. Illus., plates.

Maxwell, George. In Malay forests. London, 1907. 306 p.

DESCRIPTION - POPULAR AND SCIENTIFIC

Maxwell, W. G. Groenveldt's notes on Malay Archipelago and Malacca. JRASSB, 52 (1909): 105-110.

Maxwell, W. G. Malacca harbour. JRASSB, 52 (1909): 111-115.

Maxwell, W. G. Account of De Siqueira's voyage to Malacca. JRASSB, 57 (1911): 193-195.

McGuire, P. Westward the course' The new world of Oceania. New York, 1942. 434 p. Maps, plates. Malaya: p. 383-423.

McIntosh, Amy. Journey into Malaya. London, 1956.

McKie, Ronald. The heroes. Sydney, 1960. 285 p. Illus.

McKie, Ronald. The emergence of Malaysia. New York, 1963. 310 p.

McKie, Ronald. Malaysia in focus. Sydney, London, 1963. 236 p.

McNair, Major Fred. Perak and the Malays: "Sarong" and "Kris". London, 1878. 454 p. Illus., map.

Miller, Harry. The story of Malaysia. London, 1965. 264 p. Map.

Mills, Lennox A. Malaya. In Lennox A. Mills et al. The New World of Southeast Asia. Minneapolis, 1949: 174-215. 450 p.

Mjoberg, Eric Georg. Forest life and adventures in the Malay Archipelago. Translated by A. Barwell. London, 1930. 201 p. Map, plates.

Montano, Joseph. Voyage aux Philippines et en Malaisie. Paris, 1886. 351 p. Illus., map.

Moor, J. H. Notices of the Indian Archipelago, and adjacent countries; being a collection of papers relating to Borneo, Celebes, Bali, Java, Sumatra, Nias, the Philippine Islands, Sulus, Siam, Cochin-China, Malayan Peninsula, etc. Singapore, 1837. 117 p. Index, maps.

Moore, Donald. We live in Singapore. London, 1955. 287 p. Col. front., plates.

Moore, Donald. Where monsoons meet; the story of Malaya in the form of an anthology. London, 1956. 279 p. Front., plates.

Moore, Donald. The Sumatra. Garden City, N.Y., 1959. 286 p.

Moore, Donald, ed. Where monsoons meet; the story of Malaya in the form of an anthology. London, 1961. 125 p. Illus.

Moran, Jack William Grace. Spearhead in Malaya. London, 1959. 287 p.
    Autobiographical.

Moran, Jack William Grace. The camp across the river; further recollections of an officer in the Malayan police force. London, 1961. 191 p.

Morgenthaler, Hans O. Matahari: impressions of the Siamese-Malayan jungle. London, 1923. 240 p.

Morrison, Ian. Malayan postscript. London, 1942. 196 p. Illus., index, map.

Morrison, Ian. The Malay: lover of colour and ceremony. GM, 25 (1952): 148-156.

Nach, James. Malaysia and Singapore in pictures. Rev. ed. 1967. 64 p. (Visual Geography Series)

Neill, D. Elegant flower: first steps in China. London, 1956. 202 p.
    Author was a Malayan Civil Service cadet, and this autobiographical record begins and ends in Singapore.

Norden, H. From golden gate to golden sun: a record of travel, sport and observation in Siam and Malaya. Boston, 1923. 292 p.

Ommanney, F. D. Eastern windows. London, 1960. 245 p.
    Part One--Landscape: Singapore p. 13-116.

Ong, Tae-hae. The Chinaman abroad; or a desultory account of the Malayan Archipelago, particularly of Java. Shanghai, 1849. 80 p. (Chinese Miscellany, no. 2) Map.

DESCRIPTION - POPULAR AND SCIENTIFIC

Peet, G. L. Malayan exile. Singapore, 1934. 89 p. Illus.
Originally appeared in Straits Times as "A journal
in the federal capital."

Powell, E. A. Where the strange trails go down:
Sulu, Borneo, Celebes, Bali, Java, Sumatra,
Straits Settlements, Malay States, Siam, Cambodia,
Assam, Cochin-China. New York, 1921. 279 p.

Pratt, A. Magical Malaya. Melbourne, 1931. 278 p.

Preyer, A. Indo-Malayische Streifzüge. Leipzig, 1903.
287 p.

Ranger (pseud.). Up and down the China coast. London,
1936. 286 p. Maps, plates.
P. 48-113 deal with Malaya.

Rathborne, A. B. Camping and tramping in Malaya: fifteen
years' pioneering in the native states of the Malay
Peninsula. London, 1898. 339 p. Illus., maps, plates.

Remington, W. E. Cross winds of empire: an account
of the Malaysian Archipelago. New York, 1941. 279 p.

Robertson, E. J. Straits memories: incidents, peoples,
and life in Singapore and the Straits a generation
ago. Singapore, 1910.

Roff, William R., ed. Stories by Sir Hugh Clifford.
Selected and introduced by William R. Roff. Kuala
Lumpur, 1966. 225 p.

Roff, William R., ed. Stories and sketches by Sir Frank
Swettenham. Selected and introduced by William R.
Roff. Kuala Lumpur, 1967. 216 p.

Rogers, W. A. Fifty years in Malaya. Colombo, 1940.
96 p.

Ross, C. Heute in Indien. Durch das Kaiserreich Indien,
Ceylon, Hinterindien und Insulinde. Leipzig, 1937.
301 p.

Rutter, Owen. The pirate wind: tales of the sea-robbers
of Malaya. London, 1930. 292 p. Illus., maps.

DESCRIPTION - POPULAR AND SCIENTIFIC

Sahni, J. N. Across twentieth parallel. A narrative
study of the countries of South-east Asia and Australia.
New Delhi, 1952. 164 p. Illus.
See chaps. 8-10, p. 53-73, for Malaya.

Schnack, Friedrich. Der Maler von Malaya, Erlebnisse
in den Wäldern und an den Küsten Insulindes. Hattingen,
1951. 293 p.

Scholten, Heribert. Heisses Singapur. Würzburg, 1959.
224 p. Illus.

Shuttleworth, Charles. Hutan rimba (Safaris in the
Malayan jungle). Singapore [1963]. 167 p. Front.,
illus.

Sidney, R. J. H. Malay land--"Tanah Malayu": some phases
of life in modern British Malaya. London, 1926.
300 p. Plates.

Sidney, R. J. H. In British Malaya to-day. London,
1927. 311 p. Map, plates.

Sim, Katherine. Malayan landscape. London, 1946. 248 p.

Simpson, W. Meeting the sun. London, 1874. 413 p. Illus.

Singam, S. Durai Raja. Sir Gerald Templer's work for
a cultural revival in Malaya. MHJ, 2, 2 (1955):
131-137.

Slimming, John. Temiar jungle; a Malayan journey. London,
1958. 176 p.

Slimming, John. In fear of silence. London, 1959.

Stacey, Tom. The hostile sun: a Malayan journey. London,
1953. 182 p.

Stirling, W. G. Shadows in the Malay Peninsula. London,
1910. Illus.

Swettenham, Frank A. Journal kept during a journey
across the Malay Peninsula. JRASSB, 15 (1885): 1-37.

DESCRIPTION - POPULAR AND SCIENTIFIC

Swettenham, Frank A. About Perak. Singapore, 1893.
77 p. Reprint.
Articles on geography and history, development
of the residential system, ports, mining, agriculture,
etc.

Swettenham, Frank A. Malay sketches. London, New
York, 1895. 288 p.

Swettenham, Frank A., ed. Unaddressed letters.
London, 1898. 312 p.

Swettenham, Frank A. The real Malay. New York,
1900. 295 p.

Swettenham, Frank A. Footprints in Malaya. London,
1942. 176 p.

Talaivasingam, A. Malayan notes and sketches. Singapore,
1924. 135 p.

Taunton, H. Australind: wanderings in the Malay
East. London, 1903. 247 p.

Teeling, William. Gods of tomorrow, the story of
a journey in Asia and Australasia. London, 1936.
376 p. Illus., index, map.
See p. 40-55 for Malaya.

Thomson, John. Straits of Malacca, Indo-China and
China. New York, 1875. 546 p.

Thürk, Harry. Der Wind stirbt vor dem Dschungel.
Berlin [1961]. 389 p. Illus.

Tomlinson, H. M. In the forest of Malaya. Harper's
Monthly Magazine, 149 (Oct. 1924): 624-633.
Illus.

Tomlinson, Henry M. Tidemarks, some records of
a journey to the beaches of the Moluccas and
the forest of Malaya in 1923. London, 1924.
311 p.

Tomlinson, Henry M. Malay waters; the story of
little ships coasting out of Singapore and Penang
in peace and war. London, 1950. 199 p.

Vacher, Henry. Twelve years in India and Malaya.
A memoir of Henry Vacher, compiled from his
letters. By Francis Vacher. London, 1880. 114 p.
Plates.

Wallace, Alfred Russel. The Malay Archipelago.
The land of the orang-utan and the bird of paradise.
New York, 1869. 638 p.

Wavell, Stewart. The lost world of the East; an
adventurous quest in the Malayan hinterland.
London, 1958. 195 p. Illus.

Wavell, Stewart. The Naga King's daughter. London
[1964]. 247 p. Bibliog., plates.

Weld, Frederick A. The Straits Settlements and
British Malaya. Proc R Col Inst, 15 (1883/1884):
266-297.
Discussion, p. 297-311.

Wells, Carveth. Six years in the Malay jungle.
New York, 1925. 261 p. Illus.
Appendix compiled from official sources on
the Malay Peninsula and its resources, p. 223-255.
Bibliography of modern books relating to Malaya,
p. 256-261.

Wells, Carveth. North of Singapore. New York, 1940.
271 p.

Whitney, Caspar. Jungle trails and jungle people.
Travel, adventure and observation in the Far
East. New York, 1905. 310 p. Plates.

Wignesan, T., ed. Bunga emas; an anthology of contemporary
Malaysian literature, 1930-1963. [Kuala Lumpur,
1964]. 272 p.

Wildman, Rounsevelle. Tales of the Malayan coast,
from Penang to the Philippines. Boston, 1899.
347 p.

Wilkinson, Hugh. Sunny lands and seas. London,
1883. 324 p. Illus., map.
Notes made during a five-months' tour in India,
the Straits Settlements, Manila, China, etc.

DESCRIPTION - POPULAR AND SCIENTIFIC

Willis, Granville Pratt. It began in Singapore.
London, 1958. 189 p.

Wilson, M. C. Malaya: the land of enchantment.
Amersham, 1937. 144 p.

Winstedt, Sir Richard O. Malayan memories. Singapore,
1916. 81 p.

Winstedt, Sir Richard O. Malayan background. GM,
14 (1941-1942): 105-121. Illus.

Wittenbach, H. A. Eastern horizons. London, 1954.
99 p. Bibliog., maps, plates.
Includes Malaya.

Wolff, W. Im malaiischen Urwald und Zinngebirge.
Berlin [1909]. Illus.

CHAPTER 5

GENERAL

Allen, Richard. Malaysia: prospect and retrospect.
The impact and aftermath of colonial rule. London,
1968. 330 p. Maps.

American University, Washington, D.C., Foreign
Areas Studies Division. Area handbook for Malaysia
and Singapore. By Bela C. Maday [et al.]. Washington,
D.C., 1965 [1966]. 745 p. Illus., maps.

Asmah Binte Haji Omar. The Malaysian mosaic of
languages. In S. Takdir Alisjahbana, ed. The
Cultural Problems of Malaysia in the Context
of Southeast Asia. Kuala Lumpur [1966?]: 188-202.

Baedeker, K. Indien Handbuch für Reisende. Ceylon,
Vorderindien, Birma, die Malayische Halbinsel,
Siam und Java. Leipzig, 1914. 358 p.

Bartlett, Vernon. Report from Malaya. London, 1954.
128 p. Illus.

Bastin, John, and R. Roolvink, eds. Malayan and
Indonesian studies; essays presented to Sir
Richard Winstedt on his eighty-fifth birthday.
Oxford, 1964. 357 p.

Begbie, P. J. The Malayan Peninsula: embracing
its history, manners and customs of the inhabitants,
politics, natural history, etc. from its earliest
times. Madras, 1834. 542 p.

Begbie, P. J. The Malayan peninsula . . . . With
an introduction by Diptendra M. Banerjee. Kuala
Lumpur, New York, London, Melbourne, 1967. Various
pagination. (Oxford in Asia, Historical Reprints)

Belfield, H. Conway. Handbook of the Federated
Malay States. London, 1906. 184 p. Maps, plates.

Bottoms, J. C. Malayan glossary. MHJ, 2, 1 (1955):
82-88.

Cameron, John. Our tropical possessions in Malayan
India: being a descriptive account of Singapore,
Penang, Province Wellesley and Malacca; their
peoples, products, commerce and government.
London, 1865. 408 p. Illus.

GENERAL

Cator, G. E. Some of our Malayan problems. JRCAS,
    28 (1941): 18-32.

Chai, Hon-chan. The development of British Malaya,
    1896-1909. London, 1964. 364 p. Illus., maps.
    Concentration on administrative and social
    development of Western Malaysia.

Chapman, F. S. Travels in Japanese-occupied Malaya.
    Alpine Jl (May 1949): 36-57.

Clark, Elizabeth A. Peoples of the China Seas.
    St. Louis, 1942. 94 p.

Clark, Kathleen. Carl Gibson-Hill. JRASMB, 38,
    2 (Dec. 1965): 17-21.

Clifford, Mary Louise. The land and people of Malaysia.
    Philadelphia, 1968. 160 p. (Portraits of the
    Nations Series) Maps.

Crabb, C. H. Malaya's Eurasians--an opinion. Singapore,
    1960. 85 p. Chart.

Crawford, John. A descriptive dictionary of the
    Indian Islands and adjacent countries. London,
    1856. 459 p. Map.

Curtis, William E. Egypt, Burma and British Malaysia.
    Chicago, 1905. 399 p. Map, plates.
    P. 351-372 deal with Malaya.

Dennys, Nicholas B. A descriptive dictionary of
    British Malaya. London, 1894. 423 p.

Dodd, E. E. The new Malaya: report to the Fabian
    Colonial Bureau. London, 1946. 32 p. (Fabian
    Society Research Series, no. 115)

Ferguson, J. Ceylon, the Malay States and Java
    compared as plantation and residential colonies.
    United Empire, 2 (1911): 104-115, 165-176.

Firth, Raymond William. Report on social science
    research in Malaya. Singapore, 1948. 51 p.

German, R. L. Handbook to British Malaya. London,
    1926. 182 p. Maps. Later editions.

GENERAL

Gibbs, W. E. British Malaya: a story of empire.
Jl Manchester G Soc, 35 (1919): 8-18.

Gibson-Hill, C. A. The Malayan landscape. Seventy
camera studies. With an introduction by Malcolm
MacDonald. Singapore, 1949. 143 p. Plates.

Ginsburg, Norton Sydney. Malaya. Seattle, 1958.
533 p. Diagrs., maps.

Ginsburg, Norton Sydney, and C. F. Roberts. Malaya.
Chicago, 1955.

Gould, James W. The United States and Malaysia.
Cambridge, 1969. 275 p.

Great Britain, Central Office of Information, Reference
Division. The Federation of Malaya. London,
1963. 75 p.

Great Britain, War Office, General Staff, Geographical
Section. Gazetteer of Malaya. Published under
the authority of the Director of Survey (India).
New Delhi, 1945. 122 p. Col. map.

Guillemard, F. H. H. Malaysia and the Pacific Archipelago.
London, 1899. 574 p.
Stanford's compendium of geography and travels,
Australasia, II.

Guillemard, Laurence. British Malaya. JRCAS, 21
(1934): 394-402.

Gullick, J. M. Malaya. London, New York, 1963.
256 p. 2d. edition, expanded, 1964. 258 p. Bibliog.,
map, statistical tables.

Gullick, J. M. Malaysia and its neighbours. London,
1967. 194 p. Sketch map.

Gullick, J. M. Malaysia. New York, 1969. 304 p.
(Nations of the Modern World) Map.

Hake, H. B. E. The new Malaya and you. London,
1945. 107 p.

GENERAL

Hamilton, W. The East-India gazetteer: containing
particular descriptions of . . . Hindostan,
and the adjacent countries, India beyond the
Ganges, and the Eastern Archipelago. London,
1828. 2 v. (1) 684 p. (2) 770 p. Maps.

Hanna, Willard A. Reports on Malaya, Singapore
and Malaysia. New York, 1956.

Hanna, Willard A. Sequel of colonialism: the 1957-1960
foundations for Malaysia: an on-the-spot examination
of the geographic, economic, and political seedbed
where the idea of a Federation of Malaya was
germinated. New York, 1965. 288 p. Map.

Harrison, C. W., ed. Illustrated guide to the Federated
Malay States. London, 1923. 370 p.

Hawkins, G. Malaya. Photographs by C. A. Gibson-Hill.
Singapore, 1952. 111 p. Illus.

Haynes, A. S. British Malaya. United Empire, 25
(1934): 533-535.

Hodgson, Geoffrey. Memoir of C. A. Gibson-Hill.
JRASMB, 38, 2 (1965): 1-16.

Hughes, David R. The peoples of Malaya. Singapore,
1965. 102 p. Bibliog., illus.

Hunter, Guy. Southeast Asia: race, culture and
nation. London, New York, Kuala Lumpur, 1966.
190 p. Maps, tables.

Kanchananaga, Thuan, comp. A Malayan all-in-one
book of references and guide. Singapore, 1934.
371 p. Statistics, table.

Keane, A. H. Eastern geography: a geography of
the Malay Peninsula, Indo-China, the eastern
Archipelago, the Philippines, and New Guinea.
2d ed. rev. London, E. Standord, 1892. 192 p.
Map.

Lehmann, Heinz. Malaya unter britischer Herrschaft.
Berlin, 1941. 86 p. (Schriften des deutschen
Instituts für aussenpolitische Forschung und
des Hamburger Instituts für auswärtige Politik,
no. 90) Illus., maps.

Lin, Fang-sheng. Malaiia. Perevod s kitaisk. N.
A. Simoniia. Moscow, 1956. 103 p. Illus., map.

Malaya (Federation) Department of Information.
Federation of Malaya: Progress in pictures.
Kuala Lumpur, 1960. 70 p. Illus., map.
A photo-story of some of the more notable
progress of the Federation of Malaya under the
new nation's first five-year development plan,
1956-1960.

Malaysia. Official year book 1966. Kuala Lumpur,
1968. 494 p. Appendices, fold. map, illus.,
tables.

Malaysia, Department of Information Services, External
Information Division, Publications Section.
Malaysia at a glance. Kuala Lumpur, 1968. 106 p.
Map.

Malaysia, Ministry of Information and Broadcasting.
Malaysia, merdeka-maju (freedom and progress)
1957-1967. Kuala Lumpur, 1967. 202 p. Illus.,
part. col.
Text in Malay and English.

Malaysia Yearbook. 1962-1963/64- . Kuala Lumpur,
Malay Mail. Title varies: 1956-1962, Federation
of Malaya yearbook. Illus., tables.

Malaysian Scientific Association. Malaysian scientific
directory, 1964. Kuala Lumpur [1964]. 87 p.
Maps.

Maxwell, W. E. Malay Peninsula: its resources and
products. Proc R Col Inst, 23 (1891-1892): 3-46.

Miller, Eugene H. Strategy at Singapore. A study
of the American Council in Public Affairs. New
York, 1942. 145 p.

Miller, H. A guide to Singapore. Singapore, 1955.

Miller, Harry. Prince and premier; a biography
of Tunku Abdul Rahman Putra Al-Haj, first prime
minister of the Federation of Malaya. London,
1959. 224 p.

GENERAL

Mills, Lennox A. Malaya, a political and economic
   appraisal. Minneapolis, 1958. 234 p.

Mills, Lennox A. British Malaya, 1824-67. Singapore
   [1961]. 424 p.

Mok, S. T., and P. W. Chong. Report on the symposium
   on scientific and technological research in
   Malaysia. Mal For, 28 (Apr. 1965): 112-117.

Moore, Joanna. The land and people of Malaya and
   Singapore. London, New York, 1957. 88 p. Map,
   photos.

Morais, J. Victor, ed. Who's who in Malaysia 1963.
   Kuala Lumpur [1963]. 342 p. Illus.

Morgan, W. S. The story of Malaya. Singapore, 1940.
   98 p. 1941. 100 p.

Nazareth, Philip N. The story of Malaya and her
   neighbours. Singapore [1961]. 271 p. Illus.,
   maps.

Ogmore, Lord (earlier Lt. Col. Reeves-Williams,
   M.P.). Malaya--1946. Eastern World, 6, 8 (1952):
   15-19; 6, 9 (1952): 14-15.

Ormsby-Gore, W. G. A. Report by the Right Honorable
   W. G. A. Ormsby-Gore M.P. (Parliamentary Under-secretary
   of State for the Colonies) on his visit to Malaya,
   Ceylon and Java during the year 1928. London,
   1928. 166 p. (Command Paper, no. 3235) Map.
   Chapter 1, p. 5-67, deals with problems of
   agriculture, public health, education, forestry,
   and transportation.

Purcell, Victor. Malaya: an outline of a colony.
   London, New York, 1946. 151 p. Illus., maps.

Purcell, Victor. The memoirs of a Malayan official.
   London, 1965. 373 p. Illus.

Raghavan, Nedyam. India and Malaya; a study. Bombay,
   1954. 137 p. (India and Her Neighbours series)
   Maps.

Rawlings, G. S. Malaya. London, 1945. 38 p.

Roberts, Chester, ed. Area handbook on Malaya.
Chicago, 1955. 698 p. (Subcontractor's Monograph,
Human Relations Area Files - 17)

Robson, J. H. M. Records and recollections. Kuala
Lumpur, 1934. 207 p. Bibliog.

Ryan, N. J. The cultural background of the peoples
of Malaya. Kuala Lumpur, etc., 1962. 184 p.
Historical summary p. 1-27; Malays p. 28-73;
Chinese p. 74-129; Indians p. 130-152; the West
p. 153-172.

Schmidt, Kurt Otto. Malaysia, Singapore. Buchenhain
vor München [1965]. 72 p. (Mai's Weltführer,
Nr. 9) Illus., map.

Singam, S. Durai Raja. Sir Gerald Templer's work
for a cultural revival in Malaya. MHJ, 2, 2
(1955): 131-137.

Singam, S. Durai Raja. Malayan place names; Port
Weld to Kuantan. Singapore, 1957. 282 p.

Sutter, John Orval. Scientific facilities and information
services of the Federation of Malaya and State
of Singapore. Honolulu, 1961. 43 p. (Pacific
Science Information, no. 2) Diagrs., maps.

Thompson, Virginia. Landward side of Singapore.
PA, 14 (1941): 21-34.

Thompson, Virginia. Postmortem on Malaya. New York,
1943. 323 p. Bibliog., map.
Relates the economic conditions in the Malayan
Peninsula prior to the Japanese invasion.

Tregonning, K. G. Malaysia and Singapore. [Rev.
ed.]. Melbourne, Cheshire for the Australian
Institute of International Affairs [1966]. 113 p.
Tables.
First edition published in 1964 under title:
Malaysia.

GENERAL

United States Board on Geographic Names. Directions
for treatment of geographical names in Malaya.
Washington, D.C., 1944. 11 p. (Special publication,
no. 21)

United States Board on Geographic Names. Decisions
on names in Federation of Malaya and Singapore:
cumulative decision list. Washington, D.C.,
1952. 24 p.

United States Board on Geographic Names. British
Borneo, Singapore, and Malaya: official standard
names approved by Board of Geographic Names;
prepared in Office of Geography. Washington,
D.C., 1955. 463 p.

Wang, Gung-wu, ed. Malaysia, a survey. New York,
London, 1964. 446 p. Charts, maps, tables.

Winstedt, Richard. Britain and Malaya, 1786-1941.
London, New York, 1944. 80 p.

Wright, A., and H. A. Cartwright, eds. Twentieth
century impressions of British Malaya: its history,
people, commerce, industries and resources.
Singapore, 1908. 959 p. Illus., map.

Wright, A., and T. H. Reid. The Malay Peninsula:
a record of British progress in the Middle East.
London, 1912. 360 p. Illus., map.

Wyatt, Woodrow. Southwards from China. A survey
of South East Asia since 1945. London, 1952.
200 p.
    Chap. VII, p. 138-161, deals with Malaya.

Zinkin, Maurice. Asia and the West. London, 1951.
300 p.
    In addition to a special chapter devoted to
Malaya, the book contains numerous references
to Malaya.

CHAPTER 6

HISTORY

A. GENERAL

'Abd Allah Ibn 'Abd al-Kadir. The autobiography
of Munshi Abdullah. Translated from the Malay
by the Rev. W. G. Shellabear. Singapore, 1918.
146 p.

Ahmat, Sharom. American trade with Singapore, 1819-65.
JRASMB, 38, 2 (1965): 241-257.

Akasli, Yoji. Japanese military administration in
Malaya. [Kuala Lumpur, 1968]. 50 p. Unpublished
paper no. 42 presented at the International Conference
on Asian History, Kuala Lumpur, August 1968. Mimeographed.

Alatas, Hussein, Syed. Reconstruction of Malaysian
history. Revue du Sud-est Asiatique, 3 (1961):
221-245. Bibliog.

Albuquerque, Afonso. The commentaries of the Great
Afonso Dalboquerque, Second Viceroy of India.
Tr. and ed. by Walter de Gray Birch. London,
1875-1883. 4 v. (Issued by the Hakluyt Society,
nos. 53, 55, 62, and 69). Index, maps.

Alisjahbana, S. Takdir, Xavier S. Thani Nayagam,
and Wang Gung-Wu, eds. The cultural problems
of Malaysia in the context of Southeast Asia.
Papers presented at the first conference of the
Malaysian Society of Orientalists held in Kuala
Lumpur from the 22nd until the 25th of October
1965. Kuala Lumpur [1966].
A collection of twenty papers on a variety
of topics.

Allen, J. De Vere. Two imperialists: a study of
Sir Frank Swettenham and Sir Hugh Clifford. JRASMB,
37, 1 (1964): 41-73.

Allen, J. De Vere. The ancient regime in Trengganu,
1909-1919. JRASMB, 41, 1 (1968): 23-53.

Allen, J. De Vere. The elephant and the mousedeer--a
new version: Anglo-Kedah relations, 1905-1915.
JRASMB, 41, 1 (1968): 54-94.

Allen, J. De Vere. The Kelantan rising of 1915:
some thoughts on the concepts of resistance in
British Malayan history. JSAH, 9, 2 (1968): 211-257.

Allen, Richard. Malaysia, prospect and retrospect.
The impact and aftermath of colonial rule. London,
1968.
Book begins with the early history of Malaya,
Singapore, and Indonesia, and concentrates on
events after the defeat of Japan.

Anderson, John. Observations on the restoration
of Banca and Malacca to the Dutch, as affecting
the tin trade and general commerce of Pinang.
. . . [Prince of Wales Island], 1824. 52 p.

Anderson, John. Political and commercial considerations
relative to the Malay Peninsula and the British
settlements in the Straits of Malacca. Part I
- Consideration on the conquest of Quedah and
Perak by the Siamese. Part II - Descriptive sketch
of the tin countries on the western coast of
the Peninsula of Malacca. Prince of Wales Island,
1824. 204 p.

Anderson, John. Political and commercial considerations
relative to the Malayan Peninsula and British
settlements in the Straits of Malacca. With appendix
of the aboriginal inhabitants of the Malayan
Peninsula, and particularly of the Negroes, called
Semang. Prince of Wales Island, 1828. 391 p.

Anderson, John. Political and commercial considerations
relative to the Malayan Peninsula and the British
settlements in the Straits of Malacca. With an
introduction by Dr. J. S. Bastin. JRASMB, 35,
4 (Dec. 1962) [1965]: 204 p.

Arasaratnam, S. Some notes on the Dutch in Malacca
and the Indo-Malayan trade 1641-1670. [Kuala
Lumpur, 1968]. 15 p. Unpublished paper no. 3
presented at the International Conference on
Asian History, Kuala Lumpur, August 1968. Mimeographed.

Aspinall, A. Cornwallis in Bengal: the administrative
and judicial reforms of Lord Cornwallis in Bengal,
with accounts of the commercial expansion of
the East India Company, 1786-1793. Manchester,
1931. (Manchester University, Historical Series,
no. 60)

Association of British Malaya. The civil defence
of Malaya, a narrative of the part taken in it
by the civilian population of the country in
the Japanese invasion. Compiled by a committee
under the chairmanship of Sir George Maxwell.
London, New York, 1944. 128 p. Maps.

Azmi bin Jumid. An appraisal of "Kesah Pelayaran,
Abdullah Ka-Kelantan" as an historical work.
PS, 2, 1 (1967): 1-11.

Baker, A. C. Some account of the Anglo-Dutch relations
in the East at the beginning of the 19th century
based on the records preserved in the Colonial
Secretary's Office in Singapore, and in the Resident's
Office, Malacca. JRASSB, 64 (1913): 1-68.

Barbosa, Duarte. The book of Duarte Barbosa. An
account of the countries bordering on the Indian
Ocean and their inhabitants, written by Duarte
Barbosa and completed about the year 1518 A.D.
Tr. by M. L. Dames. London, 1918-1921. 2 v. (1)
238 p. (2) 286 p. Bibliog., index.

Bassett, D. K. The British country trader and sea
captain in South East Asia in the seventeenth
and eighteenth centuries. JHS, 1, 2 (1961): 9-16.

Bassett, D. K. The conquest of Malaya. [Review article].
JSAH, 2, 3 (1961): 91-100.

Bassett, D. K. The Portuguese in Malaya. JHS, 1,
3 (1962/1963): 18-28.

Bassett, D. K. British commercial and strategic
interest in the Malay peninsula during the late
eighteenth century. In John Bastin and R. Roolvink,
eds. Malayan and Indonesian Studies. Oxford,
1964: 122-140.

Bassett, D. K. The historical background, 1500-1815
[of Malaysia]. In Wang Gung-wu. Malaysia: A Survey.
London, 1964: 113-127.

Bassett, D. K. Anglo-Malay relations, 1786-1795.
JRASMB, 38, 2 (1965): 183-212. Map.

Bastin, Christopher, and John Bastin. Some old Penang
tombstones. JRASMB, 37, 1 (1964): 126-165.

Bastin, John. Research material for the study of
Malayan and Indonesian history in the library
of the University of Malaya in Kuala Lumpur.
JHS, 1, 2 (1961): 4-5.

Bastin, John. Problems of personality in the
reinterpretation of modern Malayan history.
In John Bastin and R. Roolvink, eds. Malayan
and Indonesian Studies. Oxford, 1964: 141-153.

Bastin, John. Sir Richard Winstedt and his writings.
In John Bastin and R. Roolvink, eds. Malayan
and Indonesian Studies. Oxford, 1964: 1-23.

Bastin, John, and Robin W. Winks, comps. Malaysia;
selected historical readings. Kuala Lumpur, London,
New York, Melbourne, 1966. 484 p. Bibliog., maps.

Bennett, Gordon. Why Singapore fell. An account
of the Japanese invasion of Malaya. London, 1944.
262 p.

Blagden, C. O. Notes on Malay history. JRASSB, 53
(1909): 139-162; 73 (1916): 127-128.

Blagden, C. O. Catalogue of manuscripts in European
languages belonging to the Library of the India
Office. V. 1 - Mackenzie collection, Part I -
The 1822 collection and the private collection.
Oxford, 1916. 302 p.

Bland, R. N. Historical tombstones of Malacca, mostly
of Portuguese origin. London, 1905. 75 p.

Blundell, E. A. Notices of the history and present
condition of Malacca. Jl Ind Archip, 2 (1848):
726-754.

Bogaars, George. The Tandjong Pagar Dock Company
1864-1905. Singapore, 1956. 117-260 p. (Memoirs
of the Raffles Museum, no. 3, December, 1956)

Bonney, R. A short history of Kuala Kubu.
JHS, 1, 1 (1960): 67-76.

Bonney, R. Francis Light, the Nonya and Penang.
JHS, 3 (1964/1965): 31-35.

Bonney, R. Francis Light and Penang. JRASMB, 38
(July 1965): 135-158.

Bonney, R. Towards Malaysian history. JHS, 4 (1965/1966):
17-21.

Bonney, R. The lease of Kuala Kedah: fact and fiction.
JHS, 6 (1967/1968): 54-77.

Bort, Balthasar. Report of Governor Balthasar Bort
on Malacca, 1678. Translated by M. J. Bremner.
With an introduction and notes by C. O. Blagden.
JRASMB, 5, 1 (1927): 1-232.
  Comprehensive survey of Dutch activities in
the Straits of Malacca.

Bowen, Charles D. British Malaya as it was. AR,
46 (1950): 896-910.

Boxer, C. R. The Achinese attack on Malacca in 1629,
as described in contemporary Portuguese sources.
In John Bastin and R. Roolvink, eds. Malayan
and Indonesian Studies. Oxford, 1964: 105-121.

Braam Houckgeest, A. E. van. Memorie over Malakka
en den tinhandel aldaar (1790). BTLV, 76 (1920):
284-290.

Braddell, Roland. An introduction to the study of
ancient times in the Malay Peninsula and the
Straits of Malacca. JRASMB, 13, 2 (1935): 70-109;
14, 3 (1936): 10-71; 15, 3 (1937): 64-126; 17,
1 (1939): 146-212; 19, 1 (1941): 21-74; 20, 1
(1947): 161-186; 20, 2 (1947): 1-19; 22, 1 (1949):
1-24; 23, 1 (1950): 1-36; 23, 3 (1950): 1-35;
24, 1 (1951): 1-27.

Braddell, Roland. Most ancient Kedah. Part I. MH,
4, 2 (1958): 18-40.

Briggs, L. P. The Khmer Emperor and the Malay Peninsula.
FEQ, 9, 3 (1950): 256-305.

Buckley, C. B. Anecdotal history of old times in
Singapore. From the foundation of the settlement
under the Hon. the East India Company on February
6th 1819, to the transfer to the Colonial Office
as part of colonial possessions of Crown on 1st
April, 1867. Singapore, 1902. 2 v. Illus.

Burney, H. The Burney papers: printed by order of
the committee of the Vajirana National Library.
Bangkok, 1910-1914. 15 v.

Chai, Hon-chan. The development of British Malaya,
1896-1909. Kuala Lumpur, London, New York, 1964.
364 p. 2d rev. ed., 1967. 366 p.

Chan, Su-ming. Kelantan and Trengganu, 1909-1939.
JRASMB, 38(July 1965): 159-198. Tables.

Chang, T. T. Sino-Portuguese trade from 1514 to
1644: a synthesis of Portuguese and Chinese sources.
Leiden, 1934. 157 p. Bibliog.

Cheng, Siok-hwa. The suppression of secret societies,
1869 to 1890. PS, 1, 1 (1966): 39-50.

Chew, Ernest. Sir Frank Swettenham and the Federation
of Malay States. MAS, 2, 1 (1968): 51-69.

Chin, Kee Onn. Malaya upside down. An account of
Malaya under the Japanese. Singapore, 1946. 208 p.

Clifford, Hugh Charles. Further India: being the
story of exploration from the earliest times
in Burma, Malaya, Siam and Indo-China. London,
1905. 378 p. Bibliog., illus., maps, plates.

Clodd, H. P. Malaya's first British pioneer: the
life of Francis Light. London, 1948. 166 p. Plates.

Collis, Maurice. British merchant adventures. London,
1942. 46 p. Illus., maps.

Coope, A. E., tr. The voyage of Abdullah; being
an account of his experiences on a voyage from
Singapore to Kelantan in A.D. 1838. Kuala Lumpur,
1967. 116 p.

Cope, Captain. A new history of the East-Indies, with brief observations of the religion, customs, manners and trade of the inhabitants; with a description of all the forts and settlements of the Europeans, and the trade carried on by the East-India Company; with an account of the wars they have been engaged in from their first settlement by Queen Elizabeth in the year 1601, to the present time. London, 1754. 392 p. Map.

Copies of all correspondence . . . relating to the proposed transfer of the Straits Settlements to the Colonial Office. . . British Parliamentary Papers, 1862, no. 40. 80 p.

Copies of correspondence . . . on the subject of the settlements in the Straits of Malacca. British Parliamentary Papers, 1857-58, no. 43. 7 p.

Copithorne, T. Recent Japanese attitudes towards Southeast Asia. JHS, 5 (1966/1967): 29-38.

Correspondence between H.M.'s Government and the East India Company on . . . the Settlements in the Straits of Malacca. London, 1858. 7 p.

Correspondence, papers, and reports respecting the protected Malay States. British Parliamentary Papers, 1882, no. 46, 46 p.; 1887, no. 58, 131 p.; 1889, no. 56, 116 p.; 1892, no. 56, 105 p.; 1896, no. 58, 71 p.

Cowan, C. D. Governor Bannerman and the Penang tin scheme 1818-1819. JRASMB, 23, 1 (1950): 52-83.

Cowan, C. D. The origins of British political control in Malaya, 1867-1878. 1955. 342 p. Ph.D. thesis (School of Oriental and African Studies) -- London.

Cowan, C. D. Ideas of history in the Journal of the Malayan (Straits) Branch of the Royal Asiatic Society, 1878-1941. In D. G. E. Hall. Historians of South East Asia. London (1961): 279-285.

Cowan, C. D. Nineteenth century Malaya: the origins of British political control. London, 1961. 286 p. Maps.

Cowan, C. D. Nineteenth century Malaya: the origins
of British political control. Kuala Lumpur, 1967.
300 p. Bibliog., maps.

Cowan, C. D., ed. Sir Frank Swettenham's Perak journals,
1874-1876. JRASMB, 24, 4 (1951): 1-148.

Crawfurd, John. History of the Indian Archipelago.
Edinburgh, 1820. 3 v.
See v. 2: 125-192.

Cullin, E. G., and W. F. Zehnder. Early history
of Penang, 1592-1827. Penang, 1905.

Dalton, Clive (pseud.). Men of Malaya. London, 1942.
165 p.

Dartford, Gerald Percy. Malacca: emporium of the
eastern trade. History Today, 10 (Dec. 1960):
856-864. Illus., map.

Dartford, Gerald Percy. A short history of Malaya.
2d ed. New impression. London, 1960. 218 p. Bibliog.,
illus.
This edition first published in 1958.

Da Silva Rego. New research material in Portuguese
on Malaysia. MH, 9, 1-2 (1965): 2-7.

Devahuti, D. India and ancient Malaya, from the
earliest times to circa A.D. 1400. Singapore,
1965. 165 p. Maps, plates.

Donnison, F. S. V. British military administration
in the Far East, 1943-46. London, 1956. 483 p.
Maps.
Includes Malaya.

Douglas, F. W. Malay place names of Hindu origin.
JRASMB, 16, 1 (1938): 150-152.

Douglas, F. W. Notes on the historical geography
of Malaya and sidelights on the Malay annals.
Klang, 1949. 50 p. Maps.

Eredia, Godinhode. Malacca, L'Inde méridionale et
le Cathay. Brussels, 1882. Quarto.

Fatimi, S. Q. In quest of Kalah. JSAH, 1, 2 (1960): 62-101.

Funakoshi, Akio. Malacca appearing in old maps--maps of the town during the Portuguese-Dutch ages. [In Japanese]. Excerpt: Tōnan Ajia Kenkyū--Southeast Asian Studies, v. 6, 4 (March 1969): 800-824. Maps.

Furnivall, J. S. The early history of the Malay Archipelago. Jl Burma Research Soc, 24, 2 (1933): 93-104.

Garnier, Grace P. Paddylands, a story of Malaya. Illustrated by Nora Hamerton. London (1947). 156 p. Illus.

George, Sidney Charles. Escape from Singapore. London, 1946. 188 p.

Gerini, G. E. Researches on Ptolemy's geography of Eastern Asia (Further India and Indo-Malay Archipelago). London, 1909. 945 p. (Royal Asiatic Society Monographs, no. 1) Map.

Gibson, J. A. The Malay Peninsula and Archipelago. London, 1928. 236 p.

Gibson-Hill, C. A. Singapore: notes on the history of the Old Strait, 1580-1850. JRASMB, 27, 1 (1954): 163-214. Bibliog., illus., maps.

Graham, Gerald S. Great Britain in the Indian Ocean: a study of maritime enterprise 1810-1850. Oxford, 1967. 479 p.
    The choice of Singapore, p. 329-346. Piracy in Malayan waters, p. 362-382.

Great Britain, Ministry of Information. The story of the Malay Peninsula. Part I -- Before the Second World War. Part II - During the Second World War. London, 1944. 2 v. in 1.

Groenveldt, W. P. Notes on the Malay Archipelago and Malacca. Verh Batav Gen Kunsten Wet, 39, 1 (1880): 144. Map.
    Compiled from Chinese sources.

Gullick, J. M. The Negri Sembilan economy of 1890's.
JRASMB, 24, 1 (1951): 38-55.

Gullick, J. M. Captain Speedy of Larut. JRASMB,
26, 3 (1953): 1-103. Bibliog., illus., map.

Gullick, J. M. Kuala Lumpur, 1880-95. JRASMB, 28,
4 (1955): 5-172.

Gullick, J. M. Malayan pioneers. Singapore, 1958.
91 p.

Gullick, J. M. Kuala Lumpur in 1884? JRASMB, 32,
1 (1959 [i.e. 1962]): 198-202. Illus.

Gullick, J. M. A history of Selangor, 1742-1957.
Singapore, 1960. 122 p. Geneal. table, illus.,
maps, plates, ports.

Hall, Daniel George Edward. From Mergui to Singapore,
1689-1819; a neglected chapter in the naval history
of the Indian Ocean. History, 40 (1955): 255-272.

Hamilton, Capt. Alexander. A new account of the
East-Indies: being the observations and remarks
of Capt. Hamilton, who resided in those parts
from the year 1688 to 1723. Edinburgh, 1727;
London, 1811. 2 v. (1) 258 p. (2) 522 p.

Harcus, A. Drummond. History of the Presbyterian
Church in Malaya. London, 1955. 16 p.

Harrison, Brian. Trade in the Straits of Malacca
in 1785. A memorandum by P. G. de Bruijn, governor
of Malacca. JRASMB, 26, 1 (1953): 56-62.

Harrison, Brian. Malacca in the eighteenth century.
Two Dutch governors' reports. JRASMB, 27, 1 (1954):
24-34.

Harrison, C. R. The last of the creepers. Memoirs
of a Malayan rubber planter 1907-1917. MH, 7,
1 (1961): 18-27.

Harun Aminurrashid. A Malay among the Portuguese.
Translated by Ahmad Hussain. Singapore, 1961.
144 p.

Helfferich, Emil. Zur Geschichte der Firmen Behn,
Meyer und Co., gegründet in Singapore am 1. November
1840, und Arnold Otto Meyer, gegründet in Hamburg
am 1. Juni 1857. Hamburg, 1957. 154 p.

Hervey, D. F. A., tr. Valentyn's description of
Malacca. JRASSB, 13 (1884): 49-74B; 15 (1885):
119-138; 16 (1885): 289-301; 17 (1886): 117-149;
22 (1890): 225-246. Map.

Hino, Iwao. Stray notes on Nippon-Malaisian historical
connections. By Iwao Hino and S. Dirai Raja Singh.
Kuala Lumpur, 1955. 164 p.

Historical maps of Malaya (Mills collection) up
to 1879. Singapore, 1936. 26 p.

Hullu, J. de. A. E. van Braam Houckgeest's memorie
over Malakka en den tinhandel aldaar (1790).
BTLV, 76 (1920): 284-309.

Hullu, J. de. De Engelschen op Poeloe Pinang en
de tinhandel der Nederlandsche Oost-Indische
compagnie in 1788. BTLV, 77 (1921): 605-614.

International Conference of South-East Asian Historians,
1st, Singapore, 1961. Papers on Malayan history.
Edited by K. G. Tregonning. Singapore, Journal
of South-East Asian History, 1962. 273 p. Illus.

Irwin, Graham. Malacca Fort. JSAH, 3, 2 (1962):
19-44.

Iskandar, T. Three Malay historical writings in
the first half of the 17th century. JRASMB, 40,
2 (1967): 38-53.

Jack-Hinton, Colin. Further investigations at Johore
Lama: preliminary notes. FMJ, n.s., 8 (1963):
24-30. Diagrs., photos.

Jack-Hinton, Colin. A note on a Ch'eng Hua Nien
Hao from Kampong Makam, Kota Tinggi, and some
remarks on the Johore river trade in the fifteenth
century. FMJ, n.s., 8 (1963): 32-35.

Jackson, J. C. Kuala Lumpur in the 1880's. The contribution
of Bloomfield Douglas. JSAH, 4 (1963): 117-127.

Jackson, J. C. Planters and speculators: Chinese
and European agricultural enterprise in Malaya
1786-1921. Kuala Lumpur, 1968. 312 p. Bibliog.,
269-281; graphs, maps, tables.

Japanese Research Division, Military History Section,
General Headquarters, Far East Command. Twenth-fifth
Army operations in Malaya and Southeast Asia
area, November 1941 - February 1942. Tokyo, 1949.

Jessy, Joginder Singh. History of Malaya (1400-1959).
Penang, 1961. 367 p. Illus., maps.

Johan, Khasnor. The bunga mas in Malay-Siamese relations.
JHS, 4 (1965/1966): 11-16.

Josselin de Jong, P. E. de. Who's who in the Malay
annals. JRASMB, 34, 2 (1961): 1-89)

Josselin de Jong, P. E. de. The character of the
Malay annals. In John Bastin and R. Roolvink,
eds. Malayan and Indonesian Studies. Oxford,
1964: 235-241.

Kennedy, J. A history of Malaya A.D. 1400-1959.
New York, London, 1962. 311 p.

Keppel, Henry. A visit to the Indian Archipelago,
in H.M. Ship Maeander. With portions of the private
journal of Sir James Brooke. London, 1853. 2 v.
in 1. Chart, plates.

Khoo, Kay-kim. A Victorian moralist in Perak's Augean
stable? JHS, 4 (1965/1966): 33-47.

Khoo, Kay-kim. The Federation of 1896: its origin.
PS, 1, 2 (1966): 6-23.

Khoo, Kay-kim. Syed Sha'aban bin Syed Ibrahim Al-Kadri.
PS, 2, 1 (1967): 40-47.

Khoo, Kay-kim. Biographical sketches of certain
Straits Chinese involved in the Klang War (1867-1874).
PS, 2, 2 (1967): 41-51.

Khoo, Kay-kim. Johor in the 19th century: a brief
survey. JHS, 6 (1967/1968): 78-96.

Khoo, Kay-kim. Recent advances in the study and
writing on Malaysian history. PS, 3, 1 (1968):
1-12.

Klein, Ira. British expansion in Malaya, 1897-1902.
JSAH, 9, 1 (1968): 53-68.

Koek, E., comp. Portuguese history of Malacca. JRASSB,
17 (1896): 117-149.

Koenig, J. G. Journal of a voyage from India to
Siam and Malacca in 1779. JRASSB, 26 (1894):
58-192, 193-201.
Koenig was a pupil of Linnaeus. Some observations
on the people as well as on the flora.

Kruijt, J. A. Straits Settlements and Malay Peninsula.
JRASSB, 28 (1895): 19-51.

Kunst, J. New light on the early history of the
Malay Archipelago. Indian Art and Letters, 12
(1938): 99-105.

Laidin bin Alang Musa. The background of the Ulu
Langat Valley in Selangor. MHJ, 2 (1955): 8-11.

Lamb, Alastair. Report on the excavation and reconstruction
of Chandi Bukit Batu Pahat, Central Kedah. FMJ,
n.s., 5 (1960): 1-108. 73 plates.

Lamb, Alastair. Early history [of Malaysia]. In
Wang Gung-wu. Malaysia: A Survey. London, 1964:
99-112.

Lamb, Alastair. Takuapa: the probable site of a
pre-Malaccan entrepot in the Malay Peninsula.
In John Bastin and R. Roolvink, eds. Malayan
and Indonesian Studies. Oxford, 1964: 76-86.

Leith, George. A short account of the settlement,
produce and commerce of Prince of Wales Island
(Penang). London, 1804. 94 p.

Lewis, Diane. Inas: a study of local history. JRASMB,
33, 1 (1960 [i.e. 1964]): 65-94. Maps.

Lim, Poh-kim. Frank Swettenham's Malayan career,
1870-1896. Historical Journal (1963/1964): 29-32.

Lim, Teck-ghee. The two faces of the Chersonese.
PS, 2, 1 (1967): 30-35.

Linehan, W. History of Pahang. JRASMB, 14, 2 (1936):
1-256. Map, plates.

Linehan, W. The identification of some of Ptolemy's
place-names in the Golden Khersonese. JRASMB,
24, 3 (1951): 86-98.

Lister, Martin. The Negri Sembilan; their origin
and constitution. JRASSB, 19 (1888): 35-53.

Loh, Philip Fook-seng. Social policy in Perak 1877-1882.
PS, 1, 1 (1966): 29-38.

Loh, Philip Fook-seng. Some aspects of British social
policy in the Protected Malay States, 1877-1895.
1967. M.A. thesis -- University of Malaya.

Loh, Philip Fook-seng. British social policy in
the Protected Malay States, 1877-1895. Oxford
University Press, 1968. 220 p. Maps, plates.

Low, J. Origin and progress of the British colonies
in the Straits of Malacca. Jl Ind Archip, 3 (1849);
4 (1850).

Low, J. Ancient connection between Kedah and Siam.
Jl Ind Archip, 5 (1851): 498-527.

Low, J. A retrospect of British policy in the Straits
of Malacca, from the period of the first establishment
of Penang, 17 July, 1786, up to April 1842, containing
historical details respecting the Straits Settlements
and the neighbouring native states. Bangkok,
1910-1914. (Burney Papers, 5, 1)

Lucas, C. P. Historical geography of the British
Colonies. V. I. The Mediterranean and Eastern
colonies. (Second edition, revised by R. E. Stubbs).
Oxford, 1906. 304 p.

Majumdar, R. C. Hindu colonies in the Far East.
Lahore, 1927.

Malaya, Museums Department. Malayan forts. (Kuala
Lumpur, 1961). 35 p. Illus., maps, ports.

The Malays in Malaya, by one of them (Hadji Abdul
Majif). Singapore, 1928. 108 p.
Deals with the origin and progress of the colonization
and settlement of the Malays in the Malay Peninsula.

Marks, Harry Julian. The first contest for Singapore,
1809-1824. 's-Gravenhage, 1959. 262 p. (Verhandelingen
van het koninklijk Instituut voor Taal-, Land- en
Volkenkunde, deel 27)

Marsden, W., tr. Memoirs of a Malayan family written
by themselves. London, 1830. 84 p.

Mat Rasip bin Manap. The importance of the Johore-Riau-Lingga
empire in the context of Malayan history. PS,
2, 2 (1967): 20-25.

Maxwell, P. B. Our Malay conquests. London, 1878.
124 p.

Maxwell, W. E. The Dutch in Perak. JRASSB, 19 (1882):
245-268.

Maxwell, W. G. Barretto de Resende's account of
Malacca. JRASSB, 60 (1911): 1-24.

Maxwell, W. G., and W. S. Gibson. Treaties and engagements
affecting the Malay States and Borneo. London,
1924. 276 p.

McHugh, J. N. Psychological warfare in Malaya: 1942-1946.
JHS, 4 (1965/1966): 48-64.

McHugh, J. N. Psychological, or political, warfare
in Malaya. JHS, 5 (1966/1967): 75-94.

McIntyre, David. Political history of Malaysia,
1896-1946. In Wang Gung-wu. Malaysia: A Survey.
London, 1964: 138-148.

McLarty, Farquhar M. Affairs of the colony, being
a history concerning the Straits Settlements
and the British protected States of the Malay
peninsula. Penang, 1893. 138 p.

Medway, Lord. The antiquity of trade in edible birds'-nests.
FMJ, n.s., 8 (1963): 36-47.

Meilink-Roelofsz, M. A. P. The forts at Kuala Selangor.
MH, 5, 2 (1959): 33-38.

Middlebrook, S. M. Yap Ah Loy (1837-1885). JRASMB,
24, 2 (1951): 1-127. Bibliog.

Mills, J. V. Three of Eredia's illustrations. JRASMB,
10, 1 (1932): 14-15. Plates.

Mills, J. V., tr. Eredia's description of Malacca,
meridional India and Cathay, 1613. Translated
from the Portuguese with notes by J. V. Mills.
JRASMB, 8, 1 (1931): 1-288.

Mills, Lennox A. British Malaya 1824-1867. JRASMB,
3, 2 (1925): 1-340. Bibliog. (276-293).
Appendix by C. O. Blagden.

Mohammad Amin Hassan. Raja Mahdi bin Raja Sulaiman.
PS, 1, 2 (1966): 53-61.

Mohd. Nor Long. Gerakan kebangsaan sa-belum perang
dunia kedua. JHS, 6 (1967/1968): 13-25.

Moorhead, F. J. A history of Malaya and her neighbors.
London, 1957.

Morley, J. A. E. The Arabs and the Eastern trade.
JRASMB, 22, 2 (1949): 143-176. Table.

Muller, Hendrick P. N. Britisch Malakka. De Gids,
77, 4 (1913): 297-334; 78, 1 (1914): 140-179.

Muller, Hendrick P. N. The Malay Peninsula and Europe
in the past. Abstracted from the Dutch by P.
C. Hoynck van Papendrecht. JRASSB, 67 (1914):
57-84.

Neilson, J. B. Travel, trade, and conquest. Singapore,
1936.
Includes Francis Light and Alfonso d'Albuquerque.

Newbold, T. J. Political and statistical account
of the British settlements in the Straits of
Malacca, viz. Pinang, Malacca and Singapore;
with a history of the Malayan States on the Peninsula
of Malacca. London, 1839. 2 v. (1) 495 p. (2) 508 p.
Illus., index, maps.

Noone, H. D. The penarikan and Bernam land-routes.
JRASMB, **17**, **1** (1939): 144-145.

Notes on Malacca. Jl Ind Archip, 9 (1855): 43-65.

Office of War Information, Bureau of Overseas Intelligence.
Political and economic changes effected by the
Japanese in Malaya. Washington, D.C., 1943. 61 p.

Oldfield, J. B. The Green Howards in Malaya, 1949-1952;
the story of a post-war tour of duty by a battalion
of the lines. Aldershot, 1953. 191 p. Illus.

O'Sullivan, W. A. The relations between southern
India and the Straits Settlements. JRASSB, 36
(1901): 67-74.

Outpost (pseud.). A story of the evacuation and
an escape to Australia. London, 1943. 68 p. Illus.,
maps, plates.

Owen, G. M. The first British occupation of the
island of Singapore. AR, 34, **117** (1938): 131-139.

Parkinson, C. N. A short history of Malaya. Singapore,
1954. 27 p. (Background to Malaya Series, no. **1**)

Parkinson, C. N. The homes of Malaya. MHJ, 2, 2
(1955): 123-130. Illus.

Parkinson, C. N. The British in Malaya. History
Today (1956): 367-375.

Parkinson, C. N. British intervention in Malaya;
1867-1877. Singapore, 1960. 388 p. Maps.

Parr, C. W. C., and W. H. Mackray. Rembau: one of
the nine states; its history, constitution and
customs. JRASSB, 56 (1910): 1-157. Map.

Percival, Arthur Ernest. The war in Malaya. London,
1949. 336 p. Maps.

Pickering, W. A. The Straits Settlements: 1 - The
early history, 2 - The protected Malay States,
3 - The Mekong Treaty of the Malay Peninsula.
London, 1896. 38 p.

Pires, Tome. The suma oriental of Tome Pires: an
account of the East, from the Red Sea to Japan,
written in Malacca and India in 1512-1515. Translated
by Armando Cortesão. London, 1944. 2 v. (578 p.).
Bibliog., illus., index, maps.

Pluvier, Jan M. The cultural aspects of the colonial
period of Malayan history. In S. Takdir Alisjahbana,
ed. The Cultural Problems of Malaysia in the
Context of Southeast Asia. Kuala Lumpur [1966]: 220-234.

Pluvier, Jan M. A handbook and chart of South-East
Asian history. Kuala Lumpur, 1967. 58 p. Chart, maps.
P. 14-21 deal with Malaysia.

Pluvier, Jan M. Malayan nationalism: a myth. JHS,
6 (1967/1968): 26-40.

Ponniah, S. M. Political trends in postwar Malaya,
1945-1951. JHS, 1, 1 (1960): 22-34.

Purcell, Victor. The colonial period in Southeast
Asia; a historical sketch. New York, 1953. 65 p.

Purcell, Victor. Malaysia. London, 1965. 224 p.

Ramani, R. In memoriam Dato Sir Roland St. John
Braddell. JRASMB, 41, 1 (1968): 1-10.

Rawling, G. S. Malaya. Bombay, 1945. 38 p. Maps.

Reid, A. J. S. A Russian in Kelantan? PS, 1, 2 (1966):
42-47.

Rentse, Anker. History of Kelantan. JRASMB, 12,
1 (1934): 44-62.

Rentse, Anker. A historical note on the northeastern
Malay States. JRASMB, 20, 1 (1947): 23-40.

Ribadeneira, Marcelo. Historia de las islas del
archipielago Filipino y reinos de la gran China,
Tartaria, Cochinchina, Malaca, Siam, Cambodge
y Japón. Edición, prólogo y notas por el P. Juan
R. de Legísima, O.F.M. Madrid, 1947. 652 p.

Roff, William R. The life and times of Haji Othman
Abdullah. PS, 1, 2 (1966): 62-68.

Roff, William R. The Persatuan Melayu Selangor:
an early Malay political association. JSAH, 9,
1 (1968): 117-146.

Roff, William R. Social history and its materials
in Malaysia. PS, 3, 1 (1968): 13-20.

Rouffaer, G. P. Was Malaka emporium voor 1400 A.D.
genaamd Malajoer? en waar lag Woerawari, Ma-hasin,
Langka, Batoesawar? BTLV, 77 (1921): 1-172.

Rudner, Martin. The organization of the British
military administration in Malaya, 1946-48. JSAH,
9, 1 (1968): 95-106.

Rudnev, Vladimir Sergeevich. Ocherki noveishei istorii
Malaii, 1918-1957. Moscow, 1959. 116 p. At head
of title: Akademiia Nauk SSSR. Institut Vostokovedeniia.

Ryan, N. J., comp. Malaya through four centuries;
an anthology 1500-1900. Kuala Lumpur, London,
1959. 162 p.

Ryan, N. J. The making of modern Malaya. Kuala Lumpur,
1963, 1965, 1967. 214+ p. Maps, plates.

Sadka, Emily, ed. The journal of Sir Hugh Low, Perak,
1877. JRASMB, 27, 4 (1954): 5-108.

Sadka, Emily. The residential system in the Protected
Malay States, 1894-1895. 1960. Ph.D. thesis --
Australian National University, Canberra.

Sadka, Emily. The colonial office and the Protected
Malay States. In John Bastin and R. Roolvink,
eds. Malayan and Indonesian Studies. Oxford,
1964: 184-202.

Sadka, Emily. The protected Malay States, 1874-95.
Singapore, 1968. 250 p. Map.

St. John, Horace. The Indian Archipelago: its history
and present state. London, 1853. 2 v. (1) 393 p.
(2) 359 p.

Sankaran, R. Prelude to the British forward movement
of 1909. PS, 1, 2 (1966): 24-43.

Sar Desai, D. R. Resident system in Malaya: 1874-1875. JHS, 3 (1964/1965): 94-106.

Shariff, Kamaruzzaman. Sejarah Melayu as a historical source. JHS, 2 (1963/1964): 41-50.

Sheehan, J. J. Three XVIIth century visitors to the Malayan Peninsula. JRASMB, 12, 2 (1934): 71-107.

Sheppard, M. C. A short history of Trengganu. JRASMB, 22, 3 (1949): 1-74. Plate, table.

Sheppard, M. C. A short history of Malaya. Kuala Lumpur, 1953. 13 p. Map.

Sheppard, M. C. Historic Malaya: an outline history. 2d ed. rev. Singapore, 1959. 29 p. Illus.

Sheppard, M. C. A short history of Negri Sembilan. Singapore, 1965. 114 p. (Malayan Historical Series, no. 3) Illus., maps.

Shorrick, N. Lion in the sky: the story of Seletar and the Royal Air Force in Singapore. Singapore, 1968. 189 p.

Sidhu, J. S. Decentralisation of the Federated Malay States 1930-34. PS, 1, 1 (1966): 17-28.

Silva, G. W. De. Popular history of Malaya and the Netherlands Indies. Kuala Lumpur, 1939. 199 p.

Sinclair, Keith. The British advance in Johore, 1885-1914. JRASMB, 40, 1 (1967): 93-110.

Skinner, A. M. Outline history of the British connection with Malaya. JRASSB, 10 (1882): 269-280.

Skinner, C. A Kedah letter of 1839. In John Bastin and R. Roolvink, eds. Malayan and Indonesian Studies. Oxford, 1964: 156-165.

Skinner, Cyril. The civil war in Kelantan in 1839. Singapore, 1966. 176 p. (Monograph no. 2, Royal Asiatic Society, Malaysian Branch) Bibliog. 169-174, maps.

Smith, T. E., and John Bastin. Malaysia. Oxford
University Press, 1967. 128 p. Map, plates.

Soedjatmoko et al., eds. An introduction to Indonesian
historiography. Ithaca, 1965. 497 p.

Solheim, Wilhelm G., and Ernestene Green. Johore
Lama excavations, 1960. FMJ, n.s., 10 (1965):
1-78. Diagr., maps, photos, plates.

Song, Ong-siang. One hundred years history of the
Chinese in Singapore. Singapore, 1923; Singapore,
1967.

Stein-Callenfels, P. V. van. The founder of Malacca.
JRASMB, 15, 2 (1937): 160-166.

Steuart, A. Francis. The foundation of Penang--Captain
Light and the Nonyah. AR, 19 (1905): 112-123.

Stevens, F. G. A contribution to the early history
of Prince of Wales Island. JRASMB, 7, 3 (1929):
377-414. Plates.

Stone, Horace. From Malacca to Malaysia, 1400-1965.
London, 1966. 248 p. Maps, tables.

Strabolgi, J. M. K. Singapore and after; a study
of the Pacific campaign. London, New York, 1942.
158 p. Maps, plates.

Sweeney, P. L. Amin. The connection between the
Hikayat Raja of Pasai and the Sejarah Melayu.
JRASMB, 40, 2 (1967): 94-105.

Swettenham, Frank. British Malaya: an account of
the origin and progress of British influence
in Malaya. London, 1948. 380 p. Fold. map, plates.

Swettenham, Frank. Sir Frank Swettenham's Perak
journals, 1874-1876. Edited by C. D. Cowan. JRASMB,
24, 4 (1951): 1-148. Map, plates.

Tan, Diana. Some activities of the Straits Chinese
British Association Penang 1920-1939. PS, 2,
2 (1967): 30-40.

Tan, Thoon-lip. Kempeitai kindness. Forewords by
E. C. S. Wade and Paul Sammy. Singapore, 1946.
142 p.

Tarling, N. British policy towards the Dutch and
the native princes in the Malay Archipelago,
1824-1871. 1956. Ph.D. thesis -- Cambridge.

Tarling, N. The relationship between the British
policies and the extent of Dutch power in the
Malay Archipelago, 1784-1871. Australian Journal
of Politics and History, 4 (1958): 179-192.

Tarling, N. Intervention and non-intervention in
Malaya. JAS, 21(1962): 523-527.

Tarling, N. The prince of merchants and the lion
city. JRASMB, 37, 1 (1964): 20-40.

Tarling, Nicholas. British policy in the Malay Peninsula
and Archipelago, 1824-1871. [London?] 1969. 236 p.
Maps.

Teeuw, A. Hikayat Raja-Raja Pasai and Sejarah Melayu.
In John Bastin and R. Roolvink, eds. Malayan
and Indonesian Studies. Oxford, 1964: 222-234.

Temple, Richard. A brief sketch of Malayan history.
Indian Antiquary, 48 (1919): 227-231; 49 (1920):
12-16. Bibliog.

Thio, Eunice. British policy in the Malay Peninsula,
1880-1909. 1957. Ph.D. thesis (School of Oriental
and African Studies) -- London.

Thio, Eunice. British policy towards Johore: from
advice to control. JRASMB, 40, 1 (1967): 1-41.

Tiele, P. A. Bouwstoffen voor de geschiedenis der
Nederlanders in den Maleischen Archipel. The Hague,
1886, 1890, 1895. 3 v. (1) 370 p. (2) 396 p.
(3) 503 p.

Tregonning, K. G. The founding and development of
Penang, 1786-1826. 1958. Ph.D. thesis -- Singapore.

Tregonning, K. G. The British in Malaya. Tucson, 1965.
186 p. (Association for Asian Studies, Monographs
and Papers, 18) Bibliog. 173-178.

Tregonning, K. G. The early land administration
and agricultural development of Penang. JRASMB,
39, 2 (1966): 34-49.

Tregonning, K. G. A history of modern Malaya. New
York, 1967. 339 p. (History of Modern South-East
Asia Series)

Tregonning, K. G. Home port Singapore: a history
of Straits Steamship Company Limited, 1890-1964.
Singapore, 1967. 321 p. Maps, plates.

Tregonning, K. G. The historical background. In
Ooi Jin-bee and Chiang Hai-ding, eds. Modern
Singapore. Singapore, University of Singapore
Press, 1969: 14-19.

Tregonning, K. G., ed. Penang and the China trade.
MH, 5, 1 (1959): 8-12.

Tregonning, K. G., ed. Malaysian historical sources.
Singapore, 1962. 130 p. Illus., tables.
   A collection of essays by various authors on
source-material in Malaysia, mostly unpublished:
Chinese language sources, English sources, Malay
historical works, microfilm in Singapore, thesis
in Singapore, etc. See review by Emily Sadka
in Singapore Library Jl 2, 2 (1962): 102-103.

Turnbull, C. M. The movement to remove the Straits
Settlements from the control of India, culminating
in the transfer to the Colonial Office in 1867.
1962. Ph.D. thesis -- London.

Turnbull, C. M. The origins of British control in
the Malay states before colonial rule. In John
Bastin and R. Roolvink, eds. Malayan and Indonesian
Studies. Oxford, 1964: 166-183.

Turnbull, Mary. The Nineteenth century of Malaysia.
In Wang Gung-wu. Malaysia: A Survey. London,
1964: 128-137.

Tweedie, M. W. F. The stone age in Malaya. JRASMB,
26, 2 (1953): 1-90. (Monographs on Malay Subjects, no. 1)

Verhoeven, F. R. J. National archives of Malaysia.
UNESCO Bulletin for Libraries, 18 (1964): 263-268.

Verhoeven, F. R. J. The lost archives of Dutch Malacca, 1641-1824. JRASMB, 37, 2 (1964): 11-27. Also published in PHR, 1, 2 (1966): 183-200.

Wake, Christopher H. Malacca's early kings and the reception of Islam. JSAH, 5, 2 (1964): 104-128. Also in Colin Jack-Hinton, ed. Papers on early South-East Asian history. Singapore, 1964: 104-128.

Wang, Gung-wu. A short history of the Nanyang Chinese. Singapore, 1959.

Wang, Gung-wu. The Melayu in Hai-huo wen-chien lu. JHS, 2 (1963/1964): 1-9.

Wang, Gung-wu. The opening of relations between China and Malacca, 1403-5. In John Bastin and R. Roolvink, eds. Malayan and Indonesian Studies. Oxford, 1964: 87-104.

Wang, Gung-wu. 1874 in our history. PS, 1, 1 (1966): 12-16.

Wang, Gung-wu. Malaysia's social history. PS, 1, 2 (1966): 1-5.

Wang, Gung-wu. The first three rulers of Malacca. JRASMB, 41, 1 (1968): 11-22.

Wheatley, P. A curious feature on early maps of Malaya. Imago Mundi, 2 (1954): 67-72.

Wheatley, P. Panarnkan. SSS, 10, 1 (1954): 1-16. Maps.

Wheatley, P. Takola emporion. A study of an early Malayan place-name. MJTG, 2 (1954): 35-47.

Wheatley, P. Ancient books containing reference to Malaya. Malayan Library Group Newsletter, 1, 2 (1955): 18-24.

Wheatley, P. Belated comments on Sir Roland Braddel's studies of ancient times in the Malay Peninsula. JRASMB, 28 (1955): 78-98.

Wheatley, P. An early Chinese reference to part of Malaya. MJTG, 5 (1955): 57-60.

Wheatley, P. The Malay Peninsula as known to the Chinese of the 3rd century, A.D. JRASMB, 28, 1 (1955): 1-23.

Wheatley, P. The Malay Peninsula as known to the West before A.D. 1000. MHJ, 3 (1956): 2-16.

Wheatley, P. Tun-sun. JRAS Gr B and I, 1-2 (1956): 17-30.

Wheatley, P. Possible references to the Malay Peninsula in the annals of the Former Han. JRASMB, 30, 1 (1957 [i.e. 1962]): 115-121.

Wheatley, P. The historical geography of the Malay Peninsula before A.D. 1500. 1958. Ph.D. thesis -- London.

Wheatley, P. The golden Khersonese. Studies in the historical geography of the Malay Peninsula before A.D. 1500. Kuala Lumpur, 1961. 388 p. Bibliog. 333-369.

Wheatley, P. Desultory remarks on the ancient history of the Malay Peninsula. In John Bastin and R. Roolvink, eds. Malayan and Indonesian Studies. Oxford, 1964: 33-75.

Wheatley, Paul. Impressions of the Malay Peninsula in ancient times. Singapore, 1964.

Wicki, Josef. D. Jorge de Santa Luzia O.P. 1. Bischof von Malakka (1558-1576). Neue Zeitschrift für Missionswissenschaft, 22 (1966): 270-284.

Wilkinson, R. J. A history of the Peninsular Malays: with chapters on Perak and Selangor. Singapore, 1920. 173 p.

Wilkinson, R. J. Early Indian influence in Malaysia. JRASMB, 13, 2 (1935): 1-16.

Winstedt, R. O. Early history of Singapore, Johore and Malacca. JRASSB, 86 (1917): 257-260.

Winstedt, R. O. Malaya, the Straits Settlements and the Federated and Unfederated Malay States. London, 1923. 283 p. Bibliog., illus., maps.

Winstedt, R. O. A history of Johore (1365-1895).
JRASMB, 10, 3 (1932): 1-167. Charts, plates.

Winstedt, R. O. A Malay history of Riau and Johore.
JRASMB, 10, 3 (1932).
Jawi text and English summary.

Winstedt, R. O. A history of Perak. JRASMB, 12,
1 (1934): 1-180.

Winstedt, R. O. A history of Selangor. JRASMB, 12,
3 (1934): 1-34.

Winstedt, R. O. Negri Sembilan: the history, policy
and beliefs of the nine states. JRASMB, 12, 3
(1934): 41-111. Bibliog., illus.

Winstedt, R. O. A history of Malaya. JRASMB, 13,
1 (1935): 1-210. Charts, map, plates.

Winstedt, R. O. Notes on the history of Kedah. JRASMB,
14, 3 (1936): 155-190.

Winstedt, R. O. A history of Malaya, 1786-1941.
London, New York, 1944. 79 p.

Winstedt, R. O. Malaya and its history. London,
1948. 158 p.

Winstedt, R. O., ed. The Malay annals or Sejarah
Melayu. The earliest recension from MS. No. 18
of the Raffles collection, in the Library of
the London Asiatic Society, London. JRASMB, 16,
3 (1938): 1-226.

Wint, Guy. The British in Asia. New York, 1954.
244 p. Index.
Two chapters deal with Malaya, 107-115, 191-200.

Wong, Choon-san. A gallery of Chinese kapitans.
Singapore, 1963. 114 p. Illus., maps.

Zainal Abidin bin Wahib. Some aspects of Malay history.
JHS, 4 (1965/1966): 6-10.

B. RAFFLES

Bastin, J. Sir Stamford Raffles's and John Crawfurd's ideas of colonizing the Malay Archipelago. JRASMB, 26, 1 (1953): 81-85.

Boulger, D. C. The life of Sir Stamford Raffles. London, 1897. 403 p.

Collis, Maurice. Raffles. London, 1966. 227 p.

Cook, John Angus Bethune. Sir Thomas Stamford Raffles, founder of Singapore, 1819 and some of his friends and contemporaries. London, 1918. 205 p.

Coupland, Reginald. Raffles 1781-1826. Oxford, 1926. 134 p. Fold. map.

Coupland, Reginald. Raffles of Singapore. 3d ed. London, 1946. 144 p.

Egerton, Hugh Edward. Sir Stamford Raffles; England in the Far East. London, 1900. 290 p.

Epton, Nina. The golden sword; being the dramatized story of Sir Thomas Stamford Raffles (1781-1826). London [n.d.]. 201 p.

Hahn, Emily. Raffles of Singapore, a biography. New York, 1946. 587 p. London, 1948. 350 p.

Hough, G. G. Notes on the educational policy of Sir Stamford Raffles. JRASMB, 11 (1933): 166-170.

Lee, Sidney, ed. Sir Stamford Raffles. In Dictionary of National Biography. London, 1906: 604-608.

Parkinson, C. N. Raffles of the Eastern Isles. MHJ, 2, 1 (1955): 59-71.

Pearson, Harold Frank. This other India; a biography of Sir Thomas Stamford Raffles. [Singapore, 1957]. 117 p.

Raffles, Lady Sophia. Memoir of the life and public services of Sir Thomas Stamford Raffles, particularly in the Government of Java 1811-1816, Bencoolen and its dependencies, 1817-1824. With details of the commerce and resources of the Eastern Archipelago, and selections from his correspondence. London, 1830, 1835. 2 v. (1) 723 p. (2) 100 p. Maps.

Raffles, T. S. Statement to the court of directors
of the East India Company of the services of
Sir Stamford Raffles, November 1824. London,
1824. 72 p.

Schnitger, Frederic M. Forgotten kingdoms of Sumatra.
Leiden, 1939. 228 p. Plates.
See p. 206-214 for Raffles.

Wurtzburg, C. E. Raffles of the Eastern Isles. London,
1954. 788 p. Bibliog., index, map, plates.

CHAPTER 7

PHYSICAL GEOGRAPHY

A. GENERAL

Alexander, J. B. The evolution of land suitability maps used for planning rural development in the Federation of Malaya. [Kuala Lumpur?], Director of Geological Survey, 1962. 11 p. (Federation of Malaya. Ministry of Rural Development Professional Paper, E-62. 3-L) Maps.

Fullard, Harold, ed. Senior Malayan Atlas. 8th ed. London, 1963.

Geno-Oehlers, Jillian, and Rudolph Wikkramatileke. The water supply of Singapore: a fundamental resource problem. In Land Use and Resources: Studies in Applied Geography. 1968: 187-202. (Institute of British Geographers, Special Publication, no. 1)

Hamzah bin Sendut. Atlas sekolah [2] rendah, Tanah-Melayu. Amsterdam, 1960. 38 p.
    Atlas of colored maps for lower secondary schools, with emphasis on Malaya.

Hamzah bin Sendut. The national atlas of Malaysia, Singapore and Brunei. Department of Surveys, 1966. 120 p. Index, 220 maps, explanatory notes. 18 miles to an inch.
    Malay language.

Hamzah bin Sendut, ed. Atlas Menengah Melayu. Kuala Lumpur, 1964.

Ho, Robert. The evolution of the Indo-Malaysian region. Proceedings of the Centenary and Bi-centenary Biological Conference (Singapore) (1958): 9-20.

Ho, Robert. Physical geography of the Indo-Australian tropics. In Symposium on the Impact of Man on Humid Tropics Vegetation. Goroka, Territory of Papua and New Guinea and UNESCO, 1960: 19-34.

Ho, Robert. Environment, man and development in Malaya. Kuala Lumpur, 1962. Maps.
    Inaugural lecture.

Ho, Robert. The environment [of Malaysia]. In Wang
    Gung-wu. Malaysia: A Survey. London, 1964: 25-43.
    Maps.

Hodder, B. W. Biogeographical aspects of settlement
    in Malaya. MJTG, 5 (1955): 12-19.

Khoo, S. G. Malaya's new series topographical maps:
    how and why. [Kuala Lumpur, 1962?]. 11 p. Maps
    (part fold.).

Ow, Yang-hong-chiew. Rivers in Malaya: their deterioration
    and remedial measures. Mal Ag Jl, 45, 1 (1965): 17-20.

Tham, Ah-kow. A preliminary study of the physical,
    chemical and biological characteristics of Singapore
    Straits. London, 1953.

Wong, Poh-poh. The changing landscapes of Singapore
    Island. In Ooi Jin-bee and Chiang Hai-ding, eds.
    Modern Singapore. Singapore, University of Singapore
    Press, 1969: 20-51.

B. CLIMATE

Bennett, Don C., and R. O. Smith. Visibility conditions
    in Malaya. Bloomington, Indiana University Foundation
    Research Division [1963]. 109 p. Maps.

Braak, Cornelius. Klimakunde von Hinterindien und
    Insulinde. Berlin, 1931. 125 p. Figs., refs.,
    tables.
        This constitutes v. 4, part R of W. Koeppen,
    and R. Geiger, eds. Handbuch der Klimatologie.

Brooks, C. E. P. Notes on the probable climate of
    a mountain station in the Malay States. JFMSM,
    10 (1921): 241-245.

Chia, Lin-sien. Meteorological observations University
    of Malaya 1962-1966. Kuala Lumpur, published
    by the Department of Geography, University of
    Malaya [1967]. 114 p. Charts, maps, tables.

Chia, Lin-sien. Solar radiation and bright sunshine in Singapore. Paper presented at 1st Annual Congress of Singapore National Academy of Science. Singapore, Aug. 1968. 8 p. Graphs. Mimeo.

Chia, Lin-sien. An analysis of rainfall pattern in Selangor. JTG, 27 (Dec. 1968): 1-18. Maps.

Dale, W. L. The rainfall of Malaya. Pt. 1 and 2. JTG, 13 (1959): 23-37; 14 (1960): 11-28.

Dale, W. L. Surface temperatures in Malaya. JTG, 17 (1963): 57-71.

Dale, W. L. Sunshine in Malaya. JTG, 19 (1964): 20-26.

Dobby, E. H. G. Winds and fronts over Southeast Asia. GR, 35 (1945): 204-218. Maps.
    The same maps were previously published by A. Grimes, in "The Journey of Fa-Hsien from Ceylon to Canton." JRASMB, 19, 1 (1941): 76-92.

Frost, R. Cumulus and cumulonimbus clouds over Malaya. Met Rep, 15 (1954).

Gan, Tong-liang. A study of some heavy rainspells on the east coast of Malaya during the northeast monsoon season. Singapore, 1962. (Memoir of the Malayan Meteorological Service, no. 6)

Gan, Tong-liang, and Tan Kong-sin. The connection between vortex development in oceanic East Asia and bad weather over Malaya and Singapore. Singapore Airport, Weather Forecast Office [1968]. 8 p. Graphs. Mimeo.

Grant, J. S. Forests and streamflow. Mal For, 20 (1957): 122-126.

Great Britain, Meteorological Office. Weather in the China Seas and in the western part of the North Pacific Ocean. London, 1937, 1938. 3 v. V. 1. Pt. 1--General information. Pt. 2--Typhoons. V. 2--Local information. V. 3--Aids to forecasting.

Greenwood, P. G. Buildings and climate in Singapore. JTG, 26 (1968): 37-47.

Haines, W. B. Summary of meteorological records,
Soils Division. Kuala Lumpur, 1931. 27 p. (RRIMB,
no. 4)

Haines, W. B. Notes on the bearing of certain meteorological
observations on agricultural problems in Malaya.
PPSC, 5 (Canada), 3 (1934): 1749-1752.

Hay, R. F. M. Wind at high levels over Singapore
(1905-1952). Great Britain, Meteorological Research
Committee, M.R.P. 770 (1952). 6 p. Figs., refs.,
tables. Mimeo.

Holshausen, C. G. Climatic data of the main towns
in Malaysia. Singapore, Singapore Polytechnic,
1963. 64 p. Maps, tables.

Holttum, R. E. The uniform climate of Malaya as
a barrier to plant migration. PPSC, 6 (Berkeley),
4 (1940): 669-671.

John, I. G. The properties of the upper air over
Singapore. Kuala Lumpur, 1950. 35 p. (Meteorological
Service Memoir, no. 4) Plates, refs., tables.

Jones, W. R. Notes on the climate of southern Burma
and the Malay Peninsula. Q Jl R Met Soc, 61 (1935):
381-386.

Kramer, Harris P., and K. Martinoff. Selective annotated
bibliography on the climate of Southeast Asia
and the East Indies. Met Abst Bibliog, 5, 2 (1954):
221-269.

Lea, C. A. A preliminary analysis of pressure observations
in Malaya. Kuala Lumpur, 1936. 8 p. (Meteorological
Service Memoir, no. 1) Figs., plates, tables.

Lockwood, J. G. Probable maximum 24-hour precipitation
over Malaya by statistical methods. Met Mag,
98, no. 1134 (Jan. 1967): 11-19.

Malaya, Department of Drainage and Irrigation. Hydrological
data, rainfall records, 1879-1958. Kuala Lumpur,
1961. 411 p. Diagrs., graphs, illus., maps, tables.

Malaya, Meteorological Service. Weather conditions
along air routes in the neighbourhood of Malaya.
Singapore, 1937. 20 p. Maps.

Malaya, Meteorological Service. Summary of observations
of winds (surface and upper), 1932-1941. Singapore,
1949. Tables.

Monteiro, Rosina. Climate and man along the East
Coast of Malaya. Kuala Lumpur, 1962. 352 p. Dissertation
(M.A.) -- University of Malaya. Bibliog., illus.,
maps. Typescript.

Nieuwolt, A. Simon. Das Klima von Singapur. Mitt
Ö G Ges, 106, 2 (1964): 157-178. Maps.

Nieuwolt, A. Simon. Evaporation and water balances
in Malaya. JTG, 20 (1965): 34-53.

Nieuwolt, A. Simon. A comparison of rainfall in
the exceptionally dry year 1963 and average conditions
in Malaya. Erdkunde, 20, 3 (1966): 169-181. Maps.

Nieuwolt, A. Simon. The urban microclimate of Singapore.
JTG, 22 (June 1966): 30-37. Diagrs.

Nieuwolt, A. Simon. Diurnal rainfall variation in
Malaya. Annals, 58, 2 (1968): 313-326. Diagr.,
maps, tables.

Oh, Kong-yew. Hydrology in Malaya, rainfall and
river discharge. Mal Ag Jl, 45, 2 (1965): 182-190.

Ramage, C. S. Diurnal variation of summer rainfall
of Malaya. JTG, 19 (1964): 62-68.

Stephenson, P. M. An index of comfort for Singapore.
Met Mag, 92, no. 1096 (1963): 338-345.

Stewart, D. C. The rainfall of Malaya. Mal Ag Jl,
18 (1930): 530-540.

Stubbs, M. W. A preliminary note on some climatological
aspects of the monsoon months of May and June
in relation to the yearly synoptic pattern found
in the Singapore and Malaysian area. Paper presented
at the First Annual Congress of the Singapore
National Academy of Science. August 1968. 10 p.
Tables. Mimeo.

Tan, Beng-cheok. An investigation of the solar radiation
at Singapore. 1962. 138 p. Ph. D. thesis (physics)
-- University of Singapore.

United Nations, ECAFE. Multiple-purpose river basin
     development. Part 2C. Water resources development
     in British Borneo, Federation of Malaya, Indonesia
     and Thailand. New York, 1959. 135 p. (Flood Control
     Series, no. 14)

United States Weather Bureau. Climate and weather
     of southeastern Asia. Pt. 1--India, Burma and
     southern China. Pt. 2--Farther India and the
     Netherlands East Indies. Washington, 1942. 2 v.
     Charts, diagr., tables.

Watts, I. E. M. The equatorial convergence lines
     of the Malayan--East Indies region. Memoirs Mal
     Met Service, no. 3 (1949): 15-40.

Watts, I. E. M. An investigation of the distribution
     of rainfall over Singapore Island. 1954. Ph. D.
     thesis -- Singapore.

Watts, I. E. M. Line-squalls of Malaya. MJTG, 3
     (Oct. 1954): 1-14.

Watts, I. E. M. Rainfall of Singapore Island. JTG,
     7 (1955): 1-68. Bibliog., p. 67-68.

Wheatley, J. J. L. Notes on the rainfall of Singapore.
     JRASSB, 7 (1881): 31-50.

Winstedt, R. O. The great flood, 1926. JRASMB, 5,
     2 (1927): 295-309.

Wycherley, P. R. Rainfall in Malaysia: a study of
     its occurrence, with tables of probability of
     rainfall of selected stations, and an introduction
     to hydrology in rubber plantations. Kuala Lumpur,
     1967. 85 p. (Rubber Research Institute of Malaya,
     Planting Manual, no. 12) Graphs, maps, tables.

C. GEOLOGY AND GEOMORPHOLOGY

Akers, R. L. Drainage of low coastal areas. RRIMPB, 27 (1956): 101-104.

Alexander, J. B. Geology and paleontology in Malaya. Nature, 183 (1959): 230-232.

Alexander, J. B. Geological appreciation summary regarding prospects of iron-ore deposits in the mukim of Bera, district of Temerloh, Pahang. Ipoh, 1961. 21 p. (Malaya. Geological Survey. Special Economic Paper, EC--61.1)

Alexander, J. B. The geology and mineral resources of the neighbourhood of Bentong, Pahang and the adjoining portions of Selangor and Negri Sembilan, incorporating an account of the prospecting and mining activities of the Bentong district. Kuala Lumpur, 1968. 250 p. (District Memoir, 8) Diagrs., maps, photos, tables.

Burton, C. K. The older alluvium of Johore and Singapore. [Kuala Lumpur?], Director of Geological Survey, 1962. 54 p. (Federation of Malaya. Ministry of Rural Development. Professional paper, E-62.2-G) Maps.

Burton, C. K. The older alluvium of Johore and Singapore. JTG, 18 (1964): 30-42.

Burton, C. K. Graptolite and tentaculite correlations and palaeography of the Siberian and Devonian in the Yunnan--Malaya geosyncline. Trans Proc Palaeont Soc Japan, N.S., no. 65 (April 1967): 27-46.

Carter, J. Mangrove succession and coastal change in south-west Malaya. Trans Papers I Brit G, 26 (1959): 79-88.

Charlton, F. G. Standard catchments in the estimation of flood flows. JTG, 18 (1964): 43-53.

Courtier, D. B. Note on terraces and other alluvial features in parts of Province Wellesley, South Kedah, and North Perak. [Kuala Lumpur?], Director of Geological Survey, 1962. 6 p. (Federation of Malaya. Ministry of Rural Development. Professional paper, E-62.1-T) Maps.

Daly, D. D. Surveys and explorations in the native
    states of the Malay Peninsula, 1875-1882. Proc
    R G Soc, 4 (1882): 393-411.

Douglas, I. Natural and man-made erosion in the
    humid tropics of Australia, Malaysia and Singapore.
    Extract from Symposium on River Morphology. Bern,
    1967: 17-29.

Douglas, I. Erosion of granite terrains under tropical
    rain forest in Australia, Malaysia and Singapore.
    Extract from Symposium on River Morphology. Bern,
    1967: 31-39.

Douglas, I. Erosion in the Sungei Gombak catchment,
    Selangor, Malaysia. JTG, 26 (1968): 1-16.

Eyles, R. J. Stream representation on Malayan maps.
    JTG, 22 (1966): 1-9.

Eyles, R. J. Laterite at Kerdau, Pahang, Malaya.
    JTG, 25 (1967): 18-23.

Eyles, R. J. Modern developments in geomorphology.
    Geographica, 3 (1967): 44-49.

Eyles, R. J. A morphometry of West Malaysia. 1968.
    196 p. Ph. D. thesis -- University of Malaya.

Eyles, R. J. Physiographic implications of laterite
    in Malaya. Paper presented to the 1st Congress,
    Singapore National Academy of Science, August,
    1968. 7 p. Map. Mimeo.

Eyles, R. J. Depth of dissection of the West Malaysian
    landscape. Paper presented to the 21st I.G.V.
    Congress, New Delhi, Dec. 1968. 13 p. Published
    in abstract.

Eyles, R. J. Depth of dissection of the West Malaysian
    landscape. JTG, 28 (June 1969): 22-31.

Fitch, F. H. Evidence for recent emergence of the
    land in east Pahang. JRASMB, 22, 1 (1949): 115-122.
    Illus., maps.

Fitch, F. H. The geology and mineral resources of
    the neighbourhood of Kuantan, Pahang. Kuala Lumpur,
    1952. 144 p. (Federation of Malaya. Geological
    Survey Department Memoir, n.s., no. 6)

Fryer, H. A. J. Notes on the physiography of Singapore with special reference to field work in the western part. Singapore, 1968. 7 p. Mimeo.

Geological Society of Malaysia. Studies in Malaysian geology: papers presented at a meeting of the Geological Society of Malaysia on 31 January 1967. Bulletin no. 1. Kuala Lumpur, 1968.

Gobbett, D. J. The formation of limestone caves in Malaya. Mal Nature Jl, 19 (1965): 4-12.

Gobbett, D. J. The Lower Palaeozoic rocks of Kuala Lumpur, Malaysia. FMJ, n.s., 9 (1964): 67-79. Illus., map, tables.

Hill, R. D. Changes in beach form at Sri Pantai, Northeast Johore, Malaysia. JTG, 23 (1966): 19-29. Maps.

Ho, R. Malayan limestone scenery. Bull Sc Soc Malay (Sept. 1956): 40-41.

Hooijer, D. A. Report upon a collection of pleistocene mammals from tin-bearing deposits in a limestone cave near Ipoh, Kinta Valley, Perak. FMJ, n.s., 7 (1962): 1-6. Tables.

Hutchinson, Charles Strachan. The basement rocks of Malaya and their paleogeographic significance in Southeast Asia. Am Jl Sci (March 1961): 181-185.

Hutchinson, Charles Strachan. Tectonic and petrological relations within three rock associations of orogenic zones in Malaysia. 1967. Ph. D. -- University of Malaya.

Ingham, F. T. The geology of the neighborhood of Tapah and Telok Anson, Perak, Federated Malay States, with an account of the mineral deposits. Singapore, 1938. 72 p. Diagr., maps, plates.

Ingham, F. T., and E. F. Bradford. Geology and universal resources of the Kinta Valley, Perak. Kuala Lumpur, 1960. 347 p. (Malaya. Geological Survey. District Memoir, 9) Diagrs., illus., maps, tables.

Klompe, Th. H. F. Igneous and structural features
of Thailand. In The Crust of the Pacific Basin.
1962: 122-134. (American Geophysical Union Monograph,
no. 6)

Koopmans, B. N. Geomorphological and historical
data of the lower course of the Perak River (Dindings).
JRASMB, 37, 2 (1964): 175-191. Bibliog., illus.,
maps.

Koopmans, B. N. A structural map of North and Central
Pahang. JTG, 22 (1966): 23-29.

Ledgerwood, E. Short geological report on the Muda
River Project (irrigation). Ipoh, Geological
Survey, 1961. 16 p. Graphs, maps. GS: 61/E/051/74.
Mimeo.

MacDonald, S. The geology and mineral resources
of North Kelantan and North Trengganu. Ipoh,
1967. 202 p. (Geological Survey West Malaysia,
District Memoir, 10) Maps, photos.

Malaya, Department of Drainage and Irrigation. Hydrological
data, stream flow records 1910-1940. Kuala Lumpur,
1962. 249 p.

Malaya, Geological Survey, Alexander, J. B. Geological
survey of Malaya, Diamond Jubilee review 1903-1963.
[Ipoh, 1963]. 26 p. Col. maps, photos.

Matsushita, Susumu. Geology of the Kinta Valley
in Malaya with special reference to its geomorphological
development. SAS, 5, 2 (1967): 93-105.

Military Engineering Experimental Establishment.
Classification of terrain intelligence, Malaya.
Fourth Combined Pool Report. Woolwich, 1964.

Mitchell, B. A. A note on land erosion in the Cameron
Highlands. Mal For, 20 (1957): 30-32.

Nossin, J. J. Relief and coastal development in
north-eastern Johore (Malaya). JTG, 15 (1961):
27-38. Maps.

Nossin, J. J. Coastal sedimentation in north eastern
Johore (Malaya). Z Geom, n.f., 6, 3-4 (1962): 296-317.

Nossin, J. J. Beach ridges on the East Coast of
Malaya. JTG, 18 (1964): 111-117.

Nossin, J. J. Geomorphology of the surroundings
of Kuantan (eastern Malaya). Geologie en Mijnbouw,
43, 5 (1964): 157-182.

Nossin, J. J. Analysis of younger beach ridge deposits
in Eastern Malaya. Z Geom, n.f., 9 (1965): 186-208.

Nossin, J. J. The geomorphic history of the northern
Pahang delta. JTG, 20 (1965): 54-64. Maps.

Nossin, J. J. Igneous rock weathering on Singapore
Island. Z Geom, n.f., 11, 1 (1967): 14-35. Map.

Oh, K. Y. Hydrology in Malaya, rainfall and river
discharge. Mal Ag Jl, 45 (1965): 182-190.

Ow, Yang-hong-chiew. Rivers in Malaya--their deterioration
and remedial measures. Mal Ag Jl, 45 (1965):
17-20.

Paton, J. R. A brief account of the geology of the
limestone hills of Malaya. BRM, 26 (1961): 66-75.

Paton, J. R. The origin of the limestone hills of
Malaya. JTG, 18 (Aug. 1964): 134-147. Figs.,
illus.

Poore, M. E. D. River control and conservation in
Malaya. In J. Wyatt-Smith, and P. R. Wycherley,
eds. Nature Conservation in Western Malaysia.
Kuala Lumpur, Malayan Nature Society, 1961: 48-51.

Renwick, A. Geohydrological investigations in the
western coastal plain of Malaya. United Nations
Water Resources Series, 24 (1963): 170-174.

Richardson, J. A. The geology and mineral resources
of the neighborhood of Raub, Pahang, Federated
Malay States. Singapore, 1939. 166 p. Maps, tables.

Richardson, J. A. An outline of the geomorphological
evolution of British Malaya. Geol Mag, 84 (1947):
129-144.

Richardson, J. A. The geology and mineral resources of the neighborhood of Chegar, Perah and Merapoh, Pahang. Kuala Lumpur, 1950. 162 p. (Malaya. Geological Survey Memoir, n.s., no. 4)

Roe, F. W. The geology and mineral resources of the Fraser's Hill area Selangor, Perak and Pahang, Federation of Malaya, with an account of the mineral resources. Kuala Lumpur, 1952. 138 p. (Geological Survey Department Memoir, no. 5) Maps, plans, plates, tables.

Roe, F. W. The geology and mineral resources of the neighborhood of Kuala Selangor and Rasa, with account of the geology of Batu Arang coal-field. Kuala Lumpur, 1954. 163 p. (Geological Survey Department Memoir, no. 7)

Samuelson, Bengt. Report to the Government of Malaysia on collection and interpretation of hydrological data. Rome, 1967. 42 p. (Food and Agricultural Organization of the United Nations, no. TA 2359)

Savage, Herbert E. A preliminary account of the geology of Kelantan. JRASMB, 3 (1925): 61-73.

Savage, Herbert E. The geology of the neighborhood of Sungei Siput, Perak, Federated Malay States, with an account of the mineral deposits. Singapore, 1937. 46 p. Maps.

Savage, Herbert E., and R. G. A. Wilshaw. An examination of the geology and soils of an area in the state of Perak. Kuala Lumpur, 1932. 15 p. (Department of Agriculture, Special Bulletin, Science Series, no. 10)

Scrivenor, J. B. A geologist's report of progress, September 1903-January 1907. Kuala Lumpur, 1907. 44 p.

Scrivenor, J. B. Note on the sedimentary rocks of Singapore. Geol Mag, decade 5, 5 (1908): 289-291. Plate.

Scrivenor, J. B. The geology and mining industries of Ulu Pahang. Kuala Lumpur, 1911. 61 p. Sketch map.

Scrivenor, J. B. Sketch of the geological structure
of Malay Peninsula. JRASSB, 59 (1911): 1-13.

Scrivenor, J. B. The geological history of the Malay
Peninsula. Q Jl Geol Soc London, 69 (1913): 343-371.
Illus.

Scrivenor, J. B. The geology and mining industry
of the Kinta District, Perak, Federated Malay
States, with a geological sketch map. Kuala Lumpur,
1913. 90 p. Diagrs., illus., fold. maps.

Scrivenor, J. B. The structural geology of British
Malaya. Jl Geol, 31 (1923): 556-570.

Scrivenor, J. B. The geology of Singapore Island.
JRASMB, 2, 1 (1924): 1-8. Map.

Scrivenor, J. B. The palaeontology of British Malaya.
JRASMB, 4, 2 (1926): 173-184.

Scrivenor, J. B. The geology of Malacca, with a
geological map and special reference to laterite.
JRASMB, 5, 2 (1927): 278-287.

Scrivenor, J. B. The geology of Malaya. London,
1928. 217 p. Bibliog., fig., map.

Scrivenor, J. B. The geology of Malayan ore deposits.
London, 1928. 216 p. Bibliog., illus.

Scrivenor, J. B. The progress of the geological
survey of Malaya. PPSC, 4 (Java), 2 (1929): 449-466.

Scrivenor, J. B. The economic geology of Kelantan
and Trengganu. Kuala Lumpur, 1931.

Scrivenor, J. B. Geological research in the Malay
Peninsula and Archipelago. Geol Mag, 78 (1941):
125-150.

Scrivenor, J. B. Geological and geographical evidence
for changes in sea-level during ancient Malay
history and late pre-history. JRASMB, 22, 1 (1949):
107-115. Bibliog.

Scrivenor, J. B., and W. R. Jones. The geology of
South Perak, North Selangor, and the Dindings.
Kuala Lumpur, 1919. 196 p. Figs., sketch map, plates.

Scrivenor, J. B., and E. S. Willbourn. The geology
of the Langkawi Islands. JRASMB, 1, 1 (1923):
338-347. Maps.

Shallow, P. G. D. River flow in the Cameron Highlands.
Kuala Lumpur, Central Electricity Board, 1956.
(Hydroelectric Technical Memorandum, 3)

Smit Sibinga, G. L. Der Malayische Archipel. Geol
Jber, 2 (1940): 393-416.

Stille, Hans. Malaiischer Archipel und Alpen. Berlin,
1943. 16 p. (Abhandlungen der Preussischen Akademie
der Wissenschaften Jahr 1943. Mathematisch-
naturwissenschaftliche Klasse, no. 1) Maps.

Swan, S. B. St. C. Maps of two indices of terrain,
Johor, Malaya. JTG, 25 (1967): 48-57.

Swan, S. B. St. C. Coastal classification with reference
to the east coast of Malaya. Zeitschrift für
Geomorphologie, Supplement 7, Küstenmorphologie--Coastal
geomorphology (1968): 114-132.

Takimoto, Kiyoshi, ed. Geology and mineral resources
in Thailand and Malaya. [Kyoto], Kyoto University,
Center for Southeast Asian Studies, 1968. 160 p.
(Reports on Research in Southeast Asia, Natural
Science Series, N-3) Maps.

Walker, D. Studies in the Quaternary of the Malay
Peninsula I. Alluvial deposits of Perak and changes
in the relative levels of land and sea. FMJ,
1/2 (1954/1955): 19-34.

Willbourn, E. S. The Pekang volcanic series. Geol
Mag, decade 6, 4 (1917): 503-514. Map.

Willbourn, E. S. An account of the geology and mining
industries of South Selangor and Negri Sembilan.
Calcutta, 1922. 115 p. Illus., fold. map, plates.

Willbourn, E. S. A general geology of the Malay
Peninsula and the surrounding countries. JRASSB,
86 (1922): 237-256.

Willbourn, E. S. The geology and mining industries
of Kedah and Perlis. JRASMB, 4, 3 (1926): 289-332.
Map.

Willbourn, E. S. The geology and mining industries
of Johore. JRASMB, 6, 4 (1928): 5-35. Illus., map.

Willbourn, E. S. The geology of Malaya. PPSC, 3
(Tokyo), 1 (1928): 443-451.

Willbourn, E. S. The relationship of geology and
civil engineering in Malaya. Kuala Lumpur, 1935.
5 p.

Wilson, J. N. Drainage and irrigation problems in
Malaya. Corona, 12 (Aug. 1960): 302-304.

Wong, P. P. The coastal types of Singapore Island.
Singapore, Department of Geography, 1968. 4 p.
Map. Mimeo.

Zeuner, F. E. Geology, climate and faunal distribution
in the Malay Archipelago. Proc R Entom Soc, ser.
A, 16 (1941): 117-123.

D. PLANT AND ANIMAL LIFE

Addison, G. H., and M. R. Henderson. Notes on the
planting of ornamental and shade trees in Malaya.
Mal For, 16 (1953): 131-146.

Alfred, Eric R. The fresh-water food fishes of
Malaya, FMJ, n.s., 9 (1964): 80-83.

Allen, Betty Molesworth. Malayan fruits; an introduction
to the cultivated species. Singapore, 1965. 245 p.
Illus., map.

Anderson, J. A. R. The ecology and forest types
of the peat swamp forests of Sarawak and Brunei
in relation to their silviculture. Edinburgh,
1961. Ph.D. thesis.

Audy, J. R., ed. Malaysian parasites I--XV. Kuala
Lumpur, 1953. 242 p. (Studies from the Institute
for Medical Research, no. 26) Illus., map, tables.

Berry, A. J. Habitats of some minute Cyclophorids,
Hydrocenids and Vertiginids on a Malayan limestone
hill. Bulletin of the National Museum, State
of Singapore, 30 (Dec. 1961): 101-105.

PHYSICAL GEOGRAPHY - Plant and Animal Life

Bunting, B. Planting of roadside trees in Malaya.
Mal Ag Jl, 27 (1939): 249-264.

Burkill, I. H. Botanical collectors, collections
and collecting places in the Malay Peninsula.
Gardens' Bulletin, 4 (1927): 113-202.

Burkill, I. H. A dictionary of the economic products
of the Malay Peninsula. London, 1935. 2 v. (2402 p.).
An invaluable storehouse of information about
fauna and flora of Malaya, with extensive ethnological
and historical notes.

Cantley, N. Notes on economic plants. JRASSB, 28
(1895): 295-334.

Chipp, T. F. A list of fungi of the Malay Peninsula.
Gardens' Bulletin, 2 (1921): 311-418.

Corbett, A. S., and H. M. Pendlebury. The butterflies
of the Malay Peninsula. 2d ed. Edinburgh, 1956. 537 p.

Corner, E. J. H. Wayside trees of Malaya. Singapore,
1940 and 1953. 772 p. V. 1. Text and text-figures.
V. 2. 228 plates.

Coulter, J. K. Development of the peat soils of
Malaya. Mal Ag Jl, 40, 3 (1957): 188-197.

Dammermann, K. W. The agricultural zoology of the
Malay Archipelago; the animals injurious and
beneficial to agriculture, horticulture and forestry
in the Malay Peninsula, the Dutch East Indies
and the Philippines. Amsterdam, 1929. 473 p.

Fernando, C. H. Notes on aquatic insects caught
at light in Malaya, with a discussion of their
distribution and dispersal. Bulletin of the National
Museum, State of Singapore, 30 (Dec. 1961): 19-31.

Foenander, E. C. Big game of Malaya; their types,
distribution and habits. London, 1952. 208 p.

Gamble, J. Sykes, and A. T. Gage. Materials for
a flora of the Malay Peninsula. Jl Proc As Soc
Bengal, 75, 22-26 (1912-1926): 544 p.

Gibson-Hill, C. A. An annotated check-list of the
birds of Malaya. Singapore, 1949. (Raffles Museum.
Bulletin, no. 29) Bibliog. p. 109-112.

Gibson-Hill, C. A. Ornithological notes from the
Raffles Museum. Nos. 15-22. BRM, 24 (1952): 220-343.

Gilliland, H. B. Geographical distribution of Malayan
grasses. JTG, 17 (1963): 20-24.

Glenister, A. G. The birds of the Malay Peninsula,
Singapore and Penang. London, 1951. 282 p.

Hamilton, A. W., and R. E. Holttum. Malayan plants.
JRASMB, 8, 2 (1930): 318-329.

Harrison, J. L. The natural food of some Malayan
mammals. Bulletin of the National Museum, State
of Singapore, 30 (Dec. 1961): 5-18.

Henderson, M. R. The flora of the limestone hills
of the Malay Peninsula. JRASMB, 17, 1 (1939):
13-87. Illus.

Henderson, M. R. Malayan wild flowers. V. 1. Singapore,
1951. 472 p. V. 2. Plates. Kuala Lumpur, 1954.
357 p.

Hewitt, B. R. The occurrence, origin and vegetation
of lowland peat in Malaya. In Proceedings of
the Linnean Society of New South Wales, 92, Pt.
1, no. 413. Sept. 1967: 58-66. Map.

Hill, J. E. The Robinson collection of Malaysian
mammals. Singapore, 1960. (Raffles Museum. Bulletin,
no. 29) Bibliog. p. 109-112.

Hill, J. E. Notes on some tube-used bats, genus
Murina from Southeastern Asia, with descriptions
of a new species and a new subspecies. FMJ, n.s.,
8 (1963): 48-59. Plates.

Holttum, R. E. The uniform climate of Malaya as
a barrier to plant migration. PPSC, 6 (California),
4 (1940): 669-671.

Holttum, R. E. A revised flora of Malaya. V. 1.
Orchids of Malaya. Singapore, 1953. 753 p.

Holttum, R. E. Adinandra Belukar: a succession of
vegetation from bare ground on Singapore Island.
MJTG, 3 (Oct. 1954): 27-32.

Holttum, R. E. Plant life in Malaya. London and
New York, 1954. 254 p. Illus., index.

Holttum, R. E. Gardening in the lowlands of Malaya.
Singapore, 1962. 323 p. Illus.

Hurrell, L. H. Migration and movements of birds
of prey over Singapore. Bulletin of the National
Museum, State of Singapore, 30 (Dec. 1961): 97-100.

Hurrell, L. H., and J. L. Riley. The Malayan National
Park. Malaya (Mar. 1960): 27-33.

Jagoe, R. B. Ecological observations on Asonopus
SPP and the grasses in Malaya. Mal Ag Jl, 32
(1949): 18-24. Bibliog., diagr., tables.

Jagoe, R. B. Beneficial effects of some leguminous
shade trees and grassland in Malaya. Mal Ag Jl,
32 (1949): 77-87. Tables.

Johnson, Anne. A student's guide to the ferns of
Singapore Island. Singapore, 1960. 121 p. Illus.

Johnson, D. S. A survey of the Malayan freshwater
life. Mal Nature Jl, 12 (1957): 57-65.

Jutting, W. S. S. van Bentham. The Malayan species
of Opisthostoma (Gastropoda Prosobranchia Cyclophoridae),
with a catalogue of all species hitherto described.
BRM, 24 (1952): 5-62. Illus.

King, George, and J. Sykes Gamble. Materials for
a flora of the Malayan Peninsula. Jl Proc As
Soc Bengal, 74, 1-21 (1905-1909): 908 p.

Lam, H. J. On a forgotten floristic map of Malasia
(H. Hollinger, 1857). Blumea, supplement, 1 (1937):
176-182.

Lord, L. Report by the economic botanist on a visit
to Malaya, Indo-China, Sumatra and Java, March-May,
1929. Colombo, 1929. 28 p. (Ceylon Papers)

Madoc, G. C. An introduction to Malayan birds. Kuala Lumpur, 1956. 234 p.

Malayan Nature Society. Nature conservation in Western Malaysia, 1961. Edited by J. Wyatt-Smith and P. R. Wycherley. Kuala Lumpur, Malayan Nature Society, 1961. 260 p. Illus., maps.

Malayan wild life. Nature, 149 (1942): 17-18.

Mayer, Charles. Trapping wild animals in Malay jungles. London, 1922. 223 p.

McKie, Ronald Cecil Hamlyn. The company of animals; a naturalist's adventures in the jungle of Malaya. New York [1966, c. 1965]. 271 p. Illus.

Medway, Lord. The Fauna [of Malaysia]. In Wang Gung-wu. Malaysia: A Survey. London, 1964: 55-66.

Merrill, E. D. The correlation of biological distribution with the geological history of Malaya. PPSC, 2 (Australia), 2 (1923): 1148-1155.

Merrill, E. D., and E. H. Walker. Bibliography of eastern Asiatic botony. Jamaica Plain, 1938. 719 p.

Newmark, G. H. Birds seen at Maxwell's Hill, April, 1955. Mal Nature Jl, 10 (July 1955): 9-12.

Norris, R. C., and J. I. Charlton. A chemical and biological survey of the Sungei Gombak. Kuala Lumpur, 1962. 57 p.

Poore, M. E. D. Vegetation and Flora [of Malaysia]. In Wang Gun-wu. Malaysia: A Survey. London, 1964: 44-54.

Pratt, Harry Charles. Malayan locust. Kuala Lumpur, 1915. 42 p. Illus., fold. map, plates.

Ridley, H. N. The poisonous plants of the Malay Peninsula. Kuala Lumpur, 1898. 199 p. (Agricultural Bulletin of the Botanic Gardens Department, Straits Settlements, no. 8) Bibliog.

Ridley, H. N. Malayan plants. JRASSB, 41 (1904): 31-51; 44 (1905): 189-211; 49 (1907): 11-52; 50 (1908): 111-152.

Ridley, H. N. Materials for a flora of the Malayan
Peninsula. Kuala Lumpur, 1907. 3 pts.

Ridley, H. N. Malay plants, new or rare. JRASSB,
54 (1910): 1-61; 61 (1912): 1-43; 68 (1915): 11-14;
73 (1916): 139-146; 75 (1917): 5-38; 79 (1919): 63-100;
82 (1920): 167-204; 86 (1922): 293-311.

Ridley, H. N. Flora of the Malayan Peninsula. London,
1922-1925. 5 v. Illus.

Ridley, H. N., and C. Curtis. Malay plant names.
JRASSB, 38 (1902): 39-122.

Steenis, C. G. G. J. van. The delimitation of Malaysia
and its main plant geographical divisions. In
M. J. van Steenis-Kruseman. Flora Malesiana,
ser. 1, v. 1. Djakarta (1950): 70-75. Maps.

Steenis, C. G. G. J. van. The mountain flora of
the Malaysian tropics. Endeavour, 21 (1962): 183-193.

Steenis-Kruseman, M. J. van. Flora Malesiana.
V. 1--Malaysian plant collectors and collections:
being a cyclopedia of botanical exploration in
Malaysia and a guide to the concerned literature
up to the year 1950. Djakarta, 1950. 639 p.

Sun, Hung-fan. The wonders of tropical plants. SSAR,
1 (1965): 1-50. Illus. In Chinese.

Symington, C. F. Flora of Gunong Tapis in Pahang
with notes on the altitudinal zonation of the
forests of the Malay Peninsula. JRASMB, 14, 3
(1936): 333-365. Illus., plates.

Symington, C. F. Foresters' manual of dipterocarps.
Kuala Lumpur, 1943. 244 p. (Malayan Forest Records,
no. 16) 114 figs.

Symposium on Ecological Research in Humid Tropics
Vegetation, Kuching, Sarawak, July, 1963. Sponsored
by the Government of Sarawak and UNESCO Science
Corporation Office for Southeast Asia. Kuching,
Sarawak, 1965. 376 p. Diagr., illus., tables.

Tenison-Woods, Julian E. Fisheries of the oriental
region. Malaysian Essays (1888): 165-255.

Tenison-Woods, Julian E. On the vegetation of Malaysia. Malaysian Essays (1889): 10-106.

Thompson, A., and A. Johnston. A host list of plant diseases in Malaya. Kew, 1953. 38 p.

Tweedie, M. W. F. The snakes of Malaya. Singapore, 1953. 139 p.

Tweedie, M. W. F. On certain mollusca of the Malayan limestone hills. BRM, 26 (1961): 49-65.

Tweedie, M. W. F., and J. L. Harrison. Malayan animal life. London, 1954. 240 p. Figs.

Watson, J. G. Malayan plant names. Singapore, 1928. 277 p. (Malayan Forest Records, no. 5)

Watson, J. G. Mangrove forests of the Malayan Peninsula. Singapore, 1928. 255 p. (Malayan Forest Records, no. 6) Illus.

Wild Life Commission of Malaya. Report. Singapore, 1932. 3 v. Bibliog., v. 1, p. 421; glossary, v. 1, p. 417-420; fold. map, plates.

Wyatt-Smith, J. The Malayan species of sonneratia. Mal For, 16 (1953): 213-216.

Wyatt-Smith, J. The vegetation of Jarak Island, Straits of Malacca. Jl Ecology, 41 (1953): 207-225. Maps, plates, tables.

Wyatt-Smith, J. A note on the fresh-water swamp, lowland and hill forest types of Malaya. Mal For, 24, 2 (1961): 110-121.

Wyatt-Smith, J. A preliminary vegetation map of Malaya with descriptions of the vegetation types. JTG, 18 (1964): 200-213. Fold. col. map.

E. SOILS

Acton, C. J. Reconnaissance soil survey report of
the north-west Selangor swamp region. Mal Ag
Jl, 45, 4 (1966): 444-471. Fold. map, tables.

Akhurst, C. G., and W. B. Haines. Description of
soils at the Rubber Research Institute Experiment
Station. JRRIM, 3 (1931): 174-181.

Alexander, J. B. The evolution of land suitability
maps in the Federation of Malaya. JTG, 18 (1964):
1-6.

Arnott, G. W. Soil survey reports, no. 6, the Kelantan
deficiency area. Mal Ag Jl, 40, 2 (1958): 60-91.
Illus., fold. col. map, tables.

Barrowcliff, M. Malayan rubber and coconut soils.
Mal Ag Jl, 2 (1931): 328-337.

Belgrave, W. N. C. Considerations on a soil survey
on Malaya. Mal Ag Jl, 17 (1929): 175-178.

Burnham, C. P. Landscape and soils in Malaya. Mal
Ag, 7 (1966/1967-1967/1968): 64-69.

Burton, C. K. The older alluvium of Johore and Singapore.
JTG, 18 (1964): 30-42.

Corbet, A. Steven. Biological processes in tropical
soils, with special reference to Malaysia. Cambridge,
1935. 156 p. Bibliog., figs., plates.

Coulter, J. K. Organic matter in Malayan soils.
Mal For, 13 (1950): 189-202.

Coulter, J. K. Peat formations in Malaya. Mal Ag
Jl, 33 (1950): 63-81.

Coulter, J. K. Soil survey reports, no. 4, the Kuala
Langat (North) forest reserve. Mal Ag Jl, 39,
3 (1956): 185-190. Diagr., maps.

Coulter, J. K. Development of the peat soils of
Malaya. Mal Ag Jl, 40, 3 (1957): 188-199. Map.

Coulter, J. K., A. R. McWalter, and G. W. Arnott.
Soil survey reports, no. 3, the Trans-Perak swamp;
with particular reference to its development
for padi cultivation. Mal Ag Jl, 39, 2 (1956):
99-120. Diagrs., map, photos.

Dennett, J. H. Preliminary results of a soil survey in Selangor. Mal Ag Jl, 17 (1929): 179-191. Diagr., map.

Dennett, J. H. The soils of Cameron Highlands. Mal Ag Jl, 18 (1930): 20-29.

Dennett, J. H. The western coastal alluvial soils. Mal Ag Jl, 20 (1932): 298-303. Sequence of coastal clays, organic soils and peats.

Dennett, J. H. The classification and properties of Malayan soils: Mal Ag Jl, 21 (1933): 347-361.

Dennett, J. H. Etudes sur les sols, classification des sols de Malaisie, d'après J. H. Dennett. Rev Bot Appl et Ag Trop, 132 (1933): 904-908.

Dennett, J. H., and W. N. C. Belgrave. Studies in Malay soils. 1--Classification and properties of Malayan soils. 2--Preliminary observation on manuring of annuals on inland soil. Mal Ag Jl, 21 (1933): 345-361.

Douglas, Ian. Erosion in the Sungei Gombak catchment, Selangor, Malaysia. JTG, 26 (1968): 1-16.

Dumansky, J., and Cheng-hok Ooi. Reconnaissance soil survey of the Temerloh Gemas Region, Malaya. Kuala Lumpur, 1966. (Malayan Soil Survey Report, no. 5/1966)

Durant, C. L. Erosion. Mal For, 5 (1936): 109-111.

Eaton, B. J. Soils, with reference to the cultivation of perennial crops in Malaya. Planter, 7 (1927): 275-277.

Eyles, R. J. Laterite at Kerdau, Pahang, Malaya. JTG, 25 (1967): 18-23.

Fermor, Lewis L. Soil destruction in Malaya, abstract. Nature, 144 (1939): 801.

Grantham, J. Some Johore soils. Mal Ag Jl, 4 (1915): 114-121.

Grantham, J. Some soils from the Kuala Pilah and Jelebu Districts. Mal Ag Jl, 4 (1915): 243-247.

Grantham, J. Soils of the Sabak District on the
Bernam River. Mal Ag Jl, 4 (1915): 298-300.

Greenstreet, V. R. Report on the soils of Lubok
Temang and Cameron Highlands. Mal Ag Jl, 10 (1922):
281-283.

Hamilton, R. A. Notes on tropical soils, with special
reference to Malayan soils for rubber cultivation.
JRRIM, 7 (1936): 27-45.

Hamilton, R. A. Soil investigations in relation
to the cultivation of rubber trees in Malaya.
Planter (Oct. 1936): 1-7.

Hartley, C. W. S. Soil erosion in Malaya. Corona,
10 (1949): 25-57.

Ives, David W. Detailed reconnaissance soil survey
of the Bukit Ibam Area, Southeast Pahang. Kuala
Lumpur, 1966. (Malayan Soil Survey Report, no.
4/1966)

Jabatan Perdana Menteri. Land Capability Classification
Report, Johore State. Kuala Lumpur, 1968. 15 p.
12 tables. Mimeo.

Jacks, G. V., and R. O. Whyte. Erosion and soil
conservation. Aberystwyth, 1938. 206 p. (Commonwealth
Bureau of Soil Science, Technical Comm., no.
36 and Herbage Publications Series Bulletin, 25)
See p. 46-47 for British Malaya.

Joseph, K. T. Sedimentary soils of Kedah and their
suggested utilization. JTG, 18 (1964): 101-110.
Maps, tables.

Joseph, K. T. The reconnaissance soil survey of
Kedah. Malaysia, Ministry of Agriculture and
Cooperatives, Oct. 1965. 39 p. (Division of Agriculture,
Bulletin, no. 117)

Kanapathy, K., and S. Thamboo. Phosphate studies
on some Kelantan soils. Mal Ag Jl, 43, 2 (1960): 104-111.

Law, Wei-min, and M. L. Leamy. Factors involved
in the genesis of some shale-derived soils in
Malaya. 1966. 104-113 p. Unpublished proceedings
of the Second Malaysian Soil Conference, Kuala Lumpur.

Law, Wei-min, and K. Selvadurai. The 1968 reconnaissance
    soil map of Malaya. May, 1968. Paper presented
    at the Third Malaysian Soil Conference, Kuching.

Leamy, M. L. The emergence of pedology in Malaya.
    Mal Ag, 6 (1966): 65-68.

Leamy, M. L. Soil classification in Malaya. 1966.
    Unpublished proceedings of the Second Malaysian
    Soil Conference, Kuala Lumpur.

Leamy, M. L., and W. P. Panton. Soil survey manual
    for Malayan conditions. Kuala Lumpur, Ministry
    of Agriculture and Co-operatives, Malaysia, 1966.
    226 p. (Division of Agriculture, Bulletin, no. 119)

Libby, David A. Schematic reconnaissance soil survey
    of the Lepar Valley in North-east Pahang. Kuala
    Lumpur, Soil Science Division, Division of Agriculture,
    1964. 15 p. (Soil Survey Report, no. 1/1964)

Low, J. Dissertation on the soil and agriculture
    of the British settlement of Penang or Prince
    of Wales Island in the Straits of Malacca, including
    Province Wellesley, on the Malaya Peninsula,
    with brief references to the settlements of Singapore
    and Malacca. Singapore, 1836. 321 p.

Malaysia. Land Capability Classification Report,
    Kuantan District, Pahang. Kuala Lumpur, Economic
    Planning Unit, Prime Minister's Department, Malaysia,
    1965.

Malaysia. Land Capability Classification Report,
    Cameron Highlands District, Pahang. Kuala Lumpur,
    Economic Planning Unit, Prime Minister's Department,
    Malaysia, 1966.

Malaysia. Land Capability Classification Report,
    Jerantut District, Pahang. Kuala Lumpur, Economic
    Planning Unit, Prime Minister's Department, Malaysia,
    1966.

Malaysia. Land Capability Classification Report,
    Lipis District, Pahang. Kuala Lumpur, Economic
    Planning Unit, Prime Minister's Department, Malaysia,
    1966.

Malaysia. Land Capability Classification Report,
    Pekan District, Pahang. Kuala Lumpur, Economic
    Planning Unit, Prime Minister's Department, Malaysia,
    1966.

Malaysia. Land Capability Classification Report,
    Raub District, Pahang. Kuala Lumpur, Economic
    Planning Unit, Prime Minister's Department, Malaysia,
    1966.

Malaysia. Land Capability Classification Report,
    Temerloh District, Pahang. Kuala Lumpur, Economic
    Planning Unit, Prime Minister's Department, Malaysia,
    1966.

Malaysia. Land Capability Classification Report,
    Pahang State. Statistical Summary. Kuala Lumpur,
    Economic Planning Unit, Prime Minister's Department,
    Malaysia, 1967.

Malaysia, Department of Agriculture, Soil Science
    Division. Present land use survey--1966. Malacca--
    Preliminary Delta. Kuala Lumpur [n.d.].

Moormann, F. R., et al. Report on the Thai-Malayan
    soil correlation meeting, 1964. Ministry of National
    Development, Thailand and Ministry of Agriculture
    and Co-operatives, Malaysia. 47 p. (Report SSR-27-1964)

Ng, Siew-kee, and K. Selvadurai. Scope of using
    detailed soil maps in the planting industry in
    Malaya. Mal Ag Jl, 46, 2 (1967): 158-163.

Ng, Siew-kee, Ignatius Fen-thau Wong, and Law Wei-min,
    eds. The Proceedings of the Second Malaysian
    Soil Conference held in February 1966, Kuala Lumpur,
    Malaya. Kuala Lumpur, 1966. 229 p. Graphs, tables.
    Processed.
        The conference was organized by the Research
    Branch, Division of Agriculture, Ministry of
    Agriculture and Co-operatives, Kuala Lumpur.

Null, W. S., C. J. Acton, and I. F. T. Wong. Reconnaissance
    soil survey of Southern Johore. Kuala Lumpur, Soil
    Science Division, Division of Agriculture, 1965.
    72 p. (Malayan Soil Survey Report, no. 1/1965)

Owen, G. A provisional classification of Malayan soils. Jl Soil Sc, 2, 1 (1951): 20-42. Also published in the Journal of the Rubber Research Institute of Malaya, Communication, 274 (1951).

Owen, G. Determination of available nutrients in Malayan soils. JRRIM, 14 (1953): 109-120.

Owen, G. Studies of the phosphate problem in Malayan soils. Ar Rubbercult Ned en Ned Ind, extra no. (May 1953): 167-172.

Panton, W. P. Soil survey reports; no. 1, Federal Experiment Station, Serdang. Mal Ag Jl, 37, 3 (1954): 136-145. Map.

Panton, W. P. Types of Malayan laterite and factors affecting their distribution. Proceedings of the Sixth International Congress of Soil Science (Paris). V. 5 (1956): 419-423.

Panton, W. P. The Federal Experiment Station, Jerangau, Trengganu. Mag Ag Jl, 40 (1957): 19-29. Maps, tables.

Panton, W. P. Reconnaissance soil survey of Trengganu. Kuala Lumpur, 1958. (Department of Agriculture, Bulletin, no. 105)

Panton, W. P. Reconaissance soil survey in Kelantan. Mal Ag Jl, 43, 2 (1960/1961): 87-103. Maps.

Panton, W. P. Malayan soils--their use and abuse. Mal Ag, 2 (1962): 35-38.

Panton, W. P. The soil resources of Johore. Johore Planters Association Annual Report (1963).

Panton, W. P. Soil survey methods in Malayan forest. Mal Ag, 3 (1963): 26-29.

Panton, W. P. The 1962 soil map of Malaya. JTG, 18 (1964): 118-124.

Panton, W. P. Reconaissance soil survey of the Southwest Johore coconut area. By W. P. Panton, Soo Swee-weng [and] Nuruddin bin Ma'arof. Kuala Lumpur, Ministry of Agriculture and Co-operatives, 1965. 40 p. (Malayan Soil Survey Report, no. 3/1965) Illus., map, col. fold. map in back pocket, tables. Processed.

Panton, W. P. Topography, geology and soils. Malayan
    Forest Records, 23 (1965): 2/2-2/20. Chapter
    2 of Part II--Environmental Factors and Tree
    Properties.

Panton, W. P., and Ang Tai-jin. Soil survey reports,
    no. 7, the Bukit Goh Forest Reserve, near Kuantan,
    Pahang. Mal Ag Jl, 41, 1 (1958): 3-9. Map, photo.

Parberry, D. B., and R. M. Venkatachalam. Chemical
    analysis of South Malayan peat soil. JTG, 18
    (Aug. 1964): 125-133. Tables.

Phillis, E. Profiles and permeability in Malayan
    padi soils. Mal Ag Jl, 44, 1 (1963): 3-17.

Robinson, A. G. The training of alluvial rivers.
    Mal For, 10 (1941): 42-48.

Rosenquist, E. A. Soils and the fertilizing of rubber
    and oil palm. JTG, 18 (1964): 148-156.

Savage, H. E. F. An examination of the geology and
    soils of an area in the state of Perak, Federated
    Malay States. Kuala Lumpur, 1932. (Department
    of Agriculture, Special Bulletin, Sc. ser., no. 10)

Scharff, J. W. New health and prosperity from tropical
    soils. Practice of composting in Malaya. Crown
    Colonist, 12 (1942): 385-386.

Shearing, C. H. Soil survey Prang Besar, Bukit Prang,
    Bukit Damar, Galloway Estates. 1962. (Harrisons
    and Crosfield, Research and Advisory Scheme,
    Soil Survey Report, no. 1)

Smallwood, Howard A. Schematic reconnaissance soil
    survey of the Kluang-Muar-Labis region of North
    Johore. Kuala Lumpur, Soil Science Division,
    Division of Agriculture, 1965. 24 p. (Malayan
    Soil Survey Report, no. 2/1965)

Soper, J. R. P. Soil erosion on Penang hills. Mal
    Ag Jl, 26 (1938): 407-418.

Speer, W. S. Report to the Government of Malaysia
    on soil and water conservation. Rome, 1963. 54 p.
    (Food and Agricultural Organization of the United
    Nations, no. 1788)

Stensland, R. W. Schematic reconnaissance soil survey
    of a part of East Pahang. Mal Ag Jl, 453 (1966): 295-310.

Tempany, H. Studies in Malayan soils. Mal Ag Jl
    (1933): 345-361, 471-491.

Wong, I. F. T. Reconnaissance soil survey of Selangor.
    Kuala Lumpur, 1966. (Malayan Soil Survey Report,
    no. 6)

Wong, I. F. T. Soil suitability classification for
    dry land crops in Malaya. 1966. Unpublished proceedings
    of the Second Malaysian Soil Conference, Kuala
    Lumpur.

CHAPTER 8

ECONOMIC, POLITICAL, AND REGIONAL GEOGRAPHY

Annandale, Nelson. The Siamese Malay States. SGM, 16 (1900): 505-523. Illus.

Bauer, Kurt Hermann. Die Kulturlandschaft von British Malaya und ihre Entwicklung aus der Naturlandschaft. Halle, 1931. 164 p.

Bouterwek, K. British Malaya. Mitt G Ges München, 22 (1929): 116-137.

Broek, Jan O. M. Malaya. Prepared with the cooperation of the American Geographical Society. Garden City, N.Y. [1958]. 63 p. Illus.

Buchanan, Keith. The Southeast Asian world. An introductory essay. London, New York, 1967. 176 p.

Cant, R. G. Pahang in 1888. The eve of British administration. JTG, 19 (1964): 4-19.

Cant, R. G. An historical geography of Pahang, 1888-1939. 1965. Ph.D. thesis -- University of Malaya.

Cherry, William T. Geography of British Malaya and the Malay Archipelago, together with brief historical outlines of the principle areas under British protection. 6th ed. Singapore, 1931. 82 p. Map.

Courtenay, P. P. Penang: the economic geography of a free port. 1962. Ph.D. -- London.

D'Almeida, W. Barrington. Geography of Perak and Salangore and a brief sketch of some of the adjacent Malay States. Jl R G Soc, 46 (1876): 357-380. Map.

Dobby, E. H. G. Some aspects of the human ecology of Southeast Asia. G Jl, 108 (1946): 40-54. Maps.

Dobby, E. H. G. Malaya and Southeast Asia. London, 1948. 224 p. Illus.

Dobby, E. H. G. Southeast Asia. London, 1950. 415 p. Bibliog., charts, illus., maps.

ECONOMIC, POLITICAL, AND REGIONAL GEOGRAPHY

Dobby, E. H. G. The Kelantan Delta. GR, 41 (1951):
226-255. Maps.

Fisher, Charles A. Southeast Asia. In W. G. East
and O. H. K. Spate. The Changing Map of Asia.
London, 1950: 179-246. 414 p. Maps, tables.

Fisher, Charles A. The problem of Malayan unity
in its geographical setting. In R. W. Steel and
C. A. Fisher, eds. Geographical Essays on British
Tropical Lands. London, 1956: 271-344.

Fisher, Charles A. The geographical setting of the
proposed Malaysian Federation. JTG, 17 (1963):
99-115.

Fisher, Charles A. The Malaysian Federation, Indonesia
and the Philippines: a study in political geography.
G Jl, 129, 3 (1963): 311-328.

Fisher, Charles A. Southeast Asia, a social economic
and political geography. London, 1964.

Fryer, Donald. Malaya. [2d ed.]. [Melbourne], Longmans
[1963]. 40 p. (Longmans' Australian Geographies, no. 14)
Illus., maps (part col.).

Gibbs, W. E. British Malaya: a story of empire.
Jl Manchester G Soc (1919): 8-18. Illus., maps.

Hall, D. G. E., ed. An atlas of Southeast Asia.
London, 1964.

Ho, Robert. Mixed farming and multiple cropping
in Malaya. In Hong Kong University. Symposium
on Land Use and Mineral Deposits in Hong Kong,
Southern China and South-East Asia. Hong Kong,
1964: 88-104. Figs., tables.

Hodder, B. W. Malayan settlement, a social geography.
[Oxford] 1954. 162 p. Dissertation (B. Litt.)
-- Oxford University. Illus.

Hodder, B. W. Man in Malaya. London, 1959. 144 p.
Diagrs., maps, plates, tables.

Iimoto, Nobuyuki. Outline of geography of Malay
Peninsula. Jl G, Tokyo G Soc, 51 (1939): 502-519.
(In Japanese)

ECONOMIC, POLITICAL, AND REGIONAL GEOGRAPHY

International Geographical Union and the University
of Malaya. Guide to tours. 9th-24th April, 1962.
Kuala Lumpur, 1962.

Jackson, James C. Batang Padang ninety years ago.
MH, 10, 1 (1965): 31-38.

Küchler, Johannes. Penang: Kulturlandschaftswandel
und ethnisch-soziale Struktur einer Insel Malaysias.
Giessen, Selbstverlag des Geographischen Instituts
der Justus Liebig-Universität Giessen, in Kommission
bei Wilhelm Schmitz Verlag, 1968. 165 p. (Giessener
geographische Schriften. Heft 13)

Marshall, Colin. Selangor. What of the future? Mal
For, 17 (1954): 50-63. Tables.

McTaggert, W. D. Malaya and its geographical interpretation
- a review article. MER, 9, 2 (1964): 83-91.

McTaggert, W. D. Historical trends or contemporary
patterns: the problem of regional geography in
a Malayan setting. Geographica, 3 (1967): 1-4.

Ooi, Jin-bee. Land, people and economy in Malaya.
London, 1963. 426 p. Bibliog., diagrs., maps,
photos.

Richardson, C. A junior geography of Malaya. Singapore,
1939. 63 p.

Richardson, C. The M.P.H. regional geography of
Malaya. Singapore, 1935. 80 p. Illus., maps.

Robequain, Charles. Le monde malais: Péninsule Malaise,
Sumatra, Java, Borneo, Célèbes, Bali et les petites
îles de la Sonde, Moluques, Philippines. Paris,
1946. 510 p.

Robequain, Charles. Malaya, Indonesia, Borneo and
the Philippines. A geographical, economic and
political description. Translated by E. D. Laborde.
London, New York, 1954. 456 p.
See especially p. 113-144 for Malaya.

Scrivenor, J. B. Physical geography of the southern
part of the Malay Peninsula. GR, 11 (1921): 351-371.

ECONOMIC, POLITICAL, AND REGIONAL GEOGRAPHY

Skinner, A. M. Geography of the Malay Peninsula.
JRASSB, 1 (1878): 52-62.

Skinner, A. M., ed. A geography of the Malay Peninsula
and surrounding countries. Singapore, 1884.

Studies in the geography of South-East Asia: a selection
of papers presented at the regional conference
of South-East Asia geographers Kuala Lumpur 1962.
London, 1964.
A reprint of JTG 17 and 18.

Thompson, Edmund R. Malaya's state idea: an application
of the unified field theory of political geography.
1959. Unpublished master's thesis (Department
of Geography) -- Syracuse University.

Tregonning, K. G. Singapore and Kuala Lumpur: a
politico-geographical contrast. PV, 7, 2 (1966):
238-241. See also note by R. Catley in PV, 8,
2 (1967): 179-180.

Uhlig, Harald. Malaysien: die Struktur des jüngsten
Staates in Südostoasien. Geographische Rundschau,
16, 4 (1964): 129-136.

Valkenburg, S. van. Agricultural regions of Asia:
Malaysia. Ec G, 11 (1935): 227-246, 325-337.

Verhoeven, F. R. J. Ayer Leleh, the transient river
that may have saved Malacca from Siamese conquest.
MH, 10, 2 (1967): 3-12.

Ward, Marion Wybourn. Recent changes in the economic
geography of Malaya. G, 45 (1960): 294-297.

West, A. J. F., and J. Rose. South-East Asia with
Malaysia and Singapore. 5th ed. 1965. 225 p.

Wikkramatileke, R. Focus on Singapore. JTG, 20 (1965): 73-83

Zaharah Binti Haji Mahmud. Change in a Malay sultanate:
an historical geography of Kedah before 1939.
1966. M.A. thesis -- Malaya.

Zaharah Binti Haji Mahmud. Moving frontiers of agricultural
settlement in 18th and 19th century Kedah. Geographica,
2 (1966): 6 p. Map.

ECONOMIC, POLITICAL, AND REGIONAL GEOGRAPHY

Zaharah Binti Haji Mahmud. The development of the State of Kedah up to the end of the nineteenth century. Unpublished paper no. 67 presented at the International Conference on Asian History. Kuala Lumpur, August, 1968. 68 p. processed.

CHAPTER 9

MAN AND CULTURE

A. PHYSICAL ANTHROPOLOGY

Annandale, Nelson. Remarks on a collection of skulls
from the Malay Peninsula. Rep Br Assoc Sc (1903):
802-803.

Annandale, Nelson, and Herbert C. Robinson. Some
preliminary results of an expedition to the Malay
Peninsula. Jl R Anthr Inst, 32 (1902): 407-417.

Annandale, Nelson, and Herbert C. Robinson. Contributions
to the physical anthropology of the Malay Peninsula.
In N. Annandale and H. C. Robinson. Fasciculi
Malayenses . . . Anthropology, Part I. London,
1903: 105-175. Illus., plates.

Annandale, Nelson, and Herbert C. Robinson. Fasciculi
Malayenses: anthropological and zoological results
of an expedition to Perak and the Siamese Malay
States, 1901-1902. Anthropology, Part I. London,
1903-1904. 180 p. Illus., plates, tables.

Duckworth, W. L. H. Malay: physical anthropology.
Notes on the anthropological observations made
by Mr. F. Laidlaw in the Skeat expedition to
the Malay Peninsula. Jl Anthr Inst, 30 (1900): 77.
(Anthropological Reviews Miscellanea, no. 75)

Duckworth, W. L. H. Human remains from rock shelters
and caves in Perak, Pahang, and Perlis and from
Selinsing. JRASMB, 12, 2 (1934): 149-167. Plate.

Finsch, O. Anthropologische Ergebnisse einer Reise
in der Südsee und dem Malayischen Archipel in
den Jahren 1879-1882. Beschreibender Catalog
der auf dieser Reise gesammelten Gesichtsmasken
von Völkertypen, herausgegeben mit Unterstützung
der Berliner anthropologischen Gesellschaft.
Berlin, 1884. 78 p. Plates.

Green, R. Anthropological blood grouping among the
Sakai. BRM, ser. B, 4 (1949): 130-132.

Hagen, Bernhard. Anthropologischer Atlas ostasiatischer
und melanesischer Völker. Wiesbaden, 1898. 113 p.
Plates.

MAN AND CULTURE - Physical Anthropology

Hagen, Bernhard. Kopf- und Gesichtstypen ostasiatischer
und melanesischer Völker. Stuttgart, 1906. 44 col. plates.

Hanny, E. T. Les races Malaiques et Américaines.
L'Anthr, 7 (1896): 129-146.

Kiffner, Fritz. Ein Beitrag zur Morphologie der
Sakei. Z Morph Anthr, 27 (1928): 179-198. Bibliog.,
tables.

Kingsbury, A. N., and P. Fasal. A nutritional survey
of the Federated Malay States. 1. Common clinical
manifestations of sub-nutrition among rural Malays
and Tamils. 2. Heights and weights tables for
young Tamils under plantation conditions. Kuala
Lumpur, 1940. (1) 14 p. (2) 8 p. (Institute for
Medical Research, Bulletin nos. 1 and 2)

Kloss, C. Boden. Measurements of some Sakai and
Slim, South Perak, with notes on the same. JFMSM,
6, 2 (1915): 71-84. Plates 1-23.

Müller, H. W. Die Kleinschädelformen Südasiens.
Ein Beitrag zum Kleinwuchsproblem. Z Rassenk,
2 (1935): 52-90, 263-296. Bibliog., illus., tables.

Nyessen, D. J. H. The Malay chin. Man, 45 (1945):
121-122. Illus.

Saller, K. Erblicher Rutilismus in der malayischen
Inselwelt. Mit allgemeinen Bemerkungen über den
Erbgang der menschlichen Haarfarbe. Z Indukt
Abst Vererb, 45 (1927): 202-231. Bibliog.

Schebesta, P., and V. Lebzelter. Schädel- und Skelettreste
von drei Semangindividuen. Anthropos, 20 (1926): 959-990.

Schebesta, P., and V. Lebzelter. Anthropological
measurements in Semangs and Sakais in Malaya
(Malacca). Anthr Praha, 6 (1928): 183-251. Illus.,
plates, tables.

Snell, C. A. R. D. Menselijke skeletresten van Gol
Ba'it, Sungai Siput, Perak, Maleisch schier-eiland.
Mens en Maatschappij, 23 (1948): 372-376.

Stevens, H. V. Anthropologische Bemerkungen über
die Eingeborenen von Malacca. Z Ethn, 29 (1897): 173-206.

131

Sullivan, Louis R. A few Andamanese skulls with
comparative notes on Negrito craniometry. Anthr
Pap Am Mus Nat Hist, 23, 4 (1921): 177-201.

Turner, W. A contribution to the craniology of the
natives of Borneo, the Malays, the natives of
Formosa and the Tibetans. Trans R Soc Edinburgh,
45, 3 (1907): 781-818. Illus., tables.

Wallace, A. R. Varieties of man in the Malay Archipelago.
Trans Ethn Soc, n.s., 3 (1865): 196-215.

B. ARCHEOLOGY AND PREHISTORY

Abdul-Aziz, Engku. Neoliths from Johore. JRASMB,
10, 1 (1932): 149-159. Plate.

Al-Rashid. Aspects of South and East Asian lower-
palaeolithic. JHS, 3 (1964/1965): 48-59.

Annandale, N., J. Coggin Brown, and F. H. Cravely.
The limestone caves of Burma and the Malay Peninsula.
Jl Proc As Soc Bengal, n.s., 9 (1913): 391-423.

Barnes, W. D. Translation of H. Kern's "Sanskrit
Inscriptions in Malay Peninsula". JRASSB, 49
(1907): 95-101.

Blagden, C. O. Antiquity of Malacca. JRASSB, 57
(1911): 189-190.

Blagden, C. O. A note on the Trengganu inscription.
JRASMB, 2 (1924): 258-263.

Claeys, J. Y. L'archéologie du Siam. Ière partie,
la péninsule malaise. 2e partie, la vallée du
Menam. 3e partie, Laos occidental. BEFEO, 31
(1931): 361-448. Figs., maps, plates.

Clark, J. G. D. Archaeological work in the Malay
Peninsula and Java. Proc Prehist Soc, n.s., 2
(1936): 251.

Collings, H. D. Report of an archaeological excavation
in Kedah, Malay Peninsula. BRM, ser. B, 1 (1936): 5-16.
Illus.

Collings, H. D. An excavation at Bukit Chuping, Perlis. BRM, ser. B, 2 (1937): 94-119.

Collings, H. D. Recent finds of iron-age sites in southern Perak and Selangor, Federated Malay States. BRM, ser. B, 2 (1937): 75-93.

Collings, H. D. An iron age find near Klang. BRM, ser. B, 4 (1949): 113-116. Illus.

Crawfurd, John. Malayan race of man and its prehistoric career. Trans Ethn Soc, n.s., 7 (1869): 119-133.

Duckworth, W. L. H. Human remains from rock shelters and caves in Perak, Pahang, and Perlis and from Selinsing. JRASMB, 12, 2 (1934): 149-167. Plate.

Dunn, Frederick L. Excavations at Gua Kechil, Pahang. JRASMB, 37, 2 (1964): 87-124. Figs., illus., tables.

Earl, George Windser. On the shell-mounds of Province Wellesley, in the Malay Peninsula. Trans Ethn Soc, n.s., 2 (1863): 119-129.

Evans, Ivor H. N. Preliminary report on the cave exploration near Lenggong, Upper Perak. JFMSM, 7 (1918): 227-235.

Evans, Ivor H. N. Preliminary report on the exploration of a rock shelter in the Batu Kurau Parish, Perak. JFMSM, 9 (1920): 34-37.

Evans, Ivor H. N. Cave-dwellings in Pahang. JFMSM, 9 (1920): 37-53.

Evans, Ivor H. N. A grave and some megaliths in Negri Sembilan with an account of some excavations. JFMSM, 9 (1921): 155-175.

Evans, Ivor H. N. On a find of stone implements at Tanjong Malim. JFMSM, 9 (1922): 257-259.

Evans, Ivor H. N. A rock shelter at Gunong Pondok. JFMSM, 9 (1922): 267-271.

Evans, Ivor H. N. An ancient clay vessel from the Langkawi Islands. JFMSM, 12 (1924): 9. Plate.

Evans, Ivor H. N. A hoard of stone implements from
Batu Gajah. JFMSM, 12 (1926): 67. Plate.

Evans, Ivor H. N. Notes on old Malay tin coins and
coin moulds. JFMSM, 12 (1927): 83-86. Plates.

Evans, Ivor H. N. Notes on the remains of an old
boat from Pontian, Pahang. JFMSM, 12 (1927):
93-96. Plates.

Evans, Ivor H. N. On slab-built graves in Perak.
JFMSM, 12 (1928): 111-119. Plates.

Evans, Ivor H. N. On ancient remains from Kuala
Selinsing, Perak. JFMSM, 12 (1928): 121-131.

Evans, Ivor H. N. On a find of stone implements
associated with pottery. JFMSM, 12 (1928): 133-135.

Evans, Ivor H. N. Further notes on remains from
Kuala Selinsing, Perak. JFMSM, 12 (1928): 139-142.
Plate.

Evans, Ivor H. N. Further notes on stone implements
associated with pottery. JFMSM, 12 (1928): 143-144.
Plate.

Evans, Ivor H. N. Further excavations of Gunong
Pondok. JFMSM, 12 (1928): 161-162. Plates.

Evans, Ivor H. N. Further notes on a find of stone
implements with pottery. JFMSM, 12 (1929): 175-176.
Plate.

Evans, Ivor H. N. A further note on the Kuala Selinsing
Settlement. JFMSM, 12 (1929): 181-184. Plates.

Evans, Ivor H. N. Recent progress in the study of
Malayan antiquities. JFMSM, 12 (1929): 185-188.

Evans, Ivor H. N. Notes on the relationship between
Philippine iron-age antiquities and some from
Perak. JFMSM, 12 (1929): 189-196.

Evans, Ivor H. N. Notes on two types of stone implements
from the Malay Peninsula. Man, 30 (1930): 157-159.

Evans, Ivor H. N. On a stone spearhead from Kelantan.
JFMSM, 15 (1930): 1-3. Plates.

Evans, Ivor H. N. On a stone implement from Kinta,
Perak. JFMSM, 15 (1930): 5. Plate.

Evans, Ivor H. N. Further notes on stone implements
from Pahang. JFMSM, 15 (1930): 7. Plates.

Evans, Ivor H. N. Malayan types of stone implements
in India, Burma and the Andamans. JFMSM, 15 (1930): 9-11.

Evans, Ivor H. N. On ancient kitchen-middens in
Province Wellesley. JFMSM, 15 (1930): 15-18.

Evans, Ivor H. N. Some problems of Malayan archeology.
JFMSM, 15 (1930): 21-24.

Evans, Ivor H. N. Notes on recent finds at Kuala
Selinsing. JFMSM, 15 (1930): 25-27. Plate.

Evans, Ivor H. N. On a pictured stone from Kelantan.
JFMSM, 15 (1930): 37. Plate.

Evans, Ivor H. N. Ancient inscriptions at Cherok
Tokun, Province Wellesley. JFMSM, 15 (1930):
35-36. Plate.

Evans, Ivor H. N. A note on beaked stone adzes.
JFMSM, 15 (1930): 67-68. Figs.

Evans, Ivor H. N. A search for antiquities in Kedah
and Perlis. JFMSM, 15 (1931): 43-50. Plates.

Evans, Ivor H. N. Excavations at Nyong, Tembeling
River, Pahang. JFMSM, 15 (1931): 51-62. Map,
plans, plates.

Evans, Ivor H. N. A further slab-built grave at
Sungkai, Perak. JFMSM, 15 (1931): 63-64. Plate.

Evans, Ivor H. N. A stone spear-head from Pahang.
JFMSM, 15 (1931): 65. Plate.

Evans, Ivor H. N. An iron implement of unusual type.
JFMSM, 15 (1931): 69. Plate.

Evans, Ivor H. N. An attempted classification of
iron age implements. JFMSM, 15 (1931): 71-76. Figs.

Evans, Ivor H. N. An ancient Cornelian bead from
Pahang. JRASMB, 11, 2 (1933): 146-147. Illus.

Evans, Ivor H. N. Melanesoid culture in Malaya.
BRM, ser. B, 3 (1937): 141-146.

Foong, See-tonn. The University of Malaya Archaeological
Society's survey of the Kuala Muda area (South Kedah),
in July 1956. JRASMB, 32, 1 (1959) [i.e. 1962]: 209-213.
Map.

Gardner, G. B. Ancient beads from the Johore River
as evidence of an early link between Malaya and
the Roman Empire. JRAS (1937): 467-470.

Gibson-Hill, C. A. Further notes on the old boat
at Pontian, in southern Pahang. JRASMB, 25, 1
(1952): 111-133. Illus.

Hale, A. Stone axes, Perak. Nature, 32 (1885): 626.

Hale, A. Evidence of Siamese work in Perak. JRASSB,
18 (1886): 356.

Hale, A. The stone age in Perak. JRASSB, Notes and
Queries, no. 3 (1886): 62.

Hale, A. Notes on stone implements from Perak. Jl
R Anthr Inst, 17 (1888): 66-67.

Harrisson, Barbara, and B. A. N. Peacock. Recent
archaeological discoveries in Malaysia 1962-1963.
JRASMB, 37, 2 (1964): 192-206. Illus.

Harrower, G. Skeletal remains from the Kuala Selinsing
excavations, Perak, Malay Peninsula. JRASMB,
11, 2 (1933): 190-210.

Heine-Geldern, R. Ein Beitrag zur Chronologie des
Neolithikums in Südostasien. In W. Kopper, ed.
Festschrift Publication d'Hommage Offerte au
P. W. Schmidt. Vienne, 1928: 9-843.

Heine-Geldern, R. Die Megalithen Südostasiens und
ihre Bedeutung für die Klärung der Megalitenfrage
in Europa und Polynesien. Anthropos, 23 (1928): 276-315.

Heine-Geldern, R. Urheimat und früheste Wanderungen
der Austronesier. Anthropos, 27 (1932): 543-619.
Illus., map.

Heine-Geldern, R. Prehistoric research in the Netherlands Indies. New York, South East Asia Institute, 1948. Contains a summary of all prehistoric research in Malaya.

Hooijer, D. A. Fossil evidence of Austromelanesian migrations in Malaysia. SWJA, 6 (1950): 416-422.

Hooijer, D. A. Austromelanesian migrations once more. SWJA, 8 (1952): 472-477.

Hooijer, D. A. Rhinoceros sondaicus Desmarest from the Hoabinhian of Gua Cha rock shelter. FMJ, n.s., 7 (1962): 23-24.

Hussein Alatas, Syed. Archaeology, history and the social sciences in Southeast Asia. FMJ, n.s., 9 (1964): 21-31.

Irby, F. W. A short account of some ancient remains found on Gunung Jerai, Kedah, with one plan. JFMSM, 1 (1905): 76-80.

Jack-Hinton, Colin. A note on a Ch'eng Hua nien hao from Kampong Makam, Kota Tinggi, and some remarks on the Johore River trade in the fifteenth century. FMJ, n.s., 8 (1963): 32-35.

Jack-Hinton, Colin. Archaeological research in South Malaya. Hemisphere, 9, 3 (March 1965): 15-19. Illus., map.

Keasberry, Benjamin. The origin of the Malay race. Inter-ocean, 48 (1927): 323ff.

Kennedy, Kenneth A. R. A biochemical analysis of human remains from Gua-cha, Kelantan, Malaya. Man, 64 (May/June 1964): 77-79.

Kern, H. Concerning some Sanskrit inscriptions in the Malay Peninsula. JRASSB, 49 (1907): 95-101.

Kloss, C. B. Notes on the Pengkalan Kempas tombstone. JFMSM, 9 (1921): 185-189. Plates.

Koenigswald, G. H. R. van. Evidence of a prehistoric Australomelanesoid population in Malaya and Indonesia. SWJA, 8 (1952): 92-96.

Kunst, J. New light on the early history of the
Malay Archipelago. Indian Art and Letters, 12
(1938): 99-105.

Lajonquiere, Lunet de. Rapport sommaire sur une
mission archéologique (Cambodge, Siam, Presqu'île
Malaise, Inde) 1907-1908. B Comm Arch Indoch
(1909): 162-187.

Lajonquiere, Lunet de. Rapport sommaire sur une
mission archéologique au Cambodge, au Siam, dans
la presqu'île malaise et dans l'Inde (1907-1908).
BEFEO, 9 (1909): 351-368.

Lamb, Alastair. Recent archaeological work in Kedah
(1958). JRASMB, 32, 1 (1959 [i.e. 1962]): 214-232.

Lamb, Alastair. Report on the excavation and reconstruction
of Chandi Bukit Batu Pahat, Central Kedah. FMJ,
5 (1960): 1-108. 73 plates.

Lamb, Alastair. Chandi Bukit Batu Pahat. Three additional
notes. Singapore, 1961. 25 p. (Papers on Southeast
Asian Subjects, no. 5) Illus.

Lamb, Alastair. Miscellaneous papers on early Hindu
and Buddhist settlement in northern Malaya and
southern Thailand. FMJ, 6 (1961): 1-90. Diagr.,
maps, photos.

Lamb, Alastair. Pengkalan Bujang, an ancient port
in Kedah. MH, 7, 1 (1961): 12-17.

Lamb, Alastair. A note on a small inscribed stone
tablet from Dr. Wales' Kedah site no. 1. FMJ,
n.s., 7 (1962): 67-68.

Lamb, Alastair. Indianised inscriptions in northwestern
Malaya. Tamil Culture, 10 (Jan. 1963): 75-86.

Lamb, Alastair. Early history. In Wang Gung-wu,
ed. Malaysia, A Survey. New York [1964]: 99-112.

Lamb, Alastair. Miscellaneous archaeological discoveries.
JRASMB, 37, 1 (July 1964): 166-168. Plates.

Lamb, Alastair. Takuapa: the probable site of a
pre-Malacca entrepôt in the Malay Peninsula.
In John Bastin and R. Roolvink, eds. Malayan
and Indonesian Studies. Oxford, 1964: 76-86.

Linehan, W. Some discoveries on the Tembeling. JRASMB, 6, 4 (1928): 66-67. Map, plates.

Linehan, W. Notes on the remains of some ancient brick structures in Pekan District. JRASMB, 6, 4 (1928): 78-81.

Linehan, W. Traces of a bronze age culture associated with iron age implements in the regions of Klang and the Tembeling, Malaya. JRASMB, 24, 3 (1951): 1-59. Plates.

Linehan, W. Malayan perforated stone discs. JRASMB, 24, 3 (1951): 73-80. Plates.

Loewenstein, John. The origin of the Malayan metal age. JRASMB, 29, 2 (1956 [i.e. 1962]): 5-78. Illus.

Loewenstein, John. The Eskimo ulu' in the Malayan neolithic. Man, 58 (1958): 37-41.

Loewenstein, John. Evil spirit boats of Malaysia. Anthropos, 53, fasc. 1/2 (1958): 203-211.

Loewenstein, John. Hollow clay stands and censers from neolithic Malaya, and their Western prototypes. JRASMB, 32, 1 (1959 [i.e. 1962]): 168-196. Illus.

Loewenstein, John. An "Ordos" bronze knife from prehistoric Malaya. Anthropos, 56 (1961): 936-937.

Loofs, H. H. E. Elements of the megalithic complex in Southeast Asia: an annotated bibliography. Canberra, Centre of Oriental Studies, in association with Australian National University Press, 1967. 114 p.
Malay Peninsula p. 37-40.

Low, James. An account of several inscriptions found in province of Wellesley, on the Peninsula of Malacca. Jl Proc As Soc Bengal, 17, 2 (1848): 62-66.

Low, James. On an inscription from Keddah. Jl Proc As Soc Bengal, 18, 1 (1849): 247-249.

Matthews, John. A check-list of "Hoabinhian" sites
excavated in Malaya, 1860-1939. Singapore, published
for the Department of History, University of Malaya,
in Kuala Lumpur by Eastern Universities Press, 1961.
59 p. (Malaya, University of, Department of History,
Papers on Southeast Asian Subjects, no. 3) Bibliog., map.

Matthews, John. A note on rock paintings recently
discovered near Ipoh, Perak, Federation of Malaya.
Man, 60 (1960): 1-3.

Matthews, John. Results of excavations in Malaya.
AP, 5 (1961): 237-242.

Maxwell, W. E. Antiquities of Province Wellesley.
JRASSB, 1 (1878): 114.

McCarthy, F. D. Comparison of the prehistory of
Australia with that of Indo-China, the Malay
Peninsula and the Netherlands East Indies. PCPE,
3, 1938 (Singapore) (1940): 30-50.

Medway, Lord. Archaeological notes from Pulau Tioman,
Pahang. FMJ, n.s., 7 (1962): 55-63. Illus.

Mohamed Sidek bin Elamdin. Stone implements and pot-sherds
found at Gua Tukang, Lenggong: a non-professional
approach. PS, 2, 2 (1967): 1-19. Illus.

Noone, H. D. Report on a new neolithic site in Ulu
Kelantan. JFMSM, 15 (1939): 170-174. Figs., map,
plates.

Paterson, H. S. An early Malay inscription from
Trengganu. JRASMB, 2, 3 (1924): 252-258. Plates.

Peacock, B. A. V. A short description of Malayan
prehistoric pottery. AP, 3 (1959): 121-156.

Peacock, B. A. V. A preliminary note on the Dong-s'on
bronze drums from kampong Sungei Loang. FMJ,
n.s., 9 (1964): 1-3. Photos.

Peacock, B. A. V. The drums at kampong Sungai Long.
MH, 10, 1 (1965): 3-15.

Peacock, B. A. V. Malaysian prehistory: some current
problems. In S. Takdir Alisjahbana, ed. The Cultural
Problems of Malaysia in the Context of Southeast
Asia. Kuala Lumpur [1966?]: 40-55.

Peacock, B. A. V. Two Dong-s'on drums. MH, 10, 2 (1967): 26-31.

Peacock, B. A. V., and F. L. Dunn. Recent archaeological discoveries in Malaysia, 1967 West Malaysia. JRASMB, 41, 1 (1968): 171-179.

Ridley, H. N. Discovery of a stone implement in Singapore. JRASSB, 23 (1891): 141-142.

Scrivenor, J. B. Notes on the petrology of stone implements from the Federated Malay States. JFMSM, 1 (1906): 123-124.

Scrivenor, J. B. Malay beliefs concerning prehistoric stone implements. Man, 8 (1908): 104-106.

Scrivenor, J. B. Geological and geographical evidence for changes in sea-level during ancient Malay history and late pre-history. JRASMB, 22, 1 (1949): 107-115. Bibliog.

Sheppard, M. C. "Batu hidop"--Megaliths in Malacca territory. BRM, ser. B, 1 (1936): 61-66. Plates.

Sheppard, Haji Mubin. Megaliths in Malacca and Negri Sembilan. FMJ, n.s., 7 (1962): 71-85. Illus.

Sieveking, A. The palaeolithic industry of Kota Tampan, Perak, northwestern Malaya. AP, 2 (1958): 91-102. 2 plates.

Sieveking, G. de G. Gua Cha and the Malayan stone age (an account of the Gua Cha expedition, April-May, 1954). MHJ, 1 (1954): 111-125.

Sieveking, G. de G. The iron age collections of Malaya. JRASMB, 29, 2 (1956 [i.e. 1962]): 79-138. Illus.

Sieveking, G. de G. Recent archaeological discoveries in Malaya (1956). JRASMB, 32, 1 (1959 [i.e. 1962]): 205-209.

Sieveking, G. de G. The prehistoric cemetery at Bukit Tengku Lembu, Perlis. FMJ, n.s., 7 (1962): 25-54. Illus.

Sieveking, G. de G., and M. W. F. Tweedie. Excavating
an important stone age site in the Malayan jungle,
at Gua Cha, in Kelantan. Illus Lond News, 226
(March 5, 1955): 405-407.

Sieveking, G. de G., P. Wheatley, and C. A. Gibson-Hill.
Recent archaeological discoveries in Malaya.
JRASMB, 27, 1 (1954): 224-233. Maps, photos.

Skinner, C. J. Ancient settlements in Penang. JRASSB,
14 (1884): 6.

Stein-Callenfels, P. V. van. The Pengkalan Kempas
inscription. JFMSM, 12 (1927): 107-110.

Stein-Callenfels, P. V. van. An excavation of three
kitchen middens at Guak Kepah, Province Wellesley,
Straits Settlements. BRM, ser. B, 1 (1936): 27-34.
Illus.

Stein-Callenfels, P. V. van. The melanesoid civilisations
of Eastern Asia. BRM, ser. B, 1 (1936): 41-51.

Stein-Callenfels, P. V. van. Report on an excavation
in the rock-shelter Gol Ba'it, near Sungai Siput
(Perak). PCPE, 3, 1938 (Singapore) (1940): 119-125.
Plans, plates.

Stein-Callenfels, P. V. van, and Ivor H. N. Evans.
Report on cave excavations in Perak. JFMSM, 12
(1928): 145-159. Diagrs., plates.

Steffen, A., and N. Annandale. Clay tablets from
caves in Siamese Malaya. Man, 2 (1902): 177-180.
Illus.

Swan, R. M. W. Note on stone implements from Pahang.
Man, 4 (1904): 54-56.

Teilhard de Chardin, P. Notes sur la paléontologie
humaine en Asie Meridionale. L'Anthr, 47 (1937):
23-33; 48 (1938): 449-456.

Trevor, J. C., and D. R. Brothwell. The human remains
of mesolithic and neolithic data from Gua Cha,
Kelantan. FMJ, n.s., 7 (1962): 6-22. Illus.,
tables.

Tweedie, Michael William Forbes. Prehistory of Malaya.
JRASMB, 10, 1 (1932): 1-8.
A general summary of results of studies, with
bibliographical references.

Tweedie, Michael William Forbes. Report on excavations
in Kelantan. JRASMB, 18, 2 (1940): 1-22. Diagr.,
maps, plates, references.
Report of 1939 expedition in South Kelantan,
15 miles north of Pahang border.

Tweedie, Michael William Forbes. Prehistory in Malaya.
JRAS (1942): 1-13.

Tweedie, Michael William Forbes. Prehistoric objects
from the Tui gold mine near Padang Tengku, Pahang.
JRASMB, 20, 1 (1947): 41-44. Diagr., plates.

Tweedie, Michael William Forbes. The Malayan neolithic.
Jl Polyn Soc, 58 (1949): 19-35. Illus.

Tweedie, Michael William Forbes. The stone age in
Malaya. JRASMB, 26, 2 (1953): 1-90. Bibliog.,
illus., maps, plates.

Tweedie, Michael William Forbes. Prehistoric Malaya.
Illustrated with drawings by K. M. Foong, and
photographs by the author. Singapore, 1955. 43 p.
(Background to Malaya Series, no. 6) Rev. ed.
Singapore, 1957. 42 p.

Wales, Dorothy C., and H. G. Quaritch Wales. Further
work on Indian sites in Malaya. JRASMB, 20, 1
(1947): 1-11. Illus., plates.

Wales, H. G. Quaritch. New light on ancient empires--
explorations reveal the southeastward spread
of Indian culture. Asia, 36 (1936): 192-197.
Illus., map.

Wales, H. G. Quaritch. Farther India: archaeological
researches in Malaya. Annual Bib Ind Arch, 12
(1937): 38-41; 13 (1938): 15-17.

Wales, H. G. Quaritch. Recent excavations in Kedah,
British Malaya. Cultureel Indië, 1 (1939): 161-166.
Illus.

Wales, H. G. Quaritch. Archeological researches
    on ancient Indian colonization in Malaya. JRASMB,
    18, 1 (1940): 1-85. Diagr., maps.

Wales, H. G. Quaritch. Recent Malayan excavations
    and some wider implications. JRASMB, 20 (1947):
    142-149.

Wallace, W. A. Plans of the Negri Sembilan grave
    and megaliths, with notes. JFMSM, 9 (1921): 175-183.
    Diagrs.

Wang, Gung-wu. Johor Lama: an introduction to archaeology.
    MHJ, 1 (1954): 18-23.

Wilkinson, R. J. Antiquities of Malaya. JRASMB,
    2 (1924): 289-291.

Wilkinson, R. J. Early Indian influences in Malayasia.
    JRASMB, 13, 2 (1935): 1-16.
    Based on Chinese and other records.

Wilkinson, R. J. Further notes upon the study of
    ancient times in the Malay Peninsula. JRASMB,
    15, 2 (1937): 167-170.

Wilkinson, R. J. The Bernam slab-graves. JRASMB,
    17, 1 (1939): 134-143.
    Slab graves connected with Sumatran megalithic
    culture.

Williams-Hunt, P. D. R. Notes on archaeology from
    the air in Malaya. JRASMB, 21, 1 (1948): 150-156.

Williams-Hunt, P. D. R. Recent archaeological discoveries
    in Malaya (1945-1950). JRASMB, 24, 1 (1951):
    186-191.

Williams-Hunt, P. D. R. Recent archaeological discoveries
    in Malaya (1951). JRASMB, 25, 1 (1952): 181-190.
    Plates.

Winstedt, R. O. Gold ornaments dug up at Fort Canning,
    Singapore. JRASMB, 6, 4 (1928): 1-4. Map, plates.

Winstedt, R. O. The prehistory of Malaya. JRASMB,
    10, 1 (1932): 1-5. Figs., plates.

Winstedt, R. O. Slab graves and iron implements.
    JRASMB, 19, 1 (1941): 93-98.

Wray, Leonard. The cave dwellers of Perak. Jl Anthr
    Inst, 26 (1897): 36-47.

Wray, Leonard. The cave dwellers of Perak. Perak
    Museum Notes, 2, 1 (1897): 7-18.

Wray, Leonard. Further notes on the cave dwellers
    of Perak. JFMSM, 1 (1905): 13-15. Plates.

C. ETHNOLOGY

1. General

Annandale, Nelson. The peoples of the Malay Peninsula.
    SGM, 20 (1904): 337-348.

Annandale, Nelson, and Herbert C. Robinson. Fasciculi
    Malayenses. Anthropological and zoological results
    of an expedition to Perak and the Siamese Malay
    states, 1901-1902. Liverpool, 1903. 180 p.

Anonymous. The piracy and slave trade of the Indian
    Archipelago. Jl Ind Archip, 3 (1849): 581-588,
    629-636; 4 (1850): 45-52, 144-162, 400-410, 617-628,
    733-746.

Bagot, H. Survey in Johore. G Jl, 83 (1934): 203-211.
    Illus., map.

Bigandet, M. Notice sur les peuples de la presqu'île
    Malaise. Nouvelles Annales des Voyages, 121 (1849):
    80-88.

Blagden, C. O. Peoples of British Malaya. Man, 31
    (1931): 49-50.

Borie, Pierre H. D. An account of the aborigines
    of the Malay Peninsula and of the Malayan and
    other tribes at present inhabiting it. Translated
    from two letters of the French Father Borie.
    Singapore [n.d.]. Original dates of letters,
    Nov. 1857 and April 1863.

Borie, Pierre H. D. La presqu'île de Malacca, les
    Malais et les sauvages. Tulle, 1886. 155 p. Illus.,
    map.

Braddell, T. Notes on a trip to the interior from
    Malacca. Jl Ind Archip, 7 (1853): 73-137.

Cole, Fay-Cooper. The peoples of Malaysia. New York,
    1945. 345 p. Bibliog., illus., maps.

Cole, Fay-Cooper. Malaysia: crossroads of the Orient.
    Eugene, 1948. 20 p. Map.

Duckworth, W. L. H. Results of Skeat's expedition
    to the Malay Peninsula. Jl Anthr Inst, 32 (1902):
    142-152.

Evans, Ivor H. N. Papers on the ethnology and archaeology
    of the Malay Peninsula. Cambridge, 1927. 154 p.
    Illus., plates.

Favre, Pierre E. L. Lettre de M. Favre. Missionaire
    apostolique des missions étrangères, à MM. les
    Directeurs du Seminaire des Missions Etrangéres.
    Ann Propag Foi (Lyon), 22 (1850): 286-295.

Hughes, David R. The peoples of Malaya. Singapore
    [1965]. 102 p. Illus.

Kloss, C. Boden. Ethnological notes. JRASSB, 50
    (1908): 73-77.

Lehmann, Johannes. Flechtwerke aus dem malayischen
    Archipel unter Zugrundelegung der Sammlungen
    des städtischen Völkermuseums. Frankfurt am Main,
    1912. 56 p. Illus., map.
    Basketwork of Malay Archipelago.

Lela, Wan. Ethnological miscellanea. JFMSM, 12 (1924):
    27-34.

Leroi-Gourham, Andre. Documents pour l'art comparé
    de l'Eurasie Septentrionale. Paris, 1943. 99 p. Illus.

Logan, James R. The ethnology of the Johore Archipelago.
    Jl Ind Archip, 1 (1847): 336-340.

Logan, James R. Five days in Naning, with a walk
to the foot of Gunong Datu in Rambau. Jl Ind
Archip, 3 (1849): 24-41, 278-287, 402-412, 489-493.

Logan, James R. The ethnology of the Indian Archipelago
embracing enquiries into the continental relations
of the Indo-Pacific Islands. Jl Ind Archip, 4
(1850): 252-347.

Logan, James R. The ethnology of Eastern Asia. Jl
Ind Archip, 4 (1850): 441-455.

Logan, James R. The ethnology of South Eastern Asia.
Jl Ind Archip, 4 (1850): 456-482.

Logan, James R. Ethnology of Eastern Asia and the
Indo-Pacific Islands. Jl Ind Archip, 4 (1850): 552-590.

Marche, Alfred. Rapport général sur une mission à la
presqu'île Malacca et aux îles Philippines. Ar Miss
Sc Lit, ser. 3, 10 (1883): 331-372.

McTaggert, W. D. The distribution of ethnic groups
in Malaya, 1947-57. JTG, 26 (1968): 69-81.

Miklucho-Maclay, N. von. Ethnologische Exkursionen
in der malayischen Halbinsel (Nov. 1874-Okt. 1875).
NTNI, 7, 6 (1876): 1-26.

Miklucho-Maclay, N. von. Ethnological excursion
in Malay Peninsula, Nov. 1874-Oct. 1875.
JRASSB, 2 (1878): 205-221.

Montane, Dr. Quelques jours chez les indigenes de
la province de Malacca. Rev d'Ethn, 1 (1882): 41-56.
Illus., tables.

Ryan, N. J. The cultural background of the peoples
of Malaya. Kuala Lumpur, 1962.

Shelford, R. S. Ethnographical collection of the
Sarawak Museum, illustrated catalogue. Pt. 1--Musical
instruments. Pt. 2--Personal ornaments. JRASSB,
40 (1903); 43 (1904). Plates.

Skeat, W. W. Report on Cambridge exploring expedition
to the Malay province of lower Siam. Rep Br Assoc
Sc, 70 (1900): 393-398.

Skeat, W. W. Notes on the ethnography of the Malay
Peninsula. Man, 1, 142 (1901): 177-180. Illus.

Skeat, W. W. Report on 2nd Cambridge expedition
to the Malay provinces of lower Siam. Rep Br Assoc
Sc, 71 (1901): 411-424.

Skeat, W. W. Blowpipe from Kuantan (Malay Peninsula).
Man, 2, 108 (1902): 145-146.

Skeat, W. W. The Malay Peninsula. In T. A. Joyce, ed.
Women of All Nations. V. 1. London, 1908: 186-201.
Illus.

Skeat, W. W. The Malay-Peninsula. In W. Hutchinson, ed.
Customs of the World. V. 1. London, 1913: 312-327.
2 v.

Skeat, W. W. The Cambridge University Expedition
to parts of the Malay Peninsula, 1899-1900. Personal
accounts by the late W. W. Skeat and F. F. Laidlaw.
Appendix by C. A. Gibson-Hill. JRASMB, 26, 4
(1953): 1-174. Bibliog., maps.
Lists all publications resulting from the expedition.

Volz, Wilhelm. Der Mensch in der malaiischen Inselflur.
Kol St, 12 (1928): 178-198.

Williams-Hunt, P. D. R. A technique for anthropology
from the air in Malaya. BRM, ser. B, 4 (1949): 44-68.
Bibliog., illus., maps.

Yule, H. Notes on analogies of manners between the
Indo-Chinese races and the races of the Indian
Archipelago. Jl R Anthr Inst, 9 (1880): 290-304.

2. Aborigines

Anderson, J. Political and commercial considerations
relative to the Malayan Peninsula and the British
Settlements in the Straits of Malacca. With Appendix:
Of the aboriginal inhabitants of the Malayan Peninsula,
and particularly of the Negroes, called Semang.
Prince of Wales Island, 1824.

Annandale, Nelson, and Herbert C. Robinson. Anthropological notes on Sai Kau, a Siamo-Malayan village in the state of Nawnchik (Tojan). Man, 2, **118** (1902): **118**-120.

Annandale, Nelson, and Herbert C. Robinson. Contributions to the ethnography of the Malay Peninsula. Part I, Semang and Sakai tribes. Part II, Coast people of Trang. In N. Annandale and H. C. Robinson. Fasciculi Malayenses . . . Anthropology, Part I. London, 1903: 1-65. Illus., plates.

Baharon Azhar bin Raffiei. An orang asli legend: "Putri buloh betong". FMJ, n.s., 9 (1964): 39-44.

Baker, A. C. An account of a journey from the Cameron Highlands to the east coast railway and of a visit to the Temiar settlements in the valleys of the Sungai Blatop and Sungai Ber. JRASMB, 11, 2 (1933): 288-295. Illus., map.

Barnard, R. C. The Sakai in Trolak forest reserve. Mal For, 2 (1933): 18-20.

Bernatzik, H. A. Die Kolonisation primitiver Völker unter besonderer Berücksichtigung des Mokenproblems. In Michael Hesch and Guenther Spannaus, eds. Kultur und Rasse, Otto Reche zum 60. Geburtstag gewidmet . . . Berlin, 1939: 254-264. Moken are Orang Laut.

Bernatzik, H. A. Freundschaft mit Urwald-Zwergen in Siam. Atlantis, 20 (1948): 66-71. Illus.

Blacking, J. A. R. Musical instruments of the Malayan aborigines. A short description of the collections in the Perak Museum, Taiping, the Selangor Museum, Kuala Lumpur, and the Raffles Museum, Singapore. FMJ, n.s., 1/2 (1954/1955): 35-52.

Blagden, C. O. Memorandum on the aborigines in the Jasin district of Malacca, dated 1892. JRASSB, 77 (1917): 177-180.

Borie, l'Abbé, P. H. D. An account of the aborigines of the Malay Peninsula. Singapore, Straits Times Press, 1863.

Bourien, P. On the wild tribes of the interior of the Malay Peninsula. Trans Ethn Soc, n.s., 3 (1865): 72-83.

Brau de Saint-Pol Lias (Marie F. X. J. J. H.). Perak
  et les Orang-Sakeys. Voyage dans l'intérieur
  de la presqu'île malaise. Paris, 1883. 302 p.
  Illus., map.

Campbell, J. A. G. The Sakais of Selangor. II. Ulu
  Langat. Selangor Jl, 3 (1895): 240-245.

Carey, Iskandar Yusof. Pem. Penasihat Orang Asli
  (Commissioner for Aborigines). Ranchangan Lima
  Tahun (A General Explanation of the Five Year
  Plan). Kuala Lumpur, October 21, 1961. Mimeo.

Carey, Iskandar Yusof. Tengleq kui serok; a study
  of the Temiar language, with an ethnographical
  summary. Kuala Lumpur, 1961. 195 p. Illus.

Carey, Iskandar Yusof. Commissioner for Orang Asli
  Affairs. The Malayan Orang Asli and their future.
  Kuala Lumpur, 1963. Mimeo.

Cerruti, G. B. The Sakai of Batang Padang. JRASSB
  (Jan. 1904): 113-118.

Cerruti, G. B. My friends the savages amongst the
  Sakais in the Malay Peninsula. Translated by
  I. Stone. Sanpietro Como, 1908. 232 p. Plates.

Cole, R. Temiar Senoi agriculture. Mal For, 22 (1959):
  191-207, 260-271.

Collings, H. D. A Temoq word list and notes. BRM,
  ser. B, 4 (1949): 69-85.

Collings, H. D. Aboriginal notes. BRM, ser. B, 4
  (1949): 86-103. Illus., plates, table.

Cooper, J. M. Andamanese-Semang-Eta cultural relations.
  Prim Man, 13 (1940): 29-47.

Croix, J. E. de la. Etude sur les Sakaies de Perak
  (presqu'île de Malacca). Rev d'Ethn, 1 (1882): 317-431.

Croix, J. E. de la. Sept mois au pays de l'étain
  Perak. B Soc G Paris, 7, 6 (1885): 395-432.

Dentan, Robert Knox. Some Senoi Semai dietary restrictions:
  a study of food behavior in a Malayan hill tribe.
  1965. 608 p. Ph.D. thesis -- Yale University.

Dentan, Robert Knox. The Samai: a non-violent people
of Malaya. New York, 1968. 110 p. Illus., map.

Evans, Ivor H. N. Notes on the non-Malayan races
of the Malay Peninsula; notes on the Besisi of
Tamboh, Kuala Langat, Selangor. JFMSM, 5, 1 (1913): 1-14.

Evans, Ivor H. N. Notes on the aborigines of Lenggong
and Kuala Kenering, Upper Perak. JFMSM, 5 (1914): 64-73.

Evans, Ivor H. N. Notes on the aborigines of the Ulu
Langat and Kenaboi districts of Selangor and Jelebu.
JFMSM, 5 (1914): 74-81.

Evans, Ivor H. N. Notes on the Sakai of the Ulu
Sungkai in the Batang Padang District of Perak.
JFMSM, 6 (1915): 85-99. Plates.

Evans, Ivor H. N. Notes on various aboriginal tribes
of Negri Sembilan. JFMSM, 6, 2 (1915): 101-114.

Evans, Ivor H. N. Notes on the aboriginal inhabitants
of Ijok in the district of Selama, Perak. JFMSM,
5 (1915): 176-186. Plate.

Evans, Ivor H. N. Notes of some aboriginal tribes
of Pahang. JFMSM, 5 (1915): 192-219.

Evans, Ivor H. N. Notes on the Sakai of the Ulu
Kampar. JFMSM, 7, 1 (1916): 23-31. Plates.

Evans, Ivor H. N. Notes on the Sakai of the Korbu
River and of the Ulu Kinta. JFMSM, 7 (1916): 75-89.

Evans, Ivor H. N. Some notes on aboriginal tribes
of Upper Perak. JFMSM, 6 (1916): 203-218.

Evans, Ivor H. N. Ethnological miscellanea. JFMSM,
7 (1918): 211-223; 9 (1922): 245-251.

Evans, Ivor H. N. Further notes on the aboriginal
tribes of Pahang. JFMSM, 9 (1920): 16-33.

Evans, Ivor H. N. On an examination of Negrito combs
from Perak. JFMSM, 9 (1922): 223-226.

Evans, Ivor H. N. Vaughan Stevens and the patterns
on Negrito combs. JFMSM, 12 (1923): 23-26.

Evans, Ivor H. N. An ethnological expedition to
South Siam. JFMSM, 12 (1926): 35-57. Plates.

Evans, Ivor H. N. Further notes on Pahang Negritos.
JFMSM, 12 (1926): 59-65. Illus., plates.

Evans, Ivor H. N. Results of an expedition to Kedah.
JFMSM, 12 (1926): 73-82. Diagr., plates.

Evans, Ivor H. N. Further notes on Lenggong Negritos.
JFMSM, 12 (1927): 101-104.

Evans, Ivor H. N. Negrito cave drawings at Lenggong,
Upper Perak. JFMSM, 12 (1927): 105-106. Plates.

Evans, Ivor H. N. Schebesta and the Negritos. Man,
28 (1928): 57-59.

Evans, Ivor H. N. A note on a Negrito funeral. JFMSM,
12 (1929): 179. Plate.

Evans, Ivor H. N. Ethnographical miscellanea. (Some
aboriginal customs and beliefs from Pahang. The
Orang Laut of Singapore). JFMSM, 9 (1929): 271-272.

Evans, Ivor H. N. The Negritos of Malaya. Cambridge,
1937. 323 p. Map.

Favre, Pierre E. L. An account of the wild tribes
inhabiting the Malayan Peninsula, Sumatra and
a few neighbouring islands, with a journey in
Johore and a journey in the Menangkabaw States
of the Malayan Peninsula. Paris, 1865. 189 p.

Forde, Cyril Daryll. Habitat, economy and society;
a geographical introduction to ethnology. New York,
1948. 500 p. Bibliog., diagrs.
    Chapter 2, p. 11-23, deals with Semang and
Sakai in Malaya.

Gibson-Hill, C. A. The Orang Laut of the Singapore
River and the sampan panjang. JRASMB, 25, 1 (1952):
161-174. Bibliog., illus.

Grubauer, Alb. Negritos. Ein Besuch bei den Ureinwohnern
Innermalakkas. PM, 51 (1905): 249-254, 271-277.

Grubauer, Alb. Orang Semang. Erdball, 1 (1926/1927):
259-266, 403-411.

Hale, Abraham. On the Sakais. Jl Anthr Inst, 15 (1886): 285-301. Illus.

Hamy, E. T. Sur les races sauvages de la péninsule malaise et en particulier sur les Jakuns. B Soc d'Anthr, ser. 2, 9 (1874): 716-723.

Holman, Dennis. Noone of the Ulu. London, Heinemann, 1958. 253 p.

Jones, Alun. The Orang Asli: an outline of their progress in modern Malaya. JSAH, 9, 2 (1968): 286-305.

Knocker, Frederic William. The aborigines of Sungei Ujong. Jl Anthr Inst, 37 (1907): 290-305. Plates.

Knocker, Frederic William. Notes on the wild tribes of the Ulu Plus, Perak. Jl Anthr Inst, 39 (1909): 142-155. Plates.

Körner, Th. Indonesien. In H. Bernatzik, ed. Die grosse Völkerkunde. V. 2. Leipzig, 1939: 251-294. Between pages 256 and 257 there is an excellent map showing the distribution of Semang and other Negritos in Malaya.

Kolinski, M. Die Musik der Primitivstämme auf Malakka und ihre Beziehungen zur samoanischen Musik. Anthropos, 25 (1930): 585-648.

Lewis, M. Blanche. Moken texts and word-list; a provisional interpretation. FMJ, n.s., 4 (1960): 1-102.

Linehan, W. The Nobat and the Orang Kalau of Perak. JRASMB, 24, 3 (1951): 60-68. Plates. The Nobat is a collection of musical instruments of the royal family.

Logan, James R. The Orang Binua of Johore. Jl Ind Archip, 1 (1847): 242-293.

Logan, James R. The Orang Sabimba of the extremity of the Malay Peninsula; the Orang Biduanda Kallang of the River Pulai in Johore; the Orang Seletar of the rivers and creeks of the old Strait and estuary of Johore. Jl Ind Archip, 1 (1847): 295-306.

Low, J. The Semang and Sakai tribes of the Malay
Peninsula. Jl Ind Archip, 4 (1850): 424-432.

Macey, Paul. Indigènes de la Péninsule Malaise.
B Soc d'Anthr, ser. 3, 8 (1885): 735-744.

Malaya, Department of the Adviser on Aborigines.
Notes on the administration, welfare and recording
of technical data relating to the Malayan aborigines.
Kuala Lumpur, 1951. 88 p.

Martin, R. Die Ureinwohner der malayischen Halbinsel.
Correspondenz-Blatt der Deutschen Gesellschaft
für Anthropologie, Ethnologie und Urgeschichte,
30 (1899): 125-127.

Martin, R. Die Inlandstämme der malayischen Halbinsel,
wissenschaftliche Ergebnisse einer Reise durch
die Vereinigten Malayischen Staaten. Jena, 1905.
1,052 p. Bibliog., map.

Martin, R. Die Inlandstämme der malayischen Halbinsel.
JFMSM, 2, 2 (1907): 61-63.

Maxwell, W. E. The Semang and Sakai tribes of the
districts of Kedah and Perak bordering on Province
Wellesley. JRASSB, 1 (1878): 111-113.

Melvin, A. G. A visit to the Sakai. Asia, 39 (1939):
692-695. Illus.

Meyners d'Estrey, H. Tribus aborigènes et autres
de la presqu'île de Malacca. Rev G, 37 (1895): 110-116.

Miklucho-Maclay, N. Über die Orang-Semang und Orang-Sakai.
Verh Berl Ges Anthr (1876): 226-227.

Morgan, Jacques de. Negritos de la presqu'île malaise.
L'Homme, 2 (1885): 545-559, 609-623, 641-656,
713-721.

Morgan, Jacques de. Exploration dans la presqu'île
malaise. B Soc Normande G, 8 (1886): 141-169,
211-227, 281-301.

Nippold, Walter. Rassen- und Kulturgeschichte der
Negritovölker Südost-Asiens. Göttingen, 1936.
425 p. Bibliog.
This constitutes volume 11 of Studien zur Völkerkunde.

Noone, H. D. Some vital statistics of the lowland
Senoi of Perak. JFMSM, 15 (1932): 195-215.

Noone, H. D. Report on the settlements and welfare
of the Ple-Temiar Senoi of the Perak-Kelantan
watershed. JFMSM, 19 (1936): 1-85. Map.

Noone, H. D. Notes on the Benua Jakun language,
spoken at Sungai Lenga, Ulu Muar, Johore. JFMSM,
15 (1939): 139-162.

Noone, H. D. The first fruits of the hill rice harvest
among the Temiar Senoi. BRM, ser. B, 4 (1949): 5-7.

Noone, R. O. Notes on the kampong, compounds and
houses of the Patani Malay village of Banggul
Ara, in the Mukim of Batu Kuran, Northern Perak.
JRASMB, 21, 1 (1948): 124-147. Diagr., illus.,
tables.
Settlement pattern, descriptions of house types
and interior furnishings.

Noone, R. O. Notes on the trade in blowpipes and
blowpipe bamboo in North Malaya. FMJ, 1/2 (1954/1955):
1-18.

Ogilvie, C. S. Che Wong word list and notes. BRM,
ser. B, 4 (1949): 11-43.

Paroissin, R. P. Souvenirs d'un missionaire en Malaisie.
Geographia (Oct. 1957): 21-24.

Preuss, K. Th. Die Zauberbilderschriften der Negrito
in Malaka. Globus, 75 (1899): 345-348, 364-369.

Preuss, K. Th. Die Zaubermuster der Orang Semang
in Malaka. Z Ethn, 31 (1899): 137-197.

Rentse, Anker. Panganerne. Malayas jungledvaerge
(The Pangan jungle dwarfs of Malaya). G Tid,
40 (1937): 110-136. Danish, with summary in English.

Robinson, H. C., and C. Boden Kloss. Additional
notes on the Semang Paya of Ijok, Selama, Perak.
JFMSM, 5, 4 (1915): 187-191. Plates.

Schebesta, Paul. Les Négrilles de la presqui'île
malaise. Etudes, 181 (1924): 206-220.

Schebesta, Paul. Die Negrito Stämme der malaiischen
    Halbinsel. Gliederung und Namen. Z Ethn, 56 (1924):
    169-175.

Schebesta, Paul. Über die Semang auf Malakka. Anthropos,
    18/19 (1924): 1002-1011.

Schebesta, Paul. Bei den Urwaldzwergen von Malaya.
    Leipzig, 1926. 278 p. Map, plates.

Schebesta, Paul. The bow and arrow of the Semang.
    Man, 26 (1926): 88-89.

Schebesta, Paul. Kubu und Jakudn (Jakun) als Protomalayen.
    Mitt Anthr Ges in Wien, 56 (1926): 192-201.

Schebesta, Paul. Sakai in Malakka. Ar Rassenbilder,
    Bildaufsatz, 9 (1926).

Schebesta, Paul. Seine Forschungsreise zu den Orang-Utan
    von Malaya (Hinterindien) 1924/1925. Mitt Anthr
    Ges in Wien, 56 (1926): 3-7.

Schebesta, Paul. Stammesnamen und geographische
    Verteilung der Orang-Utan auf Malaya (Malakka),
    Hinterindien. PM, 72 (1926): 253-257.

Schebesta, Paul. The jungle tribes of the Malay
    Peninsula. BSOAS, 4 (1926/1928): 269-278.

Schebesta, Paul. Eine Forschungsreise zu den Inlandvölkern
    von Malakka. Mitt Anthr Ges in Wien, 57 (1927): 43-46.

Schebesta, Paul. The Negritos of the Malay Peninsula.
    Man, 27 (1927): 88-94.

Schebesta, Paul. Semang. Ar Rassenbilder, Bildaufsatz,
    10 (1927).

Schebesta, Paul. Auffassung über Eigentum und Eigentumsrecht
    bei den Semang auf Malakka. Neue Ordnung, 4 (1928): 1-18.

Schebesta, Paul. Eine Forschungsreise zu den Inlandstämmen
    von Malakka 1924/25. Ethn Anzgr, I, B (1928): 27-27.

Schebesta, Paul. Gesellschaft und Familie bei den
    Semang auf Malakka. Anthropos, 23 (1928): 235-258.

Schebesta, Paul. Grammatical sketch of the Jahaij
dialect, spoken by a Negrito tribe of Ulu Perak
and Ulu Kelantan, Malay Peninsula. Translated
by C. O. Blagden. BSOAS, 4, 4 (1928): 803-826.

Schebesta, Paul. Orang-utan; bei den Urwaldmenschen
Malayas und Sumatras. Leipzig, 1928. 274 p.

Schebesta, Paul. Das Weib bei den Semang-Negrito
von Malakka. Neue Pflug, 8/9 (1928): 26-34.

Schebesta, Paul. Among the forest dwarfs of Malaya.
London, 1929. 288 p. Illus., map.

Schebesta, Paul. The decorative art of the aborigines
of the Malay Peninsula. JRAS (1929): 749-760. Plates.

Schebesta, Paul. Grammatical sketch of the Ple-Temer
language. Translated by C. O. Blagden. JRAS (1931):
641-652.

Schebesta, Paul. Das Pfeilgift der Semang (Negritos
der malaiischen Halbinsel). Ciba Z, 7 (1939):
2503-2507. Illus.

Schebesta, Paul. Les Pygmées (Traduit de l'allemand
par François Berge). Paris, 1940. 199 p. Illus., maps.

Schebesta, Paul. Bericht über meine letzte Forschungsreise
zu den ostasiatischen Negrito. Anthropos, 35/36
(1940/1941): 750-752.

Schebesta, Paul. The arrow poisons of the Semang.
Ciba Symposia, 3 (1941): 1018-1022. Illus.

Schebesta, Paul. Die letzte Pygmäen-Forschungsreise
von P. Schebesta. Z Rassenk, 12, 1 (1941): 109.

Schebesta, Paul. Die Negrito Asiens. Part 1: Geschichte,
Geographie, Umwelt, Demographie und Anthropologie
der Negrito. Studia Instituti Anthropos. V. 6.
St. Gabriel, 1952. 496 p. Bibliog., illus., indices,
maps, tables.

Schebesta, Paul. Die Zaubermuster der Orang Semang
in Malaya, Hinterindien. Z Ethn, 81 (1956): 30-57.

Schebesta, Paul. Tanah Malayu; Wanderungen und Forschungen
in den Dschungeln Malayas. Modling bei Wien [1960].
222 p. Maps, plates.

Schmidt, W. Die Sprachen der Sakai und Semang auf
Malakka und ihr Verhältnis zu den Mon-Khmer-Sprachen.
BTLV, 6 (5 of whole series), 8 (1901): 399-583.

Schmidt, W. Die Forschungsexpedition von P. P. Schebesta,
S.U.D., in 1924/25 bei den Semang-Pygmäen und
den Senoi-Pygmoiden auf der Halbinsel Malakka.
Anthropos, 20 (1925): 718-739.

Skeat, W. W. Wild tribes of the Malay Peninsula.
Jl Anthr Inst, 32 (1902): 124-141. Also in Annual
Report, Smithsonian Institution, 1902, 57 (1903):
463-478. Figs., plates.

Skeat, W. W., and C. O. Blagden. Pagan races of
the Malay Peninsula. London, 1906. 2 v. (1) 724 p.
(2) 855 p. Illus.

Stevens, H. V. Materialien zur Kenntnis der wilden
Stämme auf der Halbinsel Malacca. Veröf Kön Mus
Völk, Berlin, 2 (1892): 81-164; 3 (1894): 95-190.

Stevens, H. V. Mittheilungen aus dem Frauenleben
der Orang Belendas, der Orang Djakun und der
Orang Laut. Z Ethn, 28 (1896): 163-202.

Strong, T. A. The Sakai and shifting cultivation.
Mal For, 1 (1931/1932): 243-246.

Swettenham, F. A. On the native races of the Straits
Settlements and Malay States. Jl Anthr Inst,
16 (1888): 221-229.

Tauern, O. D. Versuch einer Sakai-Grammatik und
Vokabularium. Anthropos, 9 (1914): 529-538.

Thomson, John Turnbull. Remarks on the Sletar and
Sabimba tribes. Jl Ind Archip, 1 (1847): 341-352.

White, W. G. The sea gypsies of Malaya. Account
of the nomadic Mawken people of the Mergui Archipelago,
with description of their ways of living, customs,
boats, etc. London, 1922. 318 p.

Wilkinson, R. J. The aboriginal tribes. Kuala Lumpur,
1926. 65 p.

Williams-Hunt, P. D. R. An introduction to the Malayan
aborigines. Kuala Lumpur, 1952. 102 p. Diagr.,
plates, tables.

Winstedt, R. O. The aboriginal races. In J. E. Nathan.
The Census of British Malaya, 1921. Kuala Lumpur,
1922. 406 p. Map, plates.

Zollinger, M. N. A visit to the mountaineers, Do
Dongo, in the country of Bima. Jl Ind Archip,
2 (1848): 687-694.

3. Malays

A. Wahab Alwee. Remban: a study in integration and
conflict in a village in Negri Sembilan, Malaya.
Nedlands, Western Australia, Center for Asian
Studies, 1967. 60 p. (Working papers in Asian
Studies, no. 1) Mimeo.

Abadi, Bujang. Counting with pantuns. Eastern Horizon,
1 (Sept. 1960): 42-43.

Abdul Aziz bin Mohd. Yassin. Zakar: a perspective
on its origin and place in Malay society. Singapore,
University of Malaya, 1957.

Abdul Majid, Haji. A peculiar custom in Kuala Kangsar.
JRASMB, 3, 1 (1925): 85-86.
The sending of presents during fruit season.

Abdul Rahman bin Ahmad. The island Malays; a study
of a group of Malays in an island off Singapore:
their life, customs, beliefs, and the degree
to which they communicate with other places to
meet their various needs. Singapore, 1960.

Abdullah, Dato' Sedia Raja. The origin of pawang
and the berpuar ceremony. JRASMB, 5, 2 (1927):
310-313.

Abu Bakar bin Pawanchee. An unusual keris Majapahit.
JRASMB, 20, 2 (1947): 45-47.
A kris is a Malay dagger.

Adams, Theodore. The Malays in Malaya. AR, 40 (1944): 98-100.

Ahmad bin Mohd, Ibrahim. Islam customary law--Malaysia. Intisari, 2, 2 [n.d.]: 47-73.

Ahmad bin Mohd, Ibrahim. The legal position of the Muslims in Singapore. Intisari, 1, 1 [n.d.]: 40-49.

Ahmad bin Mohd, Ibrahim. The legal position of the Muslims in Singapore. World Muslims League Monthly Magazine, 1 (Jan. 1964): 51-57; (Feb. 1964): 45-53; (Mar./Apr. 1964): 42-52; (May 1964): 11-21.

Ahmad bin Mohd, Ibrahim. The status of Muslim women in family law in Malaysia and Brunei. Malaya Law Review, 6, 1 (1964): 40-82; 6, 2 (Dec. 1964): 327-352; 7 (Dec. 1965): 299-313; 8 (July 1966): 46-85; (Dec. 1966): 233-269.

Ahmad bin Mohd, Ibrahim. Islamic law in Malaya. Singapore, Malaysian Sociological Research Institute, 1965. 444 p.

Ahmad bin Mohd, Ibrahim. The administration of Muslim family law in Malaysia. World Muslims League Monthly Magazine, 2 (Feb. 1965): 24-44; (Mar. 1965): 22-35; (Apr. 1965): 30-46; (May 1965): 20-28; (June 1965): 45-47; (July 1965): 26-42; (Aug. 1965): 18-34; (Sept./Oct. 1965): 16-40; 3 (Nov./Dec. 1965): 35-48; (Jan. 1966): 44-60; (Feb./Mar. 1966): 26-34; (Apr. 1966): 46-57; (May 1966): 45-55; (June 1966): 39-53; (July/Aug. 1966): 32-47; (Sept. 1966): 35-49; (Oct./Nov. 1966): 27-36; (Dec. 1966): 32-46.

Ahmad, Z. A. B. The origin of some Malayan place-names. JRASMB, 3, 1 (1925): 79-82.

Alatas, Hussein, Syed. The grading of occupational prestige amongst the Malays in Malaysia. JRASMB, 41, 1 (1968): 146-156.

Al-Hadi, Alwi, Syed. Malay customs and traditions. Singapore, 1962. 128 p. Illus.
    English version of the author's "Adat resam Melayu dan 'adat isti'adat."

Alisjahbana, S. Takdir. The national language of Malaysia. Hemisphere, 8, 11 (Nov. 1964): 9-13. Illus.

Alwi bin Alhady. Malay customs and traditions. Singapore, 1962. 128 p. Photos.

Aminuddin bin Baki. The institution of debt-slavery in Perak. PS, 1, 1 (1966): 1-11.

Annandale, Nelson. Primitive beliefs and customs of the Patani fisherman. In N. Annandale and H. C. Robinson. Fasciculi Malayenses . . . Anthropology, Part I. London, 1903: 73-88. Illus., plates.

Annandale, Nelson, and Herbert C. Robinson. Contributions to the ethnography of the Malay Peninsula. Part III, Malays of Perak. In N. Annandale and H. C. Robinson. Fasciculi Malayenses . . . Anthropology, Part I. London, 1903: 67-72. Illus., plates.

Bador, A. K. Kinship and marriage among the Negri Sembilan Malays. London, 1963. M.A. thesis -- London School of Economics.

Baker, J. A. A Kedah harvesting knife. JRASMB, 18, 2 (1940): 43-45.
Description, use, and name derivation of implement.

Balai Seni Lukis Negara [National Art Gallery]. Pameran reka bentok dan seni lukis batek [Exhibition of batik design and art]. Kuala Lumpur, 1968. 23 p. Plates.

Balfour, Henry. Thorn-lined trays and their distribution. Man, 25, 1 (1925): 33-37. Illus.

Bartlett, H. H. Color nomenclature in Batak and Malay. Michigan Ac Sc, Arts, Papers, 10 (1929): 1-52.

Bazell, C. Rules for some common Malay games. JRASMB, 6, 4 (1928): 46-48.

Beamish, T. The art of Malaya. Singapore, 1955. (Malayan Heritage Series)

Bee, Reginald J. Some Kelantan place names. JRASMB, 11, 2 (1933): 138.

Blagden, C. O. Malay terminology of chess. JRAS (1898): 376-377.

Blagden, C. O. The name "Melayu". JRASSB, 32 (1899):
211-213.

Bland, Mrs. Malacca lace. JRASSB, 45 (1905): 273-277.

Bland, Mrs. A few notes on the "Anyam Gila" basket
making at Tanjong Kling, Malacca. JRASSB, 46
(1906): 1-8.

Braddell, T. The commencement of Abdullah's schooling.
Jl Ind Archip, 6 (1852): 643-652.

Brown, C. C. Kelantan bull-fighting. JRASMB, 6,
1 (1928): 74-83.

Brown, C. C. Trengganu Malay. JRASMB, 13, 3 (1935): 1-111.

Brown, C. C. Studies in country Malay. London, 1956. 270 p.

Brown, C. C. Malay sayings. 2d ed. London, 1959.

Brown, W. C. A note on rengas poisoning. JRASSB,
24 (1891): 83-85.

Browne, Laurence E. The Malays: the people of the
mouse deer. Westminister, 1934.

Bryson, H. P., and I. W. Blelloch. Ceremonial custom
in Negri Sembilan. JRASMB, 14, 3 (1936): 272-279.
Death, funeral, election of a successor.

Bucknill, J. A. S. Observations upon some coins
obtained in Malaya and particularly from Trengganu,
Kelantan and Southern Siam. JRASMB, 1 (1923): 194-217.
Illus.
A short historical account of issues of coins
in Malaya.

Burridge, K. O. L. The Malay composition of a village
in Johore. JRASMB, 29, 3 (1956): 60-77.

Burridge, K. O. L. Racial relations in Johore. Australian
Journal of Politics and History, 2, 2 (1957).

Burridge, K. O. L. Kuda Kepang in Batu Pahat, Johore.
Man, 61 (1961): 33-36.

Cabaton, A. Amulettes chez les peuples islamisés de
l'Extrême-Orient. Rev Monde Musul, 8 (1909): 369-397.

Caldecott, Andrew. Adat perpetah in Negri Sembilan. Univ Ceylon Rev, 1 (1943): 1-8.

Caldecott, Andrew, comp. Jelebu customary songs and sayings. JRASSB, 78 (1918): 3-41.

Campbell, J. Argyll. An experimental investigation concerning the effects of "tuba" (Derris elliptica) fish-poison. JRASSB, 73 (1916): 129-137. References.

Chandra, Surat. On some Malayan, Burman and Indian folk beliefs about the man-tiger or were-tiger. Anthropological Society, 15 (1933/1934).

Clifford, Sir H. C. Some Malay superstitions. Dublin Review, 148 (Jan. 1911): 134-154.

Collings, H. D. Malay notes. BRM, ser. B, 4 (1949): 104-112. Illus., plates.

Collins, G. E. P. With Malays at sea. GM, 4 (1936-1937): 329-348. Illus.

Coope, A. E., tr. The voyage of Abdullah (Pelayaran Abdullah), being an account of his experience on a voyage from Singapore to Kelantan in A.D. 1838. Kuala Lumpur, 1967. 98 p. Maps on end paper.

Coote, P. Malay psychology. AR, n.s., 19 (April 1923): 285-288.

Crandall, J. R. Social customs of Malays. Sociology and Social Research, 12 (July 1928): 567-571.

Crawfurd, John. On the Malayan and Polynesian languages and races. Jl Ethn Soc, 1 (1848): 330-374.

Crawfurd, John. Malayan race of man and its prehistoric career. Trans Ethn Soc, n.s., 7 (1869): 119-133. Comparisons of languages of various Malay peoples.

Cuisinier, Jeanne. The sacred books of India and the Malay and Siamese theatres in Kelantan. Indian Art and Letters, n.s., 8, 1 (1934): 43-50. Plates.

Cuisinier, Jeanne. Danses magiques de Kelantan. Travaux et Memoires de l'Institut d'Ethnologie, 22 (1936): 206. Illus. Reviewed in Man, 38 (1938).

Cuisinier, Jeanne. Sumangat, L'ame et son culte
en Indochine et en Indonesie. Paris, 1951. 268 p.

Cuisinier, Jeanne. Le théatre d'ombres à Kelantan.
Paris, 1957. 250 p.

Djamour, Judith. The Malay family in Singapore.
London, 1955. Ph. D. thesis -- London School
of Economics.

Djamour, Judith. Malay kinship and marriage in Singapore.
London, 1959. 151 p. (London School of Economics.
Monographs on Social Anthropology, 21)

Djamour, Judith. The Muslim matrimonial court in
Singapore. London, New York, 1966. 189 p. (London
School of Economics. Monographs on Social Anthropology,
31)

Dussek, O. T. Notes on Malay indoor games. JRASSB,
80 (1919): 69-71.

Elcum, T. B. Malay chess. JRASSB, 49 (1907): 87-92.
Origin in Malaya, rules, terms used.

Evans, Ivor H. N. Notes on the manufacture of damascened
spear and knife blades in the Malay states. JFMSM,
5 (1914): 59.

Evans, Ivor H. N. Malay filigree work. JFMSM, 6
(1915): 25-28.

Evans, Ivor H. N. Malay notes. JFMSM, 7 (1917): 117-121.

Evans, Ivor H. N. Malay beliefs: Kempunan. Man (May
1920): 38-39.

Evans, Ivor H. N. The Malay fire-piston. JFMSM,
9 (1922): 227-229. Plate.

Evans, Ivor H. N. The potting industry in Kuala
Tembeling. JFMSM, 9 (1922): 259-261.

Evans, Ivor H. N. Lucky and unlucky kris measurements.
JFMSM, 12 (1924): 11-16.

Evans, Ivor H. N. Forgeries of Malay silver-ware.
JFMSM, 12 (1926): 69-70.

Evans, Ivor H. N. The cock in Malayan art and in
relation to currency. JFMSM, 12 (1927): 87-90.
Illus., plate.

Evans, Ivor H. N. Tukung Bola. JFMSM, 12 (1929): 97-99.

Evans, Ivor H. N. Some Malay patterns and designs.
JFMSM, 12 (1929): 163-167. Figs.

Evans, Ivor H. N. Some Malay patterns from Negri
Sembilan. JFMSM, 12 (1929): 169. Figs.

Evans, Ivor H. N. Types of keris sampir and hilts
in the Malay States, Java and Celebes. JFMSM,
12 (1929): 171-173.

Firth, Raymond. The coastal people of Kelantan and
Trengganu, Malaya. G Jl, 101 (1943): 193-205.

Firth, Raymond. Malay fishermen: their peasant economy.
[2d rev. ed.]. [Hamden, Conn.] 1966. 398 p. Illus.,
maps (1 fold.).

Firth, Raymond. Ritual and drama in Malay spirit
mediumship. Comparative Studies in Society and
History, 9, 2 (1967): 190-207.

Firth, Rosemary. Housekeeping among Malay peasant
women. Man, 42, 33 (1942): 67-68.

Firth, Rosemary. Housekeeping among Malay peasants.
London, 1943. 198 p. (London School of Economics.
Monographs on Social Anthropology, 7) 2d ed.
expanded by two chapters. London, New York, 1966.

Fraser, Thomas M., Jr. Rusembilan: a Malay fishing
village in southern Thailand. Ithaca, N.Y., 1960.
299 p.

Freedman, Maurice, and M. O. Swift. Rural sociology
in Malaya. Current Sociology, 8 (1959): 1-15.

Gardner, G. B. Notes on some ancient gold coins
from the Johore River. JRASMB, 11, 2 (1933): 171-176.

Gardner, G. B. Notes on two uncommon varieties of
the Malay kris. JRASMB, 11, 2 (1933): 178-182. Plates.

Gardner, G. B. Keris and other Malay weapons. Edited by B. Lumsden Milne. Singapore, 1936. 138 p. Illus.

Ghazzali, Dato' Muhammad. Court language and etiquette of the Malays. JRASMB, 11, 2 (1933): 273-287.

Gibson-Hill, C. A. Malay hats and dish-covers. JRASMB, 24, 1 (1951): 133-158. Illus., plates.

Gibson-Hill, C. A., and A. H. Hill. Malay arts and crafts. Singapore, 1951.

Gimlette, J. D. Some superstitious beliefs occurring in the theory and practice of Malay medicine. JRASSB, 65 (Dec. 1913): 29-35.

Gimlette, J. D. Malay poisons and charms. London, 1923. 127 p.

Gordon, Shirle. Contradictions in the Malay economic structure. Intisari, 1, 2 [n.d.]: 29-40.

Gosling, L. A. P. Moslem law, custom and usage as reflected in the agricultural economy of Malaya. Annals, 50 (Sept. 1960): 322. Abstract.

Greentree, R. Poems of the Malay Peninsula. With an essay on the Malay people. London, 1901. 126 p.

Gullick, J. M. A survey of the Malay weavers and silversmiths in Kelantan in 1951. JRASMB, 25, 1 (1952): 134-148. Maps.

Gullick, J. M. Indigenous political systems of Western Malaya. London, 1965. 152 p. (London School of Economics. Monographs on Social Anthropology, 17)

H., A. B. Housekeeping and life in the Malayan rubber. Blackwood's Magazine, 221 (May 1927): 598-613.

Hale, Abraham. Folk-lore and Menangkabau code in the Negri Sembilan. JRASSB, 31 (1898): 43-61.

Hale, Abraham. List of Malay proper names. Kuala Lumpur, 1925. 20 p.
List in Roman and Arabic characters.

Hamid, Wan A. Religion and culture of the modern Malay. In Wang Gung-wu. Malaysia: A Survey. London, 1964: 179-189.

Hamilton, A. W. The Boria. JRASSB, 82 (1920): 139-144.
"Boria" is a term applied to performances of
a troupe of strolling minstrels who appear in
Penang during the first ten days of the Muharram
and at no other time of the year.

Hamilton, A. W. Malay pantuns (Pantun Malayu). 4th
ed. Singapore, 1956. 124 p. (Malayan Heritage
Series, no. 8) Text in Malay and English.

Hamilton, A. W. Malay proverbs. Singapore, 1957.
111 p. (Malayan Heritage Series, no. 6)

Hanna, Willard A. The day of the Bumiputra. Part
I: Motivating the ethnic Malay. Part II: Malayan
mutuals. American Universities Field Staff, Reports
Service, Southeast Asia Series, 15, 6, 7 (1968).

Haughton, H. T. Notes on names of places in the
island of Singapore and its vicinity. JRASSB,
20 (1889): 75-82.

Haughton, H. T. Native names of streets in Singapore.
JRASSB, 23 (1891): 49-65.

Hellier, M. Notes on the Malay game "Jongkak". JRASSB,
49 (1907): 93-94.

Hendon, Rufus S. The phonology and morphology of
Ulu Muar Malay (Kuala Pilah District, Negri Sembilan,
Malaya). New Haven, Yale University, Department
of Anthropology, 1966. 160 p. (Yale University
Publications in Anthropology, 70) Tables.

Hervey, D. F. A. Malay games. Jl Anthr Inst, 33
(1903): 284-304.

Hill, A. H. The weaving industry in Trengganu. JRASMB,
22, 3 (1949): 75-84. Illus.

Hill, A. H. Kelantan silverwork. JRASMB, 24, 1 (1951):
99-108. Illus.

Hill, A. H. Some Kelantan games and entertainments.
JRASMB, 25, 1 (1952): 20-34. Illus.

Hilton, R. N. The basic Malay house. JRASMB, 29
(1956): 134-155.

Hodgson, Geoffrey. Malay conventional sib-names.
JRASMB, 40, 2 (1967): 106-121.

Hooker, M. B. A note on the Malay legal digests.
JRASMB, 41, 1 (1968): 157-170.

Hough, G. C. A pre-Islamic element in the Malay
grave. JRASMB, 18, 2 (1940): 46-48.
Shows the non-Islamic, or indigenous, Malay
elements in actual grave structure that have
survived the Islamic cultural overlay of ceremonial
(in reference to the Jakun grave).

Howard, Joseph H., comp. Malay manuscripts: a bibliographical
guide. Kuala Lumpur, University of Malaya, Library, 1966.

Hubback, Theodore R. Elephant and seladang hunting
in the Federated Malay States. London, 1905.
288 p. 1906. 306 p. Illus.

Humphreys, J. L. A note on the north and south points
of the compass in Kedah and Trengganu. JRASMB,
4, 1 (1926): 133-135.

Husin [Husain] Ali, Syed. Social stratification
in Kampong Bagan: a study of class, status, conflict
and mobility in a rural Malay community. 1963.
M.A. thesis (Department of Malay Studies) --
University of Malaya.

Husin [Husain] Ali, Syed. Social stratification
in Kampong Bagan; a study of class, status, conflict
and mobility in a rural Malay community. Singapore,
1964. 170 p. (Monograph of the Royal Asiatic
Society Malay Branch, 1) Maps, tables.

Husin [Husain] Ali, Syed. A note on Malay society
and culture. In S. Takdir Alisjahbana, ed. The
Cultural Problems of Malaysia in the Context
of Southeast Asia. Kuala Lumpur [1966?]: 65-74.

Husin [Husain] Ali, Syed. Patterns of rural leadership
in Malaya. Kuala Lumpur, 1966. 100 p. Bibliog.,
illus., map. Mimeo.

Husin [Husain] Ali, Syed. Patterns of rural leadership
in Malaya. JRASMB, 41, 1 (1968): 95-145.

Ismael Hussein. Bibliography of works and articles on traditional Malay literature. Kuala Lumpur [n.d.]. 27 p. Mimeo.

Ismael Hussein. The study of traditional Malay literature. JRASMB, 39, 2 (1966): 1-22.

Ishmael, Zain. Ancient Malay beliefs. Hemisphere, 9, 10 (Oct. 1965): 27-31. Illus.

Jenkins, Dorothy. Malay baby. Asia, 27 (1937): 303-305.

Josselin de Jong, Patrick E. de. Minangkabau and Negri Sembilan: socio-political study in Indonesia. The Hague, 1952. 208 p. Bibliog., diagrs., illus., maps, tables.

Josselin de Jong, Patrick E. de. Islam versus adat in Negri Sembilan (Malaya). BTLV, 116, 1 (1960): 158-203.

Josselin de Jong, Patrick E. de. The rise and decline of a national hero. JRASMB, 38, 2 (Dec. 1965): 140-155.

Kempe, J. E., and R. O. Winstedt. A Malay legal miscellany. JRASMB, 25, 1 (1952): 1-19.

Kho, Lian-tie. Malayan names. Majallah Perpustakaan Singapura [Singapore Library Journal] 2, 1 (1962): 29-34.
    Essay discusses Malay and Indian Muslim names, as well as Malay titles.

Kloss, C. Boden. Malayan musical instruments. JRASSB, 45 (1906): 285-287.

Kuchiba, Masuo, and Yoshihiro Tsubouchi. Paddy farming and social structure in a Malay village; a social anthropological study of a community in Kedah. Developing Economies, 5, 3 (1967): 463-485. Graphs, tables.

Kuchiba, Masuo, and Yoshihiro Tsubouchi. Cooperation patterns in a Malay village. AS, 8, 10 (1968): 836-841.

Laidlaw, G. M. Some notes on keris-measurements. JRASMB, 20, 1 (1947): 45-46.

Lavollee, C. Les pirates Malais. Revue des Deux
Mondes, 89, 3 (1953): 579-598.

Lewis, Diane Katherine. The Minangkabau Malay of
Negri Sembilan: a study of socio-cultural change.
1963. 375 p. Ph.D. thesis -- Cornell University.
Illus.

Lewis, Martha B. A handbook of Malay script with
passages for reading and a list of commonly used
Arabic words. London, 1954.

Linehan, W. Notes on tampang. JRASMB, 9, 1 (1931):
131-133. Plates.
"Tampang" is a term used for the tin coinage
current in old Pahang.

Lister, Martin. Malay law in Negri Sembilan. JRASSB,
22 (1890): 299-319.

Lobingier, C. S. The primitive Malay marriage law.
Am Anthr, 12 (1910): 250-256.

Logan, J. R. The laws of the Indian Archipelago
and Eastern Asia. Jl Ind Archip, 1 (1847): 321-326.

Logan, J. R. Memoirs of Malays: Che Soliman's narration.
Jl Ind Archip, 2 (1848): 353-361.

Logan, J. R. Manners and customs of the Malays.
Dress. Jl Ind Archip, 3 (1849): 274-284.
Dress of women and children.

Logan, J. R. The manners and customs of the Malays.
Meals. Jl Ind Archip, 4 (1850): 433-435.

Long, E. E. Poisons and poisoning amongst the Malays.
Chambers's Journal (March 1928): 171-173.

Lopez, C. Das Verwandschaftsystem der Tagalen und
der Malaien. Ar Anthr, 22 (1930): 132-136.

Macgowan, D. J. Notes on maritime Malays. Jl Ind
Archip, 4 (1850): 687-691.

Majumdar, R. C. The Malay. Jl Greater India Soc,
3, 1 (1936): 86-96.

Marrison, G. E. The French and Dutch contributions
to Malay studies. MHJ, 2, 1 (1955): 11-20.

Marrison, G. E. Persian influences in Malay life
(1280-1650). JRASMB, 28 (1955): 52-69.

Mason, Otis T. Vocabulary of Malaysian basketwork:
a study in the W. L. Abbot collections. In Proceedings
of the U.S. National Museum, 35. Washington,
D.C., 1909: 49-51.

Maxwell, C. N. Light in the Malay language. JRASMB,
14, 3 (1936): 89-154.

Maxwell, Sir George. The Malays and the Malayans.
Nineteenth Century and After, 137 (June): 276-285.
Table.
Reply, R. Winstedt: 138 (July 1945): 45-46.

Maxwell, W. E. Folklore of Malays. JRASSB, 7 (1881): 11-29.

Maxwell, W. E. The law relating to slavery among
the Malays (with extracts from Perak code and
Malayan laws of Johore). JRASSB, 12 (1893): 257-497.

Maxwell, W. E. Modes of sitting in driving elephants.
JRASSB, Notes and Queries, 1 (1884): 10.

Maxwell, W. E. Daun tiga "lei". JRASSB, Notes and
Queries, 1 (1884): 24-27.
A Malay card game in Perak.

Maxwell, W. E. Management of elephants. JRASSB,
Notes and Queries, 2 (1885): 32-36.

Maxwell, W. E. Malay howdah. JRASSB, Notes and Queries,
2 (1885): 52.

Maxwell, W. E. Social customs; the Malay Howdah;
fighting dress of the Malays, Malay superstitions,
JRASSB, Notes and Queries, 2 (1885): 52-54.

Maxwell, W. E. Social customs: influences of the
breath in healing; modes of carrying loads. JRASSB,
Notes and Queries, 4 (1887): 120-121.

Maxwell, W. E. Tests of virginity amongst the Malays.
Indian Antiquary, 8 (1889): 61-62.

Maxwell, W. G. Mantra gahah (charm book). JRASSB,
  49 (1907): 71-86.

Mayer, Charles. My friend, the Sultan of Trengganu.
  Asia, 23 (1923): 489-493. Sketches.

McHugh, J. N. Hantu-hantu: an account of ghost belief
  in modern Malaya. Singapore, 1955.

Mills, J. V. Notes on some Malayan place names.
  JRASMB, 10, 1 (1932): 16-20.

Minattur, Joseph. The nature of Malay customary
  law. Malaya Law Review, 6 (Dec. 1964): 327-352.

Mitra, Sarat Chandra. On some Malay, Burman and
  Indian folk-beliefs about the man-tiger or wer-tiger,
  with some remarks on the origin of lycanthropy.
  Jl R Anthr Soc Bombay, 15 (1933/1934): 412-420.

Mohamad Din bin Ali. Two forces in Malay society.
  Intisari, 1, 3 [n.d.]: 15-36.

Mohamad Din bin Ali. Malay customary law--family.
  Intisari, 2, 2 [n.d.]: 33-45.

Mohamad Din bin Ali. Malay customary law and the
  family. World Muslims League Monthly Magazine,
  1 (Aug. 1964): 33-52.

Mohamad Taib bin Osman. An introduction to the development
  of modern Malay language and literature. Singapore, 1961.

Mohamad Taib bin Osman. Trends in modern Malay literature.
  In Wang Gung-wu. Malaysia: A Survey. London, 1964:
  210-224.

Mokhzani bin Abdul Rahim. The study of social stratification
  and social mobility in Malaya. East Asian Cultural
  Studies, 4, 1-4 (March 1965): 138-162.

Morgan, G. T. M. de M. Brass and white-metal work
  in Trengganu. JRASMB, 24, 3 (1951): 114-119.

Morrison, I. The Malay: lover of colour and ceremony.
  GM (Aug. 1950): 148-156. Illus.

Moubray, George Alexander de Chazal de. Matriarchy
  in the Malay Peninsula and neighboring countries.
  London, 1931. 292 p.

Mukherji, S. B. Malaya: past and present; Malay
manners and customs. UA, 2 (June 1950): 416-419.

Murphy, H. B. M. Cultural factors in the mental
health of Malay students. In Conference Proceedings
of the 1st International Conference on Student
Mental Health. The Student and Mental Health.
Princeton, 1956: 169-170.

Mustapha Albakri bin Haji Hassan, Haji. "Tun" and
"Dato". MH, 5 (1959): 7.

Nash, Manning. Tradition in tension in Kelantan.
Journal of Asian and African Studies (Jan. 1967).

Nasir bin Ismail, Syed. Malay culture. Kuala Lumpur,
1959. 15 p. (Dewan Bahasa dan Pustaka, Kuala
Lumpur, pamphlet 5) In English, with Malay translation
in Jawi script.

Needham, Rodney. Ethnographic notes on Siwang of
Central Malaya. JRASMB, 29, 1 (1956): 46-69.

Noone, R. O. D. Notes on the kampong, compounds
and houses of the Petani Malay village of Banggul
Ara, in the mukim of Batu Kuran, Northern Perak.
JRASMB, 21, 1 (1948): 124-147.

Norris, William. Malay amoks and piracies. What
can we do to abolish them? Jl Ind Archip, 3 (1849):
463-467.

Norris, William. Malay amoks referred to Mohomedanism;
sentence of death upon a Malay convicted of running
amok. Jl Ind Archip, 3 (1849): 460-463.

Osman, Mohd. Taib. A text on the rules of the Kelantan
bullfight. JRASMB, 37, 2 (1964): 1-10.

Overbeck, J. New notes on Malay game "chongkak".
JRASSB, 68 (1915): 7-10.

Oxley, T. Malay amoks. Jl Ind Archip, 3 (1849): 532-533.

Parkinson, B. K. Non-economic factors in the economic
retardation of the rural Malays. MAS, 1, 1 (1967): 31-46.

Parkinson, Brian K. The economic retardation of
the Malays: a rejoinder. MAS, 2 (1968): 267-272.

Perikatan Pemuda Melayu di luar Tanah Air. Anak
    Melayu di-Indonesia. Djakarta [1957]. 243 p.
    Illus.

Raffles, Thomas Stamford. Maritime code of the Malays.
    Calcutta (1810).

Raffles, Thomas Stamford. On the Malayan nation.
    Asiatic Researches, 12 (1818): 102-160.

Raja Samusah. The Malay game of apit. JRASMB, 10,
    1 (1932): 138-140.

Ramsay, A. B. Some notes on kampong officials in
    the Alor Gajah District of Malacca, 1932-1935.
    JRASMB, 23, 3 (1950): 97-101.

Ramsay, A. B. Indonesians in Malaya. JRASMB, 29,
    1 (1956): 119-124.

Ratnam, S. Raja. Changing Malay people. Asia, 42
    (1942): 449-453.
    Socioeconomic changes.

Rentse, Anker. Malay charms, Kelantan. JRASMB, 9,
    1 (1931): 146-157.
    A collection.

Rentse, Anker. Gantang of Kelantan. JRASMB, 11,
    2 (1933): 242-244. Plate.
    "Gantang" is the standard measure for rice, etc.

Rentse, Anker. The Kelantan shadow-play (wayang
    kulit). JRASMB, 14, 3 (1936): 284-301. Plates.

Rentse, Anker. Gold coins of the northeastern Malay
    States. JRASMB, 17, 1 (1939): 88-97. Plates.
    Notes on collected coins, some of which were
    dug up in Malaya.

Roff, William R. The Malayo-Muslim world of Singapore
    at the close of the nineteenth century. JAS,
    24, 1 (1964): 75-90.

Roff, William R. The origins of Malay nationalism.
    New Haven, London, 1967. 297 p. Illus.

Roolvink, R. Malay studies; an inaugural lecture.
[Kuala Lumpur, University of Malaya, 1962]. 15 p.
(Malaya. University. Inaugural lectures, 1962)
Translation of an inaugural lecture delivered
in Malay on June 22, 1962.

Roth, H. Ling. Oriental silverwork, Malay and Chinese.
A handbook for connoisseurs, collectors, students
and silversmiths. London, 1910. 300 p. Illus.

Ryan, Neil J. The cultural background of the peoples
of Malaya. [Kuala Lumpur, 1962]. 184 p. Illus.

Seitz, H. Two royal kerisses. Ethnos, 3 (1938):
116-124. Illus.

Shahrum bin Yub. The collections of Malay artifacts:
a brief general survey. In S. Takdir Alisjahbana, ed.
The Cultural Problems of Malaysia in the Context
of Southeast Asia. Kuala Lumpur [1966]: 75-79.

Shamsul Bahrin bin Raja Muhammad Ali, Tunku. The
Indonesians in Malaya. 1964. M.A. thesis -- Sheffield.

Shamsul Bahrin bin Raja Muhammad Ali, Tunku. The
growth and distribution of the Indonesian population
in Malaya. BTLV, 123, 2 (1967): 267-286. Maps, tables.

Sheppard, Haji Mubin. Malay courtesy. Singapore, 1956.

Sheppard, Haji Mubin. "The Magic Kite" and other
Ma'Yong stories. Federal Publications, 1960.

Sheppard, Haji Mubin. Four historic Malay timber
buildings. FMJ, n.s., 7 (1962): 86-95. Diagrs., photos.

Sheppard, Haji Mubin. Bangau: decorative guards
for sails and spars on Malay fishing boats. FMJ,
n.s., 8 (1963): 1-12.

Sheppard, Haji Mubin. Malay shadow play figures
in the Museum of Archaeology and Ethnology, University
of Cambridge. FMJ, n.s., 8 (1963): 14-17. Plates.

Sheppard, Haji Mubin. Bujam Epok Bertundan: a wedding
ceremony recalled. FMJ, n.s., 9 (1964): 32-36.

Sheppard, Haji Mubin. Leaf shadow puppets. FMJ,
n.s., 9 (1964): 37-38. Illus.

Sheridan, L. A. Malay marriages. In Patna Law College. Studies in Law; An Anthology of Essays in Municipal and International Law. Bombay, New York, 1961: 492-508.

Sim, Katherine. Costumes of Malaya. Singapore, 1963. 35 p. Illus. (part col.).

Singapore, Ministry of Education. A book of sayings, proverbs and aphorisms. Singapore, Government Printer, 1959.

Siraj, M. Status Muslim woman; family law Singapore. Intisari, 2, 2 [n.d.]: 9-17.

Siraj, M. Muslim marriages in Singapore. World Muslims League Monthly Magazine, 1 (Jan. 1964): 41-50.

Skeat, W. W. Silk and cotton dyeing by Malays. JRASSB, 38 (1902): 123-127.

Skinner, C. The influence of Arabic upon modern Malay. Intisari, 2, 1 [n.d.]: 34-47. Tables.

Skinner, C. Prosa Melayu baharu; an anthology of modern Malay and Indonesian prose. London, 1959.

Sopher, David E. The sea nomads; a study based on the literature of the maritime boat people of Southeast Asia. Kuala Lumpur, 1965. (Memoirs of the National Museum, 5)
    Part II. B--West Coast of the Malay Peninsula p. 57-83.

Stirling, W. G. The red and white flag societies. JRASMB, 3 (1925): 57-61. Illus.

Swift, M. G. L'organisation socio-economique d'un village de Malaisie. Information, 7 (Fev. 1956): 1-18.

Swift, M. G. The accumulation of capital in a peasant economy. EDCC, 5, 4 (July 1957): 325-337.

Swift, M. G. A note on the durability of Malay marriages. Man, 58 (1958): 155-159.

Swift, M. G. Rural Malay social structure and economy in Jelebu, Negri Sembilan. 1961. Ph.D. thesis -- London School of Economics.

Swift, M. G. Malay peasant society in Jelebu. London, 1965. 181 p. (London School of Economics, Monograph on Social Anthropology, 20)

Swift, M. G. Economic concentration and Malay peasant society. In Maurice Freedman, ed. Social Organization. London, 1967: 241-269.

Taylor, E. N. Customary law of Rembau. JRASMB, 7, 1 (1929): 1-289.

Taylor, E. N. Malay family law. JRASMB, 15, 1 (1937): 1-78. An essay on the law and custom relating to the distribution of property and dissolution of marriage among Malays.

Taylor, E. N. Malay legal digest. JRASMB, 21, 1 (1948): 1-67.

Taylor, E. N. Mohammedan divorce by Khula. JRASMB, 21, 2 (1948): 3-39.

Taylor, E. N. Inheritance in Negri Sembilan. JRASMB, 21, 2 (1948): 41-129.

Tisdall, C. E. G. Ideas of Mohammedan Malays. Missionary Review of the World, 39 (May 1916): 347-349.

Tisdall, C. E. G. Singapore as a centre for Moslem work. Moslem World (Jan. 1918): 5-9. Map.

Tylor, E. B. Malay divining rods. Man, 2, 40 (1902): 49-50.

Uhle, Max. Über die ethnologische Bedeutung der malaiischen Zahnfeilung. Berlin, 1887. 18 p. (Abhandlungen und Berichte des K. zoologischen und anthropologisch-enthnographischen Museums zu Dresden, 4)

Van Loon, F. H. G. Amok and lattah. Journal of Abnormal and Social Psychology, 21 (Jan. 1927): 434-444.

Vaughan, J. D. Notes on the Malays of Pinang and Province Wellesley. Jl Ind Archip, n.s., 2 (1858): 116-175.

Wehl, David. Modern Malay usage: a guide to current Malay language, with examples of usage and dictionary of definitions. Singapore, 1961.

Wells, Marian. Malayan rambles. Singapore, 1959.
39 p. Illus.

Westlake, E. Malay divining rods: a note on Dr.
Tylor's paper (Man, 1902, 40). Man, 2, 65 (1902): 91ff.

Wheeler, Leonard Richmond. The modern Malay. London,
1928. 300 p.

Wilder, William. Islam, other factors and Malay
backwardness: comment on an argument. MAS, 2,
2 (1968): 155-164.

Wilken, G. A. The sociology of Malayan peoples.
Kuala Lumpur, 1921. 172 p.

Wilkinson, R. J. The peninsular Malays. London, 1906.

Wilkinson, R. J. Some Malay studies. JRASMB, 10,
1 (1932): 67-137. Notes on ethnology, social
structure, folklore, and religion.

Wilkinson, R. J. Malay customs and beliefs. JRASMB,
30, 4 (1957): 1-87.

Wilkinson, Richard J., ed. Pantun Melayu. 2d ed.
Collected by R. J. Wilkinson and Richard O. Winstedt.
Singapore, 1957.

Williams, G. C. Griffith. Suggested origins of the
Malay keris and the superstitions attached to it.
JRASMB, 15, 3 (1937): 127-141. Bibliog.

Williams-Hunt, P. D. R. Some Malay and aboriginal
charms and methods of measuring weapons. JRASMB,
25, 1 (1952): 56-61.

Wilson, Peter J. A note on descent in a Malay village.
Behavior Science Notes, 1, 1 (1966): 7-13.

Wilson, Peter J. A Malay village and Malaysia: social
values and rural development. New Haven, 1967.
171 p. Sketch maps.

Winstedt, Richard Olof. Some notes on Malay card
games. JRASSB, 45 (1906): 85-88.

Winstedt, Richard Olof. The circumstances of Malay
life. 1909. 90 p. (Papers on Malay Subjects.
Life and customs, pt. 2)

Winstedt, Richard Olof. Three early keris. JRASSB,
62 (1912): 22-23. Plates.

Winstedt, Richard Olof. The Malay rice cycle. JRASSB,
75 (1917): 51.

Winstedt, Richard Olof. Foliated pattern in Malay
carving and silver work. JRASSB, 76 (1917): 73.

Winstedt, Richard Olof. Rules in Malay chess. JRASSB,
77 (1917): 261.

Winstedt, Richard Olof. Hindu survivals in Malay
custom. JFMSM, 9 (1920): 81-83.

Winstedt, Richard Olof. Election of a tribal chief
in Negri Sembilan. JFMSM, 9 (1920): 105-110.

Winstedt, Richard Olof. Family relationships in
Negri Sembilan. JFMSM, 9 (1920): 111-114.

Winstedt, Richard Olof. Malay charms. JFMSM, 9 (1920):
129-149; 9 (1922): 231-245.

Winstedt, Richard Olof. Kedah laws. JRASMB, 6, 2
(1928): 1-44.

Winstedt, Richard Olof. Mother-right among Khasis
and Malays. JRASMB, 10, 1 (1932): 9-13.

Winstedt, Richard Olof. A history of Malay literature.
JRASMB, 17, 3 (1940): 1-243.

Winstedt, Richard Olof. The elements of Malayan
civilization. AR, 57 (1941): 349-353.

Winstedt, Richard Olof. Malayan background. GM,
14 (1941-1942): 105-121. Illus.
Historical sketch and discussions of effects
of British rule on habits and attitudes of the
Malay.

Winstedt, Richard Olof. Old Malay legal digests
and Malay customary law. JRAS (1945): 17-29.

Winstedt, Richard Olof. Kingship and enthronement
in Malaya. JRASMB, 20, 1 (1947): 129-139. Illus.

Winstedt, Richard Olof. Malay proverbs. London [1950].
85 p. (The Wisdom of the East Series)

Winstedt, Richard Olof. The Malays: a cultural history.
(Rev. eds.). London, New York, 1950, 1958. 198 p.
Plates.

Winstedt, Richard Olof. A relic of Saktism in Muslim
Malaya. JRAS (1950): 162-165.

Winstedt, Richard Olof. An old Minangkabau legal
digest from Perak. JRASMB, 26, 1 (1953): 1-13.

Winstedt, Richard Olof. A history of classical Malay
literature. Rev. ed. JRASMB, 31, 3 (1958 [i.e. 1961]):
1-261. (Monographs on Malay Studies Subjects, 5)

Winstedt, Richard Olof, and P. E. de Josselin de Jong.
A digest of customary law from Sungai Ujong.
JRASMB, 27, 3 (1954): 1-71.

Winstedt, Richard Olof, and G. E. Shaw. Industries:
I--Arts and crafts, II--Fishing, hunting and
trapping, III--Rice cultivation. Kuala Lumpur,
1925, 1929, and 1926. (Papers on Malay Subjects--Series
I, v. 5)

Woolley, G. C. Origin of the Malay keris. JRASMB,
16, 2 (1938): 36-39.

Woolley, G. C. Keris measurements. JRASMB, 16, 2
(1938): 44-46.

Woolley, G. C. The Malay keris: its origin and development.
JRASMB, 20, 2 (1947): 60-103. Illus.

Wray, Jun. Ipoh poison of the Malay Peninsula. Jl
Anthr Inst, 21 (1892): 476-481.

Wray, Leonard. Notes on dyeing and weaving as practised
at Sitiawan in Perak. Jl Anthr Inst, 32 (1902): 153-155.
Illus.

Wray, Leonard. The Malayan pottery of Perak. Jl Anthr
Inst, 33 (1903): 24-34. Illus., plates.

Wray, Leonard. Rhinoceros trapping. JFMSM, 1 (1905): 63-65.

MAN AND CULTURE - Ethnology: Malays

Zainal-'Abidin bin Ahmad. Malay manners and etiquette.
JRASMB, 23, 3 (1950): 43-74.

Zainal Abidin bin Zahid, Raja. Malay personal names:
Singapore 1872-1955, and 1951-1955. 1957.
Thesis -- University of Malaya.

Zakaria bin Hitam. Some Chini legends. FMJ, n.s.,
9 (1964): 45-50.
Legends about Lake Chini, Pahang.

4. Chinese

Barnett, Patricia G. Malayan Chinese aid the British
war effort. FES, 11 (1942): 36-37.

Barnett, Patricia G. The Chinese in South Eastern
Asia and the Philippines. Ann Am Ac Pol Soc Sc
(1943): 32-49.

Blythe, W. L. Historical sketch of Chinese labour
in Malaya. JRASMB, 20, 1 (1947): 64-113.

Blythe, W. L. Chinese societies in Malaya. Corona,
1 (1949): 16-18.

Blythe, W. L. Interplay of Chinese secret and political
societies in Malaya. Eastern World, 3 (1950): 14;
4 (1950): 10.

Blythe, W. L. The impact of Chinese secret societies
in Malaya: a historical study. London, 1969.
566 p. Maps, plates.

Braddell, Sir Ronald St. J. Chinese marriages. Singapore,
1921.

Butwell, Richard. A Chinese university for Malaya.
PA, 36 (1953): 344-348.

Campbell, Persia Crawford. Chinese coolie emigration
to countries within the British Empire. London,
1923. 240 p. Bibliog.

Chan, Heng-chee. The Malayan Chinese Association. Singapore, 1965. 194 p. Dissertation (M.A.) -- University of Singapore. Bibliog., illus. Typescript.

Chang, Sen-dou. The distribution and occupation of Overseas Chinese. GR, 58, 1 (1968): 89-107.

Chapman, F. Spencer. The Chinese in Malaya. GM, 23 (1951): 401-411. Map.

Chen, L. M. The Chinese in British Malaya. CQ, 3 (1938): 245-254.

Chen, Mong-hock. Early Chinese newspaper of Singapore 1881-1912. Singapore, 1968. 170 p. Figs., plates.

Ch'en, S. C. Chinese in Malaya. PA, 21 (Sept. 1948): 291-295.

Chen, Ta. Chinese migration, with special reference to labor conditions. Washington, D.C., 1923. 237 p. (U.S. Department of Labor. Bulletin of Labor Statistics, no. 340)

Clarkson, James D. The cultural ecology of a Chinese village: Cameron Highlands, Malaysia. Chicago, 1968. 174 p. (University of Chicago, Department of Geography, Research Paper, no. 114) Maps.

Comber, Leon. Chinese ancestor worship in Malaya. Singapore, 1954, 1957.

Comber, Leon. Chinese magic and superstitions in Malaya. Singapore, 1955. 80 p. (Malayan Heritage Books, 5) Illus., plates.

Comber, Leon. An introduction to Chinese secret societies in Malaya. Singapore, 1957.

Comber, Leon. Chinese secret societies in Malaya: a survey of the Triad Society from 1800 to 1900. New York, 1959.

Comber, Leon. Chinese education--a perennial Malayan problem. AS, 1, 8 (1961): 30-35.

Cowgill, J. V. Chinese place names in Johore. JRASMB, 2, 3 (1924): 221-251. Tables.

Dawson, T. R. P. Tan Siew Sin, the man from Malacca.
Singapore, 1969. 81 p.

Elliott, A. J. A. Chinese spirit-medium cults in
Singapore. [London] Published for the Department
of Anthropology, London School of Economics and
Political Science [by the Royal Anthropological
Institute] 1955. 179 p. (Monographs on Social
Anthropology, no. 14) Illus.

Emerson, Rupert. The Chinese in Malaysia. PA, 7
(1934): 260-270.

Firmstone, H. W. Chinese names of streets and places
in Singapore and the Malay Peninsula. JRASSB,
42 (1905): 53-208; 64 (1906): 195-214.

Freedman, Maurice. The Chinese in South-East Asia.
In Melvin Conant, ed. Race Relations in World
Perspective. Hawaii, 1955: 47-52.

Freedman, Maurice. Immigrants and associations:
Chinese in nineteenth-century Singapore. Comparative
Studies in Society and History, 3, 1 (1960): 25-48.

Freedman, Maurice, and Marjorie Topley. Religion
and social realignment among the Chinese in Singapore.
JAS, 21, 1 (1961): 3-23.

Freeman, T. W. Recent and contemporary Chinese migration.
CR Cong Int G (Amsterdam, 1938) 2, 3a (1938): 11-22.

Gamba, Charles. Chinese associations in Singapore.
JRASMB, 39, 2 (1966): 123-168.

Gibson-Hill, C. A. The Chinese labourers' hats used
in Malaya. JRASMB, 25, 1 (1952): 35-47. Illus., plates.

Gosling, L. A. P. Migration and assimilation of
rural Chinese in Trengganu. In John Bastin and
R. Roolvink, eds. Malayan and Indonesian Studies.
Oxford, 1964: 203-221.

Haas, Roy H. The Malayan Chinese Association, 1958-1959;
an analysis of differing conceptions of the Malayan
Chinese role in independent Malaya. [1967]. 196 p.
Dissertation (M.A.) -- University of Northern
Illinois. Typescript.

Hall, D. G. E. Thoughts on the Chinese question in South-East Asia. AR, 50 (1954): 138-148.

Helbig, Karl. Die Unterwanderung Südostasiens durch die Chinesen. In Am Rande des Pazifik. Studien zur Landes- und Kulturkunde Südostasiens. Stuttgart, 1949: 144-197. 324 p. Bibliog., illus., index, maps.

Helbig, Karl. Das chinesische Element in Südostasien. Herkunft, Verteilung und Aufgaben. Erde, 2 (1950/1951): 54-61.

Ho, C. F. Chinese names of places which have commercial or other connections with the Straits Settlements. Chinese names of streets in the Straits Settlements. Singapore, 1918. 2 pts.

Huang, K. K. Malayan immigration law and the Malayan Chinese. China Weekly Review, 62 (Oct. 22, 1932): 331-332.

Jackson, Robert Nicholas. Pickering: protector of Chinese. Kuala Lumpur, London, 1965 [i.e. 1966]. 127 p. Maps, plates.

Jackson, Robert Nicholas. Grasping the nettle: first successes in the struggle to govern the Chinese in Malaya. JRASMB, 40, 1 (1967): 130-139.

Jones, Russell. Chinese names. JRASMB, 32, 3 (1959): 5-82.

Kanwar, H. I. S. The Chinese in Malaya will stay. Eastern World, 62 (1952): 12-14.

Kaye, B. Upper Nankin Street, Singapore: a sociological study of Chinese households living in a densely populated area. [Singapore] 1956. 422 p. Plates, tables. New ed., Singapore, 1960. 439 p.

Kogo, Sue Inui. Oriental immigration in British colonies and dominions. Far Eastern Review, 29 (1933): 481-487.

Kroef, Justus M. van der. Nanyang University and the dilemmas of Overseas Chinese education. CQ, 20 (Oct./Dec. 1964): 96-127.

Kühne, Dietrich. Einige Entwicklungs- und Wesenszüge chinesischer Agrar-Kolonisation in Malaysia. Geographische Rundschau, 20, 11 (1968): 432-435. English summary: On the development and pattern of Chinese agricultural colonization in Malaysia, p. 435.

Lee, Ah-chai. Policies and politics in Chinese schools in the Straits Settlements and the Federated Malay States, 1886-1941. 1958. M.A. thesis -- University of Singapore.

Leyden, John, tr. The Raja of China; with notices of the early intercourse between the Malays and the Chinese. From a Malay author. London, 1821.

Li, Tschang-fu. Abriss der Geschichte der Kolonisation von Südasien durch die Chinesen. Sinica Mitt, 2 (1927): 44, 49, 59-63.

Lo, Dorothy, and Leon Comber. Chinese festivals in Malaya. Singapore, 1958. 66 p.

Lu, Steve. Face painting in Chinese opera. Singapore, 1968. 183 p.

Maeda, K. Alor Janggus. A Chinese community in Malaya. Kyoto, 1967.

Middlebrook, S. M. Pulai: an early Chinese settlement in Kelantan. JRASMB, 11 (1933): 151-156.

Mills, L. A. The Chinese in British Malaya. Queen's Q, 33 (1926): 8-20.

Mok, To-leong. The influences of English and Malay on Chinese spoken in Malaya. MHJ, 2, 1 (1955): 28-30.

Morrison, Jan. Aspects of the racial problem in Malaya. PA, 23 (1949): 239-253.

Mosolff, H. Die chinesische Auswanderung. 1932. 525 p. Dissertation -- Rostock.

Müller-Beeck, F. G. Der Seeverkehr der Chinesen im Malayischen Archipel vor 1500. Mitt G Ges Hamburg (1882-1883): 26-35.

Mui Tsai Commission. Mui tsai in Hong Kong and Malaya.
Report of commission. London, 1937. 314 p. (Colonial
Office, no. 125)

Newell, William H. Family quarrels in a North Malayan
Toochiu Chinese vegetable-growing community.
Am Anthr, 59, 2 (1957): 266-277.

Newell, William H. A comparative study of informal
relationships in a Chinese village in Malaya
and North India. 1958. Ph.D. thesis -- Manchester.

Newell, William H. Treacherous river; a study of
rural Chinese in North Malaya. Kuala Lumpur,
1962. 233 p.

Newell, William H. Chinese place names in Province
Wellesley. JTG, 19 (1964): 58-61.

Nimbalker, D. P. Chinese in British Malaya. Penang,
1935. 46 p.

Notes on the Chinese in Pinang. Jl Ind Archip, 8
(1854): 1-27.

Nyce, Ray. The new villages of Malaya: a community
study. Hartford, 1962. 437 p. Ph.D. thesis --
Hartford Seminary Foundation. Bibliog., maps, tables.

Pickering, W. The Chinese in the Straits of Malacca.
Fraser's Magazine, 94 (Oct. 1876): 438.

Purcell, Victor. Chinese settlement in Malacca.
JRASMB, 20, 1 (1947): 115-125.

Purcell, Victor. The position of the Chinese in
Southeast Asia. Submitted by the IPR International
Secretariat as a preparatory paper for the Eleventh
Conference of the Institute of Pacific Relations
to be held at Lucknow, India, October, 1950.
New York, International Secretariat, Institute
of Pacific Relations, 1950. 78 p. (Secretariat
Paper, no. 3)

Purcell, Victor. The Chinese in Southeast Asia.
London, 1951. 801 p. Maps.

Purcell, Victor. The position of the Chinese community
in Malaya. JRCAS, 140 (1953): 70-81.

Purcell, Victor. The Chinese in Malaysia. In Wang
Gung-wu. Malaysia: A Survey. London, 1964: 190-198.

Purcell, Victor. The Chinese in Malaya. Kuala Lumpur,
Hong Kong, London, 1967. 327 p. Maps, tables.
Originally published in 1948.

Quah, Chooi-hon. The Chinese in Malaya: 1786-1941.
JHS, 4 (1965/1966): 74-82.

Ranu Dally. Yap Ah Loy, Capitan China. Singapore,
1969. 32 p. (Social Studies Programme, no. 2)

Roff, Margaret. The Malayan Chinese Association,
1948-65. JSAH, 6 (Sept. 1965): 40-53.

Sandhu, Kernial Singh. Chinese colonization of Malacca,
a study in population change, 1500 to 1957 A.D.
JTG, 15 (1961): 1-26.

Shearwood, J. O. Chinese in the Malay Peninsula.
Empire Review, 28 (1914): 167-169.

Shên, Wei-tsê, ed. Biographies of prominent Chinese
in Singapore. Compiled under the editorial supervision
of Victor Sim. Singapore, 1950. 110 p.

Skinner, G. William. Report on the Chinese in Southeast
Asia, December 1950. Ithaca, 1951. 91 p.
See p. 30-52 for Malaya.

Skinner, G. William. Overseas Chinese leadership:
paradigm for a paradox. In Gehan Wijeyewardene.
Leadership and Authority: A Symposium. Singapore,
1968: 191-207.

Somers, Mary F. Peking and the Overseas Chinese:
the Malaysian dispute. AS, 6, 5 (1966): 276-287.

Song, Ong-siang. One hundred years' history of the
Chinese in Singapore. London, 1923; Singapore,
1967. 602 p. Illus., index.

Tan, C. L. Malayan problems from a Chinese point
of view. Singapore, 1947.

Tan, Cheng-lock. A Chinese view of Malaya. In David
R. Rees-Williams. Three Reports on the Malayan
Problem. New York, Institute of Pacific Relations,
1949: 18-21. 46 p. Mimeo.

Tan, Diana. Some activities of the Straits Chinese
British Association. PS, 2, 2 (1967): 30-40.

Tan, T. H. The Chinese in Malaya. Eastern World,
7, 11 (1953): 13-16.

Topley, Marjorie. Chinese women's vegetarian houses
in Singapore. JRASMB, 27, 1 (1954): 51-67.

Topley, Marjorie. Ghost marriages among the Singapore
Chinese. Man, 55 (1955): 29-30.

Topley, Marjorie. The organisation and social function
of Chinese Women's Chai t'ang in Singapore. 1958.
Ph.D. thesis -- London.

Topley, Marjorie. The emergence and social function
of Chinese religious associations in Singapore.
Comparative Studies in Society and History, 3,
3 (1961): 170-181.

Unger, Leonard. The Chinese in Southeast Asia. GR,
34 (1944): 175-195. Maps.

Vandenbosch, Amry. Malaya: the Chinese and Hindu
problems. Current History, 23 (1952): 80-84.

Vaughan, J. D. Manners and customs of the Chinese
of the Straits Settlements. Singapore, 1879. 90 p.

Wan, Ming-sing. The history of the organisations
of the Chinese community in Selangor with particular
reference to problems of leadership, 1857-1962.
1967. M.A. thesis -- University of Malaya.

Wang, Gung-wu. Traditional leadership in a new nation:
the Chinese in Malaya and Singapore. In Gehan
Wijeyewardene. Leadership and Authority: A Symposium.
Singapore, 1968: 208-222.

Wen, Chung-chi. The nineteenth century imperial
Chinese consulate in the Straits Settlements.
Kuala Lumpur, 1968. 200 p.

Wong, C. S. Kek Loh Si, temple of paradise. Singapore,
Malaysian Sociological Research Institute [1963].
131 p. Illus.

Wong, Choon-san. A gallery of Chinese kapitans.
Singapore, 1963. 114 p. Illus., maps.

Wong, Lin-ken, and C. S. Wong. Secret societies
in Malaya. JSAH, 1, 1 (1960): 97-114.
A review article.

Yong, Ching-fatt. A preliminary study of Chinese
leadership in Singapore, 1900-1941. JSAH, 9,
2 (1968): 258-285.

5. Indians

Aiyer, K. A. N. Indian problems in Malaya: a brief
survey in relation to emigration. Kuala Lumpur,
1938. 150 p.

Ambikapath Rai. The Indian cooly in British Malaya.
Ind Rev, 15 (1914): 452-460.

Arasaratnam, S. Aspects of society and cultural
life of Indians in Malaysia. In S. Takdir Alisjahbana,
ed. The Cultural Problems of Malaysia in the
Context of Southeast Asia. Kuala Lumpur [1966?]:
101-107.

Arasaratnam, S. Indian festivals in Malaya. Kuala
Lumpur, 1966. 51 p.

Arasaratnam, S. Indians in Malaya: a historical
and contemporary sketch. In Frankfurt, Institut
für Asienkunde. Studien zur Entwicklung in Süd- und
Ostasien. Neue Folge, Teil 4, Malaysia. Berlin,
1966.

Arasaratnam, S. Social reform and reformist pressure
groups among the Indians of Malaya and Singapore
1930-1955. JRASMB, 40, 2 (1967): 54-67.

Arasaratnam, S. Social and political ferment in
the Malayan Indian community 1945-1965. In Proceedings
of the First International Conference Seminar
of Tamil Studies. Kuala Lumpur, 1968: 141-155.

Arasaratnam, S. Indians in Malaysia and Singapore.
Bombay, London, 1970. 214 p. Illus., maps.

Bozman, G. S. Some problems of Indian emigration. Asian Horizon, 1, 4 (1948): 13-25.

Conference of Employers of Indian Labour. Singapore 1903. Proceedings of a conference of employers of Indian labour held at Singapore on the 28th February and 2nd March, 1903, together with Report on a mission to India in connection with the recruitment and supply of Indian labour to the Straits Settlements and Federated Malay States. By A. W. S. O'Sullivan. [Singapore, 1903]. 53 p.

Dinkar, Desai. Indian labour in Malaya. Servant of India, 18 (1936): 565-566.

George, Charles D. V., and Thomas D. Marsh. Settlement of Indians on the land. Mal Ag Jl, 28 (1940): 240-241.

Glick, Clarence E. Leaders of Indian origin in Kuala Lumpur. A study of minority group leadership and trends toward national cohesian. In Proceedings of the First International Conference Seminar of Tamil Studies. V. 1. Kuala Lumpur, 1968: 227-241.

Jain, Ravindra K. Leadership and authority in a plantation: a case study of Indians in Malaya (c. 1900-1942). In Gehan Wijeyewardene. Leadership and Authority: A Symposium. Singapore, 1968: 163-173.

Jain, Ravindra K. Migrants, proletarians or Malayans? South Indians on the plantation frontier in Malaya. Canberra, Australian National University, 1965. 631 p. Thesis (Ph.D.) -- Australian National University. Bibliog., illus., maps.

Jain, Ravindra K. Ramnathpuram experiment: paradigm of an [Indian] estate-farm factory community in Malaya. Armidale, Faculty of Agricultural Economics, University of New England, 1966. 35 p. Diagrs., maps, tables. See also Proceedings of the First International Conference Seminar of Tamil Studies. V. 1, Kuala Lumpur, 1968: 164-196.

Kanwar, H. I. S. Indians in Malaya. Eastern World, 6, 12 (1952): 14-16; 7, 1 (1953): 19.

Khan, Latiffa. Indians in Malaya, 1900-1945. University of Hong Kong, 1963. 443 p. Dissertation (M.A.) -- University of Hong Kong. Bibliog.: 404-429, illus., map.

Kondapi, C. Indians overseas, 1838-1949. New Delhi, 1951.

Krishnan, R. B. Indians in Malaya: a pageant of
  greater India. A rapid survey of over 2,000 years
  of maritime and colonising activities across
  the Bay of Bengal. Singapore, 1916. 35 p.

Mahajani, Usha. The role of Indian minorities in
  Burma and Malaya. Bombay, New York, 1960.

Majumdar, Bimal Kanti. Malay Peninsula: Indian influence.
  Indo-Asian Culture, 12 (July 1963): 21-25.

Majumdar, R. C. Hindu colonies in the Far East.
  Calcutta, 1944. 242 p.

Marjoribanks, N. E., and A. T. Marakkayar. Report
  on Indian labour emigration to Ceylon and Malaya.
  Madras, Government Press, 1917. 99 p.

Minattur, Joseph. Dravidian elements in Malay culture.
  In Proceedings of the First International Conference
  Seminar of Tamil Studies. V. 1. Kuala Lumpur,
  1968: 261-266.

Moothedeen, A. Varkey. Our countrymen in Malaya.
  Being a review of the social, economic and political
  position of Indians in Malaya. Trivandrum, India,
  1932. 62 p.

Nair, M. N. Indians in Malaya. India, Kodnvayur
  Printing Works, 1938.

Nanjundan, S. Indians in Malayan economy; a study.
  New Delhi, Office of the Economic Adviser to
  the Government of India, 1950. 57 p. Map.

Nayagam, Xavier S. Thani, ed. Proceedings of the
  First International Conference Seminar of Tamil
  Studies, Kuala Lumpur, Malaysia, April 1966.
  V. 1. Kuala Lumpur, 1968. 764 p.

Neelakandha Aijer, K. A. Indian problems in Malaya;
  a brief survey in relation to emigration. Kuala
  Lumpur, 1938. 150 p. Bibliog., map.

Netto, George. Indians in Malaya, historical facts
  and figures. Singapore [1961]. 100 p. Illus.,
  tables.

Office of Economic Advisor to the Government of
India. Indians in the Malayan economy. New Dehli,
1950. 57 p.

O'Sullivan, W. A. Relations between southern India
and the Straits Settlements. JRASSB, 36 (1901): 67-74.

Palaniappan, M. The Young Men's Indian Association
and the Indians of Kuala Lumpur, Malaya 1945-55.
In Proceedings of the First International Conference
Seminar of Tamil Studies. V. 1. Kuala Lumpur,
1968: 209-216.

Ponnaiya, E. I., and A. T. Kulasingam. Spotlights
on the Jaffna Tamils in Malaya. Kuala Lumpur,
1935. 76 p.

Raghavan, N. India and Malaya; a study. Bombay,
published under the auspices of the India Council
of World Affairs [1954]. 137 p. (India and Her
Neighbours Series) Illus.

Rai, Ambikapathi. The Indian cooly in British Malaya.
Ind Rev, 15 (1914): 452-460.

Sandhu, Kernial Singh. Some preliminary observations
of the origins and characteristics of Indian
migration to Malaya, 1786-1957. Singapore, 1962.
40-72 p. Papers on Malayan History.

Sandhu, Kernial Singh. Indians in the modern Malayan
economy. India Q, 23 (1967): 106-126.

Sandhu, Kernial Singh. Tamil and other Indian convicts
in the Straits Settlements, A.D. 1790-1873. In
Proceedings of the First International Conference
Seminar of Tamil Studies. V. 1. Kuala Lumpur,
1968: 197-208.

Sandhu, Kernial Singh. Indians in Malaya, 1786-1957.
[n.p.], 1969. 400 p. Plates, tables, text figs.
    Sandhu is particularly concerned with the social
and economic effects on the country of such a
large settlement. He made use of the official
and private records of the Indian, Malayan, and
British governments.

Sandhu, Kernial Singh. Indians in Malaya--some aspects
    of their immigration and settlement: 1786-1957.
    Cambridge University Press, 1970. 370 p. Maps, tables.

Sastri, K. A. South Indian influence in the Far
    East. Bombay, 1949. 159 p.

Selangor Indian Association. Memorandum presented
    to the Rt. Hon. V. S. Srinivasa Sastri on deputation
    to Malaya on behalf of the Government of India.
    Kuala Lumpur, 1937. 24 p.

Settlements of Indians on the land. Mal Ag Jl, 28
    (1940): 240-241.

Settlements of Indians on the land in Malaya. B
    Rubber Growers' Assoc, 20, 10 (1938): 415-420.

The settlement of Tamil labourers on the land. Mal
    Ag Jl, 26, 11 (1938): 451-457.

Singam, S. Durai Raja. A Malayan heritage. Kuala
    Lumpur, 1962.

Singam, S. Durai Raja. Temple bells. Kuala Lumpur, 1964.

Singaravelu, S. Tamil studies in Malaysia. In Xavier
    S. Thani Nayagam. Tamil Studies Abroad: A Symposium.
    Kuala Lumpur, 1968: 204-223.

Subbiah, Rama. A lexical study of Tamil dialects
    in Lower Perak. Kuala Lumpur, 1966. 219 p.

Turner, G. E. A Perak coffee planter's report on
    the Tamil labourer in Malaya in 1902. MHJ, 2,
    1 (1955): 20-28.

Van der Velde, Edward J. Some aspects of Indian
    occupational mobility in Malaya. Michigan Ac
    Sc, Arts, Papers, 49 (1963 [i.e. 1964]): 251-260.

Verhoeven, F. R. J. Some notes on the history of
    the Tamil community in Dutch Malacca (1641-1825).
    In Proceedings of the First International Conference
    Seminar of Tamil Studies. V. 1. Kuala Lumpur,
    1968: 156-163.

Vermont, J. M. B. Immigration from India to the
    Straits Settlements. [Penang?] 1888. 61 p.

Zieseniss, Alexander. The Rama saga in Malaysia:
its origin and development. Translated by P.
W. Burch. Singapore, 1963.

D. CULTURAL HISTORY

Alisjahbana, S. Takdir. Confluence and conflict
of culture in Malaysia in world perspective.
In S. Takdir Alisjahbana, ed. The Cultural Problems
of Malaysia in the Context of Southeast Asia.
Kuala Lumpur [1966?]: 20-39.

Alisjahbana, S. Takdir. Acculturation and modernization
in Malaysia and the arising world culture. In
S. Takdir Alisjahbana, ed. The Cultural Problems
of Malaysia in the Context of Southeast Asia.
Kuala Lumpur [1966?]: 235-252.

Andrews, C. F. Hindu civilization of Malaya. Modern
Review, 50 (1931): 170-175.
A brief historical sketch.

Bladdell, R. A. How Islam came to the Malay Peninsula.
Moslem World, 32 (1942): 114-121.

Blagden, C. O. A Buddhist votive tablet (found in
Kedah). JRASSB, 39 (1903): 205-206.
Indian influence on Malay culture.

Douglas, F. W. Malay place names of Hindu origin.
JRASMB, 16, 1 (1938): 150-152.

Gullick, J. Sungei Ujong. JRASMB, 22, 2 (1949):
1-69. Map, tables.

Kanwar, H. I. S. Malaya's cultural contacts with
India. Asia, 3, 12 (1954): 536-543.

Keasberry, Benjamin. The origin of the Malay race.
Inter-ocean, 48 (1927): 323ff.

Lamb, Alastair. A copper casket from Pondicherry,
South India: a possible parallel for the stone
casket from Chandi Bukit Batu Pahat, Kedah. FMJ,
n.s., 9 (1964): 19-20. Photos.

Leroi-Gourham, Andre. Documents pour l'art comparé
de l'Eurasie septentrionale. Paris, 1943. 99 p.
Illus.
"Irrefutable evidence of contact between the
Malay world and Central Asia, from which the
Malays descended."

Minattur, Joseph. Some characteristics of Indian
culture in Malaysia. In S. Takdir Alisjahbana,
ed. The Cultural Problems of Malaysia in the
Context of Southeast Asia. Kuala Lumpur [1966?]:
90-100.

Nilakanta Sastri, K. A. Ancient contacts between
India and Southeast Asia. MJH, 1 (1954).

Peacock, B. A. V. The Kodiang pottery cones: tripod
pottery in Malaya and Thailand with a note on
the Bukit Tengku Lembu black ware. FMJ, n.s.,
9 (1964): 4-18. Illus.

Ratnam, S. Raja. Changing Malay people. Asia and
the Americas, 42 (1942): 449-453.

Roth, Henry Ling. Oriental silverwork: Malay and
Chinese. A handbook for connoisseurs, collectors,
students and silversmiths. Kuala Lumpur, 1966.
300 p. 170 plates.

Satyananda, Swami. Swami Satyananda and cultural
relations between India and Malaya; commemoration
volume. With special messages from Tunku Abdul
Rahman Putra and S. Radhakrishnan. Comp. and
ed. by V. G. Nair. Kuala Lumpur, 1960. 208 p.
Illus.

Singam, S. Durai Raja. Malaya's cultural debt to
India. 2d ed. rev. and enl. Singapore, 1955.
70 p. Illus. Mimeo.

Stutterheim, Willem Frederik. Indian influences
in the lands of the Pacific. Weltevreden, 1929.
9 p.

Wheeler, L. Richmond. The modern Malay. London,
1928. 300 p. Bibliog.

Winstedt, Richard O. Hindu survivals in Malay customs.
JFMSM, 9, 1 (1920): 81-84.

Winstedt, Richard O. Elements of Malayan civilization.
AR, 37 (1941): 349-353.

Winstedt, Richard O. Indian influence in the Malay
world. JRAS Gr B and I, 21 (1944): 186-196.

Winstedt, Richard O. The Malays, a cultural history.
Singapore, 1947. 162 p. Bibliog.

E. RELIGION

Abdullah, Dato' Sedia Raja. The leading saints in
Rembau. JRASMB, 3, 3 (1925): 101-104.

Abdullah, Dato' Sedia Raja. Mandi ayer gawar. JRASMB,
4, 2 (1926): 212-214.
A ceremony to ward off epidemics.

Abdullah, Dato' Sedia Raja. The origin of the Pawang
and the Berpuar ceremony. JRASMB, 5 (1927): 310-313.

Alatas, Hussein, Syed. The Islamic conception of
religion and social ideal. In S. Takdir Alisjahbana,
ed. The Cultural Problems of Malaysia in the
Context of Southeast Asia. Kuala Lumpur [1966?]: 108-122.

Alexander, Patrick. Spirits of the Malay jungle.
Asia, 35 (1935): 54-57.

Allard, Elizabeth. Animistic beliefs and rites on
the Malay Archipelago. Oceania, 16 (1945-1946):
87-108, 254-274, 337-352; 17 (1946): 79-91. Bibliog.

Annandale, Nelson. Notes on the popular religion
of the Patani Malay. Man, 3, 12 (1903): 27-28.

Annandale, Nelson. A magical ceremony for the curing
of a sick person among the Malays of Upper Perak.
Man, 3, 56 (1903): 100-103.

Annandale, Nelson. Religion and magic among the
Malays of the Patani states. In N. Annandale
and H. C. Robinson. Fasciculi Malayenses . .
. Anthropology. Pt. 1. London, 1903: 89-104.
Illus., plates.

Al-Attas, Naguib, Syed. Some aspects of Sufism as
understood and practiced among the Malays. Singapore,
Malaysian Sociological Research Institute, 1963.
104 p. Photos.

Al-Attas, Naguib, Syed. Islamic culture in Malaysia.
In S. Takdir Alisjahbana, ed. The Cultural Problems
of Malaysia in the Context of Southeast Asia.
Kuala Lumpur [1966?]: 123-130.

Bador, A. K. Réformisme islamique et politique en
Malaisie; un cas historique. Archives de Sociologie
des Religions, 9, 17 (1964): 68-84.

Blagden, C. O. Notes on the folklore and popular
religion of the Malays. JRASSB, 29 (1896): 1-12.

Blasdell, R. A. Use of the drum for mosque services.
Moslem World, 30 (1940): 41-45.

Blasdell, R. A. How Islam came to, the Malay Peninsula.
Moslem World, 32 (1942): 114-121.

Blasdell, R. A. Islam in Malaya. Int Rev Missions,
34 (1945): 170-172.

Browne, Laurence E. Christianity and the Malays.
London, 1936.

C., W. A Palau Tiuman superstition. JRASSB, 34 (1900): 101.

Cabaton, A. Cérémonial en usage chez les Malais
à la mort de leurs rois. Rev Monde Musul, 4 (1908):
491-501.

Camerling, Elizabeth. Über Ahnenkult in Hinterindien
und auf den Grossen Sunda Inseln. Zürich, 1928.
326 p. Bibliog.

Capra, G. Nel paisi del Buddhismo (Siam, Indo-China,
Malaya). Il Mondo (1934): 741-767.

Chelliah, D. D. The growth of unity among the churches
of Malaya. Int Rev Missions, 37 (1948): 421-426.

Chelliah, V. A., and Alexander McLeish. Malaya and
Singapore. Survey directory of churches and missions
in the Federation and Colony. London, 1948. 36 p.

Cherry, W. T. British Malaya as a mission field: a summary based on the 1921 census. Moslem World, 13 (1923): 30-38.

Clarke, W. B. The incantation and sacrifice of the Pawang Ma'yang. JRASMB, 3, 3 (1925): 106.

Clifford, Hugh. An apostle to Malaya. Asia, 26 (1926): 969-973. Father Rovellot.

Coope, A. E. The black art (ilmu jahat). JRASMB, 11 (1933): 264-272. Diagr.

Crawfurd, John. Why have Mohammedan been more successful than Christian missionaries in the Indian Archipelago? Jl Ind Archip, 3 (1849): 458-459.

Creagh, C. V. Propitiatory sacrifice of a buffalo in the Malay Peninsula. Indian Antiquary, 18 (1889): 31-32.

Cuisinier, Jeanne. L'ame et les mots qui l'expriment en Malais. B Assoc Fran Amis Or, 8 (1930): 25-35.

Cuisinier, Jeanne. Danses magiques de Kelantan. Paris, 1936. 206 p. Plates.

Danaraj, A. G. S. Mysticism in Malaya. Singapore, 1964. 90 p. Plates.

Evans, Ivor H. N. Beliefs, customs and folk-tales of the Behrang-Valley Senoi. JFMSM, 7, 4 (1918): 193-209.

Evans, Ivor H. N. Some Sakai beliefs and customs. Jl R Anthr Inst, 18 (1918): 179-197.

Evans, Ivor H. N. Kempunan (Malay beliefs). Man, 20, 38 (1920): 69-70.

Evans, Ivor H. N. Some Negrito beliefs and customs. JFMSM, 9 (1920): 1-15.

Evans, Ivor H. N. Customs of the camphor-hunters. JFMSM, 9 (1920): 53-59.

Evans, Ivor H. N. Further notes on Negrito beliefs and customs. JFMSM, 9 (1922): 191-221.

Evans, Ivor H. N. Studies in religion, folk-lore
    and custom in British North Borneo and the Malay
    Peninsula. Cambridge, 1923. 299 p. Illus., plates.

Evans, Ivor H. N. Two Malay methods of divination.
    JRASMB, 1 (1923): 247.

Evans, Ivor H. N. Some beliefs of the Lenggong Negritos.
    JFMSM, 12 (1924): 17-21.

Evans, Ivor H. N. Some Malay beliefs. JFMSM, 12,
    5 (1928): 137-138.

Fatimi, S. Q. Islam comes to Malaysia. Singapore, 1963.

Gallagher, Charles F. Contemporary Islam: a frontier
    of communalism; aspects of Islam in Malaysia.
    AUFS-SEA, 14, 10 (1966): 1-24.

Gimlette, J. D. A curious Kelantan charm. JRASSB,
    82 (1920): 116-118. Plates.

Gimlette, J. D. Smoking over a fire to drive out
    an evil spirit. Man, 24, 3 (1924): 38-39.

Gimlette, J. D. Malay poisons and charm cures. 3d ed.
    London, 1929. 301 p. Plates, tables.

Haines, Joseph Harry. A history of Protestant missions
    in Malaya during the nineteenth century, 1815-1881.
    1962. 372 p. Dissertation -- Princeton Theological
    Seminary. Maps.

Hamilton, A. W., tr. Malay love charms. JRASMB,
    4, 1 (1926): 136-137.

Ishak bin Ahmad. Malay fishermen's superstitions.
    JRASMB, 19, 1 (1941): 131-136. Diagr.
    Author, a fisheries officer, describes sacrifice
    and general ceremonies of fishing preparation.

Itagaki, Yoichi, and Koichi Kishi. Japanese Islamic
    policy in Sumatra and Malaya. Intisari, 2, 3
    [n.d.]: 11-23.

James, G. D. Missionary tours in Malaya. Singapore
    [1962]. 164 p. Illus., map.

Johns, A. H. Malay Sufism as illustrated in an anonymous collection of 17th century tracts. JRASMB, 30, 2 (1959): 5-111.

Johns, A. H. The role of Sufism in the spread of Islam to Malaya and Indonesia. JPHS, 9 (1961): 143-161.

Kempgen, Wilhelm. Mission in Malaya. Wuppertal-Barmen, 1955. 24 p.

Laidlaw, F. F. Note on the invocation of Akuan. JRASMB, 1 (1923): 376-377.
Ceremony of "medium" with a sick man.

Lela, W. Some Malay beliefs. JFMSM, 9, 4 (1922): 263-267.

Lokman Yusof. Islam and adat: as seen in land inheritance. Intisari, 1, 4 [n.d.]: 11-19.

Ma, Ibrahim T'ien-ying. What is the religion of Islam? Kuala Lumpur [1962]. 28, 20 p. Illus.
In English and Chinese.

Majid, Haji Abdul. A Malay's pilgrimage to Mecca. JRASMB, 4, 2 (1926): 269-287.

Majid, Haji Abdul. Random notes on current Malay beliefs. JRASMB, 5, 2 (1927): 360-361.

Majid, Haji Abdul. Some Malay superstitions. JRASMB, 6, 4 (1928): 41-45.

Marriott, H. Malay witchcraft. JRASSB, 39 (1903): 209-210.

Marrison, G. E. The coming of Islam to the East Indies. JRASMB, 24, 1 (1951): 28-37. Bibliog.

Marrison, G. E. Islam and the church in Malaya. Moslem World (1957): 290-298.

Maxwell, W. E. Shamanism in Perak. JRASSB, 12 (1883): 222-232.

Maxwell, W. E. Manta Sandaran. JRASSB Notes and Queries, 2 (1885): 46-47.
Invocation on going to bed.

Maxwell, W. E. Pelas Negri. JRASSB Notes and Queries,
3 (1886): 80-81.
Periodic ceremony to insure prosperity.

Maxwell, W. E. Mantra: belief in spirits and demons.
JRASSB Notes and Queries, 4 (1887): 124-130.
Notes on demonology.

McLeish, Alexander. A racial melting pot, religion
in Malaya. London, New York, 1940. 26 p. (War-time
series, no. 1) Illus., map.

McLeish, Alexander. A racial melting pot: Malaya.
Moslem World, 31 (1941): 241-253.
Deals with various denominations existing in
Malaya.

Means, Gordon P. State and religion in Malaya and
Malaysia. In M. M. Thomas and M. Abel, eds. Religion,
State and Ideologies in East Asia. [Bangalore]
1965: 101-126. Tables.

Middlebrook, S. M. Ceremonial opening of a new Chinese
temple at Kandang, Malacca, in December, 1938.
JRASMB, 17, 1 (1939): 98-106. Plates.

Noone, H. D. Customs relating to death and burial
among the Orang Ulu (Jakun) of Ulu Johore. JFMSM,
15 (1939): 180-194. Graphs, plates.

O'Sullivan, A. W. Ceremonies at seed time. JRASSB,
18 (1886): 362-365.

Overbeck, H. G. Malay customs and beliefs as recorded
in Malay literature and folk lore. JRASMB, 2,
3 (1924): 280-288; 3, 1 (1925): 53-57; 3, 3 (1925):
22-30. References.

Overbeck, H. G. The answer of Pasai. JRASMB, 11
(1933): 254-260.

Paroissin, R. P. Souvenirs d'un missionaire en Malaisie.
Geographia (Oct. 1957): 21-24.

Pekirma Wira. Islam and adat in Trengganu. Intisari,
1, 4 [n.d.]: 37-48.

Rauf, M. A. A brief history of Islam, with special
reference to Malaya. Kuala Lumpur, 1964. 128 p.
Illus., maps.

Rauf, M. A. Islamic education in Malaya. Intisari,
2, 1 [n.d.]: 14-31.

Rentse, Anker. Malay charms, Kelantan. JRASMB, 9
(1931): 146-157.

Rentse, Anker. Notes on Malay beliefs. JRASMB, 11
(1933): 245-252.

Schebesta, Paul. La conscience de la culpabilité
chez les primitivs de la Malaisie. Semaine d'Ethnologie
Religieuse, IVe Session, Milan, 1925 (1926):
186-194.

Schebesta, Paul. Das Hala- oder Medizinmannwesen
bei den Semang auf Malakka. Jahrbuch St. Gabriel,
3 (1926): 253-265.

Schebesta, Paul. Religiöses und Soziales der Urbewohner
Malakkas. Akademische Miss, 15 (1927): 23-31.

Schebesta, Paul. Jenseitsglaube der Semang auf Malakka.
In W. Koppers, ed. Festschrift publication d'Hommage
Offerte au P. W. Schmidt. Vienne, 1928: 635-644.
977 p.

Schebesta, Paul. Religiöse Anschauungen der Semang
über die Orang Hidop (die Unsterblichen). Ar Relig,
25, 1/2 (1928): 5-35.)

Schebesta, Paul. Die religiösen Anschauungen der
Semang-Zwerge von Malaya. Bonn, 1928. (Religiöse
Quellenschriften, no. 52)

Sianu. The view which more intelligent Malays give
of the present world. Indo-Chinese Gleaner, 1
(1818): 102-104.

Sianu. Malay demons. Indo-Chinese Gleaner, 2 (1819):
73-75.

Sianu. Malay witches. Indo-Chinese Gleaner, 2 (1819):
139-142.

Sianu. Magic among the Malays. Indo-Chinese Gleaner,
2 (1820): 312-315.

Skeat, W. W. Some records of Malay magic by an eye
witness. JRASSB, 31 (1898): 1-61.

Skeat, W. W. Malay magic, an introduction to the
folklore and popular religion of the Malay Peninsula.
London, 1900. 685 p.

Skeat, W. W. Malay spiritualism. Folklore, 13 (1902):
134-165.

Skeat, W. W. Vestiges of totemism in the Malay Peninsula.
Trans Int Cong History Religions, III, v. 1.
Oxford (1908): 95-102.

Skeat, W. W. Malay Peninsula. In Encyclopaedia of
Religion and Ethics, 8. New York, 1916: 348-372.

Suffian, Hashim. The relationship between Islam
and the state in Malaya. Intisari, 1, 1 [n.d.]:
7-18.

Suffian, Mohamed. Religious freedom and the position
of Islam in Malaysia. World Muslims League Monthly
Magazine, 3 (Jan. 1966): 40-43.

Topley, Marjorie. Some occasional rites performed
by the Singapore Cantonese. JRASMB, 24, 3 (1951):
120-144. Illus.

Topley, Marjorie. Chinese rites for the response
of the soul; with special reference to Cantonese
custom. JRASMB, 25, 1 (1952): 149-160. Illus.

Topley, Marjorie. Paper charms, and prayer sheets
as adjuncts to Chinese worship. JRASMB, 26, 1
(1953): 63-80. Illus.

Uno. Religious rites and ceremonies concerning rice
planting and eating in Malaysia. Tokyo, 1940.
772 p. Text in Japanese with a resume in English.

Wheeler, L. Richmond. Islam in Malaya. Int Rev Missions,
17 (1928): 342-353.

Wheeler, L. Richmond. The modern Malay. London,
1928. 300 p. Bibliog., plates.

Wilkinson, R. J. The Peninsula Malays: I--Malay
beliefs. London, 1906. 81 p.

Wilkinson, R. J. The incidents of Malay life . . .
Kuala Lumpur, 1908.
Papers on Malay subjects. Life and customs,
pt. I.

Wilkinson, R. J. Some Malay studies. JRASMB, 10,
1 (1932): 67-137.
Notes on ethnology, social structure, folklore,
religion.

Williams-Hunt, P. D. R. An up-to-date shaman. Man,
50 (1950): 116. Illus.

Williams-Hunt, P. D. R. Some Malay and aboriginal
charms and methods of measuring weapons. JRASMB,
25 (1952): 56-61.

Winstedt, R. O. The advent of Muhammadanism in the
Malay Peninsula and Archipelago. JRASSB, 77 (1917):
171-175.

Winstedt, R. O. The early Muhammadan missionaries.
JRASSB, 81 (1920): 5-6.

Winstedt, R. O. Perak birth customs. JFMSM, 9 (1920):
84-87.

Winstedt, R. O. Propitiating the spirits of a district
(menjamu negeri). JFMSM, 9 (1920): 93-95.

Winstedt, R. O. Rice ceremonies in Upper Perak.
JFMSM, 9 (1920): 116-121.

Winstedt, R. O. Rice ceremonies in Negri Sembilan.
JFMSM, 9 (1920): 122-128.

Winstedt, R. O. India and Malay beliefs. JRASSB,
83 (1921): 88-91.

Winstedt, R. O. Some Malay mystics, heretical and
orthodox. JRASMB, 1 (1923): 312-318.

Winstedt, R. O. Three peninsular charms. JRASMB,
1 (1923): 383-384.
1. To avert strife, 2. To shut the mouths of
enemies, 3. To catch a crocodile.

Winstedt, R. O. Karamat: sacred places and persons
in Malaya. JRASMB, 2, 3 (1924): 264-279.

Winstedt, R. O. Notes on Malay magic. JRASMB, 3,
3 (1925): 6-21.

Winstedt, R. O. Shaman, Saiva and Sufi: a study
of the evolution of Malay magic. London, 1925.
191 p. Bibliog.

Winstedt, R. O. More notes on Malay magic. JRASMB, 5, 3 (1927): 342-347.

Winstedt, R. O. The ritual of the rice-field. JRASMB, 7 (1929): 437-447.

Winstedt, R. O. Religious factors in Malay culture. Religions, 39 (1942): 7-11.

Winstedt, R. O. The Malay magician: being Shaman, Saiva and Sufi. Revised and enlarged with a Malay appendix. London, 1951. 160 p. Illus. First published in 1925, under the title: Shaman, Saiva and Sufi.

Zainal-'Abidin bin Ahmad. Akuan or spirit friends. JRASSB, 86 (1922): 378-384.

Zainal-'Abidin bin Ahmad. Malay festivals; and some aspects of Malay religious life. JRASMB, 22, 1 (1949): 94-106.

F. DEMOGRAPHY, IMMIGRATION, AND EMIGRATION

Abdul Aziz bin Abdul Hamid, Ungku. Poverty, proteins and disguised starvation. KEM, 2, 1 (1965): 7-48.

Abdul Razak bin Hussein, Tun, Haji. Government policy on birth control in Malaysia. KEM, 3, 1 (1966): 3-6.

Aschaimbault, Charles. Enquete préliminaire sur les populations Sam Sam de Kedah et Perlis (Malaisie). BEFEO, 49, 2 (1959): 617-636. Plates.

Brown, C. C. Perak Malays. 1921. 106 p.

Bruton, Christopher F. Some population problems in Thailand and Malaysia. Geographica, 3 (1967): 66-77. Bibliog., figs.

Caldwell, John Charles. The population of Malaya. 1962. 584 p. Thesis -- Australian National University. Illus., tables.

Caldwell, John Charles. The demographic background. In T. H. Silcock, ed. Political Economy of Independent Malaya. Kuala Lumpur, 1963: 59-92.

Caldwell, John Charles. Fertility decline and female chances of marriage in Malaya. Population Studies 17, 1 (1963): 20-32.

Caldwell, John Charles. Some implications of past population growth and likely future trends in Malaya. Population Review, 7, 2 (1963): 43-52.

Caldwell, John Charles. Urban growth in Malaya: trends and implications. Population Review, 7 (Jan. 1963): 39-50.

Caldwell, John Charles. New and old Malaya: aspects of demographic change in a high growth rate, multiracial society. Population Review, 8, 2 (1964): 29-36.

Caldwell, John Charles. Malaysia's population problem. In S. Chandrasekhar, ed. Asia's Population Problems. London, 1967: 165-188.

Chew, David D. E., and Amina H. Degani. Population and manpower. In Ooi Jin-bee and Chiang Hai-ding, eds. Modern Singapore. Singapore, University of Singapore Press, 1969: 85-108.

Colaco, L. Labour emigration from India to the British Colonies of Ceylon, Malaya and Fiji during the years 1850-1921. 1957. M. Sc. thesis (London School of Economics) -- London.

Committee on Emigration from India to the Crown Colonies and Protectorates. Report, minutes of evidence and papers. London, 1910. 3 pts. (Command Paper, no. 5192-4)

Cooper, Eunice. Urbanization in Malaya. Population Studies, 5, 2 (1951): 117-131. Tables.

Crandall, J. R. Social customs of Malays. Sociology and Social Research, 12 (1928): 567-572.

Dennery, Etienne. Asia's teeming millions and its problems for the West. London, 1931. 248 p. Bibliog., illus., maps. Chap. 6, Chinese in British Malay States, p. 161-180.

Djamour, J. Adoption of children among Singapore
   Malaysians. Jl R Anthr Inst, 82 (1953): 159-168.

Etienne, Gilbert. La grande Malaisie; vues sur l'économie
   et la population de Singapore, de la Féderation
   de Malaisie et Bornéo du Nord. Population, 18
   (1963): 111-128.

Evaluation of the population census data of Malaya.
   Economic Bulletin for Asia and the Far East,
   13, 2 (1962): 23-45.

Freedman, M. The sociology of race relations in
   South-East Asia, with special reference to British
   Malaya. 1948. M.A. thesis -- University of London.

Gordon, Shirle. Marriage/divorce in the eleven states
   of Malaya and Singapore. Intisari, 2, 2 [n.d.]:
   23-32. Tables.

Hamzah bin Sendut. Problems of rural-urban migration.
   Community Development Bulletin, 12, 3 (1961):
   86-90.

Hamzah bin Sendut. Demographic atlas of western
   Malaysia. Kuala Lumpur, 1966. 35 p. Mimeo.

Indian migration to Malaya. Industrial and Labour
   Information, 70 (1939): 643-644.

Jackson, J. C. Population changes in Selangor State,
   1850-1891. JTG, 19 (1964): 42-57. Maps.

Jones, L. W. Malaysia's future population. PV, 6,
   1 (1965): 39-51.

Lasker, Bruno. Population shifts in Southeast Asia.
   FES, 13 (1944): 201-205.

Lasker, Bruno. Asia on the move: population pressure,
   migration and resettlement in Eastern Asia under
   the influence of want and war. New York, 1945. 207 p.

Mackenzie, R. D. Race invasion of Malaya. Jl Applied
   Soc, 11 (1927): 525-540.

Malaya, Department of Statistics. 1957 population
   census of the Federation of Malaya. Reports no.
   1-14. Kuala Lumpur [1957-1960]. 14 v. Tables.

Malaysia, Department of Statistics. Vital statistics
West Malaysia 1966. Kuala Lumpur, 1967.

Marriott, H. Population of Straits Settlements and
Malay Peninsula during last century. JRASSB,
62 (1912): 31-42.

Maxwell, Sir George. The mixed communities of Malaya.
Br Mal (Feb. 1943): 115-121.

McGee, T. G. Population [of Malaysia]. In Wang Gung-wu.
Malaysia: A Survey. London, 1964: 67-81.

McTaggert, W. D. A note on age-specific fertility
in Malay 1962. Geographica, 1 (1964-1965): 23-30.
Graph, tables.

McTaggert, W. D. Distribution of ethnic groups in
Malaya 1947 and 1957. JTG, 26 (1968): 69-81.

Milne, J. C. Birth rates and race fertility in Malaya.
Mal Med Jl (Dec. 1933): 287-289.

Morrison, I. Aspects of the racial problem in Malaya.
PA, 22 (Sept. 1949): 239-253.

Mukerjee, Radhakamal. Migrant Asia; a problem in
world population. Rome, 1936. 310 p. (Comito
Italiano per la studio dei problemi della populazione,
ser. 3, v. 1) Maps.

Narasimhan, P. S. The immigrant community of Southeast
Asia. India Q, 3 (1947): 32-41.

Nathan, J. E. Census of British Malaya, 1921. London, 1922.

Neville, R. J. W. Singapore: recent trends in the
sex and age composition of a cosmopolitan community.
Population Studies, 17, 2 (1963): 99-112.

Neville, R. J. W. The areal distribution of population
in Singapore. JTG, 20 (1965): 16-25. Maps.

Neville, R. J. W. Singapore: ethnic diversity and
its implications. Annals, 56, 2 (1966): 236-253.

Neville, R. J. W. Patterns of change in a plural
society: a social geography of the city state
of Singapore. London, 1967. Ph. D. thesis --
University of London.

Neville, R. J. W. The demographic structure of Singapore
and its economic and social implications. Paper
presented at First Annual Congress of Singapore
National Academy of Science. Aug., 1968. 15 p.
Tables. Mimeo.

Neville, Warwick. The distribution of population
in the post-war period. In Ooi Jin-bee and Chiang
Hai-ding, eds. Modern Singapore. Singapore, University
of Singapore Press, 1969: 52-68.

Neville, Warwick. The demographic structure and
its economic and social implications. In Ooi
Jin-bee and Chiang Hai-ding, eds. Modern Singapore.
Singapore, University of Singapore Press, 1969:
69-84.

Noone, N. D. Some vital statistics of the lowland
Senoi of Perak. JFMSM, 15 (1932): 195-215. Charts,
tables.

Ooi, Jin-bee. The distribution of present-day man
in the tropics: historical and ecological perspective.
PPSC, 9, 1957, 20 (1958): 111-124.

Pelzer, Karl J. Die Arbeiterwanderungen in Südostasien.
Eine wirtschafts- und bevölkerungsgeographische
Untersuchung. Hamburg, 1935. 120 p.

Pelzer, Karl J. Population and land utilization.
New York, 1941. 215 p.
Constitutes Part 1 of an economic survey of
the Pacific area. See pp. 48-53 for population
of British Malaya.

Pelzer, Karl J. Mass migration and resettlement
projects in Southeast Asia since 1945. PPSC,
9, 1957, 3 (1963): 189-194.
Includes resettlement during the Emergency.

Pountey, A. M. The census of the Federated Malay
States, 1911. London, 1911.

Ramamurte, B. Demographic trends in Asian countries.
New Delhi, 1947. 18 p. (Indian Council of World
Affairs document) Mimeo.

Report of the Registrar-general on population, births
    and deaths for the year 1953. Kuala Lumpur, 1954.
    36 p. (Legislative Council Paper, no. 44) Tables.

Ridley, H. N. The Eurasian problem. Singapore, 1913.

Sandhu, Kernial Singh. The population of Malaya,
    some changes in the pattern of distribution between
    1947 and 1957. JTG, 15 (1961): 82-96.

Saw, Swee-hock. The population of Singapore and
    its social and economic implications. 1960. 193 p.
    M.A. -- University of Singapore.

Saw, Swee-hock. The demography of Malaya, with special
    reference to race differentials. 1963. Ph.D.
    thesis (London School of Economics) -- London.

Saw, Swee-hock. Trends and differentials in international
    migration in Malaya. Ekonomi, 4, 1 (1963): 47-113.

Saw, Swee-hock. The changing population structure
    in Singapore during 1824-1962. MER, 9, 1 (1964):
    90-101. Charts, tables.

Saw, Swee-hock. A note on the under-registration
    of births in Malaya during the intercensal period
    1947-1957. Population Studies, 18 (July 1964): 35-52.

Saw, Swee-hock. Sources and methods of population
    statistics in Malaya and Singapore. Ekonomi,
    5, 1 (1964): 84-91.

Saw, Swee-hock. Pattern of fertility decline in
    Malaya 1956-1965. KEM, 3, 1 (1966): 7-14.

Saw, Swee-hock. Regional differences in the structure
    of the labour force in Malaysia. KEM, 3, 2 (1966): 50-58.

Saw, Swee-hock. A note on the fertility levels in
    Malaya during 1947-1957. MER, 12, 1 (1967): 117-123.

Saw, Swee-hock, and Pearl Chu. The population of
    nineteenth century Penang. 1968. 7 p. Unpublished
    paper no. 56, presented at the International
    Conference on Asian History, Kuala Lumpur, August
    1968. Mimeo.

Saw, Swee-hock, and Ronald Ma. The economic characteristics
    of the population of Singapore, 1957. MER, 5
    (1960): 31-51.

Silcock, T. H. Migration problems of the Far East.
    In Thomas Brinley, ed. The Economics of International
    Migration. London, 1958: 251-272.

Singapore. Report on the registration of births
    and deaths, marriages and persons. 1963- . Singapore,
    Government Printing Office, 1964.

Smith, T. E. Population growth in Malaya. London,
    1952. 126 p.

Smith, T. E. The 1957 census; a preliminary report
    based on "First Country Total" returns. Kuala
    Lumpur, 1957. 57 p.

Smith, T. E. The reports on the 1957 census of the
    Federation of Malaya. Malaya (April 1962): 13-14.

Smith, T. E. Marriage, widowhood and divorce in
    the Federation of Malaya. In [Proceedings]. International
    Population Conference, New York, 1961. V. 2.
    London, 1963: 302-310.

Smith, T. E. Immigration and permanent settlement
    of Chinese and Indians in Malaya: and the future
    growth of the Malay and Chinese communities.
    In C. D. Cowan, ed. The Economic Development
    of Southeast Asia. New York [1964]: 174-185.

Snodgrass, D. R. Malaysia population projection,
    1963-70. Kuala Lumpur, Economic Planning Unit,
    October 1964. 4 p. Tables. Economic Planning
    Unit memorandum.

Tamil immigration into Kedah and Kelantan. Federated
    Malay States, Federated Council Paper (1909-1910):
    26-35.

Tufo, M. V. del. Malaya, comprising the Federation
    of Malaya and Colony of Singapore. A report on
    the 1947 census of population. London, 1949.
    597 p. Maps.

Uhlig, Harald. Die Volksgruppen und ihre Gesellschafts- und
    Wirtschaftsentwicklung als Gestalter der Kulturlandschaft
    in Malaya. Mitt Ö G Ges, 105, 1-2 (1963): 65-94.

Vlieland, C. A. British Malaya. A report on the
    1931 census and certain problems of vital statistics.
    London, 1932. 389 p.

Vlieland, C. A. The population of the Malay Peninsula;
    a study in human migration. GR, 24 (1934): 61-78.
    Diagr., illus., maps.

Vlieland, C. A. The 1947 census of Malaya. PA, 22
    (1948): 59-63.

Wikkramatileke, R. Variable ethnic attributes in
    Malayan rural land development. PV, 5, 1 (May
    1964): 35-49. Illus., map, tables.

Yeh, Stephen H. K. Some observations on fertility
    decline in Singapore. Economic Research Centre,
    University of Singapore. 15 p. (Reprint Monograph
    Series, no. 5) Mimeo.

You, Poh-seng. Population of Malaya. In Lim Tay-boh,
    ed. Problems of the Malayan Economy. Singapore,
    1956: 6-10.

You, Poh-seng. The population growth of Singapore.
    MER, 4 (1959): 56-69.

You, Poh-seng. The population of Singapore 1966:
    demographic structure, social and economic
    characteristics. MER, 12, 2 (1967): 59-96.

G. DIET, HEALTH, AND STANDARD OF LIVING

Black, K. Health and climate: with special reference
    to Malaya. Br Mal, 7 (1933): 253-256, 279-280.

Blair, R. W. The water supplies of the Federated
    Malay States. Notes on some of the water supplies
    derived from jungle streams and rivers. Kuala
    Lumpur, 1933. 162 p. (Institute for Medical Research
    Bulletin, no. 2)

MAN AND CULTURE - Diet, Health, Standard of Living

Bordier. Instructions de géographie médicale pour
la Malaisie. B Soc d'Anthr, 3d ser. 2 (1879): 45-59.

Brodie, Mabel. The health of women and children
in Malaya. Royal Sanitary Institute Journal,
58 (1937): 305-324.

Burgess, R. C., and Laidin bin Alang Musa. Health.
A report on the state of health, the diet and
the economic conditions of groups of people in
the lower income levels in Malaya. Kuala Lumpur,
1952. 80 p. (Institute for Medical Research Report,
no. 13) Illus., tables.

Burkill, I. H., and Mohamed Haniff. Malayan village
medicine; prescriptions collected by I. H. B.
and M. H. Gardens' Bulletin, 6 (1930): 165-321.

Campbell, J. A. Diet, nutrition and excretion of
the Asiatic races in Singapore. JRASSB, 76 (1917):
57-65 (medical students); 79 (1918): 107-110
(manual workers).

Chambers, W. M. The social hygiene campaign in Singapore.
Health and Empire, 13 (1938): 218-225.

Cheek, E. B. Good health through good feeding: a
Malayan guide to good health through a balanced
diet. London, 1955. 33 p. Illus., tables.

Chi, T. The leper and social work in Singapore.
Trinity Theological College Annual, 2 (1965):
27-30.

Coales, F. C., and J. A. T. Horsley. New Kinta district
water supply filtration plant. Far Eastern Review,
31 (1935): 352-356. Diagrs., tables.

Cognacq, Maurice-Charles. De la lèpre en Cochinchine
et dans la presqu'île malaise. Saigon, 1889.
172 p. Chart, plates, table.

Cross, B. Short investigation of infantile mortality
and child welfare on estates in Kedah. British
Medical Association, Malay Branch, Journal, 4
(1940): 141-163.

Federated Malay States. Report of the commission
    appointed to enquiry into certain matters affecting
    the health of estates in the Federated Malay
    States, together with a memorandum by the Chief
    Secretary to Government Federated Malay States.
    Singapore, 1924. 2 v.

Fitzgerald, R. Desmond. A thesis on two tropical
    neuroses (amok and latah) peculiar to Malaya.
    Far Eastern Association of Tropical Medicine,
    Transactions, V Congress (1923): 148-161.

Furnivall, J. S. Progress and welfare in Southeast
    Asia. New York, 1941. 83 p.

Galloway, David J. A contribution to the psychology
    of "Latah". JRASSB, 85 (1922): 140-150.
    Latah is a neurotic disturbance.

Gerrard, P. N. A vocabulary of Malay medical terms.
    Singapore, 1905. 107 p.

Gimlette, John D. Some superstitious beliefs occurring
    in the theory and practice of Malay medicine.
    JRASSB, 65 (1913): 29-35. Plate.

Gimlette, John D. A dictionary of Malayan medicine.
    Edited and completed by H. W. Thomson. London,
    New York, 1939. 259 p. Plates.

Hall, Ivan C. A pharmaco-bacteriologic study of
    two Malayan blow-gun poisoned darts. Am Anthr,
    30 (1928): 47-59.

Haridas, G. Infantile beri-beri in Singapore during
    the latter part of the Japanese occupation. Ar
    Disease Childhood, 22 (1947): 23-40.

Health service in Malaya. AR, 55 (1959): 157-160.

Hervey, D. F. A. Notes on Malacca folk medicine.
    Indian Antiquary, 18 (1889): 59-61.

Hoffman, F. L. Cancer in British Malaya and the
    Philippine Islands. Newark, 1934. 14 p.

Hooper, David. On Chinese medicine: drugs of Chinese
    pharmacies in Malaya. Gardens' Bulletin, 6 (1929):
    1-163.

Ismail Munshi. The medical book of Malayan medicine.
Translated by I. I., with notes by J. D. Gimlette
and I. H. Burkill. Gardens' Bulletin, 6 (1930):
324-474.

The Institute for Medical Research, 1900-1950. Kuala
Lumpur, 1951. 389 p. Appendix, bibliog., charts,
illus., maps, tables.

Jones, Kathleen. Social welfare in Malaya. Singapore,
1958. 45 p. Illus.

Kingsbury, A. N., and P. Fasal. A nutritional survey
of the Federated Malay States. 1. Common clinical
manifestations of sub-nutrition among rural Malays
and Tamils. 2. Heights and weights tables for
young Tamils under plantation conditions. Kuala
Lumpur, 1940. (1) 14 p. (2) 8 p. (Institute for
Medical Research Bulletin, nos. 1 and 2)

Lam, Thim-fook. The role of social welfare and its
contribution to society. JTAM (Oct.-Dec. 1967).

League of Nations, Health Organization. Conference
of Far Eastern countries on rural hygiene. Preparatory
papers: report of the Malayan delegation. Geneva,
1937. 38 p. (League of Nations Publication III
Health, Geneva, nos. 2-9)

Leong, P. C. Vitamin "A" content of Malayan bananas.
British Medical Association, Malay Branch, Journal,
3 (1939): 156-161.

Leong, P. C. Vitamin "A" content of Malayan foods.
British Medical Association, Malay Branch, Journal,
3 (1939): 219-228.

Leong, P. C. Nutrition bibliography of Malaya. Honolulu,
1952. 23 p.

Lim, Tay-boh. The planning of social security in
Malaya. MER, 1 (June 1956): 25-36.

Mair, Lucy Philip. Welfare in the British colonies.
London, 1944. 115 p.
For Malaya, see pp. 14-18 for background to
social policy, pp. 61-64 for labor, and pp. 92-93
for health.

Malaya, Chief Registration Office. Report of the Registrar-General on population, births, deaths, marriages, and adoptions for the year 1956. Kuala Lumpur, 1958. 62 p.

Malaya, Institute for Medical Research. Annual report of the Institute for Medical Research for . . . Kuala Lumpur.
Each report contains a list of publications published by members of the institute.

Malaya, Malaria Advisory Board. Annual report of the Malaria Advisory Board for the year . . . Kuala Lumpur.

Malaysia, Department of Social Welfare. Social welfare officer's kampong living experience in Kedah, 20th February to 1st March, 1967. Kuala Lumpur, Department of Social Welfare, 1967. 115 p. Maps. Mimeo.

Malaysia, Department of Social Welfare. Social welfare officer's living experience in F.L.D.A. [Federal Land Development Authority] Schemes 8th April to 6th May 1967. Kuala Lumpur, Department of Social Welfare [1967]. 353 p. Map, tables. Mimeo.

Malaysia, Ministry of Health, Division of Medical Records and Health Statistics. Statistics on health matters, West Malaysia. Report no. 1. October, 1966. 46 p. Tables. Mimeo.

Maxwell, W. E. Senna. JRASSB Notes and Queries, 4 (1887): 116-118.
Senna is a curative drug.

Maxwell, W. G. Some problems of education and public health in Malaya. United Empire, 18 (1927): 206-219.

Morland, A. Tuberculosis in Malaya. Tubercle, 31 (1950): 38 p.

Noone, R. O. Nutritional aspects of the preparations of the hill paddy among the Tĕmiar Senoi. BRM, ser. B, 4 (1949): 8-10.

Purcell, Victor. Social and medical survey. Fédération de Malaisie et de Singapore. Civilisations, 8 (1958): 631-634.

Reed, J. G. Notes on nutrition for estates. Kuala
     Lumpur, 1938.

Reid, J. A. Some new records of anopheline mosquitoes
     from the Malay Peninsula with remarks on geographical
     distribution. BRM, 21 (1950): 48-58.

Ridley, H. N. On the use of the slow loris in Malay
     medicine. JRASSB, 34 (1900): 31-34.

Russell, P. F. The Straits Settlements rural sanitation
     campaign. Mal Med Jl, 4 (1929): 79-83.

Sandosham, Arthur Anantharaj. Malariology, with
     special reference to Malaya. 2d ed. Singapore,
     1965. 327 p. Bibliog., illus., map, col. plates,
     tables.

Sansom, C. L. Notes on tropical hygiene and plantation
     work and the anti-malarial campaign in the Federated
     Malay States. Int Cong Trop Ag, 3, 1 (1914): 83-94.

Simmons, James S., et al. Global epidemiology. A
     geography of disease and sanitation. V. 1. Philadelphia,
     1944. P. 154-174 deal with Malaya.

Simpson, I. A., A.-Y. Chow, and C.-C. Soh. A study
     of the nutritional value of some varieties of
     Malayan rice. Kuala Lumpur, 1954. (Institute
     for Medical Research Bulletin, n.s., no. 5)

Singapore, Colony. Report on the registrar of births
     and deaths, marriages and persons for 1955 and
     1956. Singapore, 1958. 83 p.

Thomson, Florence A. Child nutrition: a survey in
     the Parit district of Perak, 1957. Kuala Lumpur, 1960.

Thomson, Florence A. The health of the Malayan child.
     [From] Planters' Association of Malaya, Annual
     Report, 1961. 4 p. Mimeo.

Thomson, Florence A. The birth weight of babies
     in the Federation of Malaya; effect of race and
     economic change. Journal of Tropical Pediatrics
     and African Child Health, 8 (1962): 3-9. Graphs,
     tables.

Thomson, Florence A. Food, nutrition and Malayan agricultural diversification. Mal Ag, 3 (1962): 22ff.

Thomson, Florence A. The impact of culture on birth rate and population increase in the Federation of Malaya. Paper for Seventh International Conference on Planned Parenthood, Singapore, February 1963. 8 p. Mimeo.

Thomson, Florence A., E. Ruiz, and M. Bakar. Vitamin A and protein deficiency in Malayan children. Trans R Soc Med Hyg, 58 (1964): 425ff.

United States, Interdepartmental Committee on Nutrition for National Defence. Report on a nutrition survey of the Federation of Malaya, September-October, 1962. Washington, D.C., 1964. 355 p.

Vickers, W. J., and J. H. Strahan. A health survey of the State of Kedah with special reference to rice field malaria, nutrition and water supply, 1935-1936. Kuala Lumpur, 1936.

Watson, Malcolm. Cost of disease in the tropics. Rubber Industry Bulletin (1914): 153-160.

Watson, Malcolm. Rural sanitation in the tropics; being notes and observations in the Malay Archipelago, Panama and other lands. London, 1915. 320 p.

Watson, Malcolm. The prevention of malaria in the Federated Malay States. A record of twenty years progress. 2d ed. With contributions by B. S. Hunter, A. R. Wellington, and Sir Ronald Ross. London, 1921. 408 p.

Watson, Malcolm. Twenty-five years of malaria control in the Malay Peninsula, 1901-1926. Br Mal, 1 (1927): 245-250.

Wharton, Clifton R., Jr. Food consumption and nutritional levels in Malaya: some income, locational, and racial aspects. Council on Economic and Cultural Affairs. Malayan Series, no. 2B. November 1962.

H. EDUCATION

Abdul Aziz bin Shaik Mydin. Library provision for
Malay studies in the University of Malaya. Malayan
Library Journal, 3 (1962): 23-28.

Abdul Rashid bin Ismail. School and teachers' training
college libraries: recent developments. Perpustakaan
Malaysia, 1 (June 1965): 35-41.

Arun, K. C., and G. D. Ness. Values of youth in
the Federation of Malaya. International Journal
of Adult and Youth Education, 16 (1964): 114-119.

Barnes, L. J. Report of the Committee on Malay Education.
Kuala Lumpur, 1951. 88 p. Charts, tables.

Butwell, Richard. A Chinese university for Malaya.
PA, 26 (1953): 244-248.

Carr-Saunders, Alexander. Report of the Commission
on University Education in Malay. Kuala Lumpur,
1948. 150 p.

Central Advisory Committee on Education, Federation
of Malaya. Report on the Barnes Report on Malay
Education and the Fenn-Wu Report on Chinese Education.
Kuala Lumpur, 1951. 8 p.

Chang, Min-kee. The national education system of
Malaya; its policy and structure. UMBCER, 3,
1 (1967): 28-33.

Cheeseman, H. R. Compulsory education in Malaya.
Overseas Ed, 3 (1932): 18-22.

Cheeseman, H. R. Education in Malaya, 1900-1941.
MHJ, 2, 1 (1955): 30-47.

Chelliah, David D. A history of the educational
policy of the Straits Settlements with recommendations
for a new system based on vernaculars. 2d ed.
Singapore, 1960.

Cooke, D. F. Some aspects of the history of the
mission schools in Malaya, with special reference
to the development of the grants-in-aid system.
1963. M.A. thesis -- London.

Copley, J. English as the teaching medium in the
University of Malaya. Univ Q, 8 (1954): 265-270.

Dussek, O. T. The preparation and work of rural
    school teachers in Malaya. Overseas Ed, 1 (1930): 37-44.

Education in the Malayan union. Col Rev, 5 (1948): 148-149.

Education for resettlement villages in Malaya. Col
    Rev, 7 (1952): 205-206.

Enloe, Cynthia H. Issues and integration in Malaysia.
    PA, 41, 3 (1968): 372-385.

Entwisle, A. R. Adult education in the Federation
    of Malaya. Community Development Bulletin, 55
    (1953): 53-55.

Fenn, William, and Wu Teh-yao. Chinese schools and
    the education of Chinese Malayans. Report of
    a mission invited by the Federation Government
    to study the problem of the education of Chinese
    in Malaya. Kuala Lumpur, 1951. 42 p. (Legislative
    Council Paper, no. 35)

Firth, Raymond. Report on social science research
    in Malaya. Singapore, 1948. 51 p.

Franke, E. Problems of Chinese education in Singapore
    and Malaya. Malaysian Journal of Education, 2
    (Dec. 1965): 182-191.

Furnivall, J. S. Educational progress in Southeast
    Asia. New York, 1943. 185 p.

Future development and site of the University of
    Malaya. Kuala Lumpur, 1953. (Legislative Council
    Paper, no. 87)

Garner, N. The origin and development of the secondary
    continuation schools of the Federation of Malaya,
    1961-1964. Liverpool, 1964. M. Ed. thesis.

Great Britain, Commission on Higher Education in
    Malaya. Higher education in Malaya. Report of
    commission appointed by the Secretary of State
    for the Colonies. London, 1939. 151 p. (Colonial
    Office Publication, no. 173) Illus., plan.

Gwee, Yee-hean. Education and the multi-racial society. In
    Ooi Jin-bee and Chiang Hai-ding, eds. Modern Singapore.
    Singapore, University of Singapore Press, 1969: 208-215.

Ho, Seng-ong. Education for unity in Malaya, an
  evaluation of the educational system of Malaya
  with special reference to the need for unity
  in its plural society. Penang, 1952. 209 p.
  (Malayan Educator Series, v. 1)

Kanapathy, V. Education, manpower and Malaysian
  economic development. UMBCER, 2, 2 (1967): 8-27.

Kuala Kangsar, Malay College. Malay College, 1905-1965,
  past and present. [Singapore, 1965?]. 159 p. Illus.

Lepage, R. B. Multilingualism in Malaya. In Symposium
  on Multilingualism, Brazzaville, Congo, 1962.
  Colloque sur le Multilinguisme; deuxième réunion
  du Comité Interafricain de Linguistique . . .
  [London], published under the sponsorship of
  the Committee for Technical Co-operation in Africa
  [1964]: 133-146.

Lewis, G. E. D. A comparative study of the intelligence
  and educability of Malays and Chinese in Malaya.
  1948. 264 p. Ph.D. thesis -- University of London.
  Appendices, tables.

Loh, Philip. The beginnings of higher education
  in Singapore: Raffles College 1928-1938. MH,
  9, 1-2 (1965): 9-17.

Maclusky, D. S. Agricultural education in Malaysia
  and America. Mal Ag, 5 (1964/1965): 89-95.

Malaysia. Report of the Higher Education Planning
  Committee. Kuala Lumpur, 1967. 306 p. Tables.
  [English version] p. 157-306. [Malay version] p. 1-156.

Malaysia, Ministry of Agriculture and Cooperatives.
  Revised working papers: National Training Centre
  for the Teaching of Agriculture, organised by
  the Ministry of Agriculture and Cooperatives
  and the Food and Agriculture Organization of
  the United Nations, Serdang, March 1967. [Kuala
  Lumpur] the Ministry, 1967. Various pagings,
  diagrs., tables.

Malaysia, Ministry of Education. Educational statistics
  of Malaysia 1938 to 1967. Prepared by the Educational
  Planning and Research Division, Ministry of Education.
  Kuala Lumpur, 1968. 157 p. Graphs, tables.

Mann, G. E. The school of agriculture, Malaya. Mal
    Ag Jl, 27 (1939): 390-398.

Mansor bin Othman. Mara: its role in education and
    development of attitudes. A case study. Kuala
    Lumpur, Malaysian Centre for Development Studies
    [n.d.].

Markandan, Paul S. Higher education in Malaya. Eastern
    World, 8, 3 (1954): 17-18.

Mason, Frederic. The University of Malaya; a study
    in the transmission of culture pattern. Civilisations,
    5 (1955): 363-367.

Mason, Frederic. The schools of Malaya. Rev. ed.
    Singapore, 1957. 39 p.

Maxwell, W. E. Problems of education and public
    health in Malaya. United Empire, 18 (1927): 206-219.

Nagle, J. S. Educational needs of the Straits Settlements
    and Federated Malay States. Baltimore, Johns
    Hopkins University, 1928. A dissertation submitted
    to the Board of University in conformity with
    the requirements for the Degree of Doctor of
    Philosophy, 1926.

Orata, Pedro T. Malaya headed for universal compulsory
    education. Philippine Journal of Education, 32
    (1954): 651-655.

Purcell, Victor. The crisis in Malayan education.
    PA, 26 (1953): 70-76.

Roff, Margaret. The politics of language in Malaya.
    AS, 7, 5 (1967): 316-328.

Singapore, Commission of Enquiry into Education.
    Final Report. Lim Tay-boh, chairman. Singapore,
    Government Printer, 1964.

Spector, Stanley. Students and politics in Singapore.
    FES, 25 (May 1956): 65-73.

Sutcliffe, G. A history of education in Negri Sembilan.
    1961. Ph.D. thesis (London School of Economics)
    -- London.

Vine, J. M. Public health administration and education
and training survey in the Federation of Malaya.
World Health Organisation, 1961. 98 p. Mimeo.

Wijeysingha, Eugene. A history of Raffles Institution
1823-1963. Singapore, 1963. 174 p. Photo illus.

Winstedt, Richard O. Educational system of Malaya.
In Educational Yearbook of the International
Institute of Teachers College, Columbia University,
1931. New York, 1932: 79-140.

Wong, H. K. Education and problems of nationhood.
In Wang Gung-wu. Malaysia: A Survey. London,
1964: 199-209.

Wulff, K. Fra Malajstaterne. G Tid, 29 (1926): 93-98.
Description of the Malay college at Kuala Kangsar,
Perak, its aims, its scope and general character.

Wyndham, H. A. Native education. Ceylon, Java, Formosa,
Philippines, French Indo-China, and British Malaya.
London, 1933. 264 p. Map.

Yip, Weng-kee. The occupational choices of English-medium
secondary school-leavers in relation to education
and vocational opportunity. 1965. M. Ed. thesis
-- Singapore.

Zainal-'Abidin bin Ahmad. The problem of higher
education in Malaya. Asian Horizon, 1, 3 (1948):
23-29.

Zainal Abidin Wahid. Problems of Malay--medium education.
Opinion, 1, 6 (1968): 72-74.

I. SETTLEMENT PATTERN

1. Rural

Abdul Aziz bin Mohd. Yassin, Ungku. Economic survey
of five villages in Nyalas, Malacca. Kuala Lumpur,
Rural and Industrial Development Authority, 1957.
Mimeo.

Agarwal, M. C. Some agro-economic aspects of land
    settlement in the FLDA financed schemes. Staff
    seminar paper, University of Malaya. Kuala Lumpur,
    1962.

Alexander, J. B. The evolution of land suitability
    maps used for planning rural development in the
    Federation of Malaya. Federation of Malaya, Ministry
    of Rural Development, March 1962. Also published
    in JTG, 18 (1964): 1-6.

Alliance Party of Malaya. We the Alliance; results
    in rural development. [Kuala Lumpur, 1964?].
    25 p. Illus.

Andy, J. R. Some ecological effects of deforestation
    and settlement. Mal Nature Jl, 3 (1948): 178-189.

Burridge, K. O. L. Rural administration in Johore.
    Jl Af Ad, 9, 1 (1957): 29-36.

Burridge, Kenelm O. L. Managerial influences in
    a Johore village. JRASMB, 30, 1 (1957 [i.e. 1962]):
    75-92.

Corry, W. C. S. A general survey of new villages.
    Kuala Lumpur, 1954.

Dawson, S. R. Resettlement in Malaya: the new villages
    described. Malaya, 1 (1952): 35-37.

Degani, Amina H. The land development authority.
    MER, 9, 2 (1964): 75-82.

Dobby, E. H. G. Settlement and land utilization,
    Malacca. G Jl, 94 (1939): 466-478.

Dobby, E. H. G. Settlement patterns in Malaya. GR,
    32 (1942): 211-232. Maps, plates.

Dobby, E. H. G. Resettlement transforms Malaya.
    EDCC, 1 (1952): 163-189.

Dobby, E. H. G. Recent settlement changes in South
    Malaya. MJTG, 1 (1953): 1-8. Maps.

Dow, Maynard Weston. Nation building in Southeast
    Asia. Boulder, Colorado, 1965. 279 p.
    Chapter 2, "The new villages and jungle forts
    of the Malayan emergency," pp. 17-87. Bibliog.
    on Malaya, pp. 249-254.

Downs, R. E. A rural community in Kelantan, Malaya. In Robert K. Sakai, ed. Studies on Asia. University of Nebraska, 1960: 51-62.

Federation of Malaya. Committee appointed by H. E. the High Commissioner to investigate the squatter problem: report. Kuala Lumpur, 1949.

Ferguson, D. S. The Sungei Manik irrigation scheme. MJTG, 2 (1954): 9-16.

Fiennes, D. E. M. Report on Rural and Industrial Development Authority 1950-1955. Kuala Lumpur, 1956.

Fiennes, D. E. M. The Malayan Federal Land Development Authority. Journal of Local Administration Overseas, 1, 3 (1962): 156-163.

Firth, R. W. The peasants of Southeast Asia. Inter Aff, 26 (1950): 503-514.

Fleming, J. R. Experiment in democracy; the new villages in Malaya. Int Rev Missions, 45 (1956): 101-108.

Hamzah bin Sendut. Rasah: a resettlement village in Malaya. AS, 1, 9 (1961): 21-26.

Hamzah bin Sendut. The resettlement villages in Malaya. G, 47, 1 (1962): 41-46.

Hamzah bin Sendut. Planning resettlement villages in Malaya. Planning Outlook, n.s., 1 (1966): 58-70.

Hands, John. Malay agricultural settlement Kuala Lumpur: a short history. MHJ, 2, 2 (1955): 146-162.

Hanna, Willard A. Regional development in Malaya, Part III, Bukit Tembaga: a land development project. New York, American Universities Field Staff, 1960. (American Universities Field Staff, Reports Service, Southeast Asia Series, 8, 13 (June 1960), WAH-13-60)

Herrlich, A. Schweizer Pfahlbau und Malaiensiedlung: Eine kulturmorphologische Betrachtung. Erdball, 5 (1931): 143-145. Illus.

Hill, R. D. Comments on the "Land Development Authority: an economic necessity?" MER, 10, 1 (1965): 116-121.

Ho, Robert. Land settlement projects in Malaya: an assessment of the rule of the Federal Land Development Authority. JTG, 20 (1965): 1-15.

King, J. K. Malaya's resettlement problem. FES, 23 (1954): 33-40.

Kühne, Dietrich. New villages, new towns and rural development in Malaya. Erde, 100, 2-4 (1969): 348-358. In German.

Lau, Y. S., and C. I. Fan. Investigations for the Sungei Buaya, Federal Land Development Scheme. JTAM, 13 (Apr. 1965): 36-47.

Lee, Y. L. Kukup, a Chinese fishing village in South West Malaya. JTG, 16 (1962): 131-148.

Malaya, Federal Land Development Authority. No need to be poor: a policy statement. Kuala Lumpur, 1956. 11 p.

Malaya, Federal Legislative Council. Report of the working party set up to consider the development of new areas for land settlement in the Federation of Malaya. 1956. (Legislative Council Paper, no. 11)

Malaya, Government Offices. Statistical information concerning new villages in the Federation of Malaya. Kuala Lumpur, 1952. (Government File, no. C.S. 6527/52) Mimeo.

Malayan Christian Council. A survey of the new villages in Malaya. Kuala Lumpur, 1958. Mimeo. Rev. ed. Kuala Lumpur, 1959. Mimeo.

Malaysia, Economic Planning Unit. Land capability classification report, Kuantan District, Pahang. Kuala Lumpur [Nov., 1965]. 15 p. Maps. Processed.
    Text in Malay and English. Malay title reads:
"Penyata penyama Pemetaan tanah daerah Kuantan, Pahang."

Malaysia, Economic Planning Unit. Land capability classification report, Bentong District, Pahang. Kuala Lumpur [Dec. 1965]. 17 p. Maps. Mimeo.
    Text in Malay and English. Malay title reads:
"Penyata penyama pemetaan tanah daerah Betong, Pahang."

Malaysia, Economic Planning Unit. Land capability
   classification report, Temerloh District, Pahang.
   Kuala Lumpur [April 1966]. 17 p. Maps. Mimeo.
   Text in Malay and English. Malay title reads:
   "Penyata penyama pemetaan tanah daerah Temerloh Pahang."

Malaysia, Economic Planning Unit. Land capability
   classification report, Pekan District Pahang.
   Kuala Lumpur [July 1966]. 18 p. Maps. Processed.
   Text in Malay and English. Malay title reads:
   "Penyata penyama pemetaan tanah daerah Pekan, Pahang."

Malaysia, Economic Planning Unit. Land capability
   classification report, Cameron Highlands District,
   Pahang. Kuala Lumpur [Aug. 1966]. 15 p. Maps.
   Processed.
   Text in Malay and English. Malay title reads:
   "Penyata penyama pemetaan tanah daerah Cameron
   Highlands, Pahang."

Malaysia, Economic Planning Unit. Land capability
   classification report, Raub District, Pahang.
   Kuala Lumpur [Aug 1966]. 16 p. Maps. Processed.
   Text in Malay and English. Malay title reads:
   "Penyata penyama pemetaan tanah daerah Raub, Pahang."

Malaysia, Economic Planning Unit. Land capability
   classification report, Lipis District, Pahang.
   Kuala Lumpur [Nov. 1966]. 18 p. Maps. Processed.
   Text in Malay and English. Malay title reads:
   "Penyata penyama pemetaan tanah daerah Lipis, Pahang."

Malaysia, Economic Planning Unit. Land capability
   classification report, Jerantut District, Pahang.
   Kuala Lumpur [Dec. 1966]. 18 p. Maps. Processed.
   Text in Malay and English. Malay title reads:
   "Penyata penyama pemetaan tanah daerah Jerantut, Pahang."

Malaysia, Economic Planning Unit. Report on location
   of land suitable for long-term large-scale settlement
   and agricultural development. Kuala Lumpur,
   1966. 13 p. Maps. Mimeo.

Malaysia, Economic Planning Unit. Land capability
   classification in West Malaysia: an explanatory
   handbook. Prepared by the Natural Resource Capability
   Section of the Economic Planning Unit, under
   the direction of the technical sub-committee
   on land capability classification of the National
   Development Planning Committee. Kuala Lumpur, 1967.
   11 p.

Malaysia, Federal Land Development Authority. Land
development in Malaya; Temerloh--Maran--Jerantut
(Jengka) Triangle, proposed land development
scheme by FLDA within the National Rural Development
Programme. 1962. 13 p. Illus., maps, tables. Processed.

Malaysia, Federal Land Development Authority. Land
settlement in Malaysia under the Federal Land
Development Authority. Kuala Lumpur, 1966. 46 p.
Mimeo.

Malaysia, Federal Land Development Authority. The
Jengka Triangle report. [Submitted by] Tippetts
- Abbett - McCarthy - Stratton [and] Hunting
Technical Services Limited. [Kuala Lumpur] 1967.
4 v. Diagrs., graphs, illus., maps, (part col.).
Contents--V. 1: The outline masterplan. V. 2:
Resources and development planning. V. 3: Appendices.
V. 4: Map annexe.

Malaysia, Federal Land Development Authority. A
review of the Federal Land Development Authority:
its policies and operations. Kuala Lumpur, 1969.
26 p. Mimeo.

Malaysia, Federal Land Development Authority. Annual
Report 1968. Kuala Lumpur, 1969. 53 p. Graphs,
photos., tables. Malay and English text.

Malaysia, Laws, Statutes, etc. National land code.
(Act 56 of 1965). Kuala Lumpur, 1965. 316 p.

Markandan, Paul S. Resettlement and the emergency
in Malaya. Eastern World, 7 (1953): 14-16.

Markandan, Paul S. The problems of the new villages
in Malaya. Singapore, 1954.

McMinnies, M. Operation in Johore. New Statesman,
47 (1954): 215-216.

Missen, G. J. The Malay village: two case-studies
of peasant economy. In J. Rutherford, M. I.
Logan, and G. J. Missen. New Viewpoints in Economic
Geography. Sydney, 1966: 115-136. Maps.

Ness, Gayl D. Bureaucracy and rural development
in Malaysia; a study of complex organizations
in stimulating economic development in new states.
Berkeley, 1967. 257 p. Maps.

Ness, Gayl D. Models of rural development administration: The Malaysian Ministry for Rural Development. New York, Southeast Asia Development Advisory Group, Rural Development Seminar, Asia House, 1967. 7 p. Mimeo.

Noh, Toshio. Ethnographic constitution of cultural landscape in rural settlements of Malay Peninsula. Jl G, Tokyo G Soc, 60 (1951): 179-181.

Pelzer, Karl J. Resettlement in Malaya. Yale Review, 41 (1952): 391-404.

Resettlement and the development of new villages in the Federation of Malaya. Kuala Lumpur, 1952. 20 p. (Legislative Council Paper, no. 33)

Robertson, V. C. Settlers in the rain forest [Jengka, Malaysia]. GM, 40, 12 (1968): 1049-1057. Map.

Robinson, J. B. P. Transformation in Malaya. London, 1955. 232 p. Map.
    Informative on resettlement and the New Villages, contained in Chapter II, "Resettlement and the Chinese Community."

Sandhu, Kernial Singh. Emergency resettlement in Malaya. JTG, 18 (1964): 157-183. Figs., illus., maps, tables.

Sandhu, Kernial Singh. The saga of the squatter in Malaya. JSAH, 5 (1964): 143-177. Illus., maps.

Shamsul Bahrin bin Raja Muhammad Ali, Tunku. A preliminary study of the Fringe Alienation Schemes in West Malaysia. JTG, 28 (June 1969): 75-83.

Singh, S. An evaluation of three land development schemes in Malaysia. MER, 13, 1 (1968): 89-100.

Squatter problem in the Federation of Malaya. Kuala Lumpur, 1950. 16 p. (Legislative Council Paper, no. 14)

Stead, R. The "new villages" in Malaya. GM, 27 (1955): 642-652.

A study of the settlement structure in the regional
plan for the major rural housing scheme in the
Jengka Triangle, State of Pahang, West Malaysia.
Paper presented at the Inter-Regional Seminar
for Rural Housing and Community Facilities in
Maracay, Venezuela. April 2nd-19th, 1967. Federal
Department of Town and Country Planning, Kuala Lumpur.

Taib bin Haji Andak, Tan Sri. Smallholders and
the Federal Land Development Authority. In Yun-khong
Seah. Development Seminar Sponsored by Commonwealth
Development Corporation. Kuching, 1964.

Taib bin Haji Andak, Tan Sri. The work of the Federal
Land Development Authority. Kuala Lumpur, 1964.
20 p. Tables. Mimeo.

Taib bin Haji Andak, Tan Sri. Land development
in Malaysia under the Federal Land Development
Authority; description of programme and techniques
of development implementation. In Development
Seminar. 1st. Kuala Lumpur, November 1966.

Tamil land settlements. Mal Ag Jl, 26 (1938): 448-450.

Tiga segi Jengka. Berita Mara, 2, 1 (1968): 35-45.

Weatherford, W. D. The rural development programme
in the Federation of Malaya; designed to gain
the participation of village people. Prepared
for the Government of the Federation of Malaya
by W. D. Weatherford, appointed with the U.N.
programme of technical assistance. Kuala Lumpur,
1960. 26 p. Tables. Mimeo.

Webber, M. L. Resettlement. Mal For, 14 (1951): 155-157.

Wikkramatileke, R. Mukim Pulau Rusa: land use in
a Malayan riverine settlement. JTG, 11 (1958): 1-31.

Wikkramatileke, R. A study of planned land settlement
in the eastern marshlands of Malaya. Ec G, 38,
4 (1962): 330-346.

Wikkramatileke, R. Trends in settlement and economic
development in eastern Malaya; a study of mukims
Padang Endau and Triang. PV, 3, 1 (1962): 27-50.
Illus., maps, tables.

Wikkramatileke, R. State aided rural land colonization
   in Malaya: an appraisal of the F.L.D.A. program.
   Annals, 55, 3 (1965): 377-403. Map.

Wilson, Peter J. A Malay village and Malaysia:
   social values and rural development. New Haven,
   1967. 171 p. Bibliog., glossary, index, maps,
   tables.

Wolters, O. W. Emergency resettlement and community
   development in Malaya. Community Development
   Bulletin, 3, 1 (1951): 1-8.

2. Urban

Activities of the Malayan housing trust. Ekistics,
   14, 81 (1962): 34-36.

Bellett, J. The Singapore central business district
   and its urban setting; a geographical study.
   Singapore, 1964. M.S. thesis.

Bellett, J. Singapore's central area retail pattern
   in transition. JTG, 28 (June 1969): 1-16.

Bennet, W. J. Kuala Lumpur: a town of the equatorial
   lowlands. TESG, 52, 12 (1961): 327-333.

Buchler, W. Town-planning in Singapore. Garden
   Cities and Town Planning, 21 (1931): 228-231.
   Illus.

Caldwell, J. Urban growth in Malaya: trends and
   implications. Population Review, 7, 1 (1963):
   39-50.

Chia, Gek-sim. A study of an urban community in
   Malaysia. 1967. Thesis (Department of Geography)
   -- University of Malaya.

Cho, George. The geographical setting of urban
   areas in western Malaysia. Geographica, 3 (1966):
   50-59.

Choe, Alan F. C. Urban renewal. In Ooi Jin-bee
and Chiang Hai-ding, eds. Modern Singapore.
Singapore, University of Singapore Press, 1969:
161-170.

Chong, Seck-chim. The development of Kuala Lumpur
district. MJTG, 3 (1954): 48-50.

Chua, Peng-chye. Singapore's second master plan.
JTAM, 14, 3 (1966): 4-7.

Concannon, T. A. L. A new town in Malaya. MJTG,
5 (March 1955): 39-43.

Concannon, T. A. L. Town planning in Malaya. Town
Planning Institute Journal, 44 (1958): 241-244.

Concannon, T. A. L. Petaling Jaya: a new town in
Malaya. In Hamzah Sendut, comp. Urban Development
in Southeast Asia. V. 3. Kuala Lumpur [1968]: 427-435.

Cooper, Eunice. Urbanization in Malaya. Population
Studies, 5, 2 (1951): 117-131. Tables.

Daroesman, R. Singapore sample household survey.
Report No. 2--Administrative report. Singapore.
(To be published as Survey Publication Series,
no. 2) Joint publication of Ministry of National
Development and Economic Research Centre.

Davies, D. Changing Kuala Lumpur. MH, 5, 2 (1959):
26-32.

Fraser, James M. Town planning and housing in Singapore.
Town Planning Review, 23 (1953): 5-25.

Fryer, Donald W. Megalopolis or Tyrannopolis in
Southeast Asia? New York, Southeast Asia Development
Advisory Group, Urban Development Seminar, Asia
House, 1968. 6 p. Mimeo.

Ginsburg, N. The great city in Southeast Asia.
Am Jl Sociol (1955): 455-462.

Goh, Keng-swee. Urban incomes and housing; a report
on the social survey of Singapore, 1953-54.
Singapore, Department of Social Welfare, 1956.
215 p.

Gonen, Amiram. Changing patterns of urbanization in Malaya, 1931-1957. 1960. Unpublished Master's thesis (Department of Geography) -- Syracuse University.

The greatest housing problem of the world, survey of housing conditions in South and South East Asia. UNB, 11 (1951): 39-40.

Hamzah bin Sendut. Town-size distribution in Malaya. Kuala Lumpur [n.d.]. 13 p. Mimeo.

Hamzah bin Sendut. Patterns of urbanization in Malaya. JTG, 16 (1962): 114-130. Charts, maps, tables. Reprinted, minus maps and tables, in Geographica, 1 (1964-1965): 31-54 and in Ekistics (1964).

Hamzah bin Sendut. Urbanization [of Malaysia]. In Wang Gung-wu. Malaysia: A Survey. London, 1964: 82-96.

Hamzah bin Sendut. Aspects of urbanisation in Malaysia. Hemisphere, 9, 5 (1965): 8-12. Illus.

Hamzah bin Sendut. Some aspects of administration for town and country planning. JTAM, 13 (Apr. 1965): 11-14.

Hamzah bin Sendut. Some aspects of urban change in Malaya 1931-1957. KEM, 2, 1 (1965): 87-103.

Hamzah bin Sendut. Statistical distribution of cities in Malaysia. KEM, 2, 2 (1965): 49-66.

Hamzah bin Sendut. The structure of Kuala Lumpur. Town Planning Review, 36, 2 (1965): 125-138. Reprinted in JTAM (1966).

Hamzah bin Sendut. City-size distributions of Southeast Asia. Asian Studies, 4, 2 (1966): 268-280.

Hamzah bin Sendut. Contemporary urbanization in Malaysia. AS, 6, 9 (1966): 484-491. Tables.

Hamzah bin Sendut. The impact of urban development and rural areas in Singapore. In Hamzah Sendut, comp. Urban Development in Southeast Asia. V. 4. Kuala Lumpur [1968]: 794-807.

Hamzah bin Sendut, comp. Urban development in Southeast
Asia. Kuala Lumpur [1968]. 4 v. (1) 1-161 p.
(2) 162-380 p. (3) 381-611 p. (4) 612-807 p.
(For private distribution only).
Includes 15 previously published papers dealing
with Malaya.

Hanna, Willard A. Kuala Lumpur: an amalgam of tin,
rubber and races: a brief review of the city's
history, physical, and psychological development.
New York, American Universities Field Staff,
1959. 23 p. (American Universities Field Staff,
Reports Service, Southeast Asia Series, WAH-8-59)
Illus.

Jenssen, Rolf. Planning urban renewal, and housing
in Singapore. Town Planning Review, 38, 2 (1967):
115-131.

Kuala Lumpur, Municipal Council. Kuala Lumpur 100
years. [Kuala Lumpur] 1959. 119 p. Illus.

Lam, Timothy Thim-fook. Policy for flat development
in urban areas. Town Planning Institute Newsletter,
2, 5 (Singapore, Dec. 1965). Reprinted in JTAM
(Oct.-Dec. 1965).

Lam, Timothy Thim-fook. The geographer and town
and country planning. Geographica, 2 (1966).

Lam, Timothy Thim-fook. A critique of the new master
plan of Kuala Lumpur. Geographica, 3 (1967): 60-65.

Lim, C. Geographical influences in planning for
urban Penang. 1954/1955. M.A. thesis -- University
of Singapore.

Macdonald, M. Malacca buildings. JRASMB, 12, 2
(1934): 27-37. Plates.

McGee, T. G. The cultural role of cities: a case
study of Kuala Lumpur. JTG, 17 (1963): 178-196.

McGee, T. G. The Southeast Asian city. A social
geography of the primate cities of Southeast
Asia. London, New York, 1967. 204 p. Maps.

McGee, T. G., and W. D. McTaggert. Petaling Jaya:
a socio-economic survey of a new town in Selangor,
Malaysia. Wellington, 1967. 52 p. (PV Monograph, no. 2)

McTaggert, W. D. The grading of social areas in
Georgetown, Penang. JTG, 23 (1966): 40-46.

McTaggert, W. D. Social survey of Penang. City
Council of Georgetown, City Hall, Penang, 1966.
35 p. Maps.

Missen, G. J. The big city in Malaya; a study of
Kuala Lumpur, capital of a new nation. In J.
Rutherford, M. I. Logan, and G. J. Missen. New
Viewpoints in Economic Geography. Sydney, 1966:
394-414. Maps.

Neville, R. J. W. An urban study of Pontian Kechil,
South-West Malaysia. JTG, 16 (1962): 32-56.
Maps, photographs, tables.

Newcombe, Vernon Z. Housing in the Federation of
Malaya. Town Planning Review, 27 (1956): 4-20.

Reade, Charles C. Town planning and development
in the Federated Malay States. Preliminary report
and general survey. Kuala Lumpur, 1922.

Singapore. Master plan for Singapore, 1958. Singapore,
1958. 58 p. Maps.

Singapore Planning and Urban Research Group. SPUR
1965/67. Singapore [n.d.]. 62 p. Illus.

Tan, Lam-lin. The regional influence of Kuala Lumpur.
Geographica, 2 (1966): 3 p. Maps.

Tan, Soo-hai. Case study of a squatter area in
Kuala Lumpur. JTAM, 13 (1965): 27-32.

Tan, Soo-hai. Urbanization in Malaya. JTAM, 14,
3 (1966): 8-12.

Teh, Cheang-wan. Public housing. In Ooi Jin-bee
and Chiang Hai-ding, eds. Modern Singapore.
Singapore, University of Singapore Press, 1969:
171-180.

Tsou, Pao-chun. Urban landscape of Kuala Lumpur.
A geographical survey. Institute of Southeast
Asia, Nanyang University, 1967. 68 p.

Tsou, Pao-chun. Kuala Lumpur. GM, 40, 10 (1968):
843-849. Maps.

Ullman, Edward L. The primate city and urbanization
in Southeast Asia. A preliminary speculation.
New York, Southeast Asia Development Advisory
Group, Urban Development Seminar, Asia House,
1968. 8 p. Mimeo.

Yeh, Stephen H. K., and Lee Yoke-san. Housing conditions
in Singapore. MER, 13 (1968): 11-38.

You, Poh-seng. Housing survey of Singapore, 1955.
MER, 2 (1957): 54-74.

You, Poh-seng, Stephen H. K. Yeh, Ng Kim-neo, and
Lee Yoke-san. Singapore sample household survey.
Report no. 1--Tables relating to population
and housing. Singapore, 1967. 302 p. (Survey
Publication Series, no. 1) Joint publication
of Ministry of National Development and Economic
Research Centre.

CHAPTER 10

ECONOMY

A. GENERAL

Abdul Aziz bin Abdul Hamid, Ungku. Economic survey
of five villages in Nyalas, Malacca. Kuala Lumpur,
University of Malaya Economics Department, 1957.

Abdul Aziz bin Abdul Hamid, Ungku. Facts and fallacies
about Malayan economy. Singapore, University
of Singapore, 1957.
This was published as a series of four articles
by the Straits Times, Singapore, on February
28 and March 1, 4, and 5, 1957.

Abdul Aziz bin Abdul Hamid, Ungku. Some aspects
of the Malayan rural economy related to measures
for mobilizing rural savings. Kuala Lumpur, Department
of Economics, University of Malaya, 1958. 9 p.
Tables. Mimeographed copy of a paper submitted
to the ECAFE Committee on Industry and Trade,
1951.

Abdul Aziz bin Abdul Hamid, Ungku. The interdependent
development of agriculture and other industries.
MER, 4, 1 (1959): 21-32.

Abdul Aziz bin Abdul Hamid, Ungku. Poverty and rural
development in Malaysia. KEM, 1, 1 (1964): 70-96.

Abdul Aziz bin Abdul Hamid, Ungku. Poverty, proteins
and disguised starvation. KEM, 2, 1 (1965): 7-48.

Abdul Aziz bin Abdul Hamid, Ungku. The role of the
Federal Agricultural Marketing Authority in the
development of agriculture in Malaysia. In Proceedings,
National Agriculture Marketing Seminar 13-18th
November, 1967. Kuala Lumpur, 1968: 66-74.

Abdul Majid. Cooperative movement amongst Malays.
Intisari, 1, 2 [n.d.]: 42-49.

Abdul Malek bin Hassan. Filasofah Mara dalam revolusi
pembangunan negera. Berita Mara, 1, 2 (1967): 10-13.

Abdul Razak bin Dato' Hussein, Tun. National development
with special emphasis on techniques of implementation.
KEM, 2, 2 (1965): 1-9.

Abdul Razak bin Dato' Hussein, Tun. Development
implementation in Malaysia. Kuala Lumpur, Government
Printer, 1966. 9 p.

Abdul Razak bin Dato' Hussein, Tun. Development
implementation in Malaysia. Malaysian Management
Review, 3, 1 (1968): 1-10.

Abdul Razak bin Dato' Hussein, Tun Haji. Planning
in Malaysia. In Conference on Development and
Cooperation in the South Asia Pacific Region,
Kuala Lumpur, Malaya, 1964. South Asia Pacific
Crisis; National Development and the World Community.
New York, 1964: 49-52.

Agarwal, M. C. Rural co-operative credit--a Malaysian
case study. KEM, 2, 2 (1965): 10-23.

Allen, G. C., and A. G. Donnithorne. Western enterprise
in Indonesia and Malaya: a study in economic
development. London, 1957. 320 p.

Aziz. See Abdul Aziz.

Balakrishnan, V. Protein shortage and animal industry.
Mal Ag, 4 (1963/1964): 67-73.

Barnard, Robert. Essentials of Malayan economy.
UA, 3 (1951): 196-198.

Barnett, H. L. A brief review of essential foodcrop
cultivation in Malaya. Mal Ag Jl, 30 (1947): 13-18.

Bassett, D. K. British commercial and strategic
interest in the Malay Peninsula during the late
eighteenth century. In John Bastin, ed. Malayan
and Indonesian Studies . . . Oxford, 1964: 122-140.
Map.

Beale, L. B. Review of the trade of British Malaya
in 1928. London, 1929. 90 p. (Great Britain Department
of Overseas Trade Publication)

Beaven, P. J. An engineering materials survey illustrated
by work in Malaysia. Paper presented at the First
South East Asian Conference on Foundation Engineering.
Bangkok, 1967.

Benham, Frederic Charles. Report on the trade of Penang. Kuala Lumpur, 1948.

Benham, Frederic Charles. The national income of Malaya, 1947-1949 (with a note on 1950). Singapore, 1951. 272 p.

Benham, Frederic Charles. Western enterprise in Indonesia and Malaya. MER, 2, 3 (1957): 43-52.

Benham, Frederic Charles. The national income of Singapore, 1956. London, 1959. 24 p. Charts, tables.

Benham, Frederic Charles. Economic survey, Singapore 1957. Singapore, 195?. 31 p.

Biggs, H. C. Report on the marketing of agricultural and other rural produce in Malaysia. Kuala Lumpur, 1964. 80 p.

Bilas, Richard A. Economic development of the Federation of Malaya, 1950-1960. 1962. Ph.D. thesis -- University of Virginia.

Bilas, Richard A. Growth of physical output in the Federation of Malaya: 1930-1960. MER, 8, 2 (1963): 81-90.

Blake, D. J. Patterns of Singapore's trade. MER, 13, 1 (1968): 39-69.

Bogaars, George. The effect of the openings of the Suez Canal on the trade and development of Singapore. JRASMB, 28, 1 (1955): 99-143. Bibliog., graphs, maps.

Bottomley, Anthony. The role of foreign branch plants in the industrialisation of Singapore. MER, 7, 1 (1962): 26-36.

Bottomley, Anthony. Some economic implications of the proposed Malaysia Federation from the point of view of Singapore. MER, 7, 2 (1962): 95-105.

Boulter, R. Economic conditions in Malaya to February 28, 1931. London, 1931. 66 p. (Great Britain Department of Overseas Trade Publication)

Briggs, Walter. Malaya's troubles have just begun. New Republic, 121, 5 (1949): 18-19.

Burridge, K. O. L. Managerial influences in a Johore
village. JRASMB, 25, 1 (1957): 93-114.

Butler, Harold. Problems of industry in the East,
with special reference to India, French Indochina,
Ceylon, Malaya and Netherlands Indies. Geneva,
1938. 74 p. (International Labour Office Studies
and Reports, Series B, no. 29)

Caine, Sir Sydney. Enterprise and capital in industrial
development. In Lim Tay-boh, ed. Problems of
the Malayan Economy. Singapore, 1957: 66-70.

Cant, R. G. Historical reasons for the retarded
development of Pahang State, eastern Malaya.
New Zealand Geographer, 21, 1 (1965): 26-37.
Map.

Carnell, F. G. The development of a middle class
in Burma, Thailand and Malaya. In International
Institute of Differing Civilisation. Development
of a Middle Class in Tropical and Sub-tropical
Countries. Record of XXIXth Session Held in London
from 13-16 Sept. 1955. Bruxelles, 1956: 271-279.

Carr-Gregg, John R. E. The Colombo Plan. A Commonwealth
Program for Southeast Asia. New York, 1951. 55 p.
(International Conciliation, no. 467)

Cator, G. E. Malaya: the first year. AR, 36 (1940):
751-757.

Chai, Hon-chan. The development of British Malaya,
1896-1909. Kuala Lumpur, 1964. 364 p. Bibliog.,
illus., maps.

Chalmers, W. E., and Pang Eng-fong. Industrial relations.
In Ooi Jin-bee and Chiang Hai-ding, eds. Modern
Singapore. Singapore, University of Singapore
Press, 1969: 109-126.

Chandran, J. Private enterprise and British policy
in the Malay Peninsula: the case of the Malay
Railway and Works Construction Company, 1893-1895.
JRASMB, 37, 2 (1964): 28-46.

Chen, S. J. A proposal to accelerate Malaysian economic
development through agricultural advancement.
UMBCER, 1, 1 (1965): 12-23.

Chen, S. J. Malaysia's international trade. UMBCER,
1, 2 (1965): 23-30.

Chik, Sir Louis. The economic development of Malaya.
Singapore, 1955.

Chou, K. R. The post-war trend of capital formation
in Malaya against the background of Southeast
Asia. 1955. Ph.D. thesis (London School of Economics)
-- London.

Chou, K. R. Saving and investment in Malaya (including
Singapore). [Hong Kong] 1966. 178 p.

Chow, Swee-ming. The cooperative movement amongst
the new villages in the Federation of Malaya.
Kuala Lumpur, Office of the Chinese Cooperative
Officer, 1961. (Government File, no. 926/52/30)
Mimeo.

Chu, Esme Yun-yun. Economic development in Malaya:
the problem in a plural society. Cambridge, Mass.,
1954. 272 p. Thesis (Ph.D.) -- Radcliffe College,
Harvard University. Bibliog., map, tables.

Cohen, Jerome B. The Colombo Plan for Cooperative
Economic Development. Middle East Journal, 5,
1 (1951): 94-100.

The Colombo Plan. Labor Ind Brit, 8, 4 (1950): 167-176.
Map.

The Colombo Plan for Co-operative Economic Development
in South and Southeast Asia. London, 1950. 101 p.
(Command Paper, no. 8080) (Report by the Commonwealth
Consultative Committee).

The co-operative movement in the Malay States, recent
tendencies. Rev Int Co-op, 34 (1941): 226-227.

Co-operatives. The expansion and progress of the
co-operative consumers movement since 1951. Kuala
Lumpur, 1952. 15 p. (Legislative Council Paper,
no. 46)

Corden, W. M. Prospects for Malayan exports. In
T. H. Silcock and E. K. Fisk, eds. The Political
Economy of Independent Malaya: A Case Study in
Development. Canberra, 1963: 93-111.

Crosson, Pierre R. Planning data and information
   flows in Malaysia. Philippine Economic Journal,
   4 (1965): 226-248.

Crosson, Pierre R. Economic growth in Malaysia:
   projections of gross national product and of
   production, consumption and net import of agricultural
   commodities. Washington, D.C., 1966. 185 p. (National
   Planning Association, Center for Development,
   Planning Methods Series, no. 2)

Darbishire, C. W., et al. Commerce in Singapore.
   In W. Makepeace, R. Braddell and C. E. Brooke.
   One-hundred Years of Singapore. V. 2. London,
   1921: 22-101.

Daroesman, Ruth. Economic survey of Singapore. In
   The Far East and Australasia 1969. London, Europa
   Publications, 1969.

Department of Agriculture, Negeri Sembilan. Review
   of the First Malaysia Plan: agriculture. Seremban,
   1968. 15 p. Appendices. Mimeo.

Dodd, Joseph W. The colonial economy, 1967: the
   case of Malaysia. AS, 9, 6 (1969): 438-446.

Draft development plan of the Federation of Malaya.
   Kuala Lumpur, 1950. 174 p. Illus., map.
      Discusses the development of social services,
   of national resources and utilities, of trade
   and industry.

Drake, P. J. Financial aspects of the co-operative
   movement in Malaya. MER, 11, 1 (1966): 57-83.

Drake, P. J. Financial development in Malaya and
   Singapore. Australian National University Press,
   1969. 17, 253 p.

Drake, P. J. The new issue boom in Malaya and Singapore,
   1961-64. EDCC (Oct. 1969).

Dunlop, W. R. Economic research in tropical development,
   with special reference to British Guiana and
   British Malaya. Jl R Soc Arts, 73 (1925): 312-324.

Economic Planning Unit. The role of land in the
economic development of West Malaysia, 1966-1985.
By William B. Gates, Jr., Theodore J. Goering,
and Douglas H. Keare. Kuala Lumpur, Aug. 1967.
54 p. Mimeo.

An economic review of Malaya 1945-1949. An account
of post-war reconstruction and economic progress
in Malaya and of current economic problems. London,
1950. 38 p. Bibliog. (Issued by Reference Division,
Central Office of Information).

Edwards, C. T. Public finances in the Malayan Territories.
1966. Ph.D. thesis -- Australia National University.

Eldridge, F. R. Trading with Malaysia. Washington,
D.C., 1925. 21 p. (United States Commerce Trade
Information Bulletin, no. 377)

Etienne, Gilbert. La grande Malaisie: vues sur l'économie
et la population de Singapour, de la Fédération
de Malaisie et de Bornéo du Nord. Population,
18, 1 (1963): 111-128.

Federal Agricultural Marketing Authority. Proceedings,
National Agricultural Marketing Seminar, 13-18th
November, 1967. Kuala Lumpur, 1968.

The First Malaysia Plan, 1966-1970: a short summary.
UMBCER, 2, 1 (1966): 30-35.

Fisk, E. K. The economics of the handloom industry
of the east coast of Malaya. Singapore, 1962.
72 p. Illus., maps, tables.

Fisk, E. K. Establishment cost of small rice farms:
an analytical model of returns to capital. MER,
7, 2 (1962): 45-63. Graphs, tables.

Fisk, E. K. Rural development problems in Malaya.
Australian Outlook, 16, 3 (1962): 246-259.

Fisk, E. K. Special development problems of a plural
society: the Malayan example. Economic Record,
38 (1962): 209-225.

Fisk, E. K. Features of the rural economy. In T.
H. Silcock and E. K. Fisk, eds. The Political
Economy of Independent Malaya: A Case Study in
Development. Canberra, 1963: 163-173.

Fisk, E. K. Rural development policy. In T. H. Silcock and E. K. Fisk, eds. The Political Economy of Independent Malaya: A Case Study in Development. Canberra, 1963: 174-194.

Fisk, E. K. Studies in the rural economy of South East Asia. Singapore, 1964. 108 p. Illus.

Focus on Malaysia. New Commonwealth Trade and Commerce, 48, 7 (July 1969): 23-29. Map. Brief articles on economic conditions.

Foreign Trade Association of China. British Malaya. Shanghai, 1936. 44 p. Maps, tables.

Fowler, John A. Netherlands East Indies and British Malaya: a commercial and industrial handbook. Washington, D.C., 1923. 411 p. Charts, diagrs., maps, tables.

Fredericks, J. L. Marketing boards and prospects for Malaysian agriculture. KEM, 3, 1 (1966): 41-50.

Freedman, Maurice. The growth of a plural society in Malaya. PA, 33, 2 (1960): 158-168.

Fryer, Donald W. Food production in Malaya. Australian Geographer, 6 (1952): 35-38.

Fryer, Donald W. The development of cottage and small scale industries in Malaya and in Southeast Asia. JTG, 17 (1963): 92-98.

Fryer, Donald W. Some aspects of the Malaysian rural development program. In Robert Van Niel, ed. Economic Factors in Southeast Asian Social Change. Honolulu, University of Hawaii, Asian Studies Program, 1968: 71-90.

Gamba, Charles. Rural development in Malaya. Eastern World, 6, 5 (1952): 20-21.

Gamba, Charles. Wages, unions and rubber in Malaya. Eastern World, 7 (1953): 46-49.

Gamba, Charles. Poverty, and some socio-economic aspects of hoarding, saving and borrowing in Malaya. MER, 3 (1958): 33-62.

Gamba, Charles, and Ungku A. Aziz. RIDA and Malayan
economic development. FES, 20 (1951): 173-176.

Gates, William B., Jr. Can we improve upon the First
Malaysia Development Plan? UMBCER, 3, 2 (1967): 26-31.

Goh, Chok-tong. Industrial growth, 1959-66. In Ooi
Jin-bee and Chiang Hai-ding, eds. Modern Singapore.
Singapore, University of Singapore Press, 1969: 127-146.

Goh, Keng-swee. Some problems of industrialisation.
Singapore, Ministry of Culture, 1963. 20 p. (Towards
Socialism, no. 7)

Graham, Richard. War Damage Commission Federation
of Malaya and Singapore. Report in which is included
the annual report for 1952. Kuala Lumpur, 1953.

Grant, Margaret, ed. South Asia Pacific crisis;
national development and the world community.
New York, 1964. 314 p.

Greenberg, Michael. Malaya--British dollar arsenal.
Amerasia, 5 (1941): 144-151.

Gull, E. M. British economic interests in the Far
East. London, 1943. 272 p.

Gullick, J. M. The Negri Sembilan economy of the
1890's. JRASMB, 24, 1 (1951): 38-55.

Gullick, J. M. A survey of the Malay weavers and
silversmiths in Kelantan in 1951. JRASMB, 25,
1 (1952): 134-148.

Hartland, A. Economic conditions in Malaya to 20
December, 1934. London, 1935. 66 p. (Great Britain
Department of Overseas Trade Publication)

Hartland, A. Report on economic and commercial conditions
in Malaya to March 5, 1937. London, 1937. 50 p.
(Great Britain Department of Overseas Trade Publication)

Haynes, A. S. Industrialization as an indispensable
means of maintaining the level of prosperity
in tropical regions: the position in Malaya.
In CR Cong Int G, Amsterdam, 1938. t. 2. Travaux
de la Section IIIe. Geographie coloniale.
1938: 543-549.

Hicks, Ursula K. The finance of economic development
in Malaysia. UMBCER, 3, 1 (1967): 34-39.

Holleman, L. W. J., and A. Aten. Processing of cassava
and cassava products in rural industries. Rome,
Food and Agriculture Organization of the United
Nations, 1956. 115 p. (FAO Agricultural Development
Paper, no. 54)

Home ownership in Malaya: the activities of the
Federal and Colonial Building Society. Kuala
Lumpur, 1954. (Colonial Building Notes, no. 21)

Hughes, Helen, and You Poh Seng, eds. Foreign investment
and industrialisation in Singapore. Australian
National University Press, 1969. 13, 226 p.

International Bank for Reconstruction and Development.
The economic development of Malaya; report of
a mission organized by the International Bank
for Reconstruction and Development at the request
of the Governments of the Federation of Malaya,
the Crown Colony of Singapore and the United
Kingdom. Baltimore, 1955. 707 p. Diagrs., maps,
tables.

International Bank for Reconstruction and Development.
Report on the economic aspects of Malaysia.
Kuala Lumpur, 1963.

International Bank for Reconstruction and Development.
Report on Malaysia's development prospects and
plans (in four volumes): the main report, agricultural
sector, transportation sector, education sector.
International Bank for Reconstruction and Development
[and] International Development Association.
Kuala Lumpur, Prime Minister's Department, 1966.
Various pagings processed. Diagrs., maps.

International Labour Office. Expanded Programme
of Technical Assistance. Report to the Government
of the Federation of Malaya on manpower information.
Geneva, 1962. (ILO/TAP/Malaya/R. 16)

Jack-Hinton, C. A synopsis of the report on the
economic aspects of Malaysia by a mission of
the International Bank for Reconstruction and
Development under the chairmanship of Jacques
Rueff. Singapore, 1963. 26 p.

Jacoby, Erich H. Agrarian unrest in Southeast Asia.
New York, 1949. 287 p.
See chap. 4 for Malaya, p. 101-133.

Jacquelin, Dorothy Grant. British Malaya and British
Borneo; preliminary survey on relief and rehabilitation
problems in Southeastern Asia. Washington, D.C., 1943.
60 p. (Office of Foreign Relief and Rehabilitation
Operations Publication)

Jacquelin, Dorothy Grant. The economic structure
of British Malaya. Washington, D.C., 1944. 154 p.
(Country Monograph, no. 2)

Jago, E. Malaya and the economic war. AR, 36, 125
(1940): 134-136.

Jenks, J. W. Report on certain economic questions
in the English and Dutch colonies in the Orient.
Washington, D.C., 1902. 176 p.

Jones, Gavin W. The employment characteristics of
small towns in Malaya. MER, 10, 1 (1965): 44-72.

Jones, Gavin W. Female participation in the labour
force in a plural economy; the Malayan example.
MER, 10, 2 (1965): 61-82.

Kanapathy, V. The role of financial institutions
in Malaysian economic development. UMBCER, 1,
1 (1965): 1-11.

Kanapathy, V. Industrialization of Malaysia. UMBCER,
1, 2 (1965): 1-22. Illus.

Kanapathy, V. Industrialization of Malaysia. Geographica,
2 (1966): 16 p.

Kanapathy, V. International trade and Malaysian
economic development. UMBCER, 2, 2 (1966): 6-19.

Kanapathy, V. The role of research in economic development.
UMBCER, 3, 2 (1967): 6-21.

Kertas Kerja (Working Papers). Konggeres Ekonomi
Bumiputra Malaysia. Kuala Lumpur, 1965. 132 p. Illus.
In English or Malay.

King, A. W. Plantation and agriculture in Malaya,
with notes on the trade of Singapore. G Jl, 93,
2 (1939): 136-148.

Koepfle, L. G. British Malaya: major commercial changes
will follow its liberation, new plans and calculations
will stem from basic facts. Foreign Commerce
Weekly, 20 (July 14, 1945): 14-17.

Lam, Timothy Thim-fook. Relationship between physical
and economic planning in national development.
KEM, 3, 1 (1966): 51-57.

Lam, Timothy Thim-fook. Aspects of planning in Malaysia.
Australian Planning Institute Journal, 5, 3 (1967).

The Land Development Ordinance, 1956. Kuala Lumpur,
1956. (Federation of Malaya, no. 20 of 1956) Mimeo.

Langdon, Wm. R. Malaya's rubber and tin. Current
History, 23 (1952): 144-149.

Langley, G. A. Telecommunication in Malaya. JTG,
17 (1963): 79-91. Maps.

Lee, S. Y. Financial and credit institutions. In
Ooi Jin-bee and Chiang Hai-ding, eds. Modern
Singapore. Singapore, University of Singapore
Press, 1969: 147-160.

Lehmann, H. Malaya unter britischer Herrschaft.
Berlin, 1941. 86 p. Maps.
    Highly biased examination of British economic
policy.

Lembaga Pemasaran Pertanian Persekutuan (Federal
Agricultural Marketing Authority--FAMA). Annual
Report and Statement of Accounts, 1965 and 1966.
Kuala Lumpur, 1967.

Li, Dun-jen. British Malaya, an economic analysis.
New York [1955]. 123 p. Bibliog.

Lim, Chong-yah. Export taxes on rubber in Malaya--a
survey of post-war development. MER, 5, 2 (1960):
46-58.

Lim, Chong-yah. The Malayan rubber replanting taxes.
MER, 6, 2 (1961): 43-52.

Lim, Chong-yah. Economic development of modern Malaya.
1964. D.Phil. thesis -- Oxford.

Lim, Chong-yah. Asian economic development: Malaya.
In Cranley Onslow, ed. Asian Economic Development.
London, 1965: 95-117.

Lim, Chong-yah. Economic development of modern Malaya.
Kuala Lumpur, 1967. 388 p. Bibliog. p. 359-369,
graphs, maps, tables.

Lim, Chong-yah. Money and monetary policy. Singapore,
1969. 42 p.

Lim, Chong-yah. West Malaysian external trade, 1947-65.
In T. Morgan, ed. Economic Interdependence in
Southeast Asia. Madison, Wisconsin, 1969: 203-237.

Lim, Tay-boh. The co-operative movement in Malaya.
Cambridge, 1950. 37 p. (Malayan Questions Series)
Chart.

Lim, Tay-boh. Economic and financial aspects of
social security with special reference to Malaya.
1955. Ph.D. thesis (London School of Economics)
-- London.

Lim, Tay-boh. The development of Singapore's economy.
Singapore, 1960. 74 p.

Lim, Tay-boh, ed. Problems of the Malayan economy.
Singapore, 1956. 68 p. (Background to Malaya
Series, no. 10) [1957, 102 p.].

Low, F. A. An outline for a plan of implementation
for the Muda River Project. Kuala Lumpur, Bahagian
Peranchang Ekonomi, August, 1967. 14 p. Diagr.

Lyall and Evatt, Singapore. Handbook of Malayan
and Singapore stocks and shares. Singapore, 1961.

Ma, Ronald. Company profits and prices in the rubber
industry in Malaya, 1947-58. MER, 4, 2 (1959): 27-44.

Ma, Ronald. Singapore--the economic challenge of
a growing population. Australian Outlook, 16
(1962): 47-62.

Ma, Ronald, ed. The Malayan economy in transition;
    lectures presented at the symposium organized
    by the Singapore Institute of Management, held
    at the University of Singapore, March 1965. [Singapore],
    1965. 46 p.

Ma, Ronald, and Poh-seng You. The economic characteristics
    of the population of the Federation of Malaya
    1957. MER, 5, 2 (1960): 10-45.

Ma, Ronald, and Poh-seng You. The economy of Malaysia
    and Singapore. Singapore, 1966. 62 p.

Mackenzie, K. E. Malaya; economic and commercial
    conditions in the Federation of Malaya and Singapore.
    London, 1952. 189 p. Map, tables.

Malaya. Report on economic planning in the Federation
    of Malaya in 1956 and on the outcome of the financial
    talks held in London from December the 21st 1956
    to January the 10th, 1957. Kuala Lumpur, 1957. 23 p.

Malaya. Rural thrift and credit; report of the working
    party set up by the cabinet to consider the Cohen
    Report on the proposed Bank Ra'ayat. Kuala Lumpur,
    Economic Secretariat, 1959. 12 p.

Malaya. Second Five-year Plan. 1961-1965. Kuala
    Lumpur, 1961. 67 p.

Malaya, Department of Drainage and Irrigation. Brief
    details of some development projects in the 1961-65
    Plan. Kuala Lumpur, 1962.

Malaya, Laws, statutes, etc. The land development
    ordinance, 1956. [Kuala Lumpur, 1956]. (Its Ordinance,
    no. 20 of 1956)
        Published in Supplement to the Federation of
    Malaya Government Gazette of June 27, 1956, no.
    14, v. 14, Notification Federal, no. 1369.

Malaya, Laws, statutes, etc. The land development
    (amendment) ordinance, 1957. [Kuala Lumpur, Government
    Printer, 1957]. 268-269 p. (Its Ordinance, no.
    35 of 1957)
        Published in Supplement to the Federation of
    Malaya Government Gazette of 15th Aug., 1957,
    no. 18, v. 10, Notification Federal, no. 2003.

Malaya, Laws, statutes, etc. The land development
(amendment) ordinance, 1958. [Kuala Lumpur, Government
Printer, 1958]. 391-393 p. (Its Ordinance, no.
56 of 1958)

Malaya: Malayan statistics. London, 1932. 178 p.
Tables.

Malaya: the R.I.D.A. (Rural and Industrial Development
Authority) story. AR, 50 (1954): 159-163. Plate.

Malayan Collieries, Ltd. A description of the property,
operations and social organization at Batu Arang
Colliery. Kuala Lumpur, 1950.

Malaysia. First Malaysia Plan 1966-1970. Kuala Lumpur,
1965. 190 p.

Malaysia. Report on 1st seminar on development 24th
October-3rd. November, 1966. Kuala Lumpur, 1967.
112 p.

Malaysia. Report on 2nd. seminar on development
22nd June-30th. June 1967. Kuala Lumpur, 1967.
121 p.

Malaysia. Mid-term review of the First Malaysia
Plan 1966-1970. Kuala Lumpur, 1969. 135 p. Map.

Malaysia, Department of Statistics. Survey of manufacturing
industries in West Malaysia. Kuala Lumpur, 1967.

Malaysia, Economic Planning Unit. Report on: location
of land suitable for long-term large-scale settlement
and agricultural development; a report by a sub-committee
of the Technical Sub-Committee on Land Capability
Classification. 13 p. Tables.

Malaysia, Economic Planning Unit. Canadian assistance
to the Federation of Malaya under the Colombo
Plan technical cooperation scheme. Kuala Lumpur,
1963. 2 v. (various pagings). Mimeo.

Malaysia, Economic Planning Unit. Interim review
of development in Malaya under the Second Five-year
Plan, 1961-65. Kuala Lumpur, 1963. 76 p.

Malaysia, Economic Planning Unit. Interim review
of development in Malaya under the Second Five-year
Plan, December, 1963. Kuala Lumpur, Jabatan Chetak
Keraja, 1964. 76 p. Diagrs., tables.

Malaysia, Economic Planning Unit. Requests for Canadian
assistance 1964/65. By William T. Phillips. Kuala
Lumpur, 1964. 39 p. Tables. Mimeo.

Malaysia, Economic Planning Unit. United Kingdom
assistance to Malaysia under the Colombo Plan
for technical cooperation scheme. Kuala Lumpur,
1964. 2 v. (various pagings). Tables. Mimeo.

Malaysia, Economic Planning Unit. United Nations technical
assistance country programme for Malaysia 1965-1966.
Kuala Lumpur, May, 1964. 1 v. (various pagings).

Malaysia, Economic Planning Unit. Malaysia: projections
of exports and production of major export commodities
up to 1970. Kuala Lumpur, February, 1965. 19 p.
Fold. tables. Mimeo.

Malaysia, Economic Planning Unit. Malaysia: projections
of exports and production of major export commodities
up to 1970. Kuala Lumpur, September, 1965. 25 p.
Rev. August 1966. Tables. Mimeo.

Malaysia, Economic Planning Unit. Location of land suitable
for immediate settlement and agricultural development;
a report by a sub-committee of the Technical Sub-
Committee on Land Capability Classification. Kuala
Lumpur, the Unit, June, 1966. 22 p. Fold. map.
Processed.

Malaysia, Economic Planning Unit. Report on the
Trengganu River Project. [Submitted by] Binnie
and Partners in association with Preece, Cardew
and Rider. October, 1966. 39 p. Maps, tables.

Malaysia, Kementerian Kemajuan Nasional dan Luar
Bandar. Techniques used for developing Malaysia.
Kuala Lumpur, 1965. 18 p. Illus. (part col.).

Malaysia, Ministry of Agriculture and Co-operatives.
A food technology research and development centre
for Malaysia; outline of a proposed request to
the United Nations Special Fund for assistance
in food technology research and development in
Malaysia. Kuala Lumpur, the Ministry [1965?].
27 p. Tables. Mimeo.

Malaysia, Ministry of Agriculture and Co-operatives.
Report of the Government of Malaysia to the Food
and Agriculture Organisation of the United Nations,
1964-1966. Kuala Lumpur, the Ministry, 1967. 47 p.

Malaysia, Ministry of Agriculture and Co-operative,
Federal Agricultural Marketing Authority. National
agricultural marketing seminar proceedings, 13-18
Nov., 1967. Kuala Lumpur, 1968. 209 p. Diagrs.,
graphs, tables.

Malaysia, Ministry of National and Rural Development.
Techniques used for developing Malaysia. Kuala
Lumpur, Government Printer, 1965. 19 p. Photos.

Malaysia, National Development Planning Committee.
First Malaysia Plan, 1966-1970. V. I. Allocations
of public investment recommended by N.D.P.C.
Kuala Lumpur, Economic Planning Unit, September, 1965.
147 p. Tables. Mimeo.

Malaysia, National Development Planning Committee.
First Malaysia Plan, 1966-70. V. II. Record of
discussions between N.D.P.C. technical working
group and representatives of ministries and departments
on allocations of public investment. 132 p. Mimeo.

Malaysian Centre for Development Studies, Development
Seminar, 1st, Kuala Lumpur, November 1966. The
aims and tools of economic development planning,
panel discussion; verbatim report. Chairman,
C. L. Robless. Sponsored by the Malaysian Centre
for Development Studies. Kuala Lumpur, the Centre,
1966. 46 p. Mimeo.

Malaysian Centre for Development Studies, Development
Seminar, 1st, Kuala Lumpur, November 1966. Community
development, panel discussion; verbatim report.
Chairman, Sa'ad bin Walad. Sponsored by the Malaysian
Centre for Development Studies. Kuala Lumpur,
the Centre, 1966. 31 p. Mimeo.

Malaysian Centre for Development Studies, Development
Seminar, 1st, Kuala Lumpur, November 1966. Economic
growth through investment in education, panel
discussion; verbatim report. Chairman, C. L. Robless.
Sponsored by the Malaysian Centre for Development
Studies. Kuala Lumpur, the Centre, 1966. 32 p. Mimeo.

Malaysian Centre for Development Studies, Development
Seminar, 1st, Kuala Lumpur, November 1966. The
implementation of development; the role of politician,
panel discussion; verbatim report. Chairman,
C. L. Robless. Sponsored by the Malaysian Centre
for Development Studies. Kuala Lumpur, the Centre,
1966. 58 p. Mimeo.

Malaysian Centre for Development Studies, Development
Seminar, 1st, Kuala Lumpur, November 1966. Land
development, panel discussion; verbatim report.
Chairman, Sa'ad bin Walad. Sponsored by the Malaysian
Centre for Development Studies. Kuala Lumpur,
the Centre, 1966. 41 p. Mimeo.

Malaysian Centre for Development Studies, Development
Seminar, 1st, Kuala Lumpur, November 1966. Planning:
the Malaysian experience. By Thong Yaw Hong.
Kuala Lumpur, 1966. 13 p. Mimeo.

Malaysian Centre for Development Studies, Development
Seminar, 1st, Kuala Lumpur, November 1966. Report
on 1st seminar on development, 24th October-3rd.
November. Kuala Lumpur, Malaysian Centre for
Development Studies, 1966. 240 p. Mimeo.

Malaysian Centre for Development Studies, Development
Seminar, 2nd, Kuala Lumpur, June 1967. Report
on 2nd seminar on development, 22nd June-30th
June 1967. Sponsored by Malaysian Centre for
Development Studies. Kuala Lumpur, Jabatan Chetak
Kerajaan, 1967. 121 p.

Mamajiwala, R. K. Ownership and control of public
limited rubber planting companies incorporated
in the Federation of Malaya, 1948-1958. 1963.
M.A. thesis -- University of Malaya.

Markandan, Paul, ed. Federation of Malaya, 1960;
report on finance, commerce and industry. Singapore,
1960. 126 p. Bibliog., illus., tables.

Mayer, Philip. Reading list on rural conditions
and betterment in the British colonies. London,
1947. 121 p.
Numerous references pertaining to Malaya.

McHale, T. R. The Malayan economy and stereo-regular
rubbers. AS, 1, 4 (1961): 25-28.

McHale, T. R. Changing technology and shifts in
the supply and demand for rubber: an analytical
history. MER, 9, 2 (1964): 24-48.

Meek, John Paul. Malaya: a study of governmental
response to the Korean boom. [Ithaca, N.Y.] 1955.
32 p. (Cornell University. Southeast Asia Program.
Data Paper, no. 17) Bibliog., illus.

Merican, M. A. Finance in post-war Malaya. 1959.
B.Litt. -- Oxford.

Mills, L. A. Malaya: a political and economic appraisal.
London, 1958.

Missen, G. J. Manufacturing in Malaya; a survey
with special reference to the impact of political
changes. In J. Rutherford, M. I. Logan, and G.
J. Missen. New View Points in Economic Geography.
Sydney, 1966: 296-313.

Mitchell, Kate L. Industrialization of the Western
Pacific. New York, 1942. 322 p.
Constitutes Part 3 of An Economic Survey of
the Pacific Area. See p. 178-189 for British
Malaya.

Mohamad bin Jamil. The role of farmers' associations
in marketing agricultural produce. In Proceedings,
National Agricultural Marketing Seminar, 13th-18th
November, 1967. Kuala Lumpur, 1968: 55-63.

Mohamad bin Jamil, and Koh Theam-hee. The development
of Farmers' Association in Malaysia as a unit
for extension program planning and implementation
of agricultural projects. Kuala Lumpur, Department
of Agriculture, 1966. 20 p. Appendices, charts.
Mimeo.

Mohar bin Raja Badiozaman, Raja. Report of the committee
on investment incentives. Kuala Lumpur, Ministry
of Commerce and Industry, 31st December, 1966.
36 p. Mimeo.

Mokhzani bin A. Rahim. The economy of a Perlis village,
Malaya, with special reference to the problems
of capital accumulation. 1963. M.A. thesis (London
School of Economics) -- London.

Montgomery, John D. Development administration in
    Malaysia; report to the Government of Malaysia.
    By John D. Montgomery and Milton J. Esman, Ford
    Foundation consultants. Kuala Lumpur, 1966. 27 p.

Murakami, Makoto. Geographical analysis of the
    industrialization in Singapore. Geographical
    Review of Japan, 41, 9 (1968): 541-570. Maps.
    In Japanese, with English summary, p. 569-570.

Nanjundan, S. Economic development of Malaya. India
    Q, 8 (1952): 289-311.

Ness, Gayl D. Community development and public investment:
    the programming of economic development in Malaysia.
    Developing Economies, 2 (Dec. 1964): 397-417.

Ness, Gayl D. Economic development and the goals
    of government in Malaya. In Wang Gung-wu. Malaysia:
    A Survey. London, 1964: 307-320.

Newboult, A. T. Reconstruction in Malaya. Jl R Soc
    Arts, 96 (1948): 331-350.

Onn bin Jaffar, Dato Sir. Report on community development
    in the Federation of Malaya. Kuala Lumpur, Government
    Printer, 1954.

Ooi, Jin-bee. Geographical problems of rural development
    in tropical areas, with special reference to
    Malaya. 1957. D.Phil. -- Oxford.

Ooi, Jin-bee. Rural development in tropical areas,
    with special references to Malaya. JTG, 12 (1959):
    1-222. Maps.

Oshima, Harry T. Growth and unemployment in Singapore.
    MER, 12, 2 (1967): 32-58.

Pang, Eng-fong. Study of taxation in postwar Singapore.
    Singapore, 1967. 104 p. Thesis -- University
    of Singapore.

Pasupathy, V. The significance of geomorphic controls
    in the development of the Malayan economy. Geographica,
    1 (1964/1965): 60-67.

Penerangan Negri Pahang. Pembangunan Pahang 1961-1965.
    Kuantan [n.d.]. 405 p. Photos., tables.

Phillips, Joseph D. Foreign trade in the Pacific
area. In Katrine R. C. Greene and Joseph D. Phillips.
Transportation and Foreign Trade. New York, 1942:
105-208. 208 p.
Constitutes Part 2 of An Economic Survey of
the Pacific Area. See p. 136-137, 151-153, and
177-178 for British Malaya.

Prichard, N. F. Lloyd. The value of rubber and tin
to Malaya and the sterling area. Eastern World,
8, 10 (1954): 42-44.

Progress report on the development plan of the Federation
of Malaya, 1950-1952. Kuala Lumpur, 1953. 128 p.

Purcal, J., ed. The monetary system of Singapore
and Malaysia: implications of the split currency.
Singapore [n.d.].

Purvis, Malcolm J. Evaluation and use of underdeveloped
agricultural statistics: the food economy of
Malaysia. 1966. 457 p. Ph.D. thesis -- Cornell
University.

Purvis, Malcolm J. Research report on the food economy
of Malaysia and Brunei. Ithaca, submitted to
the National Planning Association, by the Department
of Agricultural Economics, New York State College
of Agriculture, Cornell University, 1965. 417 p.
Mimeo.

Puthucheary, J. J. Ownership and control in the
Malayan economy; a study of the structure of
ownership and control and its effect on the development
of secondary industries and economic growth in
Malaya and Singapore. Singapore, 1960. 187 p. Tables.

Rao, V. K. R. The Colombo Plan for economic development.
Lloyd Bank Review (July 1951): 21 p.

Rawlins, J. Sig. D. French enterprise in Malaya.
JRASMB, 39, 2 (1966): 50-94. Bibliog.

Reeth, C. F. van. Singapore et la péninsule malaise;
interêts économiques belges. Bruxelles, 1904.
55 p. Map.

Report of the Hawkers Inquiry Commission, 1950.
Chairman T. H. Silcock. Singapore, 1950. 96 p.

Richter, H. V. Indonesia's share in the entrepot
trade of Malaya and Singapore prior to confrontation.
MER, 11, 2 (1966): 28-45.

Rueff, Jacques. Report on the economic aspects of
Malaysia. Mission of the International Bank for
Reconstruction and Development. Kuala Lumpur, 1963.

Scheme for the Reorganisation of the Rural and Industrial
Development Authority, Federation of Malaya;
and subsequent progress reports. Kuala Lumpur,
1951, 1952, 1953, and 1954. (Legislative Council
Papers, nos. 10; 24, 35, and 65; 35; and 45 and
84 respectively)

Sedky, A. An attempt in estimating local production
and consumption of food commodities [in Malaya].
Kuala Lumpur, 1961. 26 p. Mimeo.

Sedky, A. The situation of food production and consumption
in Malaya. Kuala Lumpur, Food and Agriculture
Organization of the United Nations, 1962. (FAO
Report Series on Malayan Food Commodities, no. 1)

Silcock, T. H. Some determinants of economic development.
MER, 2 (1957): 1-15.

Silcock, T. H. A note on future trading and the
Singapore rubber market. MER, 3 (1958): 63-66.

Silcock, T. H. Some problems of economic growth
in the British territories in Southeast Asia.
Weltwirtschaftliches Archiv, 80, 2 (1958).

Silcock, T. H. The Commonwealth economy in Southeast
Asia. Durham, N.C., 1959. 259 p.

Silcock, T. H., ed. Readings in Malayan economics.
Singapore, 1961. 501 p. Tables.

Silcock, T. H., and E. K. Fisk, eds. The political
economy of independent Malaya; a case study in
development. Berkeley, Singapore, Canberra, 1963.
306 p. Tables.

Singapore, Economic Planning Unit, Prime Minister's Office.
First Development Plan, 1961-1964. Review of progress
for the three years ending 31st December, 1963.
Singapore, 1964. 57 p.

Singh, Bhupinder. Post-war Japanese competition
in Malaya. MER, 1 (1956): 48-54.

Snodgrass, D. R. Background data for the First Malaysia
Plan. Kuala Lumpur, Economic Planning Unit, October,
1964. 6 p. (Economic Planning Unit memorandum) Tables.

Soper, J. R. P. Government and the small-holder.
Mal Ag Jl, 31 (1948): 214-218.

Sparrow, H. R. Electrical development in Malaya.
Far Eastern Review, 34 (1938): 307-308.

Stenton, Jean E. Rural development in Malaysia.
Can G Jl, 77, 3 (1968): 84-93. Map.

Stepanek, Joseph E. Measures for the development
of small industries in the Federation of Malaya.
[Kuala Lumpur] 1960. 141 p. Diagrs., tables.

Strickland, Claude F. Report on co-operation in
Malaya. Kuala Lumpur, 1929. 19 p. (Legislative
Council Paper, no. 26)

Strickland, Claude F. The co-operative movement
in the East. Inter Aff, 11 (1932): 812-823.

Stuchen, Philip. Industrial development survey and
new industry possibilities, prepared for the
government of the Federation of Malaya. [Kuala
Lumpur, Ministry of Commerce and Industry, 1963].
2 v.

Sumitro Djojahadikusumo. Trade and aid in South-East
Asia. V. 1, Malaysia and Singapore. Melbourne,
1968. 311 p.

Surridge, B. J. Report on co-operation in the Federation
of Malaya. Kuala Lumpur, 1953. (Legislative Council
Paper, no. 41)

Swift, M. G. The accumulation of capital in a peasant
economy. EDCC, 5, 4 (1957).

Swift, M. G. Capital, saving and credit in a Malay
peasant economy. In Raymond Firth and B. S. Yamey.
Capital, Saving and Credit in Peasant Societies.
Studies from Asia, Oceania, the Caribbean, and
Middle America. Chicago, 1964: 133-156.

Tan Ee-Leong. The Chinese banks incorporated in
Singapore and the Federation of Malaya. JRASMB,
26, 1 (1953): 113-139. Illus., tables.

Tan, Siew-sin. The Malaysian economy: its present
position and future problems. KEM, 2, 1 (1965): 1-6.

Thompson, A. M. Report to the Government of the
Federation of Malaya on the marketing of rice.
Rome, Food and Agriculture Organization of the
United Nations, 1954. (FAO Report, no. 278)

Thong, Yaw-hong. Building institutions for preparing
and executing development plans: Malaysian experience.
Paper prepared for the Conference on Economic
Planning in Southeast Asia, 1-5 February, 1965.
Honolulu, East-West Center, 1965. 23 p. Mimeo.

Tjoa, Soei-hock. Institutional background to modern
economic and social development in Malaya, with
special reference to the East Coast. Kuala Lumpur,
1963. 283 p. Diagrs., maps, tables.

Tregonning, K. G. Singapore in Malaysia, a brief
study of its industrial potential. Singapore,
J. M. Sassoon, 1963. 28 p.

Tufo, M. V. del. Rural development in Malaya. In
International Institute of Differing Civilizations.
Programmes and Plans for Rural Development in
Tropical and Sub-tropical Countries. Bruxelles,
1953: 247-256.

Tufo, M. V. del. Aspects de l'économie malaise en
1954. Civilisations, 5 (1955): 309-318.

United Nations, Economic Commission for Asia and
the Far East. Industrial developments in Asia
and the Far East. Vol. III: country reports:
Laos, Malaysia, Nepal, New Zealand, Pakistan,
Philippines, Singapore, Thailand, Republic of
Vietnam. Selected documents presented to Asian
Conference on Industrialization, Manila, December
1965. New York, United Nations, 1966. 7, 376 p.
Tables.

United Nations. Klang Valley Plan; part of the U.N.
Adviser's preliminary report on Klang Valley
Development. Prepared by Vlado Antolic. [1961?].
Various pagings. Mimeo.

United Nations. Klang Valley Plan: 6 vols. Report
by U.N. Adviser, Vlado Antolic. 1961. 6 v. Tables
(some fold.). Mimeo.

United States, Embassy, Kuala Lumpur. Economic trends
in Malaysia and their implications for the United
States. 1967. 9 p. Mimeo.

Waide, Bevan. Agricultural credit and marketing
in Malaysia. In Proceedings, National Agricultural
Marketing Seminar 13-18th November, 1967. Kuala
Lumpur, 1968: 36-42.

Ward, Marion W. The trade of the ports of Malaya.
Minneapolis, 1960. 337 p. Ph.D. thesis -- University
of Minnesota. Bibliog. p. 331-337, illus., maps.

Ward, Marion W. A review of problems and achievements
in the economic development of independent Malaya.
Ec G, 44, 4 (1968): 326-342.

Watherston, D. C. Report on community development
in the Federation of Malaya. Community Development
Bulletin, 6, 1 (1954): 13-17.

West, Henry W. Current economic production in the
Malay Peninsula. Jl Manchester G Soc, 55 (1952):
91-107.

Wharton, C. R., Jr. Marketing, merchandising, and
moneylending: a note on middleman monopsony in
Malaya. MER, 7, 2 (1962): 24-44.

Wharton, C. R., Jr. The economic meaning of subsistence.
MER, 8, 2 (1963): 46-58.

Wharton, C. R., Jr. Rubber supply conditions: some
policy implications. In T. H. Silcock and E.
K. Fisk, eds. The Political Economy of Independent
Malaya. Canberra, 1963: 131-162.

Wheelwright, E. L. Reflections on some problems
of industrial development in Malaya. MER, 8,
1 (1963): 66-80.

Wheelwright, E. L. Industrialization in Malaya.
In T. H. Silcock and E. K. Fisk. Political Economy
of Independent Malaya. Canberra, 1963: 210-241.

Wheelwright, E. L. Industrialization in Malaysia. Melbourne, London, New York, 1965. 153 p. Tables.

Wilcox, Clair. Regional cooperation in Southeast Asia. MER, 9, 2 (1964): 106-112.

Wilcox, Clair. The planning and execution of economic development in Southeast Asia. Harvard, Center for International Affairs, 1965. 37 p. (Occasional Papers in International Affairs, no. 10, September 1965)

Williams, W. J. Electricity supply of the Federated Malay States. Far Eastern Review, 32 (1936): 406-410.

Willmot, R. B. Report on economic and commercial conditions in Malaya to March, 1939. London, 1939. 114 p. (Great Britain Department of Overseas Trade publication)

Wilson, Joan. The Singapore rubber market. Singapore, 1958. 75 p. Diagrs.

Wolfstone, Daniel. The Malays move in. FEER, 42 (Oct. 1963): 187-194.

Wright, Philip G. Trade and trade barriers in the Pacific. Honolulu, 1935. 530 p. Chap. 13, British Malaya, p. 388-406.

Yamada, Isamu. Measuring changes in economic structure with special reference to the industrial population in Malaya. KEM, 1, 1 (1964): 59-69.

Yeh, Stephen H. K. The size and structure of households in Singapore, 1957-1966. MER, 12, 2 (1967): 97-115.

Zin, U Thet. Report to the Government of Malaysia. The rice processing industry. Rome, Food and Agriculture Organization of the United Nations, 1967. 42 p. (FAO/MAL/TF, 9)

B. AGRICULTURE

1. General

Abdul Razak bin Dato' Hussein, Tun. Jayadiri--a
drive for greater progress. Speech delivered
April 18, 1968. Chawangan Perkembangan, Jabatan
Pertanian. Kuala Lumpur, 1968. 21 p. Mimeo.

Allee, Ralph H., and Clifton R. Wharton. Observations
on methods to intensify Malayan agricultural
diversification. Kuala Lumpur, University of
Malaya, 1962. 17 p. Mimeo.

Allen, E. F. The cultivation of Colocasia Esculenta
(L) Schott in Malaya. Mal Ag Jl, 28 (1940): 392-398.

Alunan, Rafael R. Agricultural development in Southeastern
Asia and Malaysia. Manila, 1931. 105 p. (Chap. 3
Malay archipelago).

Arnot, David Blair, and J. S. Smith. Shifting cultivation
in Brunei and Trengganu. Mal For, 6 (1937): 13-17.

Barlow, Colin, and Ng Choong-sooi. Some principles
of estate budgeting. Kuala Lumpur, 1966. 6 p.
(Rubber Research Institute of Malaya, Planters'
Conference, July 1966. Preprint no. 14) Tables.

Barnett, H. L. A brief review of essential foodcrop
cultivation in Malaya. Mal Ag Jl, 30 (1947): 13-18.

Baumgarten, F. L. Agriculture in Malacca. Jl Ind
Archip, 3 (1849): 707-721.

Bean, K. W. Muda River Project. World Crops, 21,
1 (March/April 1969): 13-16. Map.

Belgrave, W. N. C. The cultivation of food crops
on estates. Mal Ag Jl, 27 (1939): 209-213.

Birkinshaw, F. Reclaiming old mining land for agriculture.
Mal Ag Jl, 19 (1931): 470-476.

Blaut, James M. The economic geography of a one-acre
farm on Singapore Island: a study in applied
micro-geography. MJTG, 1 (1953): 37-48. Map.

Blaut, James M. Chinese market gardening in Singapore: a study in functional microgeography. Ann Arbor, Mich., 1958.

Bocquet. Les plantations indochinoises en 1940. Comparaison avec celles de la Malaisie Britannique et des Indes Néerlandaises. Rev Gen du Caoutchouc, 18 (1941): 327-332. A part reproduced in "Etat actuel des plantations d'Hevea en Indochine." Rev Bot Appl et Ag Trop, 22 (Mars-Avril 1942): 180-190.

Boyd, M. A. Malaysian agriculture. Mal Ag, 4 (1963/1964): 4-16.

Brandt, Karl, J. Norman Efferson, and Don Paarlberg. Policies and measures leading toward greater diversification of the agricultural economy of the Federation of Malaya; report submitted to the Government of the Federation of Malaya by the survey team provided by the Ford Foundation. Kuala Lumpur, 1963. 64 p.

Brown, David W. A reconnaissance study of farming organization in the Ama Keng food production area. Singapore, 1960. Illus.

Brown, David W. A reconnaissance study of farming organization in a coastal area of West Johore; a preliminary report. Singapore, 1960. Illus.

Bunting, B. The culture of vegetables in Malaya. Kuala Lumpur, 1930. (Department of Agriculture, Special Bulletin, General Series, no. 1)

Bunting, B. Agricultural possibilities of Cameron Highlands for the proprietory planter and small holder. Mal Ag Jl, 20 (1932): 154-163.

Bunting, B., and J. N. Milsum. Agriculture at Cameron's Highlands. Mal Ag Jl, 18 (1930): 5-19.

Bunting, B., and J. N. Milsum. Cultivation of coffee in Malaya. Mal Ag Jl, 18 (1930): 481-496.

Chandran, M. R. Background of plantation agriculture. Planter, 37, 11 (1961): 600-602.

Corbett, G. H., and C. Dover. Life history and control of some Malayan insects of economic importance. Mal Ag Jl, 15 (1927): 239-269. Bibliog.

Courtenay, P. P. Water control and irrigation in North Malaya. G, 44 (1959): 46-47.

Craig, J. A. Agriculture in Trengganu. Mal Ag Jl, 22 (1934): 177-182.

Craig, J. A. Agriculture in Kelantan. Mal Ag Jl, 23 (1935): 369-374.

Degani, Amina Hatim. Land use for rubber and rice in Malaya, 1947-1960. [1962]. 220 p. Thesis -- University of British Columbia. Maps, tables.

Deshmukh, G. B. Agriculture in Greater India. Poona, 1928. 86 p. Illus., maps, plate.

Dobby, E. H. G. Agricultural questions of Malaya. Cambridge, 1949. 38 p. Diagr., map.

Dobby, E. H. G. The development of Malaya's uplands. In The Development of Upland Areas in the Far East. V. 2. New York, 1951: 1-21. Map.

Donaldson, R. D. The present land use of Malacca. Kuala Lumpur, 1968. 11 p. (Present Land Use Report, no. 1) Appendices, maps. Mimeo.

Economic Planning Unit, Prime Minister's Department. Economic analysis of the Kemubu Drainage and Irrigation Project. Kuala Lumpur, September 1965. 19 p. Tables.

Economic Planning Unit, Prime Minister's Department. Implementation Workshop Muda River Project, Sub-Project No. 5. The management of the project. Kuala Lumpur, 1967. 6 p. Appendices. Mimeo.

The estate management hand-book 1967. Kuala Lumpur, 1967. 76 p. (Rubber Research Institute of Malaya, Economic and Planning Division: Report no. 3)

Ferguson, D. S. Construction of coastal lands in Malaya. Mal Ag Jl, 34 (1951): 3-9.

Fisk, E. K. Malaysia. In R. T. Shand, ed. Agricultural
Development in Asia. Canberra, Australian National
University Press, 1969: 181-214.

Fisk, Ernest K. The mechanisation of agricultural
smallholdings in underdeveloped areas. MER, 6
(1961): 53-60.

Focus on agricultural diversification. Mal Ag, 5
(1964/1965): 1-11.

Food production in Malaya. Great Britain and the
East, 65 (1948): 36-37.

Fryer, D. W. The plantation industries - the estates.
In Wang Gung-wu. Malaysia: A Survey. London,
1964: 227-245.

Gething, P. A. Agricultural extension in the Kuala
Langat District, Selangor. Mal Ag Jl, 40, 1 (1957):
9-18.

Glover, E. Maurice. Pioneer farming in Malaya. FEER,
15 (1953): 171.

Greenstreet, V. R., and J. Lambourne. Tapioca in
Malaya. Kuala Lumpur, 1938. 78 p. (Department
of Agriculture, Special Bulletin, General Series,
no. 13)

Grist, D. H. Malayan agricultural trade in 1937.
Mal Ag Jl, 26 (1938): 186-191.

Grist, D. H., comp. An outline of Malayan agriculture.
Kuala Lumpur, 1936. 388 p. (Department of Agriculture,
Malayan Planting Manual, no. 2) Bibliog., illus.,
maps. Also published in London, 1950.

Hamilton, A. W., and R. E. Holttum. A Malay garden.
JRASMB, 11, 2 (1933): 139-143.

Haynes, A. S. Agricultural research work and problems
in Malaya. Kuala Lumpur, 1927.

Haynes, D. W. A census of agricultural machinery
in the Federation of Malaya. Mal Ag Jl, 39, 3
(1956): 200-216.

Henshall, H. J. Mechanical cultivation and belukar crushing. RRIMPB, n.s., 12 (1954): 53-56.

Hill, R. D., and Ani bin Arope. Agriculture in Trengganu, Malaysia. Paper presented at Congress of National Academy of Science. Singapore, August 1968. 10 p. Graphs, maps. Mimeo.

Ho, Robert. Mixed farming and multiple cropping in Malaya. JTG, 16 (1962): 1-17.

Ho, Robert. The evolution of agriculture and land ownership in Saiong Mukim. MER, 13, 2 (1968): 81-102.

Holttum, Richard E. The effects of the introduction of exotic plants in the Malay Peninsula. PPSC, 5 (Canada), 3 (1933): 1749-1752.

Holttum, Richard E. Gardening in the lowlands of Malaya. Singapore, 1953. 323 p.

Hsu, Yu-chu, and Cheam Soon-tee. A methodology of farm management research in newly developing areas. Malaysian Management Review, 3, 1 (1968): 65-77.

Jack, H. W. Brief notes on agricultural conditions on the east coast of Malaya. Mal Ag Jl, 16 (1928): 88-91.

Jackson, James C. Smallholding cultivation of cash crops. In Wang Gung-wu. Malaysia: A Survey. London, 1964: 246-273.

Jackson, James C. Chinese and European agricultural enterprise in Malaya, 1786-1921: a geographical study of expansion and change. 1965. Ph.D. thesis -- University of Malaya.

Jackson, James C. Chinese agricultural pioneering in Singapore and Johore. JRASMB, 38 (1965): 77-105.

Jackson, James C. Planters and speculators: Chinese and European agriculture in Malaya 1786-1921. Kuala Lumpur, 1968. 334 p. Bibliog., figs., maps, tables.

Jagoe, R. B. Beneficial effects of some leguminous shade trees on grassland in Malaya. Mal Ag Jl, 32 (1949): 77-90.

Johnston, Anthony. Common diseases and pests of
crops in Malaya, with suggestions for their control.
Kuala Lumpur, 1959. (Department of Agriculture,
Bulletin, no. 110)

Johnstone, J. R. Observations on agricultural development
in Malaya. Trop Ag, 32 (1955): 274-277.

Joseph, K. T. Problems of agriculture. In Wang Gung-wu.
Malaysia: A Survey. London, 1964: 274-292.

Kanapathy, V. The place of agriculture in Malaysian
economy. UMBCER, 2, 1 (1966): 6-29.

Kanapathy, V. The place of agriculture in Malaysian
economic development. Geographica, 3 (1967): 21-43.

Kennaway, M. J. Some agricultural enterprises in
Malaya, 1933-1934. Kuala Lumpur, 1934. 132 p.
(Articles originally appeared in the Straits Times).

Khairi bin Haji, Mohamed, and Mohamed Tamin bin
Yeop. Socio-economic survey and its implication
to the Muda Irrigation Project. Kubang Sepat
Pilot Scheme: a case study. Kuala Lumpur [1967].
16 p. Tables. Mimeo.

King, A. W. Plantation and agriculture in Malaya,
with notes on the trade of Singapore. G Jl, 93
(1939): 136-148.

Koh, Theam-hee. Agricultural development and farmers'
association - a case study. Kuala Lumpur, Malaysian
Centre for Development Studies [n.d.].

Koh, Theam-hee. Farmers' association: the development
of decision making bodies. A paper presented
at the Regional Seminar on Development 4th February
- 14th February, 1968. Kuala Lumpur, 1968. 22 p.

Koh, Theam-hee, and Liao Hsing-chia. A scheme for
supervised farm credit. [Kuala Lumpur, n.d.].
26 p. Appendices. Mimeo.

Koh, Theam-hee, and Liao Hsing-chia. Farm surveys,
and farmers association business service plan.
Kuala Lumpur, Department of Agriculture, 1966.
7 p. Appendices.

Ladejinsky, W. L. Agriculture in British Malaya.
For Ag, 5 (1941): 103-125.

Ladejinsky, W. L. Agricultural policies of British
Malaya. For Ag, 5, 4 (1941): 159-164.

Lambourne, J. The Brazil nut in Malaya. Kuala Lumpur,
1930. (Department of Agriculture, Special Bulletin,
General Series, no. 2)

Lee, Peng-choong. The implications of the land capability
classification on forest reservation in Malaysia.
Mal For, 31, 2 (1968): 74-77.

Le Mare, D. W. Pig-rearing, fish-farming and vegetable
growing. Mal Ag Jl, 35 (1952): 156-166.

Lew, Sip-hon. Some economic aspects of agricultural
diversification in Malaysia. Mal Ag Jl, 45, 1
(1965): 6-16.

Lim, Joo-jock. Tradition and peasant agriculture
in Malaya. MJTG, 3 (Oct. 1954): 44-47.

Lowe, B. A. Vegetable production of Cameron Highlands.
Mal Ag Jl, 30 (1947): 5-12.

MacAndrew, W. R. The growing of possible economic
crops in British Malaya. Ipoh, 1932.

Malaya. Annual report of the Division of Agriculture,
Malaya for the year 1965. By Mohamad bin Jamil.
Kuala Lumpur [n.d.]. 89 p. Mimeo.

Malaya, Department of Agriculture and Co-operatives.
Census of Agriculture, 1960. Technical report
on the sample design for the Agriculture Census.
By S. Tsukibayashi. Kuala Lumpur, 1960.

Malaya, Department of Agriculture and Co-operatives.
Census of Agriculture, 1960. Census Monograph
One. Comparison of data from the 1960 agriculture
census with data from other sources. Kuala Lumpur,
1961.

Malaya, Department of Agriculture and Co-operatives.
Census of Agriculture, 1960. Administrative Report.
Census Documents, by T. B. Wilson. Kuala Lumpur, 1962.

Malaya, Department of Agriculture and Co-operatives.
Census of Agriculture, 1960. Report no. 1. Number
of farms. Kuala Lumpur, 1960.

Malaya, Department of Agriculture and Co-operatives.
Census of Agriculture, 1960. Report no. 2. Size
of farms. By T. B. Wilson. Kuala Lumpur, 1960.

Malaya, Department of Agriculture and Co-operatives.
Census of Agriculture, 1960. Report no. 3. Type,
tenure and fragmentation of farms. By T. B. Wilson.
Kuala Lumpur, 1961.

Malaya, Department of Agriculture and Co-operatives.
Census of Agriculture, 1960. Report no. 4. Farm
equipment and power. By T. B. Wilson. Kuala Lumpur,
1961.

Malaya, Department of Agriculture and Co-operatives.
Census of Agriculture, 1960. Report no. 5. Livestock.
By T. B. Wilson. Kuala Lumpur, 1961.

Malaya, Department of Agriculture and Co-operatives.
Census of Agriculture, 1960. Report no. 6. Farms
reporting rubberland. By T. B. Wilson. Kuala
Lumpur, 1961.

Malaya, Department of Agriculture and Co-operatives. Census
of Agriculture, 1960. Report no. 6A. Rubberland: area
and production. By S. Selvadurai. Kuala Lumpur, 1962.

Malaya, Department of Agriculture and Co-operatives.
Census of Agriculture, 1960. Report no. 7. Coconuts.
By S. Selvadurai. Kuala Lumpur, 1962.

Malaya, Department of Agriculture and Co-operatives.
Census of Agriculture, 1960. Report no. 8. Land
use and tenure. By T. B. Wilson. Kuala Lumpur, 1962.

Malaya, Department of Agriculture and Co-operatives.
Census of Agriculture, 1960. Report no. 9. Temporary
crops: area and production. By S. Selvadurai.
Kuala Lumpur, 1962.

Malaya, Department of Agriculture and Co-operatives.
Census of Agriculture, 1960. Report no. 10. Permanent
crops: compact areas and scattered trees. By
S. Selvadurai. Kuala Lumpur, 1962.

Malaya, Department of Agriculture and Co-operatives.
Census of Agriculture, 1960. Report no. 11. The
farmer: age, sex, livelihood, household. By S.
Selvadurai. Kuala Lumpur, 1962.

Malaya, Department of Agriculture and Co-operatives.
Census of Agriculture, 1960. Report no. 12. Farm
labour. By S. Selvadurai. Kuala Lumpur, 1962.

Malaya, Department of Agriculture and Co-operatives.
Census of Agriculture, 1960. Report no. 13. Usage
of irrigation, fertilizers and chemicals. By
S. Selvadurai. Kuala Lumpur, 1962.

Malaya, Department of Agriculture and Co-operatives.
Census of Agriculture, 1960. Report no. 14. Fish
and wood production. By S. Selvadurai. Kuala
Lumpur, 1962.

Malaya, Department of Agriculture and Co-operatives.
Census of Agriculture, 1960. Report no. 15. i.
Government farms; ii. Group settlements. By S.
Selvadurai. Kuala Lumpur, 1962.

Malaya, Department of Agriculture and Co-operatives.
Census of Agriculture, 1960. Report no. 16. Estates.
By S. Selvadurai. Kuala Lumpur, 1963.

Malaya (Federation), Department of Statistics. Kementerian
Pertanian dan Sharikat Kerjasama. A report of
progress achieved ... during the period January
1958 to December 1960, for submission to Food
and Agricultural Organization of the United Nations.
[Kuala Lumpur] 1962. 41 p.

Malaya: prospects for agriculture. Kuala Lumpur,
Department of Technical Operations, Sept. 1960.
Mimeo.

Malaysia, Department of Agriculture. Regulations
governing the budget making and budgetary control
of Farmers' Association. (Draft). Kuala Lumpur
[n.d.]. 25 p. Mimeo.

Marsh, T. D., and N. Kanagarantnam. The cultivation
of tobacco in Malaya. Mal Ag Jl, 20 (1932): 557-574.

Marshal, C. Land use and abuse in Malaya. Mal For,
15 (1952): 132-136.

McConnell, Robert M. A survey of agriculture in
   Malaysia. Washington, D.C., 1964. 55 p. (U.S.
   Department of Agriculture, Economic Research
   Service Foreign Report, no. 95) Illus., map.

Milsum, J. N. Fruit culture in Malaya. Kuala Lumpur,
   1919. (Department of Agriculture, Special Bulletin,
   o.s., no. 29)

Milsum, J. N. Cultivation of coffee in Malaya. Mal
   Ag Jl, 18 (1930): 481-496.

Milsum, J. N. Cultivation of allotments by Tamil
   labourers. Kuala Lumpur, 1932. 12 p. (Department
   of Agriculture, Circular, no. 3)

Milsum, J. N., and D. H. Grist. Vegetable gardening
   in Malaya. Kuala Lumpur, 1941. 206 p. (Malayan
   Planting Manual, no. 3)

Mohamad bin Jamil, and Koh Theam-hee. The development
   of Farmers' Association in Malaysia as a unit
   for extension program planning and implementation
   of agricultural projects. Kuala Lumpur, Department
   of Agriculture, 1966. 20 p. Appendices. Mimeo.

Mohd. Tamin bin Yeop. The Sungei Muda Irrigation
   Scheme and Kubang Sepat Double-cropping Pilot
   Scheme. 1967. 10 p. Maps. Mimeo.

Moubray, G. A. de C. de. The Sungei Manik irrigation
   scheme. Mal Ag Jl, 24 (1936): 160-166.

Muda Irrigation Project. Estimate proposal for protecting
   the catchment (Project No. 14). Kuala Lumpur,
   Aug. 1968. 25 p. Appendices A-K, maps. Mimeo.

Ng, Kay-fong, Tan Chee-lian, and R. Wikkramatileke.
   Three farmers of Singapore: an example of the
   mechanics of specialised food production in an
   urban unit. PV, 7, 2 (1966): 169-198.

Ormsby-Gore, W. G. Tropical agriculture in Malaya,
   Ceylon and Java. United Empire, n.s., 19 (1928):
   459-475.

Pendleton, R. L. Land use in Southeast Asia. FES,
   16 (1947): 25-29.

Phang, S., and T. K. Wong. Some possible crops for
    diversification. Mal Ag, 4 (1964): 22-36.

Pim, Alan. Colonial agricultural production; the
    contribution made by native peasants and by foreign
    enterprise. London, 1946. 190 p.
    For Malaya, see p. 13-76, especially p. 45-59.

Pinto, Constance. The development of an agricultural
    policy in the Federated Malay States 1874-1914.
    Singapore, 1961. M.A. thesis -- University of
    Malaya.

Research stations and training centres under the
    Ministry of Agriculture and Co-operatives. Mal
    Ag Jl, 46, 2 (1967): i-ii.

Sandison, S. Notes on the burning of jungle. Planter,
    39, 1 (1963): 15-17.

Sarle, C. R. Census of Agriculture, Federation of
    Malaya, 1960. New York, Council on Economic and
    Cultural Affairs, August, 1962.

Scarlett, Sally. Some comments on farmers' associations
    in Malaysia and Taiwan. Mal Ag, 7 (1966/1967-1967/1968):
    21-31.

Simpson, J. J., and Lau Sing Nam. Chinese market
    gardening. Mal Ag Jl, 22 (1934): 119-124.

Smith, H. V. Report on marketing problems in the
    fruit industry of Malaya, July-September, 1957.
    Kuala Lumpur [n.d.]. Mimeo.

Spencer, J. E. Seasonality in the tropics: the supply
    of fruit to Singapore. GR, 49 (1959): 475-484.

Spring, F. G. Food-stuffs in Malaya. Trop Agriculturalist,
    49 (1917): 256-260.

Spring, F. G., and J. N. Milsum. Food production
    in Malaya. Kuala Lumpur, 1919. 112 p. (Department
    of Agriculture, Special Bulletin, o.s., no. 30)

Stanton, W. R. An agricultural policy for Malaya.
    World Crops, 17, 1 (1965): 20-25.

Stockdale, Frank. Report by Sir Frank Stockdale
on a visit to Malaya, Java, Sumatra and Ceylon,
1938. London, 1938. 108 p.

Stockdale, Frank. Abstract of a report on a visit
to Malaya. Mal Ag Jl, 27 (1939): 371-374.

Strickland, C. Contrasts of the Indian and the Malayan
countryside. Journal of the Central Asian Society
(London), 17 (1930): 43-54.

Valkenburg, S. van. Agricultural regions of Asia.
Part 8--Malaysia. Ec G, 11 (1935): 227-246, 325-337.

Wharton, Clifton R. Farm management and Malayan
rural development. [Kuala Lumpur, 1964]. 20 p.
Tables.

Wheatley, Paul. Land use in the vicinity of Singapore
in the eighteen-thirties. MJTG, 2 (1954): 63-66.

Williams, C. N. Temperature and cultivation of high
altitude areas in Malaysia. Mal Ag, 7 (1966/1967-
1967/1968): 41-50.

Willis, J. C. Report upon agriculture in the Federated
Malay States. Selangor, 1905. 106 p.

Wilson, J. N. The Sri Menanti, Senggarang and Muar
drainage schemes, Johore. Mal Ag Jl, 40, 4 (1957):
241-252. Illus., map.

Wyatt-Smith, J. A land utilisation map of Malaya.
Singapore, submitted to the Food and Agriculture
Organization Forestry Commission Conference,
1952. (FAO/APFC-52/80) A table analyzing the
types of forests in forest reserve and on state
land in the Federation of Malaya is reproduced
in the Malayan Forester, 17 (1954): 84.

2. Land tenure

Abdul Aziz bin Abdul Hamid, Ungku. Land disintegration
and land policy in Malaya. MER, 3, 1 (1958): 22-29.

Abdul Aziz bin Abdul Hamid, Ungku. Subdivision of
estates in Malaya 1951-1960. Kuala Lumpur, 1962. 3 v.

ECONOMY - Agriculture: Land tenure

Abdul Aziz bin Abdul Hamid, Ungku. Subdivision of
estates in Malaya 1951-1960. Author's reply.
MER, 11, 2 (1966): 46-62.

Akib, S. The attitude of the Malayan peasant toward
the tenure problem of Malaya. Proc Conf World
Land Tenure Prob, 1 (1951): 113-115.

An annotated bibliography on land tenure in the
British and British protected territories in
South East Asia and the Pacific. London, 1952.
164 p. (Colonial Research Studies, no. 6)

Aziz. See Abdul Aziz.

Bibliography of "Statutory and legal sources; Proceedings
and legislative council debates; Official statements
and investigations" regarding land tenure in
Federated Malay States. In An Annotated Bibliography
on Land Tenure in the British Protected Territories
in South East Asia and the Pacific. London, 1952: 2-27.

Bridges, William F. N. Surveys for title in the
Federated Malay States, with notes on the revenue
surveys of the Unfederated Malay States. Kuala
Lumpur, 1930. 68 p. Map, tables.

Bryson, H. P. Land tenure and documents of title
in Malaya. Malaya (1963): 26-27.

Chua, B. L. Land registration in Singapore and the
Federation of Malaya. UMLR, 1 (1959): 318-330.

Coulson, N. System of land tenure in Kelantan. Mal
Ag Jl, 16 (1929): 118-126.

Cowgill, J. V. System of land tenure in the Federated
Malay States. Mal Ag Jl, 16 (1928): 187-193.

Das, S. K. The Torrens system in Malaya. With an
introduction by Dato' Sir James Thomson. Singapore,
Malayan Law Journal, 1963. 542 p.

Dobby, E. H. G. Malaya: rubber and rice. Current
History, 25 (1953): 295-300.

Grist, D. H. Land tenure. In An Outline of Malayan
Agriculture. London, 1933: 13-24.

275

Harrison, C. W. Land laws and land administration
in the Federated Malay States. Singapore, 1923.

Hill, R. D. Agricultural land tenure in West Malaysia.
MER, 12, 1 (1967): 99-116.

Innes, J. R. Treatise on registration of titles
in the Federated Malay States, with reports of
cases from 1907-1913. Kuala Lumpur, 1913.

Jacoby, Erich H. Agrarian unrest in Southeast Asia.
New York, 1949. 287 p.
    See Chapter 4, p. 101-133, on Malaya.

Jacoby, Erich H. Types of tenure and economic development.
MER, 4, 1 (1959): 10-20.

Jacoby, Erich H. Agrarian unrest in Southeast Asia.
2d rev. and enl. ed. London, 1961. 279 p.
    Part 5 deals with the Federation of Malaya,
    p. 109-147.

Jarret, N. R. Land tenure in Malaya. Eastern World,
5, 3-4 (1951): 9-10.

Joseph, K. T. Malacca land laws, 1825-1886. Singapore,
1953. Thesis -- University of Malaya.

Land administration and surveys. Singapore, 1923.
    49 p. (Malayan Series X)

Leake, H. M. Studies in tropical land tenure. Trop
Ag, 9 (1932): 244-249, 320-325.

Leake, H. M. Further studies in tropical land tenure.
IV. The eastern colonies. Malaya. Trop Ag, 15
(1938): 243-245.

Lim, Teck-ghee. Aspects of British land and agricultural
policy in Perak, 1874-1897. 1968. 321 p. M.A.
thesis -- University of Malaya.

Lim, Teck-ghee. The origins of a colonial land policy.
1968. 38 p. Unpublished paper no. 44, presented
at the International Conference on Asian History,
Kuala Lumpur, August 1968. Mimeo.

Liversage, V. Land tenure in the colonies. Cambridge,
1945. 151 p. Bibliog., index.

Mahmud bin Mat. Land subdivision and fragmentation.
Intisari, 1, 2 [n.d.]: 11-17.

Malaysia. National Land Code. Act of Parliament
No. 56 of 1965. Kuala Lumpur, 1965.

Malaysia, Development Administration Unit. Prime
Minister's Department. Land administration: a
study on some critical areas. Kuala Lumpur, 1968.
49 p. Charts, table. Mimeo.

Maxwell, George. Malay reservations. United Empire,
37 (1946): 125-126.

Maxwell, W. E. Straits Settlements: present and
future land systems. Rangoon, 1883. 34 p.

Maxwell, W. E. The law and customs of the Malays
with reference to the tenure of land. JRASSB,
13 (1884): 75-219.

Maxwell, W. E. Memorandum on the introduction of
a land code in the native states in the Malay
peninsula. Singapore, 1894. 112 p.

Meek, Charles K. Land law and custom in the colonies.
London, 1946. 337 p.
See chapters 3 and 4, p. 32-56 for Malaya.

Mohar bin Raja Badiozaman. Malay land reservation
and alienation. Intisari, 1, 2 [n.d.]: 19-25.

Moor, I. M. Local land tenure. Mal Ag Jl, 10 (1922):
13-17.

Ness, Gayl D. Subdivision of estates in Malaya 1951-1960:
a methodological critique. MER, 9, 1 (1964): 55-62.

Padi Cultivators (Control of Rent and Security of
Tenure) Act, 1967. Malaysia, Act of Parliament,
No. 43 of 1967.

Pelzer, Karl J. Population and land utilization.
New York, 1941. 215 p.
Constitutes Part 1 of An Economic Survey of
the Pacific Area. See p. 143-147 for land tenure
of Malaya.

Quirin, G. David. Estate subdivision and economic development: a review article. MER, 9, 1 (1964): 63-79.

Reports of committees and variety of subjects and bills dealing with land and land transfers during the occupation period. Kuala Lumpur, 1949. (Legislative Council Papers, no. 15, 35, 43, 50 and 51)

Sinclair, Keith. Hobson and Lennin in Johore: Colonial Office policy towards British concessionaires and investors, 1878-1907. MAS, 1, 4 (1967): 335-352.

Singh, S. Economic aspects of three new land development schemes organized by the Federal Land Development Authority in the Federation of Malaya. Canberra, 1965. Ph.D. thesis -- Australian National University.

Singh, S. An evaluation of three land development schemes in Malaysia. MER, 13, 1 (1968): 89-100.

Smith, Eldon, and Peter R. Goethals. Tenancy among padi cultivators in Malaysia. A study of tenancy conditions and laws affecting land lord-tenant relations. Kuala Lumpur, 1965. 150 p.

Talog Davies. "Malay" as defined in the States Malay reservation enactments. Intisari, 1, 2 [n.d.]: 27-28.

Tippetts, Abbett, McCarthy, and Stratton. The Jengka Triangle report. [Kuala Lumpur] 1967. 4 v. Illus., maps. Contents: V. 1, The outline master plan. V. 2, Resources and development planning. V. 3, Appendices. V. 4, Maps.

Watson, R. G. The land laws and land administration of the Federated Malay States. Kuala Lumpur, 1908. 36 p.

Wilson, T. B. Some economic aspects of padi-land ownership in Krian. Mal Ag Jl, 37 (1954): 125-135.

Wilson, T. B. The inheritance and fragmentation of Malay padi lands in Krian, Perak. Mal Ag Jl, 38, 2 (1955): 71-77. Tables.

3. Rice

Agarwal, M. C. An account of the Tanjong Karang
    Project. MER, 9, 2 (1964): 64-74. Tables.

Ahmad bin Yunus. Review of work on major insect
    pests of rice in Malaysia. Mal Ag Jl, 45, 1 (1965):
    28-56.

Allan, F. H., and E. J. H. Berwick. The development
    of new rice lands in Malaya. U N Sci Conf Conserv
    and Util Resources Proc, 6 (1951): 588-590.

Allen, E. F. The effects of crop rotation on growth
    and yield of padi. Mal Ag Jl, 39, 2 (1956): 133-139.
    Tables.

Allen, E. F., and D. W. M. Haynes. A review of investi-
    gations into the mechanical cultivation and harvesting
    of wet padi with special reference to the latter.
    Mal Ag Jl, 36 (1953): 61-80. Map.

Allen, E. F., and J. R. Milburn. Double cropping
    of wet padi in Province Wellesley. MER, 39, 1
    (1956): 48-62. Diagrs., tables.

Ashby, J. K. Off-season padi trials in the Salor
    irrigation area, Kelantan, in 1953. Mal Ag Jl,
    37 (1954): 3-11.

Aston, A. V. Review of the Sungei Manik padi irrigation
    scheme. Mal Ag Jl, 28 (1940): 322-329. Map.

Barnett, H. L. Rice in Malaya, season 1947-1948.
    Mal Ag Jl, 32 (1949): 4-17. Tables.

Beamish, Tony. The black rice of Padang Masirat.
    MHJ, 1 (Dec. 1954): 125-127.

Bean, K. W. Muda River Project. World Crops, 21,
    1 (1969): 13-16.
    Irrigation in Kedah and Perlis.

Berwick, E. J. H. Pure strains of padi in Krian.
    Mal Ag Jl, 28 (1940): 429-433.

Berwick, E. J. H. Wet padi mechanical cultivation
    experiments, Kelantan, season 1950-1951. Mal
    Ag Jl, 34 (1951): 166-184.

Berwick, E. J. H. Dry padi mechanical cultivation experiments, Kelantan, season 1950-1951. Mal Ag Jl, 34 (1951): 185-206.

Berwick, E. J. H. Mechanical cultivation of rice in Malaya. World Crops, 3 (1951): 207-210.

Birkinshaw, F. A. A review of field experiments on paddy in Malaya. Mal Ag Jl, 28 (1940): 507-516.

Blagden, C. O. An account of the cultivation of rice in Malaya. (Romanized by Inche Muhammad Ja'far, tr. by C. O. B.) JRASSB, 30 (1897): 285-304.

Britisch Malakka: rijstoogst-seizoen 1939-1940. Ec Weekbl Ned Ind, 10 (1941): 441.

Brown, F. B. Varietal extension trials with wet padi, 1952-1953. Mal Ag Jl, 36 (1953): 218-225.

Brown, F. B. Hybrid vigor in rice. Mal Ag Jl, 36 (1953): 226-236.

Brown, F. B. Rice variety trial in Malaya, 1954-58. Kuala Lumpur, 1959. (Department of Agriculture, Bulletin, no. 109)

Buckley, T. A. Improvement of rice yields in Malaya by the use of fertilizers. Mal Ag Jl, 34 (1951): 119-126.

Cheng, Siok-hwa. Rice imports into Malaya: a brief historical survey. 1968. 14 p. Unpublished paper no. 85 presented at the International Conference on Asian History, Kuala Lumpur, August 1968. Mimeo.

Coleman, P. G. Wet padi mechanisation investigations in Province Wellesley during the 1950-1951 season. Mal Ag Jl, 36 (1953): 3-19.

Cook, J. Fallow season cultivation of padi-land in Malacca. MER, 31 (1948): 115-118.

Cooke, E. M. Rice cultivation in Malaya. Singapore, 1961. 55 p. (Malayan Studies Series, no. 2)

Dobby, E. H. G. The North Kedah Plain (Malaya); a study in the environment of pioneering for rice cultivation. Ec G, 27 (1951): 287-315.

Dobby, E. H. G. Malaya's rice problem. PA, 27 (1954): 58-60.

Dobby, E. H. G., et al. Padi landscapes of Malaya. MJTG, 6 (1955): 94 p. and atlas; 10 (1957): 143 p. Maps.

Farm Economic Survey of the Muda River Project 1966. A joint-study report prepared by the Division of Agriculture and the Economics and Statistics Section of the Ministry of Agriculture and Co-operatives, West Malaysia. Kuala Lumpur, 1967.

Federated Malay States. Report on the progress of schemes for the improvement and extension of rice cultivation. Kuala Lumpur, 1935. 12 p. 7 key plans.

Goor, G. A. W. van de, and G. Zijlstra. Irrigation requirements for double cropping of lowland rice in Malaya. Wageningen, 1968. 68 p. (International Institute for Land Reclamation and Improvement, Publication 14) Maps.

Grantham, W. Malaya's position with regard to rice production. In Federation of Malaya. Annual Report of the Drainage and Irrigation Department for the Year 1948. Kuala Lumpur, 1949: 31-39.

Grist, D. H. Wet padi planting in Negri Sembilan. Kuala Lumpur, 1922. 93 p. (Department of Agriculture, Special Bulletin, o.s., no. 33)

Grist, D. H. Rice in Malaya in 1939. Mal Ag Jl, 28 (1940): 164-170.

Grist, D. H. Rice in Malaya in 1940. (Prices and price control, import and exports, areas and yield, consumption vs production). Mal Ag Jl, 29 (1941): 155-162.

Grist, D. H. Rice. London, 1953.

Grist, D. H. The rice problem. MJTG, 5 (1955): 20-25.

Hai, Ding-eng (Tan). The rice industry in Malaya, 1920-1940. Singapore, 1963. 60 p. (Singapore Studies on Borneo and Malaya, no. 2) Illus.

Hartley, C. W. S. Establishment of new rice areas in Malaya. World Crops, 3 (1951): 171-175.

Hartley, C. W. S. Experiments with the mechanization of rice culture in Malaya. Agricultura e Pecuaria, 23 (1951): 46-49, 66. In Portuguese.

Haynes, A. L. Extension of rice cultivation in the Federated Malay States: need of a definite policy. Kuala Lumpur, 1933. 7 p. (Legislative Council Paper, no. 28)

Hill, A. H. Kelantan padi planting. JRASMB, 24, 1 (1951): 56-76. Bibliog., illus.

Hill, R. D. Dry rice cultivation in peninsular Malaya. OG (Dacca), 10, 1 (1966): 10-14.

Hill, R. D. Rice cultivation systems in Malaya. World Crops, 18, 3 (1966): 72-74.

Jack, Henry W. Rice in Malaya. Kuala Lumpur, 1923. 96 p. (Department of Agriculture, Special Bulletin, o.s., no. 35)

Jack, Henry W. Present position in regard to rice production in Malaya. PPSC, 4 (Java), 4 (1929): 33-44.

Jack, Henry W. Tractor ploughing for padi cultivation. Mal Ag Jl, 13 (1935): 142-144.

Jagoe, R. B. Photoperiodism of Oryza sativa in Malaya. Experiments on the effects of a small difference of light period on flowering of the padi plant. Mal Ag Jl, 35 (1952): 85-102. Bibliog.

Jagoe, R. B., and L. N. H. Larter. Improvement of padi varieties in Malaya. Mal Ag Jl, 34 (1951): 127-130.

Kandiah, Punithavathy. Some of the major problems of achieving selfsufficiency in the rice production in Malaya. Geographica, 1 (1964/1965): 55-59.

Khatijah Binti Ahmad. Padi/rice marketing in West Malaysia. In Proceedings, National Agricultural Marketing Seminar, 13th-18th November, 1967. Kuala Lumpur, 1968: 98-122.

Kimura, N. Chemical control of padi stem-borer in
Malaya (1959-1960). Kuala Lumpur, 1965. 33 p.
(Division of Agriculture Bulletin, no. 116)

Kok, L. T. Rice leaf and plant hoppers--their significance
and control with special reference to Malaysia.
Mal Ag, 7 (1966/1967-1967/1968): 51-58.

Kuchiba, Masuo, and Yoshihira Tsuhouchi. Maraya
hokuseibu no inasaku--noson--konin, rikon, kazoku
no tokushitsu ni tsuite (A Malay padi-farming
community in the northwestern part of Malaya--a
sociological analysis of marriage, divorce, and
family). Tonan Ajia Kenkyu, 4, 1 (1966).

Kuchiba, Masuo, and Yoshihira Tsuhouchi. Paddy farming
and social structure in a Malay village. Developing
Economies, 5, 3 (1967): 463-485.

Kuchiba, Masuo, Yoshihira Tsuhouchi, and Maeda.
Maraya hokuseibu no inasaku--noson--nochi shoyu
no reisai-ka ni tsuite (A padi-farming community
in the northwestern part of Malaya--the fragmentation
of landholding). Tonan Ajia Kenkyu, 3, 1 (1965): 48-51.

Kuilman, L. W. Rice during and after the war: a
bibliography of the literature on rice during
the period 1940-1947. Buitenzorg, 1949. 244 p.
(Communications of the General Agricultural Research
Station Buitenzorg, Java, no. 87)

Kyoto University, Centre for Southeast Asian Studies.
Rice culture in Malay, improvement in rice culture
in Malaya by Japanese experts. Kyoto, 1965.

Lambourne, J. Mechanical cultivation of rice. Mal
Ag Jl, 19 (1931): 218-228.

Larter, L. N. H. Rice variety trials in Malaya,
1947-1950. Kuala Lumpur, 1953. 88 p. (Department
of Agriculture, Special Bulletin, Science Series,
no. 25)

Laycock, Harold G. Rice production in Malaya. Malaya
(1954): 278-281.

Lee, Sin-fook, and Koh Theam-hee. Experience in
introducing double-cropping of paddy at Tanjong
Karang, Selangor, Malaysia. Farm Management Notes,
Asia Far East, 3, 2 (1967): 38-46. 2 figs.

Lim, Guan-soon, and Goh Kee-guan. Leafhopper transmission
of a virus disease of rice locally known as "padi
jantan" in Krian, Malaysia. Mal Ag Jl, 46, 4
(1968): 435-450.

Lim, Joo-jock. Padi-farming activities and rainfall
regimes. 1954. M.A. thesis -- University of Singapore.

Lockard, R. G. The effect of depth and movement
of water on the growth and yield of rice plants.
Mal Ag Jl, 41, 4 (1958): 266-281.

Lockard, R. G. Mineral nutrition of the rice plant
in Malaya, with special reference to penyakit
merah. Kuala Lumpur, 1959. 148 p. (Department
of Agriculture Bulletin, no. 108)

Malaya. Action taken by the Federation government
on the report of the Rice Production Committee.
Kuala Lumpur, 1954. 22 p. (Legislative Council
Report, no. 30)

Malaya. Rice Committee interim report. Kuala Lumpur,
Government Printer, 1955.

Malaya, Federation of. Investigations into the mechanical
cultivation of padi in Malaya, August, 1950.
Kuala Lumpur, 1952. 120 p. (Department of Agriculture
Mechanisation Series, no. 1) Illus., tables.

Malaya, Federation of. Government trading in rice.
Kuala Lumpur, 1954. 23 p. (Legislative Council
Paper, no. 27)

Malaya, Ministry of Agriculture and Co-operatives.
Muda River Project; report on the supply of irrigation
water from the River Muda and Padang Terap for
double rice cultivation in the coastal plains
of Kedah and Perlis. Kuala Lumpur, 1961. 32 p.
Diagrs., graphs, illus., maps, tables.

Malaya, Rice Committee. Final report of the Rice
Committee. Kuala Lumpur, 1956. 139 p. Graphs,
tables.

Malaya, Rice Production Committee. Report of the
Rice Production Committee. Kuala Lumpur [n.d.].
156 p. Graphs, map.

Malaysia, Department of Statistics. Rice statistics
for the States of Malaya, 1965. Kuala Lumpur,
1966. The same statistics were issued for 1966.
Kuala Lumpur, 1967.

Marsden, R. H. A small rice thresher for peasant
growers. Mal Ag Jl, 42, 4 (1959): 199-206. Illus.

Matsushima, Seizo. Some experiments on soil water
plant relationship in rice. Kuala Lumpur, Division
of Agriculture, Ministry of Agriculture and Co-
operatives [1962]. 35 p. (Division of Agriculture
Bulletin, no. 112) Graphs, illus., tables.

Matsushima, Seizo. Theory and techniques of rice
cultivation, determination of yield and its application.
Kuala Lumpur, Department of Agriculture, 1961.
257 p. Mimeo.

Miller, J. I. Administration of the Sungei Manik
padi irrigation scheme. Mal Ag Jl, 25 (1937):
370-375. Maps, plates.

Moubray, G. A. de C. de. Sungei Manik irrigation
scheme. Mal Ag Jl, 24 (1936): 160-166. Illus.,
plates, tables.

Muhammad Ja'far. An account of the cultivation of
rice in Malacca. JRASSB, 30 (July 1897): 285-296.

Narkswasdi, Udhis, and S. Selvadurai. Report no.
1--Selangor. Economic survey of padi production
in West Malaysia. Kuala Lumpur, 1967. 211 p.

Narkswasdi, Udhis, and S. Selvadurai. Report no.
2--Collective padi cultivation in Bachang, Malacca.
Kuala Lumpur, 1967. 272 p.

Narkswasdi, Udhis, and S. Selvadurai. Report no.
3--Malacca. Kuala Lumpur, Ministry of Agriculture
and Co-operatives, 1967. 187 p.

De ontwikkeling van de rijstcultuur in British Malakka.
Ec Weekbl Ned Ind, 10 (1941): 473-476.

Padi planting methods in Malaya. Mal Ag Jl, 27 (1939):
40-59.

Pratt, Harry Charles. Padi cultivation in Krian.
   Kuala Lumpur, 1911. 19 p. (Department of Agriculture,
   Special Bulletin, o.s., no. 12)

Purcal, J. Marketing of paddy from four villages
   in Province Wellesley, Malaya. Food and Agriculture
   Organization of the United Nations/Economic Commission
   for Asia and the Far East Meeting, New Delhi,
   February-March 1963.

Purcal, J. Labour utilization among men in a padi
   village in Province Wellesley. MER, 10, 2 (1965):
   49-60.

Ramiah, K. Notes on field visits. (In Burma, Philippines
   and Malaya). Int Rice Comm News Letter, 2 (1952): 12-20.

Ramiah, K. Factors affecting rice production. Rome, 1954.

Die reisländer Hinterindiens, 4. Malaya. Gordian,
   47 (1942): 11-12.

Report on the progress of schemes for the improvement
   and extension of rice cultivation. Kuala Lumpur,
   1935. 12 p. 7 plans.

Report of the Rice Cultivation Commission. Harold
   A. Tempany, Chairman. Singapore, 1931.
   2 v. (1) 54 p. (2) 196 p.

Report of the Rice Production Committee. V. 1.
   J. G. Black, Chairman. Kuala Lumpur, 1953. 158 p.
   (Legislative Council Paper, no. 52) Graphs, map,
   tables.

Rice cultivation in British Malaya. United Empire,
   28 (1937): 159-161.

Robinson, A. G. Irrigation of riverine areas: Bota-Lambor
   Kanan pumping scheme, Perak River. Mal Ag Jl,
   24 (1936): 524-528.

Rutherford, J. Double cropping of wet padi in Penang,
   Malaya. GR, 56, 2 (1966): 239-255. Maps.

Rutherford, J. Intensive padi farming in Malaya:
   developmental problems and general effects of
   government planning. In J. Rutherford, M. I.
   Logan, and G. J. Missen. New Viewpoints in Economic
   Geography. Sydney, 1966: 71-92.

Rutherford, J. Case studies of Malayan rice areas:
some dominant features of seven irrigation projects.
In J. Rutherford, M. I. Logan, and G. J. Missen.
New Viewpoints in Economic Geography. Sydney,
1966: 93-114.

Samoto, Shiro. Report on the rice varietal improvement
in Malaya, 1961-1963. Province Wellesley, 1963.
240 p. Mimeo.

Sands, W. N. Vegetation of the rice lands in North
Kedah. Mal Ag Jl, 21 (1933): 379-386.

Sedky, A. Production and processing of rice in Malaya.
Kuala Lumpur, Ministry of Agriculture and Cooperatives,
August, 1962. (Food and Agriculture Organization
of the United Nations, Report Series on Malayan
Food Commodities)

Selangor, Department of Agriculture. Farm economic
survey of the Muda River Project, 1966; a joint-study
report prepared by the Department of Agriculture
and Co-operatives, West Malaysia. Kuala Lumpur,
September, 1967. 109 p.

Shaw, G. E. Malay industries; pt. 3: rice planting.
Kuala Lumpur, 1926. 40 p. (Papers on Malay Subjects,
ser. 1, 5)

Simpson, H. J. Wet rice cultivation. Kuala Lumpur,
1933. 7 p. (Department of Agriculture Circular, no. 4)

Simpson, I. A., A. Y. Chow, and C. C. Soh. A study
of the nutritional value of some varieties of
Malayan rice. Kuala Lumpur, 1951. 28 p. (Institute
for Medical Research Bulletin, n.s., no. 5)

Stout, B. A. Equipment in rice production. Rome,
Food and Agriculture Organization of the United
Nations, 1966. 169 p. (Food and Agriculture Organization
of the United Nations, Agricultural Development
Paper, no. 84) Bibliog. of 322 items.

Tahir Abd. Rahim. Malay practices and beliefs connected
with the cultivation of padi in Malacca. Singapore,
1957. Thesis -- University of Malaya.

Tan, Ding-eing. The rice industry in Malaya, 1920-1940.
Singapore, University of Singapore, 1963.

Tang, Teng-lai, and P. Vamathevan. Adaptability
trials of West Malaysian padi varieties during
the seasons 1961-62 to 1963-64. Mal Ag Jl, 46,
1 (1967): 119-129.

Tempany, Harold A. Widespread efforts to expand
rice production. Times Rev Br Colonies, 12 (1953):
7-9. Illus., map, statistics.

Thompson, V. War and further India's rice. FES,
10 (1941): 183-188.

Thomson, A. M. Report on the marketing of rice in
the Federation of Malaya. New York, United Nations,
1954. (Food and Agricultural Organization of
the United Nations, Report no. 278)

Van, T. K. Present status of rice breeding in Malaya.
Mal Ag Jl, 43, 2 (1960/1961): 112-116.

Van, T. K. Rice variety trials in Malaya, 1958-1961.
Kuala Lumpur (1963). 51 p. (Division of Agriculture
Bulletin, no. 114)

Van, T. K. The breeding and selection of two new
hybrid varieties, Malinja and Mahsuri, for double
cropping in the States of Malaya. Mal Ag Jl,
45, 4 (1966): 332-344.

Wickizier, Vernon D., and M. K. Bennett. The rice
economy of Monsoon Asia. Palo Alto, 1941. 358 p.
Diagrs., maps, tables.

Wilshaw, R. G. H. Padi manurial and minor cultural
trials, seasons 1937-1938 and 1938-1939. Mal
Ag Jl, 27 (1939): 513-529.

Wilson, T. B. Sungei Manik padi farm survey; composition
and land tenure, 1956. Mal Ag Jl, 40, 2 (1957): 92-109.

Wilson, T. B. The economics of padi production in
North Malaya. Kuala Lumpur, Ministry of Agriculture,
Federation of Malaya, 1958.

Wulff, A. De rijstcultuur in Malakka. Landbouw,
15 (1939): 101-135.

Wyatt, I. J. Field investigations of padi stem-borers,
1955-1956. Kuala Lumpur, 1957. 42 p. (Department
of Agriculture Bulletin, no. 102)

4. Rubber

Achieving an optimum stand. RRIMPB, 34 (1958): 5-10.

Agoes Salim. The market for small farm rubber in
    Malaya. 1967. 199 p. Ph.D. thesis -- University
    of Wisconsin.

Allen, E. F. Cultivating other crops with rubber.
    RRIMPB (Jan. 1955): 10-21.

Application of stimulants to the virgin bark in
    clone trials. RRIMPB, 80 (Sept. 1965): 150-157.

Asimont, W. F. C. Hevea brasiliensis or para rubber
    in the Malay Peninsula. London, 1908. 64 p. Tables.

Balley, Walter. The production of estates and of
    native holdings in the world production of rubber.
    Int Rev Ag, 30 (1939): 95E-102E.

Baptist, E. D. C. Improvement of yields in Hevea
    brasiliensis. Kuala Lumpur, 1953. 9 p. (Originally
    appeared in World Crops, 5, 1953.)

Baptist, E. D. C. Recent progress in Malaya in the
    breeding and selection of clones of Hevea brasiliensis.
    Report of the 13th International Horticultural
    Congress, 2 (1953): 1100-1121.

Barlow, C., with B. R. Buttery, and P. R. Wycherly.
    Density of planting and degree of thinning: an
    experiment on Sepang Estate. RRIM, 62 (Sept.
    1969). Mimeo.

Barlow, C., with C. K. Chan. Towards an optimum
    size of rubber holding. JRRIM, 21, pt. 5 (1969).

Barlow, C., with C. S. Ng, and C. K. Chan. Factors
    affecting the profitability of rubber production
    on West Malaysian estates. JRRIM, 21, pt. 5 (1969).

Barlow, Colin. The marketing of smallholders' rubber.
    Kuala Lumpur [1968?]. 14 p.

Barlow, Colin. Towards improved marketing for rubber
    smallholders. In Proceedings, National Agricultural
    Marketing Seminar 13th-18th November 1967. Kuala
    Lumpur, 1968: 187-191.

Barlow, Colin, and Chan Chee-kheong. Towards an
optimum size of rubber holding. Kuala Lumpur,
Natural Rubber Conference, 1968. 41 p. Preprint.

Barlow, Colin, Lim Poh-loh, and Ong Yong. An assessment
of smallholders' central processing and marketing
schemes. Kuala Lumpur, Natural Rubber Conference,
1968. 12 p. Preprint.

Barlow, Colin, and Lim Sow-ching. A report on the
survey of Malay group processing centres, 1964.
April, 1965. 36 p. (Rubber Research Institute
of Malaya, Statistics Division, Economic Report,
no. 1)

Barlow, Colin, and Lim Sow-ching. A report on the
RIDA central latex processing factory at Meru.
Kuala Lumpur, 1965. 61 p. (Rubber Research Institute
of Malaya, Statistics Division, Economic Report,
no. 2)

Barlow, Colin, and Lim Sow-ching. Effect of density
of planting on the growth, yield and economic
exploitation of Hevea brasiliensis. Part II.
The effect on profit. JRRIM, 20, 1 (1967): 44-64.

Barlow, Colin, Lim Sow-ching, and P. O. Thomas.
Effect of planting systems on times of tapping
and collection. JRRIM, 19, 4 (1966): 196-204.

Barlow, Colin, and Ng Choong-sooi. Budgeting on
the merits of a shorter replanting period. [Kuala
Lumpur] 1966. 8 p. (Rubber Research Institute
of Malaya, Planters' Conference, July 1966. Preprint
no. 15) Tables.

Bateman, L. Natural rubber takes the strain. Planter,
40, 7 (1964): 326-336.

Bauer, P. T. Rubber production costs during the
great depression. Ec Jl, 53 (1943): 361-369.
Tables.

Bauer, P. T. Some aspects of the Malayan rubber
slump, 1929-1933. Economica, n.s., 11 (1944):
190-198.

Bauer, P. T. Notes on cost. Economica, n.s., 12
(1945): 90-100.

Bauer, P. T. The economics of planting density in rubber growing. Economica, n.s., 13 (1946): 131-135.

Bauer, P. T. The working of rubber regulation. Ec Jl, 56 (1946): 391-414.

Bauer, P. T. Malayan rubber policies. Economica, n.s., 14 (1947): 81-107.

Bauer, P. T. Malayan rubber policies. India Rubber World, 116 (1947): 629-634, 783-786.

Bauer, P. T. Report on a visit to the rubber growing smallholdings of Malaya. London, 1948. 92 p. (Colonial Research Publication, no. 1)

Bauer, P. T. The rubber industry: a study in competition and monopoly. Cambridge, 1948. 404 p.

Bauer, P. T. The working of rubber regulation: a rejoinder. Ec Jl, 58 (1948): 236-243.

Bauer, P. T. What remedy for rubber in Malaya. New Commonwealth, 29 (1955): 14-15.

Bauer, P. T. Malayan rubber policy. Political Science Quarterly, 72 (1957): 83-99.

Benham, Frederic. The rubber industry. Economica, n.s., 16 (1949): 355-368.

Bevan, J. W. L. Report on the marketing of smallholders' rubber with special reference to the first buyer level. Kuala Lumpur, 1956. 28 p.

Bevan, J. W. L. A study of yields, labour inputs and incomes of rubber smallholders in the coastal areas of Selangor, a preliminary summary of data. Kuala Lumpur, Department of Agriculture, University of Malaya, November, 1962.

Bolle-Hones, E. W. Nutrition of Hevea brasiliensis. I. Experimental methods. JRRIM, 14 (1954): 183-207.

Brown, Judith J. P. Careers in rubber: a guide to employment possibilities within the rubber industry of the states of Malaya. Published by the Rubber Producers' Council [n.p., n.d.]. 67 p.

Buddings and clonal seedlings. RRIMPB, 36 (1958): 51-59.

Bugbee, H. C. The Malayan rubber smallholders' income.
NRN (Feb. 1954): 4-5.

Bugbee, H. C., and Warren S. Lockwood. A visit to
the Malayan front. NRN (Oct. 1951): 1-6.

Burbridge, F. W. Gutta-percha and caoutchouc producing
trees. JRASSB, 3 (1879): 52-59. Postscript by
H. J. Murton, p. 59-61. Correction, v. 4 (1880): 6.

Carrie, J. Gordon. A review of Federated Malay States
statistics--relating to rubber production. Mal
Ag Jl, 18 (1930): 40-43. Diagr.

Chan, Kwong-wah. Economic aspects of Malayan rubber
supply after the Second World War (1949-1961).
University of Malaya, July, 1962.

Chan, Kwong-wah. A study of the supply response
of Malayan rubber estates between 1948 and 1959.
MER, 7, 2 (1962): 77-94.

Cook, J. Purchase and bulk processing of smallholder
latex. Mal Ag Jl, 33 (1950): 136-143.

Cook, J. Further notes on the marketing of small-holding
latex. Mal Ag Jl, 36 (1953): 181-189.

Covers and fertilizers for immature rubber. RRIMPB,
89 (March 1967): 66-72.

Cramer, P. J. S. High yield rubber material. Planter
(1950): 1-4.

Cumming, C. M. Rubber planting in Malaya, with particular
hints on planting, also statistics showing the
growth of the industry in Malaya. London, 1920. 60 p.

Davidson, L. R. Rubber small-holders' problems and
progress. World Crops, 5 (1953): 190-193.

Davidson, L. R., and Mohd. Rouse bin Mohd. Amin.
Centralized processing of smallholder's latex
and rubber. JRRIM, 12 (1950): 203-211.

Dijkman, M. J. Hevea. Thirty years of research in
the Far East. Coral Gables, 1951. 329 p.

Drabble, John H. The plantation rubber industry
in Malaya up to 1922. JRASMB, 40, 1 (1967): 52-77.
Tables.

Drabble, John H. Investment in the plantation rubber
industry in Malaya, c. 1900-1922. 1968. 25 p.
Unpublished paper no. 79, presented at the International
Conference on Asian History, Kuala Lumpur, August
1968. Mimeo.

Drabble, John H. The plantation rubber industry
in Malaya: its origin and development to 1922.
1968. Ph.D. thesis -- London University.

Dutch Technical Aid Mission, Malaysia, 1967. Agro- and
socio-economic study questionnaire: rubber small
holdings. Kuala Lumpur, 1967.

Eaton, B. J., and Mungo Park. Rubber and its uses
in mining. Kuala Lumpur, 1926. (Rubber Propaganda
Committee).

The economic evaluation of tapping systems: a further
explanation. RRIMPB, 83 (1966): 28-34. Chart, tables.

Edgar, A. T., comp. Manual of rubber planting (Malaya).
Kuala Lumpur, 1958. 705 p.

Estate and factory practice for the production of
SMR [Standard Malaysian Rubber]. RRIMPB, 78 (May
1965): 89-98.

Evans, Geoffrey. The Rubber Research Institute of
Malaya. Nature, 147 (1941): 15-16.

Figart, D. M. The plantation rubber industry in
the Middle East. Washington, D.C., 1925. (United
States Department of Commerce. Trade Promotion
Series, no. 2)

Final report of the Rubber Smallholdings Enquiry
Committee. Kuala Lumpur, 1952.

Fisk, E. K. Productivity and income from rubber
in an established Malay reservation. MER, 6,
1 (1961): 13-22.

Fryer, D. W., and James C. Jackson. Peasant producers or urban planters? The Chinese rubber smallholders of Ulu Selangor. PV, 7, 2 (1966): 198-228. Maps.

Gain, Francois. Contribution à l'étude technique et économique de la saignée de l'hyvéa en Malaisie britannique. Nancy, 1935. 164 p. Diagr., illus., tables.

Gamba, Charles. Wages, unions and rubber in Malaya. Eastern World, 7 (1953): 46-49.

Gamba, Charles. Synthetic rubber and Malaya. Singapore, 1959.

Greenwood, J. M. F. Rubber smallholdings in the Federation of Malaya. Kuala Lumpur, Rubber Research Institute, 1962.

Greenwood, J. M. F. Rubber smallholdings in the Federation of Malaya. JTG, 18 (1964): 81-100.

Grist, D. H. Nationality of ownership and nature of constitution of rubber estates in Malaya. Kuala Lumpur, 1933. (Department of Agriculture, Special Bulletin, Economic Series, no. 2)

Growth of the rubber industry. Competition between synthetic and natural products. Times Rev Br Colonies, 2 (1951): 11-13, 15. Graphs, illus., map, statistics.

Guha, M. M., and G. A. Watson. Effects of cover crops on soil nutrient status and on growth of hevea. I. Laboratory studies on the mineralisation of nitrogen in different soil mixtures. JRRIM, 15, 4 (1957/1958): 175-188.

Haines, W. B. The uses and controls of natural undergrowth on rubber estates. Kuala Lumpur. (Rubber Research Institute of Malaya, Planting Manual, no. 6)

Haines, W. B., and E. Guest. Recent experiments on manuring hevea and their bearing on estate practice. Empire Journal of Experimental Agriculture, 4 (1936): 300-324.

Hawkins, D. W. In Malaya today. The strains of a rubber planter's life. Times Rev Br Colonies, 1 (1951): 4.

Hilton, R. N. Maladies of hevea in Malaya. Kuala
Lumpur, 1959.

Ho, Robert. Labour inputs of rubber producing smallholders
in Malaya. MER, 12, 1 (1967): 79-89.

Ho, Robert. Rubber production by peasants of the
Terachi Valley, Malaya. Institute of British
Geographers, Transactions and Papers, 41 (1967):
187-201. Map.

Holt, Everett G. Report on Malayan and British Borneo
rubber industry. Washington, D. C., United States
Department of Commerce, 1946.

Hotchkiss, H. Stuart. Operations of an American
rubber company in Sumatra and the Malay Peninsula.
Ann Am Ac Pol Soc Sc, 112 (1924): 154-162.

Hutchinson, F. W. Defoliation of Hevea brasiliensis
by aerial spraying. (Report on an investigation
into the possibility of aircraft spraying to
defoliate rubber trees as a method of eradicating
an outbreak of South American leaf blight). JRRIM,
15, 5 (1957/1958): 241-274.

Jackson, J. C. A Malayan rubber estate. In The Geographical
Association. Asian Sample Studies. 1968: 42-51.
Maps. (Tanah Getah Estate, located 12 miles west
of Kuala Lumpur.)

Jackson, James C. Smallholding rubber cultivation
in Malaya, 1952-1962. OG, 9, 1 (1965): 33-40.
Maps.

Jenkins, R. O. Rubber--I, introduction and expansion
with special reference to Malaya. Br Mal, 26
(1951): 296-299.

Jenkins, R. O. Rubber--II, the development of plantation
systems of upkeep. Br Mal, 26 (1951): 323-327.

Knorr, K. E. Rubber after the war. Stanford University,
Food Research Institute, 1944. 46 p. (War-Peace
Pamphlets, no. 4)

Knorr, K. E. World rubber and its regulation. Stanford,
1945.

Latex foam from Malayan rubber. New Commonwealth,
22 (1925): 23-25. Illus.

Lew, Sip-hon. The place of Malaysian natural rubber
in the world rubber economy. Planter, 42, 5 (1966):
218-221.

Lewis, Harrison A. Rubber regulation and the Malayan
plantation industry. Washington, D.C., 1935.
46 p. (United States Bureau of Foreign and Domestic
Commerce: Trade Promotion Series, no. 159) Diagr.,
illus., map, tables.

Lim, Chong-yah. The Malayan rubber replanting taxes.
MER, 6, 2 (1961): 43-52.

Lim, Sow-ching, and Colin Barlow. A study of inputs
and outputs of selected catch crops on immature
rubber smallholdings in West Malaysia. Rubber
Research Institute of Malaya, Economics and Planning
Division, Part I, Feb. 1967. 33 p.; Part II,
Nov. 1967. 37 p. Mimeo.

MacFadyean, A. The history of rubber regulation
1934/43. London, 1944. 239 p.

Malaya. Taxation and replanting in the rubber industry;
statement of the Federal Government on the report
of the Mudie Mission and on certain proposals
made by the Rubber Producers' Council. Kuala
Lumpur, 1955. 41 p. Tables.

Malaya, Federation of. Rubber industry (replanting)
ordinance, 1952, scheme no. 2 for the administration
of Fund B. Kuala Lumpur, 1952. 4 p. (Legislative
Council Paper)

Malaya, Rubber Research Institute of. Annual Report,
1966. Kuala Lumpur, 1967. 112 p.

Malayan Rubber Fund Board, Natural Rubber Bureau.
Natural rubber, 1962; a survey of the aims and
achievements of the research and development
organizations financed by the Malayan Rubber
Fund. [Kuala Lumpur, 1962]. 39 p. Illus.

The Malayan rubber industry. Commonwealth Survey,
158 (1954): 45-48.

Malaysia, Department of Statistics. Rubber statistics
    handbook, 1966. Kuala Lumpur, 1967. 155 p.

Mann, C. E. T. Improvement in the quality of rubber
    planting material. Rubber Research Institute
    of Malaya, Transactions, 15 (1940): 251-270.

Mann, C. E. T. Improving the quality of natural
    rubber. Rubber India, 3 (1951): 23-25.

Mann, C. E. T. The Rubber Research Institute of
    Malaya. World Crops, 5 (1953): 189-190.

Mann, C. E. T., and C. C. T. Sharp. The history
    and description of clones of Hevea brasiliensis.
    Kuala Lumpur, 1937. (Rubber Research Institute
    of Malaya, Planting Manual, no. 5)

McGavack, J. The future of natural rubber. NRN (Mar.
    1959): S-1 to S-6.

McHale, Thomas R. The Malayan economy and stereo-regular
    rubbers. AS, 1, 4 (1961): 25-28.

McHale, Thomas R. Commodity control schemes for
    rubber, retrospective and prospective. KEM, 1,
    2 (1964): 13-29.

McHale, Thomas R. Natural rubber and Malaysian economic
    development. MER, 10, 1 (1965): 16-43.

McHale, Thomas R. Rubber smallholdings in Malaya,
    their changing nature, role and prospects. MER,
    10, 2 (1965): 35-48.

McHale, Thomas R. Rubber and the Malaysian economy.
    Singapore, 1967. 111 p. Graphs, tables.
    Contains several chapters which are based on
    articles previously published in the Malayan
    Economic Review and in Kajian Ekonomi Malaysia.

Meads, H. D. Bark consumption and bark reserves
    on small rubber holdings in Malaya. Kuala Lumpur,
    1934. (Department of Agriculture, Special Bulletin,
    Economic Series, no. 4)

Mudie, R. F., J. R. Raeburn, and B. Marsh. Report
    of the Mission of Enquiry into the Rubber Industry
    of Malaya. Kuala Lumpur, 1954.

Murray, R. K. S. Report on a visit to Malaya, Java and Sumatra. Colombo, 1937. 46 p. (Rubber Research Scheme "Ceylon," Bulletin, no. 54)

Ng, Choong-sooi. Some aspects of estate replanting and new planting costs. RRIMPB, 92 (Sept. 1967): 164-175.

Ng, Choong-sooi, Colin Barlow, and Chan Chee-kheong. Factors affecting the profitability of rubber production on West Malaysian estates. Kuala Lumpur, Natural Rubber Conference, 1968. 28 p. Preprint.

Ng, Eng-kok, Ng Choong-sooi, and Lee Chew-kang. Economic analysis of tapping experiments. Kuala Lumpur, Natural Rubber Conference, 1968. 28 p. Preprint.

Ong, Chan-chuan. Development of rubber industry in Malaya. Commerce, 1, 5 (1962): 38-43.

Ong, Yong. A report on the survey of smokehouses used by smallholders in Malaya. Kuala Lumpur, 1966. 26 p. (Smallholders Advisory Service: Report no. 2, Rubber Research Institute of Malaya)

Ong, Yong. A report on three group processing centres at Pekan established with Mara grants during 1965. Kuala Lumpur, 1966. (Smallholders Advisory Service: Report no. 3, Rubber Research Institute of Malaya)

Ooi, Jin-bee. The rubber industry of the Federation of Malaya. JTG, 15 (1961): 46-65.

Owen, G., D. R. Westgarth, and G. C. Iyer. Manuring hevea: effects of fertilizers on growth and yield of mature rubber trees. JRRIM, 15, 1 (1957): 29-52.

Paardekooper, E. C. A forecast of Malayan rubber production, 1960-70. Kuala Lumpur, March, 1961. (Research Archives of the Rubber Research Institute of Malaya, Document no. 13)

Petch, T. Notes on the history of the plantation rubber industry of the East. Ceylon R Bot Gdns, 5 (1914): 433-520.

Proceedings of a latex symposium, held at Kuala
    Lumpur on February 19-21st., 1951. JRRIM, 13
    (1951): 98-219.

Proceedings of the meeting to discuss the quality
    and grading of natural rubber, September 12th-14th
    1949 in Kuala Lumpur. JRRIM, 12 (1950): 212-277.

Rao, B. Sripathi. Pests of hevea plantations in
    Malaya. With watercolors by Hoh Choo-chuan. Kuala
    Lumpur, 1965. 198 p. Col. illus.

Ratchaga, P. C. The future of Malaya's natural rubber.
    MER, 1, 1 (1956): 42-47.

Rawlings, E. H. The small-holders in Malaya. Eastern
    World, 6, 3 (1952): 36-37.

Reorganisation in the Malayan rubber industry -
    Special Report. Economist Intelligence Unit Rubber
    Trends, 28 (Dec. 1965): 11-19.

Report on the Commission of Enquiry into the Constitution,
    Administration and Working of the Rubber Research
    Institute appointed by His Excellency the High
    Commissioner. Kuala Lumpur, 1933.

Report of the Mission of Enquiry into the Rubber
    Industry of Malaya. Kuala Lumpur, 1954. 76 p.

Ridley, H. N. Story of the rubber industry. With
    an appendix by L. Lewton-Brain showing the growth
    of the rubber industry in Malaya. 1905-1910.
    London, 1911. 31 p.

Rowe, J. W. F. Studies in the artificial control
    of raw material supplies: no. 2. Rubber. London,
    1931. 87 p. (Royal Economic Society, London,
    Memorandum, no. 29)

Rubber-growing: elementary principles and practice.
    Kuala Lumpur, 1938. 82 p. (Rubber Research Institute
    of Malaya, Planting Manual, no. 7) Illus., plates.

Rudner, Martin. The state and peasant innovation
    in rural development: the case of Malaysian rubber.
    Israel, Institute of Asian and African Studies,
    the Hebrew University of Jerusalem, 1969. 32 p.
    (Franz Oppenheimer Memorial Symposium, Paper no. 5)
    Mimeo.

Schulz, Anneliese. Der Plantagenkautschuk in Britisch
Malaya. Berlin, 1936. 96 p. (Veröffentlichungen
des Institutes für Meereskunde. N.F.B. Reihe,
Heft 11) Maps.

Seow, Boon-chiew. Smallholders' rubber production--prospects
of improving production. Geographica, 2 (1966): 3 p.

Sharples, A., and A. R. Sanderson. The root disease
problem on old rubber trees in Malaya. Kuala
Lumpur, 1931. 43 p. (Rubber Research Institute
of Malaya, Bulletin, no. 3)

Silcock, T. H. A note on the working of rubber regulation.
Ec Jl, 58 (1948): 228-235. Rejoinder by P. T.
Bauer, p. 236-243.

Silcock, T. H. A note on future trading and the
Singapore rubber market. MER, 3 (1958): 63-66.

Singapore Chamber of Commerce Rubber Association.
Singapore type descriptions. NRN (August 1954):
S24-S29.

Small-holder's crisis in Malaya. The need for new
rubber plantings. Times Rev Br Colonies, 4 (1951): 5.

Smith, H. F. A sampling survey of tapping on smallholdings,
1939-40. JRRIM, 12 (1947): 77-125.

Soliva, R. An economic view of rubber planting.
Singapore, 1930. 137 p.

Soosai, J. S., and Kow Hun-woon. A bibliography
of contributions to natural rubber research from
the Rubber Research Institute of Malaya: 1927-1967.
Kuala Lumpur, 1968.

Standard Malaysian rubber (SMR) progress report
and present trends. RRIMPB, 91 (July 1967): 121-126.

Standard Malaysian rubbers: specifications and sampling
procedure for producers. RRIMPB, 78 (May 1965): 81-88.

Stern, Robert Mitchell. Malayan rubber production,
inventory holdings, and the elasticity of export
supply. Southern Economic Journal, 31 (Apr. 1965):
314-323.

Stocktaking in natural rubber research. RRIMPB, 34 (1958): 1-5.

Sulaiman bin Mohd. Haniff. Study of industrial use of rubber wood in Kedah and Penang. Paper presented at the Second Pan-Malaysian Forestry Conference. 1968. 11 p. Map. Mimeo.

Tan, Augustine Hui-hong. Natural rubber: problems and techniques of stablization. 1965. 237 p. M.A. thesis in Economics -- University of Singapore.

Tapping system on mature rubber. RRIMPB, 80 (Sept. 1965): 226-235.

Tapping systems. RRIMB, 11 (1954): 32-37.

Thomas, P. O. A method of testing differences among seasonal indices of smallholders' rubber production. KEM, 3, 1 (1966): 21-24. Chart, tables.

Thomas, P. O., and A. Fong Chu-chai. Rubber industry statistics. Kuala Lumpur, Rubber Research Institute of Malaya, 1968. 39 p.

Vonk, H. De voorlichting van de small-holders in Malaka op het gebied van de rubbercultuur. Landbouw, 17 (1941): 259-290.

Voon, Phin-keong. Rubber smallholdings--problems and prospects. Geographica, 2 (1966): 5 p. Graph.

Voon, Phin-keong. Chinese rubber smallholding industry in Selangor. 1967. M.A. thesis in geography -- University of Malaya.

Voon, Phin-keong. The rubber smallholding industry in Selangor, 1895-1920. JTG, 24 (1967): 43-49. Maps.

Wah, Francis Chan-wong. A preliminary study of the supply response of the Malayan rubber estates between 1948 and 1959. MER, 7 (1962): 77-94.

Ward-Jackson, C. Rubber planting. A book for the prospective estate assistant in British Malaya. Kuala Lumpur, 1920.

Watson, G. A. Cover plants in rubber cultivation.
JRRIM, 15, 1 (1957): 2-18. Bibliog.

Watson, G. A. Rubber cultivation in a diversified
agriculture--notes on its relegation to the poorer
soils of Malaya, North Borneo and Sarawak. A
paper presented to the Conference of Southeast
Asian Geographers. April, 1962. Tables. Also
published in SMJ, 10, no. 19-20 (1962): 590-597.
Mimeo.

Westorp, A. R. The use of fertilizers on Malayan
rubber estates. Kuala Lumpur, 1939.

Whitford, H. N. Estate and native plantation rubber
in the Middle East, 1929. New York, 1930. 120 p.
Diagrs., illus., map, tables.

Whitford, H. N. Estate and native plantation rubber
in the Middle East, 1930. New York, 1931. 169 p.
Diagr., tables.

Whitford, H. N. Fourth report on plantation rubber
in the Middle East, 1932. New York, 1932. 88 p.
Charts, tables.

Whitford, H. N. Fifth report on plantation rubber
in the Middle East, 1933. New York, 1934. 74 p.
Charts, tables.

Whittlesey, Charles R. Governmental control of crude
rubber. The Stevenson Plan. Princeton, N.J.,
1931. 235 p.

Wycherley, P. R. Variation in the performance of
hevea in Malaya. JTG, 17 (1963): 143-171.

5. Coconut and oil palm

Arnott, G. W. The Malayan oil palm and the analysis
of its products. (Division of Agriculture, Federation
of Malaya, Bulletin, no. 113)

Bevan, J. W. L., T. Fleming, and B. S. Gray. Planting
techniques for oil palms in Malaysia. Kuala Lumpur,
1966. 156 p.

Bevan, J. W. L., and T. J. Goering. The oil palm
in Malaysia: an estimate of product prices and
returns to investment. In P. D. Turner, ed. Oil
Palm Developments in Malaysia. Kuala Lumpur,
1968: 152-164.

Bevan, J. W. L., and B. S. Gray. Germination and
nursery techniques for the oil palm in Malaysia.
Planter, 42, 4 (1966): 165-187.

Bevan, J. W. L., and B. S. Gray. The organisation
and control of field practice for large-scale
oil palm plantings in Malaysia. Kuala Lumpur,
Incorporated Society of Planters, 1969. 166 p.
Graphs, photos., tables.

Brown, David W. A visit with Rajab bin Harun--a
Malay coconut producer and fisherman. CECA Paper.
New York, Council on Economic and Cultural Affairs,
March 1963. 8 p.

Bull, R. A. The production of oil palm seedlings
for field planting. Planter, 42, 6 (1966): 248-290.

Bunting, B. Culture du palmier à huile et production
de l'huile de palme en Malaisie. Rev Bot Appl
et Ag Trop, 15 (1935): 534-544.

Bunting, B., and C. D. V. Georgi. Oil palm in Malaya.
Mal Ag Jl, 12, 6-7 (1924): 145-153.

Bunting, B., C. D. V. Georgi, and J. N. Milsum.
The oil palm in Malaya. Kuala Lumpur, 1935. 293 p.
(Malayan Planting Manual, no. 1) Tables.

Coghlan, H. L. Coconuts in Malaya. Trop Ag, 41 (1913):
100-102.

Coghlan, H. L. Coconut industry in Malaya. London,
1914. 42 p. Illus. [1920, 39 p.].

Cooke, F. C. Investigations on coconuts and coconut
products. Kuala Lumpur, 1932. 99 p. (Department
of Agriculture Special Bulletin, General Series,
no. 8) Diagr.

Corbett, G. H. Insects of coconuts in Malaya. Kuala
Lumpur, 1932. 106 p. (Department of Agriculture
Special Bulletin, General Series, no. 10)

Coulter, J. K. Mineral nutrition of the oil palm in Malaya. Mal Ag Jl, 41, 3 (1958): 131-151.

Deasy, George F. The oil palm in Malaya. Jl G, 41 (1942): 21-32.

Fiennes, D. E. M. The Malayan oil palm industry. Kuala Lumpur [n.d.]. 15 p. Mimeo.

Gray, B. S. The potential of the oil palm in Malaya. JTG, 17 (1963): 127-132.

Gray, B. S., and J. W. L. Bevan. Research needs for the oil palm in Malaysia. In P. D. Turner, ed. Oil Palm Developments in Malaysia. Kuala Lumpur, 1968: 138-151.

Gray, B. S., and Hew Choy-kean. Cover crops experiments in oil palms on the west coast of Malaysia. In P. D. Turner, ed. Oil Palm Developments in Malaysia. Kuala Lumpur, 1968: 56-65.

Gunn, J. S., and W. Boa. Mechanical maintenance of oil palm plantations. World Crops, 14, 7 (1962): 214-219.

Haddon, A. V., and Y. L. Tong. Oil palm selection and breeding: a progress report. Mal Ag Jl, 42, 3 (1959): 124-156. Graphs, illus., tables.

Hartley, C. W. S. The oilpalm. London, 1967. 706 p. Most important book on industry; contains numerous references to industry in Malaysia.

Jack, H. W., and W. N. Sands. Observations on the dwarf coconut palm in Malaya. Mal Ag Jl, 17 (1929): 140-165.

Jagoe, R. B. Notes on the oilpalm in Malaya. Mal Ag Jl, 22 (1934): 541-549.

Jagoe, R. B. Deli oil palms and early introduction of Elaeis guineensis to Malaya. Mal Ag Jl, 35, 1 (1952): 3-11.

Jagoe, R. B. The "dumpy" oil palm. Mal Ag Jl, 35 (1952): 12-21.

Khoo, Swee-joo. The Malayan oil palm industry. KEM, 1, 1 (1964): 1-13.

Lever, R. J. A. W. A new coconut pest in Singapore.
Mal Ag Jl, 34 (1951): 79-82.

Malaya, Department of Labour. Report on the coconut
industry in Malaya. Kuala Lumpur, 1955. Mimeo.

Malaya, Department of Labour. Report on the oilpalm
estates in Malaya. Kuala Lumpur, 1956. 14 p. Mimeo.

Malaysia, Department of Statistics. West Malaysia
oil palm, coconut and tea statistics, 1966.
Kuala Lumpur, 1967. 35 p.

Malaysia, Economic Planning Unit. Report on a proposal
for land development for oil palm in Trengganu.
Submitted by the E.P.U. team comprising Thong
Yaw Hong, W. P. Panton [and] Sulaiman bin Abdullah.
Kuala Lumpur, the Unit, April, 1966. 15 p. Map,
fold. tables.

Malaysia, Ministry of Agriculture and Co-operatives.
The oil palm in Malaya. Kuala Lumpur, Ministry
of Agriculture and Co-operatives, 1966. 255 p.
Graphs, illus., some in col., map (fold.), tables.

Mann, Charles. Oil palms in Malaya. Malaya, 1 (1952):
25-27.

Mendham, N. J. A study of the Malaysian oilpalm
industry, with reference to possible development
in Papua and New Guinea. Papua and New Guinea
Agricultural Journal, 18, 4 (1967): 150-157. Illus.

Muttukumaru, Emmanuel. Report to the Government
of Malaysia. Economic survey of the coconut growing
industry. Rome, Food and Agriculture Organization
of the United Nations, 1968. 246 p. (Food and
Agriculture Organization of the United Nations,
no. TA 2441)

Ng, Siew-kee. Soil suitability for oil palms in
West Malaysia. In P. D. Turner, ed. Oil Palm
Developments in Malaysia. Kuala Lumpur, 1968: 11-17.

Ng, Siew-kee, and S. Thamboo. Nutrient contents
of oil palms in Malaya. I. Nutrients required
for reproduction: fruit bunches and male inflorescence.
Mal Ag Jl, 46, 1 (1967): 3-45. Graphs, tables.

Ng, Siew-kee, and P. De Souza. Nutrient contents of oil palms in Malaya. II. Nutrients in vegetative tissue. Mal Ag Jl, 46, 3 (1968): 332ff.

Ng, Siew-kee, Cheah Thean-eng, and S. Thamboo. Nutrient contents of oil palms in Malaya. III. Micronutrient contents in vegetative tissues. Mal Ag Jl, 46, 4 (1968): 421-434. Graphs, tables.

Raymond, D. Proposals for the organisation of palm fruit processing by F.L.D.A. small holders in Malaya. Kuala Lumpur, Tropical Products Institute, 30 April, 1963. 66 p. Diagrs., maps, tables. Mimeo.

Raymond, W. D. The palm oil industry. Tropical Science, 3 (1963): 68-89.

Report of a Committee Appointed by His Excellency the Officer Administering the Government of the Straits Settlements and High Commissioner for the Malay States to Investigate and Report on the Present Economic Condition of the Coconut and Other Vegetable Oil Producing Industries in Malaya. Kuala Lumpur, 1934.

Report of the Working Committee on Coconut and Coconut Products. Kuala Lumpur, 1957. Mimeo.

Rosenquist, E. A. The prospect of the oil palm industry in Malaya. Mal Ag Jl, 2 (1962): 42-45.

Sankar, N. S. Fruit collection and evacuation by road. Planter, 42, 2 (1966): 59-68.

Sedky, A. Production and processing of coconut in Malaya. Kuala Lumpur, 1962. (Food and Agriculture Organization of the United Nations Report Series on Malayan Food Commodities, no. 3)

Selvadurai, S. A preliminary report on the survey of coconut smallholdings in West Malaysia. Kuala Lumpur, 1968. 170 p.

Selvadurai, S., and Othman bin Mohamed Lela. An evaluation of the Minyak Beku (Johore) coconut replanting and rehabilitation scheme. Kuala Lumpur, 1967.

Sharples, A. Palm diseases in Malaya. Mal Ag Jl, 16, 9-10 (1928): 313-358.

ECONOMY - Agriculture: Coconut and oil palm

Sharples, A. Coconut research in Malaya. Mal Ag
    Jl, **18** (1930): 71-77.

Smith, A. C. Coconut industry in Malaya. Malaya
    (1952): 26-27.

Tan, Koon-lin. The oilpalm industry in Malaya. 1965.
    265 p. M.A. thesis -- University of Malaya.

Turner, P. D. Fungicides in the control of some
    fungus diseases of oil palm in Malaysia. Mal
    Ag Jl, 46, **1** (1967): 46-58. Photos., tables

Turner, P. D., ed. Oil palm developments in Malaysia.
    Proceedings of the First Malaysian Oil Palm Conference.
    Kuala Lumpur, 1968.

Turner, P. D., and R. A. Bull. Diseases and disorders
    of the oil palm in Malaysia. Kuala Lumpur, 1967.
    247 p.

Veldhuis, J. Methods of assisted pollination for
    oilpalms. <u>In</u> P. D. Turner, ed. Oil Palm Developments
    in Malaysia. Kuala Lumpur, 1968: 72-82.

Walker, T. M. The Malayan oil palm industry. Report
    to the Persatuan Ekonomi Melayu. University of
    Malaya. October 11, 1962.

Wilson, T. B. The West Johore coconut production
    survey. Kuala Lumpur, 1958. 47 p. (Department
    of Agriculture, Bulletin, no. 104)

Wood, B. J. Insect pests of oil palms in Malaya.
    Planter, 42, 7 (1966): 311-315.

6. Pineapple

Armstrong, D. S. The pineapple industry recovers.
    Foreign Trade, 12, 310 (1952): 14-16.

Brown, F. B. Pineapple varieties and selection in
    Malaya. Mal Ag Jl, 36 (1953): 237-246.

Courtenay, C. E. The reconstruction of the Malayan
    canned pineapple industry. Mal Ag Jl, 30 (1947):
    183-190.

Courtenay, C. E. Demand exceeds output for Malayan
    pineapple. Western Canner and Packer, 43, 11
    (1951): 38-40.

Dunsmore, J. R. The pineapple in Malaya. Mal Ag
    Jl, 40, 3 (1957): 159-187. Illus.

Grist, D. H. The Malayan pineapple industry. Mal
    Ag Jl, 18 (1930): 188-191.

Grist, D. H. Pineapple canning. Mal Ag Jl, 18 (1930).

Grist, D. H. Pineapple cultivation. Mal Ag Jl, 18
    (1930).

Johnson, W. J. B. Recent developments in the Malayan
    pineapple canning industry. Mal Ag Jl, 25 (1937):
    270-276.

Lewis, W. R. Pineapple canning in Malaya. Food,
    20 (1951): 417-419.

Malaya, Federation of. Memorandum on the resuscitation
    of the Malayan canned pineapple industry. Kuala
    Lumpur, 1949. (Legislative Council Paper, no. 14)

Malaya, Pineapple Industry. Report of the Commission
    of Enquiry into the Pineapple Industry in Malaya
    and the Statement of the Government's Future
    Policy for the Industry. 1960. 39 p. (Legislative
    Paper, no. 19)

Malaysia, Ministry of Agriculture and Co-operatives.
    An economic survey of pine-apple smallholdings
    in Pontian, Johore. Kuala Lumpur, 1968.

Neville, R. J. W. The pineapple canning industry
    of Malaya. OG, 7, 1 (1963): 59-82.

Neville, R. J. W. The plantation in Malaya; case
    study of a pineapple plantation in South Johore.
    TESG, 55, 3 (1964): 57-69.

Olds, G. D. P. The Malayan pineapple industry. Mal
    Ag Jl, 23 (1935).

The pineapple canning industry in Malaya. Mal Ag
    Jl, 19 (1931): 425-445.

Recherches sur la culture des ananas en Malaisie
  britannique. Rev Bot Appl et Ag Trop, 17 (1937):
  762-767.

Tay, T.-H., Wee Y.-C., and Chong W.-S. The nutritional
  requirements of pineapple (Ananas Comosus L.
  Merr. Var. Singapore Spanish) on peat soils in
  Malaya. I. Effect of nitrogen, phosphorus and
  potassium on yield, sugar and acid content of
  the fruit. Mal Ag Jl, 46, 4 (1968): 458-468.

Thomson, R. K. Pineapple industry in Malaya is recovering
  from war effects. Foreign Trade, 8 (1950): 598-600.

Wee, Y.-C., and Ng J.-C. Some observations on the
  effect of month of planting on the Singapore
  Spanish variety of pineapple. Mal Ag Jl, 46,
  4 (1968): 469-475.

7. Cacao, coffee, and tea

Allen, G. F. Investigations into the cultivation
  of cacao in Malaya. Mal Ag Jl, 36 (1953): 147-163.

Cheeseman, Ernest Entwisle. Report on potentialities
  for the cultivation of cocoa in Malaya, Sarawak
  and North Borneo. London, 1948. 44 p. (Colonial
  Office Publication, no. 230)

Faulkner, O. T., and J. N. Milsum. Cacao. An introductory
  note. Mal Ag Jl, 26 (1938): 20-26.

Gamble, G. Report on visits to India, Malaya and
  Ceylon, with some notes for the guidance of tea
  planters in Kenya. Nairobi, 1951. 94 p.

Gillett, David. Report to Cadbury Bros. Ltd. Bournville,
  on the suitability of cocoa growing in the territories
  of Malaya, Sarawak and British North Borneo,
  December 1947-March 1948. London, 1948. 24 p.

Greig, J. The cultivation of lowland tea at the
  central experimental station, Serdang. Kuala
  Lumpur, 1937. 31 p. (Department of Agriculture
  Special Bulletin, General Series, no. 29) Plates.

Haddon, A. V. Variety trials of seedling cocoa in
  Malaya. Mal Ag Jl, 43 (1961): 169-205.

Lever, R. J. A. W. Tea growing in Malaya. World
    Crops, 14, 11 (1962): 374-377.

Lockard, R. G., V. Vamathevan, and S. Thamboo. Mineral
    deficiency symptoms of cacao grown in sand-culture.
    Kuala Lumpur, 1959. 20 p. (Department of Agriculture,
    Bulletin, no. 107)

Malaya. Report of the working party set up to consider
    the development of a cacao industry in the Federation
    of Malaya. Kuala Lumpur, 1955. 16 p.

Malaya, Department of Labour. Report on the tea
    planting industry. Kuala Lumpur, 1955. Mimeo.

Rosenquist, E. A. Cocoa selection and breeding in
    Malaya. Mal Ag Jl, 33 (1950): 181-193.

Shepherd, R. Selection of cocoa planting material
    in Malaysia. In Cocoa and Coconuts in Malaya.
    Kuala Lumpur, 1968: 3-11.

Simpson, J. J. Propagation of tea from cuttings.
    Mal Ag Jl, 32 (1949): 70-76. Illus.

Tea at the agricultural station Cameron Highlands.
    Mal Ag Jl, 26 (1938): 137-153.

Thompson, A. Blister blight of tea. Mal Ag Jl, 32
    (1949): 25-27.

Vanter, Warner. There in the jungle Malaya's cacao
    grows. World Crops, 8, 5 (1956): 180-182.

Whitehead, C. The vegetative propagation of tea
    on the lowlands of Malaya. Mal Ag Jl, 41, 2 (1958):
    79-87. Illus.

8. Other crops

Barrett, R. J. R. A description of existing practices
    in the cultivation of Mandarin oranges in Telok
    Anson area. Mal Ag Jl, 42, 2 (1959): 93-97. Illus.

Fairweather, J. The sago industry in Malaya. Mal
    Ag Jl, 25 (1937): 329-333.

Hill, R. D. Pepper growing in Johore. JTG, 28 (June 1969): 32-39.

Jackson, James C. Nutmeg "mania" in Singapore in the 1840's. Geographica, 1 (1964/1965): 1-10. Map.

Jackson, James C. Nutmeg mania in Singapore in the 1840's. KEM, 2, 2 (1965): 24-30.

Jackson, James C. European tapioca planters in the Straits Settlements in the late 19th century. MH (1966).

Jackson, James C. Tapioca, the plantation crop which preceded rubber in Malaya. MH, 10, 2 (1967): 13-24. Maps, photos.

Lambourne, J. A preliminary report on tapioca as a catch crop with oil palm. Mal Ag Jl, 15, 4 (1927): 104-113.

Mahmood bin Yaacob, Haji. Dry season cultivation of vegetables and food crops on islands and river banks in Kelantan. Mal Ag Jl, 41, 3 (1958): 156-162. Illus., map.

Mason, F. R. The clove and nutmeg industry of Penang and Province Wellesley. Mal Ag Jl, 19 (1931): 4-8.

Malaysia, Ministry of Agriculture and Co-operatives. West Malaysia acreages of miscellaneous crops; crops other than rubber, padi and oilpalm. Kuala Lumpur, August, 1967. 80 p. Tables. Mimeo.

C. ANIMAL HUSBANDRY

Arnott, G. W., and H. K. Lim. Animal feeding stuffs in Malaya. Mal Ag Jl, 45, 4 (1966): 370-386, 387-403. Bibliog., graphs, tables.

Crotty, Raymond. An economic survey of the livestock industry in West Malaysia. Kuala Lumpur, Ministry of Agriculture and Co-operatives, May, 1967. 86 p. Tables.

Crotty, Raymond. Livestock marketing in West Malaysia.
In Proceedings, National Agricultural Marketing
Seminar, 13th-18th November 1967. Kuala Lumpur,
1968: 77-91.

Devendra, C. Towards improved animal production.
Mal Ag, 4 (1963/1964): 33-44.

Devendra, C. Studies in the nutrition of the indigenous
goat in Malaya. Mal Ag Jl, 46, 1 (1967): 80-118;
46, 2 (1967): 191-216. Graphs, tables.

Eswaran, H. Cattle as contributors to East Coast
development. Mal Ag, 4 (1963/1964): 17-21.

George, C. D. V. Fodders and feeding stuffs in Malaya.
Kuala Lumpur, 1934. 35 p. (Department of Agriculture,
Special Bulletin, General Series, no. 17)

Gosling, Lee Anthony Peter. Patterns and problems
of livestock production in Malaya. Ann Arbor,
1958. 308 p. Ph.D. thesis -- University of Michigan.

Gunn, L. T. Fodders and feeding-stuffs in Malaya.
Kuala Lumpur, 1951. 88 p. (Department of Agriculture,
Federation of Malaya, Scientific Series, no. 24)

Henderson, R. M. C. The cultivation of fodder grasses
in Malaya. Mal Ag Jl, 38 (1955): 71-77, 141-150,
250-255.

Holland, E. H. The place of livestock on the estate
in South East Asia. Third Food and Agriculture
Organization of the United Nations Far East Meeting
on Animal Production and Health. Bangkok, 1961.

Kelly, R. B. Asian environments and livestock production.
Kuala Lumpur, Department of Agriculture, University
of Malaya, 1962.

Lim, Han-kuo. Animal feeding stuffs. Part 4, compositional
data of grasses and fodders. Mal Ag Jl, 46, 4
(1968): 405-420. Tables.

Malaysia, Ministry of Agriculture and Co-operatives.
West Malaysia: Census of commercial poultry farms
and hatcheries. Kuala Lumpur, 1967.

Malaysia, Ministry of Agriculture and Co-operatives, Veterinary Division. First Malaysia Plan, 1960-1970, draft federal proposals. Kuala Lumpur, November, 1964. 47 p. Tables. Mimeo.

Malaysia, Ministry of Agriculture and Co-operatives, Veterinary Division. Proposals for the development of the livestock industry and the reorganization of the veterinary services. Kuala Lumpur, the Ministry, June, 1965. 111 p. Mimeo.

Marsh, T. D., and V. Dawson. Animal husbandry in Malaya. 1. Cattle in Malaya. Mal Ag Jl, 30 (1947): 133-142.

Marsh, T. D., and V. Dawson. Animal husbandry in Malaya. 2. The buffalo in Malaya. Mal Ag Jl, 31 (1948): 102-114.

Marsh, T. D., and V. Dawson. Animal husbandry in Malaya. 3. The improvement of cattle and buffaloes in Malaya. Mal Ag Jl, 31 (1948): 157-179.

D. FISHERIES

Alfred, Eric R. An annotated bibliography of Malayan fresh-water fisheries. JRASMB, 39, 1 (1966): 145-165.

Berube, Louis. Outlook of the fish marketing problem in Malaysia, report of a survey. Summary and recommendations of the general report. Kuala Lumpur, Ministry of Agriculture and Co-operatives, 1966. 75 p. (Economic Research Progress Report, no. 3) Mimeo.

Birtwistle, W. Rearing of carp in ponds. Mal Ag Jl, 19 (1931): 372-383.

Burdon, T. W. The fishing methods of Singapore. JRASMB, 27, 2 (1954): 5-76. Illus.

Burdon, T. W. The fishing industry of Singapore. Rev. ed. Singapore, 1957. 50 p.

Chung, Choeng-hoy. Fish culture and the rural farmer. Mal Ag, 4 (1963/1964): 45-53.

Dew, A. T. The fishing industry of Krian and Kurau,
Perak. JRASSB, 23 (1891): 95-119. Diagrs.

Dunn, I. G. Notes on mass fish death following drought
in South Malaya. Mal Ag Jl, 45, 2 (1965): 204-211.

Firth, Raymond. Economics of a Malayan fishing industry.
Man, 41, 58 (1941): 69-73. Illus.

Firth, Raymond. Coastal people of Kelantan and Trengganu,
Malaya. G Jl, 101 (1943): 193-205.

Firth, Raymond. Malay fishermen: their peasant economy.
London, 1945. 354 p. Bibliog., glossary, illus.,
index, map.

Fraser-Brunner, A. Sea fishes of Malaya. Malayan
Shell, 5 (1958): 10-14.

Gibson-Hill, C. A. The boats of local origin employed
in the Malayan fishing industry. JRASMB, 27,
2 (1954): 145-174.

Gopinath, K. The Malayan purse seine (Pukat Jerut)
fishery. JRASMB, 23, 3 (1950): 75-96. Diagr.,
illus., maps, tables.

Heath, R. G. Fish production in the Krian irrigation
area. Mal Ag Jl, 22 (1934): 186-188.

Hickling, C. F. Incentives to greater production
in the fishing industry. Times Rev Br Colonies,
13 (1954): 8-9, 11.

Kesteven, G. L., ed. Malayan fisheries. A handbook
prepared for the inaugural meeting of the Indo-Pacific
Council, Singapore, March 1949. Singapore, 1949.
88 p. Illus., maps.

Kesteven, G. L., and T. W. Burdon. An introduction
to the fisheries survey of the Colony of Singapore,
with a consideration of the methodology employed.
Singapore, 1952. 119 p. (Fisheries Survey Report,
no. 1) Diagrs., tables.

Le Mare, D. W. Application of the principles of
fish culture to estuarine conditions in Singapore.
In Proceedings, Indo-Pacific Fisheries Council,
Apr. 1950. Bangkok, 1951: 180-183.

Le Mare, D. W. Malaya's fishing industry. Malaya
    (1954): 390-393.

Ling, S. W. Report to the Government of Malaysia
    on development of inland fisheries, with special
    emphasis on fish culture. Rome, 1965. 93 p. (Food
    and Agriculture Organization of the United Nations,
    no. 2095)

Malaya. Report of the Committee to Investigate the
    Fishing Industry. Kuala Lumpur, 1956. 28 p.

Malaya, Department of Labour. Report on the fishing
    industry. Kuala Lumpur, 1955. Mimeo.

Malaysia, Fish Research Institute. Tropical fish
    culture Research Institute Report for 1966.
    Batu Berendam, 1967.

Maxwell, C. N. Malayan fishes. JRASSB, 84 (1921):
    179-280. Plates.

Mohammed Idris Yassin. Economic organization in
    production and marketing of fish and its effect
    on the fishermen at Beserah. Geographica, 2 (1966):
    5 p. Chart, map.

Nair, Ragavan. Fish marketing in Malaysia. In Proceedings,
    National Agricultural Marketing Seminar, 13th-18th
    November 1967. Kuala Lumpur, 1968: 126-152.

Ommanney, Francis Downes. Malayan offshore trawling
    grounds; the experimental and exploratory fishing
    cruises of the F.R.V. Manihine in Malayan and
    Borneo waters, 1955-56, with a note on temperatures
    and salinities in the Singapore Strait. London,
    1962. 95 p. Maps, tables.

Parry, M. L. The fishing methods of Kelantan and
    Trengganu. JRASMB, 27, 2 (1954): 77-144. Illus., map.

Scott, J. S. An introduction to the sea fishes of
    Malaya. Kuala Lumpur, 1959. 180 p. Bibliog.

Slack, H. D. The maturation of Chinese grass-carp
    (Ctenopharyngodon idellus C. et V.) in tropical
    waters. Mal Ag Jl, 43, 4 (1962): 299-306.

Soong, Min-kong. Fishes of the Malayan padi fields.
Mal Nature Jl, 3 (1948): 87-89; 4 (1949): 29-31;
5 (1950): 88-91.

Soong, Min-kong. The role of science and technology
in fisheries development in Malayasia. Mal Ag
Jl, 45, 1 (1965): 21-27.

Stead, David G. General report upon the fisheries
of British Malaya with recommendations for future
development. Sydney, 1923. 366 p.

Tham, Ah-kow. The food fishes in the Singapore Straits.
London, 1950.

Tweedie, M. W. F. Malay names of freshwater fishes.
JRASMB, 25, 1 (1952): 62-67.

Tweedie, M. W. F. Notes on Malayan fresh-water fishes:
3, the Anabantoid fishes; 4, new and interesting
records; 5, Malay names. BRM, 24 (1952): 63-108.

Wilkinson, Berkeley, and Robinson. Report on the
fishing industry of the Straits Settlements and
the Federated Malay States on the west coast
of the Peninsula. Kuala Lumpur, 1904.

E. FORESTS AND FORESTRY

Abdul Majid. Report on forest administration in
West Malaysia for the year 1965. Kuala Lumpur
[n.d.]. Mimeo.

Allen, Betty Molesworth. Some common trees of Malaya.
[Singapore], 1957. 100 p. Illus.

Allouard, P., and P. Sallenave. Les services forestiers
à Java et en Malaisie. Bulletin Economique de
l'Indochine, 38 (1935): 730-794. Maps, plates.

Baharuddin bin Haji Ghazali. Development prospects
for forest industries in Malaya. 1964. Thesis
for diploma in forestry (Forest Department) --
University of Oxford.

Beversluis, A. J. Het boschwezen in Malakka. Tectona,
27 (1934): 46-70.

Burgess, P. F. An ecological study of the hill forests
of the Malay Peninsula with special reference
to the regeneration of three species of economic
importance. Paper presented at the Second Pan-Malaysian
Forestry Conference. September, 1968. 16 p. Mimeo.

Carson, G. L. The "spot" method of enumeration survey
in the Matang. Mal For, 16 (1953): 206-212.

Chong, Peng-wah. Part of Pekan District, Pahang.
Kuala Lumpur, 1965. (Forest Resources Reconnaissance
Survey of Malaya, Report, no. 1)

Chong, Peng-wah. Sawmilling and conversion efficiency
in N.W. Malaysia. Mal For, 30, 2 (1967): 145-154.
Diagrs.

Coulter, J. K. The Kuala Langat (North) Forest Reserve.
Mal Ag Jl, 39 (1956).

Cousens, J. E. Some notes on the composition of
lowland and tropical rain forest in Rengam Forest
Reserve, Johore. Mal For, 14 (1951): 131-139.

Cubitt, G. E. S. Wood in the Federated Malay States;
its use, misuse and future provision. Kuala Lumpur,
1920. 31 p.

Cubitt, G. E. S. Report on forestry in the Federated
Malay States. Proc Br Emp For Conf (London, 1920)
(1921): 55-58.

Cubitt, G. E. S. Forestry in the Malay Peninsula:
statement prepared for the British Empire Forestry
Conference, London, 1924. London, 1924. 24 p.

Cubitt, G. E. S. Forestry in Malaya. London, 1926. 25 p.

Cubitt, G. E. S. Report on forestry in the Federated
Malay States. Proc Br Emp For Conf, 3 (Australia,
1928) (1928): 29-30.

Cubitt, G. E. S. Forestry in Malaya. Br Mal, 18
(1943): 225-227.

Desch, H. E. The forests of the Malay Peninsula
and their exploitation. Mal For, 7 (1938): 169-180.

Desch, H. E. Malayan forests and their utilization.
AR, 34 (1938): 719-728. Far Eastern Review, 35
(1939): 23-27.

Desch, H. E. The contribution of tropical forests
to war economy. Mal For, 10 (1941): 123-130.

Desch, H. E., and A. V. Thomas. Timber utilization
in Malaya. Kuala Lumpur, 1940. 70 p. (Malayan
Forest Records, no. 13) Plates.

Durant, C. L. Vegetable cultivation as an aid to
forest improvement. Mal For, 10 (1941): 48-54.

Durgnat, P. A. Swamp forests in lower Perak. Mal
For, 15 (1952): 127-131.

Durgnat, P. A. Some aspects of Malaya's sawmilling
industry. Mal For, 21 (1958): 215-230.

Forest research programme, 1950. Silvi-culture and
forest botany. Mal For, 13 (1950): 28-40.

Forest resources of Malaya. PPSC, VI (California)
4 (1940): 830-833.

Foxworthy, F. W. Commercial woods of the Malay Peninsula.
Kuala Lumpur, 1921. 135 p. (Malayan Forest Records,
no. 1)

Foxworthy, F. W. Minor forest products of the Malay
Peninsula. Kuala Lumpur, 1922. 65 p. (Malayan
Forest Records, no. 2)

Foxworthy, F. W. Forest reconnaissance in Malaya.
Empire Forestry Journal, 3 (1924): 78-86.

Foxworthy, F. W. Malayan forests, their composition
and value. Proc Br Emp For Conf (London, 1926):99-116.

Foxworthy, F. W. Commercial timber trees of the
Malay Peninsula. Singapore, 1927. 195 p. (Malayan
Forest Records, no. 3)

Francke, A. Aus der Waldwirtschaft Britisch-Malayas,
ein Beispiel zum Waldbau in tropischen Regenwald.
Kolonialforstliche Mitteilungen, 4 (1941): 93-140.

H. Wald und Forstwirtschaft der Malaiischen Halbinsel.
Z Weltforst, 9 (1941): 162-173.

Hodgson, D. H. The elements of Malayan silviculture.
Mal For, 1 (1931/1932): 85-91.

Ismail bin Haji Ali. The impact of land development
on forest resources and management in Selangor.
Mal For, 28 (Oct. 1965): 264-270.

Junghaus, W. Die Forstwirtschaft in Malacca.
Z Weltforst, 1 (1934): 552-554.

Leong, Hing-nin. Highlights of forestry during the
first decade of independence in West Malaysia.
Mal For, 31 (1968): 3-14. Graphs, tables.

Lian, Kwen-koo. Timber exports from West Malaysia--1966.
Mal For, 30, 3 (1967): 191-198. Tables.

Liew, Khooi-cheng, and Donald T. Lopez. Development
of the sawmilling industry in West Malaysia.
Mal For, 31, 1 (1968): 33-42.

Malaya. Report on forest administration, 1957. Kuala
Lumpur, 1958.

Malaya. Report on forest administration, 1958. Kuala
Lumpur, 1959.

Malaya, Forest Service. The need for reorganisation
and expansion of the Malayan Forest Service,
with a chapter on forestry education in Malaysia.
Kuala Lumpur, Malayan Forest Service, 1965. 63 p.

Malaysia. Jabatan Hutan. Report of the special committee
on the establishment of quick growing species.
Kuala Lumpur, 1968. 67 p. Appendices. Mimeo.

Malaysia, Forest Department. Report on the establishment
of quick growing pulpwood plantations; laporan
badan istimewa jadian konifer. [Kuala Lumpur],
the Department, 1 April, 1968. 100 p. Graphs, tables.

Mead, J. P. Forestry in the Malay Peninsula. Indian
Forester, 60 (1935): 25-28.
A paper read at the Fourth British Empire Forestry
Conference.

Mok, S. T. A note on the forest resources of Kuantan district, Pahang. Mal For, 30, 3 (1967): 217-221. Map, tables.

Noakes, D. S. P. The mangrove charcoal industry in Matang. Mal For, 13 (1950): 80-83.

Noakes, D. S. P. Notes on the silviculture of the mangrove forests of Matang, Perak. Mal For, 14 (1951): 183-196.

Noakes, D. S. P. The job of forestry. Malaya (1954): 385-388.

Oliphant, J. N. Artificial or natural regeneration. Mal For, 1 (1931/1932): 186-192.

Oliphant, J. N. Some economic aspects of timber production in Malaya. Empire Forestry Journal, 13 (1934): 45-57.

Oliphant, J. N. Save the vegetation. Mal For, 4 (1935): 3-7.

Rule, Alex. Exploitation of tropical forests and the problem of secondary species. Empire Forestry Review, 26 (1947): 83-86.

Salleh bin Mohd. Nor. A note on the forest resources of West and South Johore. Mal For, 30, 3 (1967): 212-216. Map, tables.

Salleh bin Mohd. Nor. A note on the forest resources of Segamat district, Johore. Mal For, 31, 1 (1968): 28-32. Map, tables.

Setton, G. G. K. What does Malaya get from the forest? Mal For, 17 (1954): 114-128.

Smith, C. Logging and regeneration of Malayan rain forest. Mal For, 3 (1934): 130-133.

Strugnell, E. J. Silviculture in Malaya. Empire Forestry Journal, 17 (1938): 188-194.

Strugnell, E. J. Development in silvicultural practice in Malayan evergreen forests. Mal For, 11 (1947/1948): 37-41.

Symington, C. F. The study of secondary growth on rain forest sites in Malaya. Mal For, 2 (1933): 107-117.

Thomas, A. V. Notes on some timber from Cameron Highlands. Mal For, 4 (1935): 188-196.

Thomas, A. V. Prospects of pulp production in Malaya. Mal For, 13 (1950): 75-79.

Thomas, A. V. Forestry. A brief description of the timbers included in the Malayan grading rules. Kuala Lumpur, 1954. 15 p.

Walton, A. B. Artificial regeneration. Mal For, 1 (1931/1932): 107-110.

Walton, A. B. Some considerations for the future management and silvicultural treatment of Malayan forests. Mal For, 11 (1947/1948): 68-74.

Walton, A. B. Land planning and forestry. Mal For, 14 (1951): 212-220.

Walton, A. B., R. C. Barnard, and J. Wyatt-Smith. Silviculture of lowland Dipterocarp forest in Malaya. Unasylva, 7 (1953): 19-23. Also in Mal For, 15 (1952): 181-197.

Watson, J. G. Mangrove forests of the Malay Peninsula. Singapore, 1928. 260 p. (Malayan Forest Record, no. 6)

Watson, J. G. Forest research in Malaya. Empire Forestry Journal, 13 (1934): 223-231.

Watson, J. G. The regeneration of tropical rain-forest. Mal For, 5 (1936): 20-23.

Watson, J. G. Forestry and tin mining. Mal For, 8 (1939): 145-149.

Watson, J. G. Forests and timber production. Mal For, 10 (1941): 93-96.

Watson, J. G. Some materials for a forest history of Malaya. Mal For, 13 (1950): 63-72.

Webb, B. E. Trouble in the sawmilling industry. Mal For, 17 (1954): 147-150.

Webber, M. L. The mangrove ancestry of a freshwater swamp forest suggested by its Diatom flora. Mal For, 17 (1954): 25-26.

Wyatt-Smith, J. Save the Belukar. Mal For, 11 (1947/1948): 24-26.

Wyatt-Smith, J. Forestry, agricultural settlements and land planning. Mal For, 14 (1951): 206-212.

Wyatt-Smith, J. Malayan forest types. Mal Nature Jl, 7 (1952): 45-55; 8 (1953): 52-58.

Wyatt-Smith, J. A note on the fresh-water swamp, lowland and hill forest types of Malaya. Mal For, 24, 2 (1961): 110-121.

F. MINERALS AND MINING

Adams, Frank D. Tin mining in Malaya. Montreal, 1928. 32 p. (McGill University Publication Series V, no. 18) Illus., maps.

The alluvial tin mining industry of the Federated Malay States. Far Eastern Review, 29 (1933): 222-226.

Attenborough, L. G. Tin mining in Malaya. Kuala Lumpur, 1925. 32 p. (Institute of Mining and Metallurgy, no. 245)

Bain, H. Foster. Singapore's control of key mineral resources. FA, 7 (1929): 666-669.

Barnard, Robert. Malaya holds key to world tin empire. Great Britain and the East, 67 (1951): 45.

British Malaya's dependence on rubber and tin. Board of Trade Journal, 126 (1931): 823-825.

Courtenay, P. P. International tin restriction and its effect on the Malayan tin industry. G, 46 (1961): 223-231.

Crookewit, H. The tin mines of Malacca. Jl Ind Archip, 8 (1854): 112-133.

Doyle, P. Tin mining in Larut. London, 1879.

Eastham, J. K. Rationalisation in the tin industry. Review of Economic Studies IV (London) (1936): 13-32.

Fermor, Lewis L. Coal veins in Malaya. Geol Mag, 76 (1939): 465-472.

Fermor, Lewis L. The mineral resources of Malaya. B Imperial Inst, 38 (1940): 69-82.

Fermor, Lewis L. Report upon the mining industry of Malaya. Kuala Lumpur, 1940. 240 p. Diagr., maps, tables.

Fermor, Lewis L. Malaya's mineral resources and the war. AR, 37 (1941): 371-391.

Fraulob, K. Vorkommen, Untersuchung und Bewertung alluvialer Zinnerzlagerstätten unter besonderer Berücksichtigung der Malaiischen Halbinsel. Metallhüttenbetriebe, 22 (1934): 395-401, 427-430, 502-511.

Greig, G. E. Mining in Malaya. London, 1931. 76 p. Illus.

Groves, J. J. D. Batu Arang coal mine. R Engineers Jl, 65 (1952): 435-441.

Hale, Abraham. On the mines and miners in Kinta, Perak. JRASSB, 16 (1886): 303-320.

Harris, Florence E., and Mary E. Trought. United States tin mission report, Malaya 1951. Mineral Trade Notes, Special Supplement no. 39 to v. 35, no. 3. (1952). 26 p. Map. Mimeo.

Harris, H. G. B., and E. S. Willbourn. Mining in Malaya. London, 1936. 96 p. Illus. Revised 1940. 108 p.

Hughes, A. D. Alluvial tin mining in Malaya. Mining Engineering, 1, 3 (1949): 65-74. Illus.

Ingham, F. T. Deep alluvial tin deposits of Malaya near the granite limestone contact. Far Eastern Review, 36 (1940): 410-412. Figs., plate.

Iron-mining boom in Malaya. FEER, 17 (1954): 455-456.

Jackson, J. C. Malay mining methods in Kinta in 1884. MH, 8, 2 (1964): 12-18.

Jones, W. R. On the supposed case of tin in statu nascenti in the Malay Peninsula. Geol Mag, 51 (1914): 537-541.

Jones, W. R. Tinfields of the world. London, 1925.

King, Arthur W. Changes in the tin mining industry of Malaya. G, 25 (1940): 130-134. Map.

Knorr, K. E. Tin under control. Stanford, 1945.

Lian, Hock-lian. European mining enterprises in Selangor, 1873-1896. Historical Journal (1963/1964): 23-28.

Lock, Charles G. Warnford. Mining in Malaya for gold and tin. London, 1907. 195 p. Illus., map.

Lowinger, Victor A. Malaya's great tin mining industry. Far Eastern Review, 33 (1937): 357-359.

Malaya, Department of Mines. Bulletin of statistics relating to the mining industry. 1956- . Kuala Lumpur. (Published annually).

Malayan Tin Bureau. Tin News. Washington, D.C. Monthly.

Malaysia, Department of Statistics. Census of mining industries in West Malaysia, 1965. Kuala Lumpur, 1966. 58 p.

Middleton, W. B. Prospecting tin land in Malaya. Institute of Mining and Metallurgy, Transactions, 24 (1914/1915): 300-328.

The mineral resources of Johore. B Imperial Inst, 34 (1936): 54-57.

Mitchell, B. A. Malayan tin tailings--prospects of rehabilitation. Mal For, 20 (1957): 181-186.

Ooi, Jin-bee. Tin mining landscapes of Kinta. A
    study of some of the major environmental problems
    of mining in the Kinta Valley. Singapore, 1954.
    M.A. thesis.

Ooi, Jin-bee. Mining landscapes of Kinta. MJTG,
    4 (Jan. 1955): 1-58. Extensive bibliog., illus.,
    maps.

O'Reilly, J. M. H. An assessment of the Malayan
    tin mining industry in the twentieth century.
    JTG, 17 (1963): 72-78.

Pentzlin, H. Aufbau und Bewährung des Kartells der
    Zinnstaaten. Z Geopol, 16 (1939): 80-87.

Present conditions of mining in British Malaya.
    Jl Geol, 50 (1938): 269-279. [In Japanese].

Roe, F. W. Coalfields at Batu Arang. In Chamber
    of Mines Yearbook. Kuala Lumpur, 1946.

Savage, Herbert E. F. The stanniferous deposits
    of Trengganu, Unfederated Malayan States. Mining
    Journal, 162 (1928): 723-726.

Savage, Herbert E. F. The mineral prospects of Trengganu.
    Kuala Lumpur, 1931.

Scrivenor, J. B. Notes on prospecting for tin ore
    in the Federated Malay States. Mining Journal,
    95 (1911): 991-992, 1032-1034, 1043-1044, 1086-1088.

Scrivenor, J. B. Report on Rantau Panjang coal measures
    by government geologist. Kuala Lumpur, 1911. 7 p.

Scrivenor, J. B. A sketch of Malayan mining. London,
    1928. 76 p. Illus., map.

Siew, Nim-chee. Labour and tin mining in Malaya.
    Ithaca, 1953. 48 p. (Cornell University Southeast
    Asia Program, Data Paper, no. 7) Illus., map.

Siew, Nim-chee. The International Tin Agreement,
    1953. MER, 2 (1957): 35-53.

Simms, George. Malayan tin, a rich endowment. Optima,
    18, 2 (1968): 74-79.

Thomson, A. G. Mineral resources of Malaya. MER, 2 (1952): 12-13.

Tin in Malaya. Kuala Lumpur, 1951. 12 p. Illus.

Tin in Malaya and Nigeria. Times Rev Br Colonies, 7 (1952): 7-9. Graphs, illus., statistics.

United Nations Tin Conference. 1953 International Tin Agreement. Kuala Lumpur, Government Printer, 1953.

Villa, E. M. de. The study of mines in China, Indochina and Malaya. Hongkong, 1935. 226 p. Plates.

Willbourn, E. S. Notes on the occurrence of lode tin-ore in the Kinta Valley. Kuala Lumpur, 1924.

Willbourn, E. S. List of minerals found in British Malaya together with a description of their properties, occurrences and uses. JRASMB, 3, 2 (1925): 57-100.

Willbourn, E. S. The geology and mining industries of Johore. JRASMB, 6, 4 (1928): 5-35.

Willbourn, E. S. A short account of the geology of those tin-deposits of Kinta that are mined by alluvial methods. Engineering Assoc of Malaya Jl, 4 (1936): 1-10.

Wong, Lin-ken. The Malayan tin industry to 1914, with special reference to the states of Perak, Selangor, Negri Sembilan and Pahang. 1959. Ph.D. thesis (School of Oriental and African Studies) -- London.

Wong, Lin-ken. Western enterprise and the development of the Malayan tin industry to 1914. In C. D. Cowan, ed. The Economic Development of Southeast Asia. New York [1964]: 127-153.

Wong, Lin-ken. The Malayan tin industry to 1914, with special reference to the states of Perak, Selangor, Negri Sembilan and Pahang. Tucson, 1965. 302 p. Illus., tables.

Wray, L. Tin mines and the mining industry of Perak, and other papers. Perak Museum Notes, 3 (1894): 1-25; 2 (1897): 19-33; 2 (1898): 81-88.

Yip, Yat-hoong. The marketing of tin-ore in Kampar.
MER, 4 (Oct. 1959): 45-55.

Yip, Yat-hoong. Malaya in the 1953 international
tin agreement. Singapore, 1960. M.A. thesis.

Yip, Yat-hoong. Malaya under the pre-war international
tin agreement. MER, 8, 1 (1963): 81-97.

Yip, Yat-hoong. The mining industry. In Wang Gung-wu.
Malaysia: A Survey. London, 1964: 293-306.

Yip, Yat-hoong. Post-war international tin control
with special reference to Malaysia. KEM, 1, 2
(1964): 51-87.

Yip, Yat-hoong. Development prospects of the Malayan
tin mining industry. KEM, 3, 1 (1966): 25-40. Tables.

Yip, Yat-hoong. Tin export earnings and the early
economic growth of Malaya. KEM, 3, 2 (1966): 21-31.

Yip, Yat-hoong. The development of the tin mining
industry in Malaysia. 1967. Ph.D. thesis -- University
of Malaya.

Yip, Yat-hoong. Recent changes in the ownership
and control of locally incorporated tin dredging
companies in Malaya. MER, 13, 1 (1968): 70-88.

G. LABOR

Abdul Aziz bin Mohd. Yassin, Ungku. Development
and utilisation of labour resources in Southeast
Asia. In Philip W. Thayer and W. T. Phillips.
Nationalism and Progress in Free Asia. Baltimore,
1956: 193-203.

Awbery, S. S., and S. W. Dalley. Labour and trade
union organisation in the Federation of Malaya
and Singapore. Kuala Lumpur, London, 1948. 70 p.
(Colonial Office, no. 234) Tables.

Banner, Hubert S. Labour in British Malaya. AR,
27 (1931): 669-673.

Benson, W. Labour protection in Malaya. AR, 25 (1929):
31-38.

Blake, D. J. Compilation, chronicle or history?
A review of Charles Gamba, "The origins of trade
unionism in Malaya". MER, 8, 2 (1963): 91-103.

Blythe, W. L. Historical sketch of Chinese labour
in Malaya. JRASMB, 20, 1 (1947): 64-114.

Chalmers, W. Ellison. Crucial issues in industrial
relation in Singapore. Singapore, 1967. 312 p.

Conditions of labour and methods of recruiting in
Malaya. Int Labour Rev, 21 (1930): 426-428.

Employment in Singapore and the Federation of Malaya
in 1953. Industry and Labour, 12, 9 (1954): 424-425.

Gamba, Charles. Malayan labour, merdeka and after.
India Q, 14 (1948): 280-292.

Gamba, Charles. Wages, unions and rubber. Eastern
World, 7 (1953): 46-49.

Gamba, Charles. Trade unionism in Malaya. FES, 23
(1954): 28-30.

Gamba, Charles. The National Union of Plantation
Workers: the history of the plantation workers
of Malaya, 1946-1958. Singapore [1962]. 292 p.
Map, tables.

Gamba, Charles. The origins of trade unionism in
Malaya; a study in colonial labour unrest. Singapore,
1962. 511 p. Charts, col. map, tables.

Gammans, L. D. Co-operative societies amongst Indian
labourers in Malaya. Planter (May 1933): 384-385.

Gilman, E. W. F. Labour in British Malaya. London,
1924. 44 p.

Hadow, Patrick. Labour conditions in Malaya. In
International Rubber Congress and Exhibition,
Batavia, 1914. Batavia, 1914: 60 p.

Hyde-Clarke, Meredyth. The labour problem: Britain's research into human relations. Times Rev Br Colonies, 15 (1954): 7-9.

Indian labour in Ceylon, Fiji and British Malaya. Int Labour Rev, 42 (1940): 57-76.

International Labour Office. Recruiting of labour in colonies and other territories with analogous conditions. Geneva, 1925. 282 p.

International Labour Office. Report to the Government of the Federation of Malaya on manpower information. Geneva, 1962. 20 p. Tables. "ILO/TAP/Malaya/R.16."

International Labour Office. The trade union situation in the Federation of Malaya. Report of a mission from the International Labour Office. Geneva, 1962. 108 p.

International Labour Organization, Committee on Work on Plantations. Basic problems of plantation labour. Geneva, 1950. 166 p.
    Contains numerous references to labor conditions in Malaya.

Jackson, R. N. Immigrant labour and the development of Malaya, 1786-1920; a historical monograph. Kuala Lumpur, 1961. 161 p.

Jenks, J. W. Report on certain economic questions in the English and Dutch colonies in the Orient. Washington, D.C., 1902. 176 p. (War Department Document, no. 168)

Jones, G. W. The growth of Malaya's labour force. Canberra, 1966. 472 p. Ph.D. thesis -- Australian National University. Bibliog., p. 454-472.

Josey, Alex. Trade unionism in Malaya. Singapore, 1954. 52 p. (Background to Malaya Series, no. 4)

Josey, Alex. Labour laws in a changing Singapore. Singapore (1968). 110 p.

Kanapathy, V. Education, manpower and Malaysian economic development. UMBCER, 3, 1 (1967): 8-27.

Kleinsorge, Paul L. Singapore's industrial arbitration court: collective bargaining with compulsory arbitration. Industrial and Labor Relations Review, 17 (July 1964): 551-565.

Labour. Report and award of a Board of Arbitration to settle the wage dispute in the rubber industry, 1952. Kuala Lumpur, 1952. (Legislative Council Paper, no. 81)

Labour in British Malaya. Singapore, 1924. 44 p. (Malayan Series, no. 11)

Labour in British Malaya in 1931. Int Labour Rev, 27 (1933): 397-402.

Labour in British Malaya in 1934. Int Labour Rev, 34 (1936): 789-794.

Labour in British Malaya in 1935. Int Labour Rev, 36 (1937): 91-96.

Labour protection in Malaya. Int Labour Rev, 17 (1928): 258-262.

Loh, Philip. The British approach to slavery in the Straits Settlements and the Malay States 1819-1910. JHS, 3 (1964/1965): 1-14.

Malaya, Department of Labour and Industrial Relations. Report on employment, unemployment and under-employment, 1962. [Kuala Lumpur] 1963. 26 p. Tables.

Malaya, Registry of Trade Unions. Annual report of the trade union registry for the year . . . 1953- . Kuala Lumpur. Annual.

Malaya, South Indian Labour Fund Board. Annual report. 1960- . Kuala Lumpur.
The board was established on September 1, 1958. Commissioner of Labour is ex-officio chairman of the board. First report covered the year 1959. Published annually since then.

Malaysia, Department of Statistics. Report on employment and unemployment in metropolitan towns, states of Malaya, 1965. Kuala Lumpur, 1965. 44 p.

Memorandum on the report of the committee appointed
by His Excellency the High Commissioner to "enquire
into the incidence of unemployment in Selangor
and to make recommendations" and the report of
the Selangor Unemployment Enquiry Committee.
Kuala Lumpur, 1938. 18 p. (Legislative Council
Paper, no. 5)

Moresco, E., and D. G. Stibbe. Le contrat de travail
dans les colonies asiatiques. Bull Colonisation
Comparée, 7 (1910): 545-570; 8 (1911): 1-11;
9 (1912): 289ff., 527ff.; 10 (1913): 1ff., 145ff.

Mui Tsai Commission. Mui tsai in Hong Kong and Malaya.
Report. London, 1937. 314 p. (Colonial Office,
Colonial no. 125) Tables.

The mui tsai system in China, Hongkong and Malaya.
Int Labour Rev, 34 (1936): 663-676.

Narayanan, P. P. Malayan workers and their future.
UA, 12 (1960): 252-259.

Nijhar, K. S. Growth of union membership and size
of trade union units in Malaya. KEM, 2, 2 (1965):
32-48.

Orde-Browne, G. St. J. Labour conditions in Ceylon,
Mauritius and Malaya. Report presented by the
Secretary of State for the Colonies. London,
1943. 113 p. (Command Paper, no. 6423) Diagr.,
index, tables.

Parmer, J. Norman. Colonial labor policy and administration:
a history of labor in the rubber plantation industry
of Malaya, 1910-1941. New York, 1960. 294 p.
(Monographs of the Association for Asian Studies, 9)

Parmer, J. Norman. Chinese estate workers' strikes
in Malaya in March 1937. In C. D. Cowan, ed.
The Economic Development of Southeast Asia.
New York [1964]: 154-173.

Pelzer, Karl J. Die Arbeiterwanderungen in Südostasien;
eine wirtschafts- und bevölkerungsgeographische
Untersuchung. Hamburg, 1935. 126 p. (British
Malaya als Arbeiterbedarfsgebiet, p. 60-87).

Pillai, P. P., ed. Labour in Southeast Asia. New
    Delhi, Indian Council of World Affairs, 1947.

Planters' Association of Malaya. Interim report
    of the special labour committee on matters relating
    to wages for Indian estate labourers. Kaula Lumpur,
    1928.

Planters' Association of Malaya. Matters relating
    to Indian Immigration Committee. By C. Ward-Jackson.
    In The Yearbook, 1929-30.

Purcal, J. Labour utilisation in a padi village
    in Province Wellesley. MER, 10, 2 (1965): 49-60.

Report of the commission appointed to enquire into
    the conditions of indentured labour in the Federated
    Malay States. Kuala Lumpur, 1911. 49 p. Diagr.,
    forms, map, tables. Also published in Proceedings
    of the Federal Council of the Federated Malay
    States, Kuala Lumpur, 1909-1910, Paper no. 11
    (1911): C60-C111.

Rubber Growers' Association. Memorandum on labour
    in Malaya with particular reference to South
    Indian labour. London, Rubber Growers' Association,
    1935.

Sastri, Srinivasa. Report on the conditions of Indian
    labour in Malaya. New Delhi, 1937. 28 p. Also
    published in Kuala Lumpur under same title as
    Legislative Council Paper no. 10, 1937. 32 p.

Saw, Swee-hock. Regional differences in the structure
    of the labour force in Malaysia. KEM, 3 (1966): 50-58.

Saw, Swee-hock. The structure of the labour force
    in Malaya. Int Labour Rev, 98, 1 (1968): 55-72.

Shamsul Bahrin bin Raja Muhammad Ali, Tunku. Indonesian
    labour in Malaya. KEM, 2, 1 (1965): 53-70.

Siew, Nim-chee. Labour and tin mining in Malaya.
    Ithaca, N.Y., 1953. 48 p. (Cornell University,
    Southeast Asia Program, Data Paper, no. 7) Illus.,
    map. Mimeo.

Smith, M. Mead. Labor conditions in British Malaya.
    Washington, D.C., 1944. 16 p. Tables.

Smith, M. Mead. Labour conditions in British Malaya.
Monthly Labor Rev, 57 (1944): 279-294.

Thompson, Virginia. Labour supply in Southeast Asia.
FES, 14 (1945): 70-73.

Thompson, Virginia. Notes on labor problems in Malaya.
New York, 1945. 36 p.

Thompson, Virginia. Labor in Southeast Asia. FES,
20 (1951): 129-135.
For British policy in Malaya, see p. 133.

Thompson, Virginia, and Richard Adloff. Labor problems
in Southeast Asia. New Haven, Conn., 1947. 283 p.
Index.
Chap. 3, Malaya, p. 62-116.

Turner, G. E. A. A Perak coffee planter's report
on the Tamil labourer in Malaya in 1902. MHJ,
2 (1955): 20-28.

Vreede, A. G. Rapport omtrent de arbeidstoestanden
in en de werving van arbeidskrachten voor de
Straits Settlements, de Federated Malay States
en Ceylon. Weltevreden, 1928. 109 p. (Publicaties
van het Kantoor van Arbeid, no. 4)

Weaver, George L. P. The NUPW [National Union of
Plantation Workers] in Malaya. SAIS Review, 2
(1958): 10-20.

H. POWER

Batang Padang Hydro-Power Scheme in Malaysia. Executed
by Hochtief AG, Philipp Holzmann AG, Joint Venture
Batang Padang. [Essen, n.d.]. Diagrs., maps, photos.

Kinloch, Robert F. The growth of electric power
production in Malaya. Annals, 56, 2 (1966): 220-235.

Malaya, Central Electricity Board. Raub hydro-electric
development, an economic assessment. Kuala Lumpur,
1965. 15 p. Mimeo.

Malaya, National Electricity Board of the States
of Malaya. Annual report . . . Kuala Lumpur.
Annual series, started in 1951.

I. TRANSPORTATION

Abdul Aziz bin Abdul Hamid, Ungku, S. J. Gilani,
Jock Hoe, and Lim Chong-yah. Traffic flow through
Port Swettenham projected to 1975. Kuala Lumpur,
Department of Economics, University of Malaya,
1964. 155 p. Selected bibliog. p. 149-155, tables.

Allen, D. F. Report on the major ports of Malaya.
Kuala Lumpur, 1951. 176 p. Maps.

Allen, D. F. Report on the minor ports of Malaya.
Singapore, 1953. 174 p. Map, plates, tables.

Barnes, W. D. Singapore's old straits and new harbour.
JRASSB, 60 (1911): 25-36.

Brandreth, Harold Gordon. The Malayan railway and
road/rail competition in the states of Malaya.
Kuala Lumpur, 1964. 94 p. Diagrs., tables.

Courtenay, P. P. Penang: a port study. In The Geographical
Association. Asian Sample Studies. 1968: 52-63. Maps.

Dalton, H. Goring. Some Malay boats and their uses.
JRASMB, 4, 2 (1926): 192-197. Figs., plates.

Development of the Port of Penang. Kuala Lumpur,
1954. 4 p. (Legislative Council Paper, no. 50)

Federated Malay States Railways. Fifty years of
railways in Malaya, 1885-1935. Kuala Lumpur,
1935. 136 p.

Federation of Malaya. Report of the Federal Ports
Committee. Kuala Lumpur, 1952.

Fifty years of railways in Malaya, 1885-1935. Far
Eastern Review, 32 (1936): 157-165.

Fisher, C. A. The railway geography of British Malaya.
SGM, 64 (1948): 123-136. Illus., maps, plates.

Fitzgerald, R. T. D. The Jong, a model boat with an out-rigger, from Malaya. Man, 39, 149 (1939): 156-157. Illus.

Gibson-Hill, C. A. Cargo boats of the east coast of Malaya. JRASMB, 22, 3 (1949): 106-125.

Gibson-Hill, C. A. The Indonesian trading boats reaching Singapore. JRASMB, 23, 1 (1950): 108-138. Bibliog., diagr., illus.

Gibson-Hill, C. A. Tongkang and lighter matters. JRASMB, 25, 1 (1952): 84-110. Bibliog., illus. Tongkang is a fairly large, heavy, bargelike cargo-carrying sailboat, usually seagoing, mostly built by Chinese.

Gibson-Hill, C. A. The Orang Laut of the Singapore River and the sampan panjang. JRASMB, 25, 1 (1952): 161-174.

Gibson-Hill, C. A. The steamers employed in Asian water, 1819-1839. JRASMB, 27, 1 (1954): 120-162. Bibliog.

Greene, Katrine R. C. Transportation. In Katrine R. C. Greene, and Joseph D. Phillips. Transportation and Foreign Trade. New York, 1942: 1-101. Constitutes Part 2 of An Economic Survey of the Pacific Area. See p. 56-62 for British Malaya.

Hughes, William B. Malaya case studies in highway impact. Washington, D.C., Brookings Institution, Transport Research Program, 1965.

Kandaouroff, P. Die malayischen Eisenbahnen. Archiv für Eisenbahnwesen, 58 (1935): 187-210.

Mactier, R. S. The ports of Malaya. Malaya (Oct. 1952): 29-35.

Malaya. Malayan railways. Report of the Malayan Railway Economics Commission, March, July 1961. Kuala Lumpur, 1961. 2 v.

Malaya and its communications. B Inter News, 18 (1941): 2003-2007.

Malaya, Federal Ports Committee. Report and supplementary report. Kuala Lumpur, Government Printer, 1952.

Malaya, Prime Minister's Department, Economic Planning Unit. Report of the inter-departmental working party on roads and bridges. Kuala Lumpur, 1959. 30 p. Mimeo.

Malaysia, Economic Planning Unit. The general transport study of Malaysia: a proposal. Kuala Lumpur, 1966. 35 p. Mimeo.

Marschall. Zum Ausbau der Vereinigten Malayischen Staatsbahnen. Archiv für Eisenbahnwesen, 55 (1932): 773-777.

Marshall, R. A. Kuala Lumpur: an important Malayan railway centre. Railway Magazine (Oct. 1950): 701-706. Illus.

Mildenstein, L. von. Die Strassen in Malaya und Straits Settlements. Strasse, 5 (1938): 518-520.

Millbourn, Sir Eric. Report of the inquiry into the port of Port Swettenham. Kuala Lumpur, 1958. 36 p.

Paterson, D. The Johore causeway. Inst Civil Engineers, 220 (1925): 250-290.

Polunin, Ivan. Traditional boats of Malaya. G Mag, 25 (1952/1953): 334-345.

Sidhu, Jagjit Singh. Railways in Selangor 1882-1886. JRASMB, 38 (1965): 6-22.

Thompson, Virginia. Farther India's communications. FES, 11 (1942): 4-9.

Tregonning, K. G. The origin of the Straits Steamship Company in 1890. JRASMB, 38, 2 (Dec. 1965): 274-289.

Tregonning, K. G. Home port Singapore: a history of the Straits Steamship Company Limited 1890-1963. Oxford University Press, 1967. 300 p. Front., maps, plates.

Trimer, George. The ports of the Straits Settlements.
Far Eastern Review, 33 (1937): 349-351, 360.

Ward, Marion W. The trade of the ports of Malaya.
Ann Arbor, Mich., University Microfilms, 1960.
347 p.

Ward, Marion W. Malayan fishing ports and their
inland connections. TESG, 55, 5 (1964): 113-122.
Maps.

Ward, Marion W. Port Swettenham and its Hinterland,
1900-1960. JTG, 19 (1964): 69-78.

Ward, Marion W. Major port hinterlands in Malaya.
TESG, 57, 6 (1966): 242-251. Maps.

Warrington Smyth, H. Boats and boat building in
the Malay Peninsula. Jl R Soc Arts (1920): 570-586.

White, Bruce. Malaysia transport survey, a proposal.
Prepared for the International Bank for Reconstruction
and Development, acting as executing agency for
the Government of Malaysia. London, 1967. 78 p.
Diagr., graph.

CHAPTER 11

STATE

A. GENERAL

Abdul Rahman, Tunku. Malaysia: key area in Southeast
Asia. FA, 43, 4 (1965): 659-670.

Abdul Rahman Putra Al-Haj, Tunku. May 13. Before
and after. Kuala Lumpur, 1969. 207 p.

Abdul Tai bin Mahmud. The role of Muslims in nation
building in the Federation of Malaysia. Islamic
Review, 52 (Dec. 1964): 22-23.

Alatas, Hussein, Syed. Modernization and national
consciousness. In Ooi Jin-bee and Chiang Hai-ding,
eds. Modern Singapore. Singapore, University
of Singapore Press, 1969. 216-232.

All Malaya Council of Joint Action. The people's
constitutional proposal for Malaya. Kuala Lumpur,
1947. 57 p.

Allen, James de V. The Malayan Union. New Haven,
Yale Southeast Asia Studies, 1967. (Monograph
Series, no. 10)

Allen, James de V. Malayan civil service, 1874-1941:
colonial bureaucracy/Malayan élite. 1968. 52 p.
Unpublished paper no. 10, presented at the International
Conference on Asian History, Kuala Lumpur, August,
1968. Mimeo.

Allen, Richard. Malaysia: prospect and retrospect.
The impact and aftermath of colonial rule. London,
New York, Kuala Lumpur, 1968. 330 p. Maps.

Ardizzone, Michael. A nation is born, being a defence
of Malayan union. London [1946]. 95 p. (Forum Books)

Asian nationalism and Western politics. New York,
1950. 66 p. (11th Conference, Institute of Pacific
Relations. Lucknow, 1950).

Bartlett, Vernon. Die Zukunft Malayas. Aussenpolitik,
7 (1956): 177-182.

Bass, Jerome R. Malaysia and Singapore: moving apart?
AS, 9, 2 (1969): 122-129.

Bass, Jerome R. Malaysia: continuity or change?
AS, 10 (1970): 152-160.

Bauer, P. T. Nationalism and politics in Malaya.
FA, 25 (1947): 503-517. Map.

Bedale, Harold. Report on the establishment, organization
and supervision of local authorities in the Federation
of Malaya. Kuala Lumpur, 1953. 28 p. (Legislative
Council Paper, no. 14)

Bilainkin, G. Malaya at the cross roads. Contemporary
Review, 140 (1931): 749-756.

Bilainkin, G. The new Malaya. Fortnightly Rev, 141
(1934): 69-76.

Bondarevsky, G. L. The postwar struggle of the Malay
peoples for national liberation. Soviet Press
Translations (Sept. 15, 1950): 483-503.

Bondarevsky, G. L. Crisis of the colonial system;
national liberation struggle of the peoples of
East Asia; reports presented in 1949 to the Pacific
Institute of the Academy of Science, USSR. Bombay,
1951. 268 p.

Boyce, Peter. Policy without authority: Singapore's
external affairs power. JSAH, 6 (1965): 87-103.

Boyce, Peter, and R. K. Davis. Malaysia tests the
Commonwealth. Australian Quarterly, 37 (1965):
59-68.

Brackman, Arnold C. Southeast Asia's second front;
the power struggle in the Malay Archipelago.
Singapore, 1966. 341 p.

Braddell, Roland. The legal status of the Malay
States. Singapore, 1931.

Bradley, C. Paul. Malaysia's first year. Current
History, 48 (1965): 82-88.

Bradley, C. Paul. Rupture in Malaysia. Current History,
50 (1966): 98-105.

Brecher, Michael. The new states of Asia: a political
analysis. London, 1963. 226 p.

Burns, Creighton. City of strife. Age (Sept. 17, 1964).

Burns, Creighton. Race parley in Malaysia. Age (Sept. 25, 1964).

Burns, Creighton. Passions in Malaysian politics. Age (Dec. 14, 1964).

Burns, Creighton. Bombs, invaders and race riots. Age (April 5, 1965).

Burns, Creighton. Fraying nerves in Malaysia. Age (July 26, 1965).

Burridge, K. O. L. Rural administration in Johore. Jl Af Ad, 9, 1 (1957): 29-36.

Butwell, Richard. Malaysia and its impact on the international relations of Southeast Asia. AS, 4 (1964): 940-946.

Cady, John F., Patricia B. Barnett, and Shirley Jenkins. The development of self-rule and independence in Burma, Malaya and the Philippines. New York, 1948. 104 p. Mimeo.
   For Malaya, see Part II, p. 51-78.

Caine, Sir Sydney. The passing of colonialism in Malaya. Political Quarterly, 29 (1958): 258-268.

Caine, Sir Sydney. The political economy of independent Malaya. Journal of Commonwealth Political Studies, 2 (May 1964): 161-164.

Carnell, F. G. British policy in Malaya. Political Quarterly, 23 (1952): 269-281.

Carnell, Francis G. Malayan citizenship legislation. Int Comp Law Q, 1 (1952): 504-518.

Carnell, Francis G. Constitutional reform and elections in Malaya. PA, 27 (1954): 216-235.

Catley, R. Malaysia: the lost battle for merger. Australian Outlook, 21, 1 (1967): 44-60.

Cator, G. E. Some of our Malayan problems. JRCAS, 28, 1 (1941): 18-32.

Cator, G. E. Malaya: a retrospect. AR, 38 (1942): 375-379.

Chai, Hon-chan. The development of British Malaya 1896-1909. London, 1965. 364 p. 5 maps. Concentrates on administrative and social developments.

Clark, Margaret F. The Malayan Alliance and its accommodation of communal pressures, 1952-1962. Kuala Lumpur, 1964. 235 p. Thesis (M.A.) -- University of Malaya. Tables. Typescript.

Constitutional proposals for Malaya: report of the working committee appointed by a conference of His Excellency the Governor of the Malayan Union, the Honorable the Rulers of the Malay States and the Representatives of the United Malays National Organisation. Revised to December 19, 1946. Kuala Lumpur, 1947. 92 p.

Corry, W. C. S. Malaya and the English press. Spectator, 191 (1953): 537.
    Reply by F. Carnell, p. 632-633.

Corry, W. C. S. The present picture in Malaysia. JRCAS, 52, 3/4 (1965): 249-259.

Dartford, Gerald P. Plan for Malaysian federation. Current History, 43 (1962): 278-282.

Das, S. K. Japanese occupation and ex-post facto legislation in Malaya. Singapore, 1960. 148 p.

Dobby, E. H. G. (pseud., Guy Roberts). Making Malaya a nation. GM, 19 (1946): 141-150.

Dobby, E. H. G. (pseud., Guy Roberts). Malayan prospect. PA, 23 (1950): 392-401.

Dodd, E. E. Reconstruction in Burma and Malaya. Pt. 6. In S. Gore-Brown, Rita Hinden, C. W. Greenidge, and E. E. Dodd. Four Colonial Questions: How Should Britain Act? London, 1945: 41-56. (Fabian Research Series, no. 88) Illus., maps. 56 p.

Edgeton, T. Malaya reaches political adolescence. Eastern World, 8, 8 (1954): 9-11.

Emerson, Rupert. Malaysia: a study in direct and indirect rule. New York, 1937. 536 p.

Emerson, Rupert. The outlook in Southeast Asia.
Netherlands Indies, French Indochina, British
Malaya. For Policy Reports, 15 (1939): 206-216.

Emerson, Rupert, L. A. Mills, and V. Thompson.
Government and nationalism in Southeast Asia.
New York, 1942. 242 p.

Enloe, Cynthia H. Issues and integration in Malaysia.
PA, 41, 3 (1968): 372-385.

Esslemont, Don. Politics before the split. Venture
(London), 17 (Sept. 1965): 18-20.

The Federation of Malaya Agreement, 1948. Kuala
Lumpur, 1952. 77 p.

Finkelstein, Lawrence S. Prospects of self-government
in Malaya. FES, 21 (1952): 9-17.

Fisher, Charles A. The geographical setting of the
proposed Malaysian Federation. JTG, 17 (1963): 99-115.

Fisher, Charles A. Malaysia: a study in the political
geography of decolonisation. In C. A. Fisher.
Essays in Political Geography. London, 1968: 75-145.

Fistie, Pierre. Singapour et la Malaisie. Paris,
1960. 128 p. (Collection Que sais-je? 869)

FitzGerald, C. P. The expulsion of Singapore.
Nation, 201 (Oct. 1965): 208-212.

Fletcher, Nancy McHenry. The separation of Singapore
from Malaysia. Ithaca, Department of Asian Studies,
Cornell University, 1969. 98 p. (Southeast Asia
Program, Data Paper, no. 73)

Freedman, Maurice. Colonial law and Chinese society.
Jl R Anthr Inst, 80 (1952): 97-125. Bibliog.
Deals with the Chinese in Singapore.

Freedman, Maurice. The growth of a plural society
in Malaya. PA, 33 (June 1960): 158-160.

Furnivall, John S. Progress and welfare in Southeast
Asia; a comparison of colonial policy and practice.
New York, 1941. 84 p.

Gamba, Charles. Malaya and self-government. Eastern
   World, 6, 9 (1952): **16-17**, 32.

Gamer, Robert E. Urgent Singapore, patient Malaysia.
   Int Jl, 21, 1 (1965-1966): 42-56.

Gamer, Robert E. Parties and pressure groups. In
   Ooi Jin-bee and Chiang Hai-ding, eds. Modern
   Singapore. Singapore, University of Singapore
   Press, 1969: 197-207.

Gammans, L. D. The situation in Malaya. World Affairs,
   2 (1948): 353-356.

Gordon, Bernard K. The dimensions of conflict in
   Southeast Asia. Englewood Cliffs, N.J., 1966.

Grant, Margaret, ed. South Asia Pacific crisis.
   New York, 1964.

Great Britain Colonial Office. Federation of Malaya:
   summary of the revised constitutional proposals.
   London, 1947. 20 p. (Command Paper, no. 7171)

Grossholtz, Jean. An exploration of Malaysian meanings.
   AS, 6, 4 (1966): 227-240.

Groves, Harry E. The constitution of Malaysia. Singapore,
   1964. 239 p.

Groves, Harry E. Constitutional problems. In Wang
   Gung-wu, ed. Malaysia: A Survey. London, 1964: 356-364.

Gullick, J. M. Indigenous political systems of Western
   Malaya. London, 1965. 152 p. (London School of
   Economics, Monograph on Social Anthropology, no. 17)

Gullick, J. M. Malaysia. 1969. 304 p. Illus., maps.

Guyot, James F. Creeping urbanism and political
   development in Malaysia. Chapel Hill, N.C., 1967.
   38 p. Mimeo.

Hagan-Shaidali, S. A. E. Communalism and racialism
   in Malayan politics. Eastern World, 7, 9 (1953): 20-21.

Hake, H. B. Egmont. The new Malaya and you. London,
   1945. 107 p. Illus., map.

Hall, J. Duncan. Post war and politics of British
Southeast Asia. Jl Politics, 9 (1947): 692-716.

Han Suyin. Singapore separation. FEER, 49 (Aug.
1965): 349-352.

Hanna, Willard A. The formation of Malaysia, new
factor in world politics; an analytical history
and assessment of the prospects of the newest
state in Southeast Asia, based on a series of
reports written for the American Universities
Field Staff. New York [1964]. 247 p. Map.

Hanna, Willard A. Sequel to colonialism: the 1957-1960
foundations for Malaysia. New York, American
Universities Field Staff, 1965.

Harrison, Cuthbert W. Some notes on the government
services in British Malaya. London, 1929.

Hawkins, David C. Britain and Malaysia - another
view: was the decision to withdraw entirely voluntary
or was Britain pushed a little? AS, 9, 7 (1969):
546-562.

Hawkins, G. First steps in Malayan local government.
PA, 26 (1953): 155-158.

Hayden, R. Malaya and the Philippines: colonial
contrasts. FA, 5 (1927): 327-331.

Hazra, Niranjan Kumar. Malaya's foreign relations,
1957-1963. Singapore, 1965. 267 p. Dissertation
(M.A.) -- University of Singapore. Mimeo.

Herms, L. Widerstand der Völker gegen Malaysia.
Deutsche Aussenpolitik, 2 (1964): 127-136.

Hill, L. Report on the reform of local government.
Singapore, 1952. 143 p. Tables.

Hinton, Wilfred J. Government of Pacific dependencies:
British Malaya. Honolulu, 1929. 64 p.

How, Mun-heng. The Federal Council of the F.M.S.
as a colonial legislature. JHS, 5 (1966/1967): 39-46.

Hunter, Guy. Southeast Asia: race, culture and nation.
London, New York, Kuala Lumpur, 1966. 190 p. Maps,
tables.

Indonesien, Burma und Malaya im Kampf um Unabhängigkeit
und Demokratie. Berlin, 1961. 202 p. Maps.
Articles by D. N. Aidit and S. N. Rostowski.

Innes, J. R. Some notes on the constitution and
legislation of the Federated Malay States. Society
of Comparative Legislation, n.s., 16 (1916): 24-29.

Innes, J. R. The protectorate system in the Malay
States. National Review, 78 (1921): 398-406.

Ireland, Alleyne. The Far Eastern tropics: studies
in the administration of tropical dependencies.
Hong Kong, British North Borneo, Sarawak, Burma,
the Federated Malay States, Straits Settlements,
French Indo-China, Java, the Philippine Islands.
Boston, 1905. 339 p. Bibliog., index.

Ishak bin Tadin. Dato Onn and Malay nationalism,
1946-1951. JSAH, 1 (1960): 56-88.

Ismail bin Dato Abdul Rahman, Dato. Alliance Malaysian
Malaysia in two stages: 1. interracial harmony;
2. non-communal Malaysia. Petaling Jaya, Kuala
Lumpur, Federal Department of Information, Malaysia
[196-?]. 12 p.

Itagaki, Yoichi. Nationalism in Indonesia and Malaya:
Japanese policy in Indonesia and Malaya during
the war. FEER, 13 (1952): 173-176.

Jeyaratnam, K. Communalism and political process
in the Federation of Malaya. London, 1960.
Ph.D. thesis.

Jones, S. W. Public administration in Malaya. London,
New York, 1953. 229 p.

Jones, S. W. Public administration in Malaya.
Jl R Inst Int Aff, 32 (1953): 134-138.

Josey, Alex. Malayan affairs. Malaya, 1950. 46 p.
Broadcast from Radio Malaya, Public Relations
Department.

Kaberry, Phyllis M. British colonial policy in Southeast
Asia and the development of self-government in
Malaya. London, 1944; New York, 1945. 91 p.

Kahin, George McT. Malaysia and Indonesia. PA, 37,
    3 (1964): 253-270.

Kennedy, Raymond. Malaya: a colony without a plan.
    FES, 14 (1945): 225-226.

Kennedy, Raymond. Status quo for Malaya. FES, 15
    (1946): 134-137.

Khoo, Kay-kim. The origin of British administration
    in Malaya. JRASMB, 39, 1 (1966): 52-91.

King, Frank H. H. The new Malayan nation, a study
    of communalism and nationalism. New York, Institute
    of Pacific Relations, 1957. 89 p. Map.

Kroef, J. M. van der. Problems of national reconstruction
    in Malaya. Indonesië, 6, 2 (1952): 97-125.

Kroef, Justus M. van der. Malaysia--Singapore: neutrality
    or regional defence? World Review, 8, 1 (1969): 3-15.

Landon, Kenneth P. Malay nationalism. FEQ, 2 (1943):
    145-147.

Lee, Kuan-yew. The battle for merger. Singapore,
    1962. 207 p. Illus.
    A series of twelve radio talks on the struggle
    for independence through merger between Singapore
    and the Federation of Malaya. Also in Malay:
    Perjuangan untok perchantuman.

Lee, Kuan-yew. Are there enough Malaysians to save
    Malaysia? Singapore, Ministry of Culture, 1965.
    24 p. Illus.

Lee, Kuan-yew. The battle for a Malaysian Malaysia.
    Singapore, Ministry of Culture, 1965. 2 v. (1) 68 p.
    (2) 61 p. Illus. (part col.).

Lee, Kuan-yew. Malaysia comes of age. Singapore,
    Ministry of Culture, 1965. 27 p. Illus.

Leifer, Michael. Anglo-American differences over
    Malaysia. World Today, 20, 4 (1964): 156-167.

Leifer, Michael. Communal violence in Singapore.
    AS, 4 (1964): 1115-1121.

Leifer, Michael. Politics in Singapore: the first
term of the People's Action Party, 1959-1963.
Journal of Commonwealth Political Studies, 2
(1964): 102-117.

Leifer, Michael. Singapore in Malaysia: the politics
of federation. JSAH, 6 (1965): 54-70.

Leifer, Michael. Singapore leaves Malaysia. World
Today, 21 (1965): 361-364.

Linehan, W. The relations between Thailand and the
southern states of the Malay Peninsula. Singapore,
1941.

Lister, T. Report on the administration of the Federated
Malay States. Rangoon, 1920.

Lock, Tan-cheng. Malayan problems, from a Chinese
point of view. Singapore, 1947. 182 p.

Lowe, John. The Malayan experiment. London, 1960.
41 p. (Fabian Society, London. Research Series, 213)
Illus.

MacFadyen, Eric. A political future for British
Malaya. PA, 17 (1944): 49-55.

MacKeen, A. M. M. An Islamic constitutional document
in Malaysia. In S. Takdir Alisjahbana, ed. The
Cultural Problems of Malaysia in the Context
of Southeast Asia. Kuala Lumpur [1966?]: 131-138.

MacMichael, Harold A. Report on a mission to Malaya.
London, 1946. 16 p. (Colonial, no. 194)

Malaya after the emergency: conditions for constitutional
advance. Round Table, 172 (1953): 350-358.

Malaya: Britain's problem colony. New Statesman,
47 (1954): 665-690.

Malayan constitution. New Statesman, 47 (1954): 146.

Malayan Union and Singapore. Statement of policy
on future constitution. London, 1946. 10 p. (Command
Paper, no. 6724)

Malayan Union and Singapore. Summary of proposed
    constitutional arrangements. London, 1946.
    10 p. (Command Paper, no. 6749)

Malaysia. Agreement concluded between the Federation
    of Malaya, United Kingdom of Great Britain and
    Northern Ireland, North Borneo, Sarawak and Singapore.
    Kuala Lumpur, 1963. 232 p.

Malaysia, Development Administration Unit. Organisation
    of the Government of Malaysia, 1967. Kuala Lumpur,
    1967. 417 p. Maps, tables.

Malaysia, National Operations Council. The May 13
    tragedy. A report. Kuala Lumpur, 1969. 96 p.

Malaysia's case in the United Nations Security Council.
    Kuala Lumpur, 1965.

Mander, Linden A. The British Commonwealth and colonial
    rivalry in Southeast Asia. Pacific Historical
    Rev, 11 (1942): 19-27.

Mani, Lawrence G. A nation in the making; an independent
    survey. By Lawrence G. Mani, Ken Jalleh, and
    Donald K. Ellery. With introduction by S. Rajaratnam.
    Singapore, 1965. 115 p. Illus.

Martin, P. Les institutions politiques de Singapour
    et de la Malaisie. Politique Etrangère, 25 (1960):
    152-167.

Maxwell, Sir George. Problems of administration
    in British Malaya. New York, Institute of Pacific
    Relations, 1943. Mimeo.

McDougall, Derek J. The Malaysia-Singapore area
    and Australian security: some selected aspects.
    [Melbourne] 1968. 266 p. Thesis -- University
    of Melbourne. Bibliog. p. 246-266.

McGee, T. G. The Malayan elections of 1959, a study
    in electoral geography. JTG, 16 (1962): 70-99.

McKerron, Patrick. Malaya: the essential problem.
    United Empire (S-O 1952): 264-269.

Means, Gordon P. Malaysia--a new federation in Southeast
    Asia. PA, 36, 2 (1963): 138-159.

Menon, K. P. K. Politics and parties in Malaya.
India Quarterly (1950): 44-57.

Merdeka. Malaya becomes the tenth dominion. Round
Table, **188** (1957): 350-357.

Middlebrook, S. M., and A. W. Pinnick. How Malaya
is governed. London, 1949. **188** p. Illus., maps.

Miller, Harry. The story of Malaysia. London, 1965.
By a journalist.

Mills, Lennox A. British rule in Eastern Asia; a
study of contemporary government and economic
development in British Malaya and Hong Kong.
London, 1942. 581 p. Bibliog., maps.
See p. 1-372 for Malaya.

Mills, Lennox A. Malaya to-day. World Affairs, 5
(1951): 26-36.

Milne, R. S. Politics and government. In Wang Gung-wu.
Malaysia: A Survey. London, 1964: 323-335.

Milne, R. S. Singapore's exit from Malaysia: the
consequences of ambiguity. AS, 6 (1966): 175-184.

Milne, R. S. Government and politics in Malaysia.
Boston, 1967. 259 p.

Montgomery, John Dickey. Development administration
in Malaysia; report to the government of Malaysia.
By John D. Montgomery and Milton J. Esman. Kuala
Lumpur, 1966. 27 p.

Moore, Daniel Eldredge. The United Malay National
Organization and the 1959 Malayan elections;
a study of a political party in action in a newly
independent society. Berkeley, 1960. Thesis --
University of California.

Moore, Joanna. The law and people of Malaya and
Singapore. London, 1957.

Morkill, A. G. The Malay union. AR, 42 (1946): **181-187.**

Ness, Gayl D. Expressive and instrumental leadership
and the goals of government in Malaysia. In Gehen
Wijeyewardene, ed. Leadership and Authority:
A Symposium. Singapore, 1968: 39-64.

Oh, John C. H. The Federation of Malaysia: an experiment
in nation-building. American Journal of Economics
and Sociology, 26, 4 (1967): 425-437.

Oliver, A. S. Outline of British policy in East
and Southeast Asia 1945. Jl R Inst Int Aff, 29
(1950): 83.

Ongkilli, J. P. The Borneo response to Malaysia
1961-1963. Singapore, 1967. 148 p.

Osborne, Milton E. Singapore and Malaysia. Ithaca,
N.Y., 1964. 115 p. (Cornell University. Southeast
Asia Program. Data Paper, no. 53) Map.

Ott, Marvin. Malaysia: the search for solidarity
and security. AS, 8, 2 (1968): 127-132.

Parmer, J. Norman. Trade unions and politics in
Malaya. FES, 24 (Mar. 1955): 33-39.

Parmer, J. Norman. Malaysia. In George McT. Kahin,
ed. Governments and Politics of Southeast Asia.
2d ed. Ithaca, N.Y., 1964: 281-371.

Parmer, J. Norman. Malaysia 1965: challenging the
terms of 1957. AS, 6, 2 (1966): 111-118.

Parmer, J. Norman. Malaysia: changing a little to
keep peace. AS, 7, 2 (1967): 131-137.

Peet, G. L. Political questions of Malaya. Cambridge,
1949. 39 p. Maps.
A Malayan Questions series.

Peritz, René. American-Malay relations: substance
and shadows. Orbis, 11, 2 (1967): 532-550.

Peterson, A. D. The birth of the Malayan nation.
Inter Aff, 31 (July 1955): 311-316.

Pluvier, J. M. Malayan nationalism: a myth. JHS,
6 (1967/1968): 26-40.

Png, Poh-seng. The Kuomintang in Malaya, 1912-1941.
JSAH, 2 (1961): 1-32.

Population and citizenship in Malaya. FEER, 16 (1954):
270-271.

Purcell, Victor. A Malayan Union: the proposed new constitution. PA, 19 (1946): 20-40.

Purcell, Victor. Malaya in peace and in turmoil. World Today, 4 (1948): 421-429.

Purcell, Victor. Malayan constitution. Problems of equal citizenship. Times Rev Br Colonies, 5 (1952): 6.

Puthucheary, M. The operations room in Malaysia as a technique in administrative reform. Paper presented in seminar on "Administrative Reform and Innovation" at the tenth meeting of Eastern Regional Organization for Public Administration. Kuala Lumpur, 1968. 42 p. (GA 5/Pre-Conference/D24) Mimeo.

Pye, Lucien W. A new class in Malaya. New Leader, 43 (May 30, 1960): 12-14.

Races and parties in Malaya. Round Table, 42 (1952): 234-239.

Ratnam, K. J. Government and the plural society. JSAH, 3 (1961): 1-10.

Ratnam, K. J. Political parties and pressure groups. In Wang Gung-wu, ed. Malaysia: A Survey. London, 1964: 336-345.

Ratnam, K. J. Communalism and the political process in Malaya. Kuala Lumpur, 1965. 248 p. Map, tables.

Ratnam, K. J., and R. S. Milne. The Malayan parliamentary election of 1964. Singapore, 1967. 467 p. Maps, fold. tables.

Rees-Williams, David R. The Malayan situation in 1948. In Rees-Williams et al. Three Reports on the Malayan Problem. New York, Institute of Pacific Relations, 1949: 1-17. 46 p. Mimeo.

Rees-Williams, David R., et al. Three reports on the Malayan problem. New York, Institute of Pacific Relations, 1949. 46 p. Mimeo.

Report of the Committee on the Malayanisation of
the Government Service. D. Gray, Chm. Kuala Lumpur,
1954. 124 p.
Committee set up to investigate, inter alia,
the extent to which locally domiciled Malayans
have been promoted or newly appointed to higher
posts in all branches of the Public Service in
Malaya since 1948.

Report on Community Development. Kuala Lumpur, 1954.
30 p. (Legislative Council Paper, no. 39)

Report of the Select Committee on the Village Councils
Bill, 1952. Kuala Lumpur, 1952. 11 p. (Legislative
Council Paper, no. 40)

Rogers, Marvin L. Politization and political development
in a rural Malay community. AS, 9 (1969): 919-933.

Roll, C. Der malayische Staatenbund und Singapur.
Aussenpolitik, 10 (1959): 756-760.

Rolofson, William M. Relations between the Chinese
and the British government of Malaya up to 1942.
Chicago, 1951. Dissertation (M.A.) -- University
of Chicago.

Royal Institute of International Affairs. Problems
of the post-war settlement in the Far East.
C. British Malaya. London, 1942. 33 p. (United
Kingdom Paper, no. 1/c)

Sadka, Emily. Malaysia: the political background.
In T. H. Silcock, ed. Political Economy of Independent
Malaya. 1963: 28-58.

Scott, J. C. Political ideology in Malaysia. Reality
and beliefs of an elite. New Haven, 1968. 302 p.

Shearn, E. D. National elections for Malaya: despatches
exchanged between the Secretary of State and
the High Commissioner. Malaya (1954): 323-325.

Sheridan, L. A. The Federation of Malaya constitution.
(Text, annotation, commentary). Singapore, 1961.

Sheridan, L. A. Constitutional problems of Malaysia.
Int Comp Law Q, 13 (1964): 1349-1367.

Sheridan, L. A., ed. Malaya and Singapore. The Borneo
Territories. The development of their laws and
constitutions. London, 1961. 510 p.

Sheridan, L. A., and Harry E. Groves. The constitution
of Malaysia. 1967. 398 p.

Silcock, T. H. Dilemma in Malaya. London, 1949.
43 p. (Fabian Research Series, no. 135) Maps.

Silcock, T. H. Forces for unity in Malaya. Inter
Aff, 25 (1949): 453-465.

Silcock, T. H. Policy for Malaya, 1952. Inter Aff,
28 (1952): 445-451.
Reply by E. D. Shearn, 29 (1953): 271-272.

Silcock, T. H. Singapore in Malaya. FES, 29 (Mar.
1960): 33-39.

Silcock, T. H. Development of a Malayan Foreign
Policy. Australian Outlook, 17, 3 (1963): 42-53.

Silcock, T. H., and A. Aziz. Nationalism in Malaya.
Submitted by the I.P.R. International Secretariat
as a preparatory paper for the eleventh conference
of the Institute of Pacific Relations to be held
at Lucknow in October 1950. New York, International
Secretariat, Institute of Pacific Relations,
1950. 48 p. (Secretariat Paper, no. 8)

Silcock, T. H., and A. Aziz. Nationalism in Malaya.
In W. L. Holland, ed. Asian Nationalism and the
West. New York, 1953: 267-345.

Singapore. Malaysia: agreement concluded between
the United Kingdom of Great Britain and Northern
Ireland, the Federation of Malaya, North Borneo,
Sarawak and Singapore. Singapore, Government
Printer, 1963. (Command Paper 22 of 1963)

Singh, T. Bhagwan. Concept of "Malaysian Malaysia".
JHS, 6 (1967/1968): 41-50.

Singh, Vishal. Recent political developments in
Malaya. Foreign Affairs Reports, 5 (Jan. 1956): 1-15.

Sington, Derrick. Malayan perspective. London, 1953.
25 p. (Fabian Controversy Series, no. 10) Tables.

Slimming, John. Malaysia; death of a democracy.
London, 1969. 82 p. Map.

Smith, Rennie. The future of Malaya. PA, 6 (1933): 394-398.

Smith, T. E. The background to Malaysia. London,
1965. (Chatham House Memoranda) Mimeo.

Spear, Percival. Towards self-government in Malaya.
World Aff Interp, 23 (1952): 38-40.

Spencer, J. E. Independent Malaya: the problems
of Malayanization. Foreign Affairs Reports, 7
(1958): 53-63.

Starner, Frances L. Malaysia and the North Borneo
territories. AS, 3, 11 (1963): 519-534.

Starner, Frances L. Malaysia's first year. AS, 5,
2 (1965): 113-119.

Strix. Pot-shot at a proconsul. Spectator, 192 (1954): 141.
Discussion, p. 176, 204, 231, 259, 290, 324,
and 352.

Swift, M. Malayan politics: race and class. Civilisations,
12 (1962): 237-245.

Tan, Siew-sin. The alliance and the minorities in
Malaya. Eastern World, 9 (Mar. 1955): 21-22.

Tan, Siew-sin. Citizenship, Malay rights and Chinese
education. Kuala Lumpur, Federal Department of
Information, Malaysia, 1965.

Tan, Siew-sin. The concept of a Malaysian Malaysia
was born on the day the Alliance was born. Kuala
Lumpur, Federal Department of Information, Malaysia,
1965. 17 p.

Tan, Siew-sin. The truth behind a major tragedy.
Kuala Lumpur, Malaysian Chinese Association Headquarters, 1965. 12 p. English and Chinese text
of a speech.

Taylor, J. C. Local government in Malaya. Alor Star,
1953. 70 p.

Templer, Gerald. Building a Malayan Nation. The
Dalhousie Review, 34, 2 (1954): 131-137.

Thio, Eunice. Some aspects of the Federation of
the Malay States, 1896-1910. JRASMB, 40, 2 (1967): 3-15.

Thompson, Virginia, and Richard Adloff. Empire's
end in Southeast Asia. New York, 1949. 62 p.

Thompson, Virginia, and Richard Adloff. Malaya.
In Lawrence K. Rossinger et al. The State of
Asia: A Contemporary Survey. New York, 1951: 332-361.
Index. 522 p.

Thompson, Virginia, and Richard Adloff. Malaya's
three way problem. For Policy Bul, 31, 6 (1951): 5-8.

Tilman, Robert O. Malaysia: the problems of Federation.
Western Political Quarterly, 16 (1963): 899-911.

Tilman, Robert O. Malaysian foreign policy: the
dilemmas of a committed neutral. Public Policy,
16 (1967): 115-159.

Tilman, Robert O., ed. Man, state, and society in
contemporary Southeast Asia. New York, 1969.
515 p. Bibliog., charts, index, maps.

Tilman, Robert Oliver. The Malay administrative
service, 1910-1960. Indian Journal of Public
Administration, 7 (1961): 145-157.

Tilman, Robert Oliver. Public service commissions
in the Federation of Malaya. JAS, 20, 2 (1961): 181-196.

Tilman, Robert Oliver. The public services of the
Federation of Malaya. Durham, N.C., 1961. Ph.D.
thesis (Department of Political Science, Graduate
School of Arts and Sciences) -- Duke University.

Tilman, Robert Oliver. The nationalization of the
colonial services in Malaya. South Atlantic Quarterly,
61 (1962): 183-196.

Tilman, Robert Oliver. Bureaucratic transition in
Malaya. Durham, N.C., Published for the Duke
University Commonwealth-Studies Center by Duke
University Press, 1964. 175 p. (Duke University,
Durham, N.C. Commonwealth Studies Center. Publication,
no. 21)

Tilman, Robert Oliver. Policy formulation, policy
    execution and the political elite structure of
    contemporary Malaya. In Wang Gung-wu, ed. Malaysia:
    A Survey. New York, 1964: 346-355. Tables.

Tilman, Robert Oliver. Bureaucratic development
    in Malaya. In Ralph Braibanti, ed. Asian Bureaucratic
    Systems Emergent from the British Imperial Tradition.
    Durham, N.C., 1966: 550-604. Tables.

Tinker, Irene. Malayan elections: electoral pattern
    for plural societies. Western Political Quarterly,
    9 (June 1956): 258-282. Map, tables.

Training of Malayans by government for higher posts
    in the government service. Kuala Lumpur, 1953.
    4 p. (Legislative Council Paper, no. 12)

Tregonning, K. Malaya, 1955. Australian Quarterly,
    28, 2 (1956): 20-35.

Turnbull, C. M. Constitutional development 1819-1968.
    In Ooi Jin-bee and Chiang Hai-ding, eds. Modern
    Singapore. Singapore, University of Singapore
    Press, 1969: 181-196.

United States, Department of State. Survey of British
    Malaya. Washington, D.C., 1942. 108 p. (Office
    of Intelligence Research, no. 750) Maps.

United States, Department of State. Political and
    economic changes effected by Japanese in Malaya.
    Washington, D.C., 1943. 61 p.

Venkatarangaiya, M. Political postwar developments
    in Burma, Indonesia, Indochina and Malaya. FEER,
    15 (1953): 140-144.

Von der Mehden, Fred R. Some aspects of political
    ideology in Malaysia. Studies on Asia, 5 (1964):
    95-104. Table.

Wales, Horace G. Q. Years of blindness. New York,
    1943. 323 p.
    A discussion of the rise of nationalism in
    Southeast Asia and the blindness of the Western
    powers to the significance of this movement as
    it developed in their various colonies.

Wang, Gung-wu. Malayan nationalism. JRCAS, 49 (1962): 317-328.

Wang, Gung-wu. Traditional leadership in a new nation: the Chinese in Malaya and Singapore. In S. Takdir Alisjahbana. The Cultural Problems of Malaysia in the Context of Southeast Asia. Kuala Lumpur (1966): 170-187.

Warner, Denis. The second fall of Singapore. Reporter (Sept. 9, 1965): 27-29.

Whittingham-Jones, Barbara. Should Britain quit Malaya? Contemporary Review, 178 (1950): 14-18.

Wiersbitzky, Kurt. Südostasien: Ein Kampffeld der Zukunft zwischen Weiss, Rot und Gelb. Leipzig, Berlin, 1938. 69 p.

Wijeyewardene, Gehan, ed. Leadership and authority: a symposium. Singapore, 1968. 337 p.
A collection of nineteen papers, four of which deal with Western Malaysia.

Winks, Robin W. Malaysia and the Commonwealth: an inquiry into the nature of Commonwealth ties. In Wang Gung-wu, ed. Malaysia: A Survey. New York, 1964: 375-399.

Winstedt, R. O. The constitution of the colony of the Straits Settlements and the Federated and Unfederated Malayan States. London, 1931. 20 p.

Wray, Leonard. Settlements on the Straits of Malacca. Proc R Col Inst, 5 (1873/1874): 103-125.

Zainal Abidin bin Abdul Wahid. Malaysia, Southeast Asia and world politics. In Wang Gung-wu, ed. Malaysia: A Survey. London, 1964: 365-374.

B. COMMUNIST MOVEMENT AND EMERGENCY

Bartlett, Vernon. Malaya: "Jungle Bashing" for C.T.'s. NY Times Mag (May 23, 1954): 12-13, 62, 64, and 67.

Bauer, P. T. Malaya: background and prospects; the stakes are large in the struggle in Malaya between the government and the Communists. Cambridge Journal, 2 (1949): 598-621.

Brazier-Creagh, K. R. Malaya (the type of war being fought and problems of the government), with discussion. R United Service Inst Jl, 99, 594 (1954): 175-190.

Brimmell, Jack Henry. A short history of the Malayan Communist Party. Singapore, 1956. 26 p.

Carnell, Francis G. Communalism and Communism in Malaya. PA, 26 (1953): 99-117.

Chapman, F. S. How to win the jungle war. Spectator (1952): 346-354.

Clutterback, Richard L. (Col.). Malaya: a case study. Military Review, 43 (Sept. 1963): 63-78.

Clutterback, Richard L. (Col.). The long long war: the emergency in Malaya, 1948-1960. London, 1967. 206 p. Map, plates.

The Communist Party of Malaya, its origins and development. SE Asia Rev, 1 (1952): 25-27.

The Communist threat to the Federation of Malaya. Kuala Lumpur, 1959. 31 p.

Creech-Jones, A. The Asian crisis and the Malay Peninsula. Int Jl, 6 (1950/1951): 29-42.

Danwar, H. I. S. Curtain off the Malayan scene. UA, 4 (1952): 183-187.

Dartford, Gerald. The Communist threat to Malaya and Singapore. Current History, 38 (Feb. 1960): 82-87.

Dougherty, James E. The guerrilla war in Malaya. USNIP, 84 (1958): 40-49. Illus.

The emergency in Malaya. World Today, 10 (Nov. 1954): 477-487.

From banditry to revolt in post-war Malaya. SE Asia Rev, 1 (1952): 15-24.

General Templer's policy in Malaya: operations to ensure cooperation against terrorists by villages. Illus Lond News, 223 (1953): 235. Plate.

Great Britain, Colonial Office. Malaya, the facts behind the fighting. London, 1952. 19 p. Illus.

Great Britain, Regional Information Office for the United Kingdom in Southeast Asia. Handbook to Malaya (Federation of Malaya and the Colony of Singapore) and the emergency. Singapore, 1951. 37 p. Maps.

Greene, H. C. In Malaya the front is everywhere. NY Times Mag (Mar. 4, 1952): 12-13.

Gwee, Hock-aun. The emergency in Malaya. [Penang] 1966. 116 p. Maps, photos.

Han, Su-yin (pseud.). Malaya: the "emergency" in its seventh year. Reporter, 11, 11 (1954): 23-27.

Handbook to Malaya and the emergency. Kuala Lumpur, 1953. 43 p. Illus., map.

Hanrahan, Gene F. Chinese Communist guerrilla tactics. Washington, D.C., Collection and Dissemination Branch, Army G-2, unclassified, July, 1952. 134 p.

Hanrahan, Gene F. The Communist struggle in Malaya. New York, 1954. 146 p.

Henniker, M. C. A. Red shadow over Malaya. Foreword by Sir John Harding. London, 1955. 316 p. Illus., maps.

Henniker, M. C. A. The emergency in Malaya 1948-60. JRCAS, 51 (1964): 32-42.

How a planter lives in Malaya today: precautions against terrorist attacks. Illus Lond News, 220 (1953): 662-663.

Insurrection in Malaya. Round Table (Dec. 1948): 24-31.

Kroef, Justus M. van der. Communism in Malaysia and Singapore: a contemporary survey. The Hague, 1967. 268 p.

Long, George. Malaya meets its emergency. Nat G Mag, 103 (1953): 185-228. Map, plates.

Lyttelton, Oliver. Malaya. United Empire, 43 (1952):
128-132.
   Speech by Lyttelton, reporting on the emergency.

Malaya: how planters endure a sneak war . . . and
a new commander plans to beat Reds. NRN (May
1952): S 15-S 17. Reprinted from: Newsweek, April
28, 1952.

Malaya, Department of Information. Communist banditry
in Malaya; the emergency, with a chronology of
important events, June 1948-June 1951. Kuala
Lumpur (1951). 121 p. Illus.

Malaya, Department of Information. Communist terrorism
in Malaya. The emergency. With a chronology of
important events, June 1948-June 1952. Kuala
Lumpur, 1952. 170 p. Illus.

Malaya, Department of Information. Handbook to Malaya
and the emergency. Singapore, 1955.

Malaya, Department of Information, Public Relations
Office. Handbook to Malaya (Federation of Malaya
and the Colony of Singapore) and the emergency.
Singapore, 1954. 58 p.

Malaya, Legislature. The Communist threat to the
Federation of Malaya. Kuala Lumpur, Government
Printer, 1959. (Legislative Council Paper, no.
23 of 1959)

Malaya, Public Relations Department. Anatomy of
Communist propaganda. Kuala Lumpur, 1950. 60 p.

Malaya, Public Relations Department. Communist banditry
in Malaya: extracts from speeches by the High
Commissioner, Sir Henry Gurney. Kuala Lumpur,
1950. 11 p.

Malaya, Public Relations Department. Emergency situation:
chronology of important events during the emergency
in Malaya for the period July to December, 1949.
Kuala Lumpur, 1950. 20 p.

Markandan, Paul S. General Templer and Malaya. Eastern
World, 8, 7 (1954): 14-15.

Markandan, Paul S. Shooting war in Malaya continues.
Eastern World, 91 (1955): 17-18.

Mellersh, Francis. The campaign against the terrorists in Malaya. Jl R United Service Inst, 96 (1951): 401-415.

The militant Communist threat to West Malaysia. Kuala Lumpur, 1966.

Miller, Harry. The Communist menace in Malaya. New York, 1954. 248 p. Plates.
    London edition titled: Menace in Malaya.

Mills, Neil B. (Lt. Col., USMC). Civic action in Malaya. In Counterinsurgency Case History: Malaya 1948-1960, Reference Book RB 31-2. Fort Levenworth, Kansas, United States Army Command and General Staff College, November 1, 1965: 43-53.

Morrison, Ian. The Communist uprising in Malaya. FES, 17 (1948): 281-286.

Morrison, Ian. Aspects of the racial problem in Malaya. PA, 22 (1949): 239-253.

Nasmyth, J. Pattern of terrorism. Spectator, 190 (1953): 539-540.

Noll (pseud.). The emergency in Malaya. Army Quarterly, 68 (April 1954): 46-65.

O'Ballance, Edgar. Malaya: the Communist insurgent war, 1948-1960. London, 1966. 188 p. Map.

Ogmore, The Rt. Hon. Lord. A Governor-General for Malaya. Eastern World, 8, 4 (1954): 15-16.

Paget, Julian. Counter-insurgency campaigning. London, 1967. 189 p. Maps.
    The emergency in Malaya (1948-1960), p. 43-79.

Park, Bum-joon Lee. The British experience of counter-insurgency in Malaya: the emergency, 1948-1960. 1965. 284 p. Thesis -- American University.

Peterson, Alec. Telling the people of Malaya. New Commonwealth, 28 (1954): 553-555. Graph, plates.
    Use of information services to overcome the Communist challenge and the "apathy, ignorance, separation and racial intolerance" of the country.

Plum, Patrick. End of the emergency. Blackwood's
Magazine, 288 (Nov. 1960): 385-393.

Purcell, Victor. Strong arm in Malaya. New Statesman
and Nation, 45 (1953): 59-60.

Purcell, Victor. General Templer. 20th Century,
155 (1954): 118-129.
Discussion, p. 231-234 and 327-331.

Purcell, Victor. General Templer in Malaya.
Z Geopol, 25 (1954): 277-286.

Purcell, Victor. Malaya: Communist or free? Palo
Alto, Calif., 1954. 288 p. Index.

Pye, Lucian W. Guerrilla Communism in Malaya--its
social and political meaning. Princeton, N.J.,
1956. 369 p.

Scalapino, Robert A., ed. The Communist revolution
in Asia: tactics, goals, and achievements.
Englewood Cliffs, N.J., 1965.

Short, Anthony. Communism and the emergency. In
Wang Gung-wu, ed. Malaysia: A Survey. London,
1964: 149-160.

Starner, Frances L. Communism in Malaysia: a multifront
struggle. In Robert A. Scalapino, ed. The Communist
Revolution in Asia: Tactics, Goals and Achievements.
Englewood Cliffs, N.J., 1965: 221-250.

Templer, Malayan pacifier. US News and World Report,
32 (Jan. 25, 1952): 65-66.

Thompson, Elizabeth M. Red terrorism in Malaya.
Editorial Research Reports, 24 (1952): 503-522.

Thompson, Sir Robert Grainger Ker. Defeating Communist
insurgency; experiences from Malaya and Vietnam.
London, 1966. 171 p. (Studies in International
Security, 10) Illus., maps.

United States Army Command and General Staff College.
Counterinsurgency case history: Malaya 1948-1960,
Reference Book RB31-2. Fort Leavenworth, Kansas,
November 1, 1965.

CHAPTER 12

SINGAPORE

Attiwill, Kenneth. Fortress; the story of the siege
    and fall of Singapore. [1st ed.]. Garden City,
    New York, 1960 [c. 1959]. 243 p. Illus.
    First published in London in 1959 under title:
    The Singapore Story.

Balk, Arvid. Singapur, Englands Panzerfeste im Fernen
    Osten. Berlin, 1937. 79 p. Map, plates.

Barber, Noel. A sinister twilight. The fall of Singapore,
    1942. 1968. 364 p.

Blake, D. J. Patterns of Singapore's trade. MER,
    13, 1 (1968): 39-69.

Boyce, P. J. Singapore as a sovereign state. Australian
    Outlook, 19, 3 (1965): 259-271.

Braddell, Roland. The lights of Singapore. London,
    1934, and other editions. 218 p.

Buckley, Charles B. An anecdotal history of old
    times in Singapore. Singapore, 1902. 2 v.

Buest, Tristan. The naval base at Singapore.
    PA, 5 (1932): 306-318.

C. S. C. La base navale de Singapore. Rev Pacifique,
    4 (1925): 965-968.

Child Welfare and Social Work, Section of Maris
    Stella Girls' School, Franciscan Missionaries
    of Mary, Singapore. Teen-age girls' family problems
    Singapore. Survey on sixteen to seventeen year-old
    girls of Chinese descent from Queenstown and
    the Farrer Road Kampong--their attitudes towards
    life and patterns of behaviour, with special
    emphasis on their family relationships and values.
    Singapore, 1965. 158 p.

Chong Peng-khaun. Problems in political development:
    Singapore. 1968. 114 p.

Cook, John A. B. Sunny Singapore; an account of
    the place and its people, with a sketch of the
    results of missionary work. London, 1907. 183 p.
    Plates.

Cornish, Vaughan. Singapore and naval geography.
United Empire, 16 (1925): 500-512. Maps.

Danjou, Andre. Singapore et le "British Malaya".
Rev Pacifique, 2 (1924): 28-42.

Dewar, K. G. B. The Singapore naval base. Contemporary
Review, 138, 775 (1939): 22-28.

Dobby, E. H. G. Singapore, town and country. GR,
30 (1940): 84-109. Fig., maps, plates.

Doraisamy, T. R., ed. One hundred fifty years of
education in Singapore. Singapore, Teachers'
Training College, 1969. 150 p.

Elliot, Alan J. A. Chinese spirit-medium cults in
Singapore. London, 1955.

Fletcher, Nancy McHenry. The separation of Singapore
from Malaysia. Ithaca, 1969. 98 p. (Southeast
Asia Program, Data Paper, no. 73)

Focus on Singapore. New Commonwealth, 45, 9 (1967):
413-432. Economic conditions in Singapore.

Fraser, J. M. The work of the Singapore Improvement
Trust, 1927-1947. Singapore, 1948.

Gamba, Charles. Housing and town planning in Singapore.
Eastern World, 7, 8 (1953): 35-38.

Gibson-Hill, C. A. Singapore. Twenty-four camera
studies. Singapore, 1948. Plates.

Gibson-Hill, C. A. The Singapore Chronicle (1824-37).
JRASMB, 26, 1 (1953): 175-199. Bibliog.

Gibson-Hill, C. A. Singapore. Old Strait and New
Harbour 1300-1870. Singapore, 1956. 11-116 p.
(Memoirs of the Raffles Museum, no. 3, December, 1956)

Goh, Keng-swee. Urban incomes and housing. Singapore,
Government Printer, 1956.

Hanna, Willard A. The separation of Singapore. New
York, American Universities Field Staff, 1965.

Hodder, B. W. Racial groupings in Singapore. MJTG
(1953): 25-36. Maps.
Also in Hamzah Sendut. Urban Development in
Southeast Asia. p. 706-722.

Josey, Alex. Report from Singapore (a weekly newsletter).
Singapore, Donald Moore Press.

Josey, Alex. Lee Kuan Yew and the Commonwealth.
Singapore, 1969. 112 p.

Kaye, Barrington. Upper Nankin Street, Singapore.
Singapore, 1960.

Krell, H. Singapur. Z Erdk, 6 (1938): 41-44.

Leasor, James. Singapore. The battle that changed
the world. London, Garden City, 1968.

Lee, Kuan-yew. The winds of change; 8 speeches by
Lee Kuan Yew, Prime Minister of Singapore, on
present political situation. [Singapore, PAP
Political Bureau, 1964]. 48 p. Illus.

Leifer, Michael. Communal violence in Singapore.
AS, 4 (Oct. 1964): 1115-1121.

Leifer, Michael. Politics in Singapore: the first
term of the People's Action Party 1959-1963.
Journal of Commonwealth Political Studies, 2,
2 (1964): 102-119.

Leifer, Michael. Singapore in Malaysia. The politics
of Federation. JSAH, 6, 2 (1965): 54-70.

Local Produce Working Committee. Food supplies for
Singapore. Singapore, 1951. 25 p. (Legislative
Council Paper, no. 63)

Lockwood, R. There are still weak spots in Singapore.
Austral-Asiatic Bulletin, 3 (1939): 16-17.

Lockwood, William W. Showdown at Singapore? New
York, San Francisco, 1941. 31 p.

Lohau, P. Die Gründung und Entwicklung der britischen
Kolonie Singapore. Z Kol -politik, -recht, -wirtschaft,
9 (1912): 721-737.

SINGAPORE

Macleish, Kenneth. Singapore, reluctant nation.
Nat G Mag, 130, 2 (1966): 269-300. Maps.

Makepeace, W., R. St. J. Braddell, and G. E. Brooke.
100 Years of Singapore. London, 1921. 2 v. Illus.

Malan, L. N. Singapore. The founding of the new
defences. R Engineers Jl, 52 (1938): 213-235.

Maxwell, W. E. Founding of Singapore. JRASSB, Notes
and Queries, 4 (1886): 104-113.

McKie, R. C. H. This was Singapore. London, 1942.
209 p.

Medan Sastera. Majallah Tiga Bulanan. Berdasar:
Bahasa, Sastera, Budaya. V. 1- ; 1964- .
Pustaka Melayu, Singapura.

Miller, Eugene H. Singapore naval base controversy,
1921-1938. Amerasia, 5 (1942): 487-493.

Miller, Eugene H. Strategy at Singapore. New York,
1942. 145 p.

Milne, R. S. Singapore exit from Malaysia; the consequences
of ambiguity. AS, 6, 3 (1966): 175-184.

Mohr, F. M. Singapore. Preussische Jahrbücher, 2,
1 (1925): 19-39.

Mohr, F. M. Singapore. Z Geopol, 2 (1925): 741-758.

Moore, Donald. We live in Singapore. London, 1955.
287 p. Photos.

Moore, Donald, and Joanna Moore. The first 150 years
of Singapore. Singapore, 1969. 731 p. Illus., maps.

Nam, Tae-yul. Singapore's one-party system: its
relationship to democracy and political stability.
PA, 48, 4 (1969/1970): 465-480.

Nathan, Andrew. The Jurong story: a special survey
of Singapore's new industrial complex. FEER,
45 (August 27, 1964): 381-396.

Onraet, Rene Henry de Solminihac. Singapore, a police
background. London, 1947. 152 p.

Ooi, Jin-bee. Singapore: the balance-sheet. In Ooi
  Jin-bee and Chiang Hai-ding, eds. Modern Singapore.
  Singapore, University of Singapore Press, 1969: 1-13.

Ooi, Jin-bee, and Chiang Hai-ding, eds. Modern Singapore.
  Singapore, University of Singapore Press, 1969.
  285 p. Bibliog., diagrs., maps, photos.

Oshima, Harry J. Growth and unemployment in Singapore.
  MER, 12, 2 (1967): 32-58.

Outpost (pseud.). Singapore nightmare; a story of
  the evacuation and an escape to Australia.
  London, 1943. 68 p.

Owen, Frank. The fall of Singapore. London [1960].
  216 p. Illus.

Papineau Studios. Guide to Singapore. Singapore,
  1953. 208 p. Illus., maps.

Parkinson, C. N. Britain in the Far East: the Singapore
  naval base. Singapore, 1955. 55 p. (Background
  to Malaya Series, no. 7)

Pearson, Harold Frank. Stories of early Singapore.
  London, 1953. 128 p.

Pearson, Harold Frank. People of early Singapore.
  London, 1955. 128 p.
    Covers the period 1819-1836.

Pearson, Harold Frank. A history of Singapore. London,
  1956. 192 p. Illus., maps.

Peritz, René. The evolving politics of Singapore:
  a study of trends and issues. 1964. 486 p.
  Thesis -- University of Pennsylvania.

Phayre, I. Britain's bulwark against Japan: fifty-million
  naval base at Singapore. Current History, 45
  (1937): 75-80. Illus., map.

Plotkin, David G. Rage in Singapore; the cauldron
  of Asia boils over. New York, 1942. 315 p.

Poetry Singapore. No. 1- ; Aug. 1968- . Publication
  of this journal is sponsored by the National
  Theatre Trust, Singapore.

Pondeveaux, L. La Malaise Britannique et la base de Singapour. La G, 70 (1938): 18-23.

Raffles, Sir T. S. Singapore local laws and institutions, 1823. London, 1824.

Raffles, Sir T. S. Founding of Singapore. JRASSB, 2 (1878): 175-182.

Ransonnet-Villez, Eugen. Skizzen aus Singapur und Djohor. Braunschweig, 1876. 88 p.

Reith, George M. Handbook to Singapore. Singapore, 1907. 133 p. Map.

Report of the Singapore Riots Inquiry Commission. Chairman, Lionnel Leach. Singapore, 1951. 98 p. Maps. An inquiry into the disorders on the 11th December, 1950.

Roosevelt, N. The strategy of Singapore. FA, 7 (1929): 317-322.

Roucek, J. S. Notes on the geopolitics of Singapore. Jl G, 52 (1953): 78-81.

Sansom, Sir George. The story of Singapore. FA, 22 (1944): 279-297.

Simpich, Frank. Singapore, crossroads of the East. Nat G Mag, 49 (1926): 235-269. Map.

Simpich, Frank. Behind the news in Singapore. Nat G Mag, 78 (1940): 83-110. Map.

Singapore. Master plan. Singapore, 1955. 3 v. Diagrs., illus., maps.

Singapore. External Trade Statistics (including trade with the Federation of Malaya) for the year 1959-- . Compiled by the Department of Statistics. Singapore, Government Publications Bureau, 1960.

Singapore. Estimates of the Revenue and Expenditure of the State of Singapore for the year 1963- . Singapore, Government Printer, 1963.

SINGAPORE

Singapore. Directory. Istana, Judiciary, Audit,
    Public Service Commission, Cabinet, Parliament,
    Ministries, Statutory Boards, Advisory Committees,
    Universities, Commonwealth and Foreign Representatives,
    United Nations Agencies. Singapore, Government
    Printing Office, 1967.

Singapore. Report on the Census of Industrial Production
    1965. By P. C. K. Tan, Chief Statistician, Department
    of Statistics, Singapore. Singapore, Government
    Printing Office, 1968. 92 p.

Singapore, Department of Civil Aviation. Annual
    Report. 1962- . Singapore, Government Printing
    Office, 1963.

Singapore, Department of Education. Annual Report.
    1958- . Singapore, Government Printing Office,
    1959.

Singapore Harbour Board. The port of Singapore.
    Singapore, 1949. Plates.

Singapore, Immigration Department. Annual Report.
    1960- . Singapore, Government Printer, 1962.

Singapore, Inland Revenue Department. Annual Report.
    1964- . Singapore, Government Printing Office, 1967.

Singapore Institute of Management. Annual Report.
    1965- . Singapore, 1966.

Singapore, Labour Department. Annual Report. 1958- .
    Singapore, Government Printer, 1960.

Singapore, Ministry of Culture. A year of decision.
    The Yang di-Pertuan Negara's policy address,
    delivered October 31, 1961. Singapore, 1961.
    24 p. (Towards Socialism, v. 6. A Ministry of
    Culture Series)

Singapore, Ministry of Culture. The merger plan.
    Singapore, 1961. 14 p.

Singapore, Ministry of Culture. Malaysian heritage.
    Singapore, 1962.

Singapore, Ministry of Culture. Year of fulfilment,
    June 1961--June 1962. Singapore, Government Printer,
    1962.

Singapore, Ministry of Culture. Social transformation in Singapore. Singapore, Government Printer, 1963.

Singapore, Ministry of Culture. Separation. Singapore, 1965.

Singapore municipality obtains new water supply from Johore. Far Eastern Review, 28 (1932): 220-227.

Singapore, Postal Services Department. Annual Report. 1958- . Singapore, Government Printing Office, 1959.

Singapore, Public Service Commission. Annual Report. 1959-60- . Singapore, Government Printing Office, 1962.

Singapore, Social Welfare Department. A social survey of Singapore; a preliminary study of some aspects of social conditions in the municipal area of Singapore. Singapore, 1947. 166 p. Map, tables.

Singapore, Social Welfare Department. Social welfare. Singapore, 1950. 48 p. Illus., map.

Singapore, Social Welfare Department. Annual Report. 1959- . Singapore, Government Printer, 1961.

Singapore, Survey Department. Singapore guide and street directory with sectional maps. Singapore, Government Printer, 1954. 2nd ed., 1955; 3rd ed., 1956; 4th ed., 1957; 5th ed., 1958; 6th ed., 1961; 7th ed., 1963; 8th ed., 1966.

Singapore Year Book. 1964- . Singapore, Government Printing Office, 1966.

Smith, P. The future of Singapore. PA, 6 (1933): 394-398.

Spaniger, R. Die Kolonie Singapur. Mitt G Ges Wien, 91 (1949): 52-55.

Thomas, K. C. Singapore, a Straits Settlement. Home Geographic Monthly, 2, 4 (1932): 37-42.

Thomson, G. G. Singapore's new housing. Corona, 7 (1955): 23-25. Plates.

Tiltman, H. H. The Far East comes nearer. Sydney, 1937. 298 p. Plates.
    Chap. 17 deals with the Singapore naval base.

Tregonning, K. G. Singapore in Malaysia, a brief
study of its industrial potential. Singapore,
J. M. Sassoon, 1963. 28 p.

Trimmer, G. W. G. The port of Singapore. Far Eastern
Review, 30 (1934): 277-281.

Tsuji, Masanobu. Singapore, the Japanese version.
Translated by Margaret E. Lake. Edited by H.
V. Rowe, with an introduction by H. Gordon Bennett.
Sydney [1960]. 358 p. Illus.

Warsfold, William B. A visit to Japan with an account
of the founding of Singapore. London, 1893. 283 p.

Weller, George A. Singapore is silent. New York,
1943. 312 p.

Wilkinson, R. J. Old Singapore. JRASMB, 13, 2 (1935):
17-21.

Wong, Lin-ken. The trade of Singapore, 1819-69.
JRASMB (1961).

Wright, A. Singapore and Sir Stamford Raffles. Quarterly
Review, 232 (1919): 265-283.

You, Poh-seng. Fertility and the increase of population
in Singapore. In Proceedings of the World Population
Conference. New York, United Nations, 1955: 989-999.

You, Poh-seng. The housing survey of Singapore,
1955. MER, 2 (1957): 54-74.

Zappa, Paolo. Die Schlüsselstellung britischer Macht
in Asien, Singapur. Leipzig, 1942. 175 p.

EXPLANATORY NOTE TO AUTHOR INDEX

Citation references in this index are an indication of the location within the body of the book of complete bibliographic citations. References are to chapters by arabic numerals, chapter sections by letters, and subsections by secondary arabic numerals.

A single index reference may refer to more than one bibliographic entry by a single author. For example: there are a total of eleven bibliographic entries by the single author Abdul Aziz bin Abdul Hamid, which may be found in three places in the body of the bibliography. Chapter 9, section F, contains one citation; chapter 10, section A, contains seven citations; and chapter 10, section B, subsection 2, contains three citations.

Several entries in this index may appear to be obvious variations of a single author's name. Because some of these apparent variations may actually indicate distinct authors or significant distinctions of a single author's works, each entry was made to reflect the form used in the full bibliographic citation by the author of this volume.

A. Wahab Alwee. 9C3
Abadi, Bujang. 9C3
'Abd Allah Ibn 'Abd al-Kadir. 6A
Abdul Aziz bin Abdul Hamid, Ungku. 9F, 10A, 10B2
Abdul Aziz bin Abdul Hamid, Ungku, S. J. Gilani, Jock Hoe, and Lim Chong-yah. 10I
Abdul Aziz bin Mohd. Yassin. 9C3
Abdul Aziz bin Mohd. Yassin, Ungku. 9I1, 10G
Abdul Aziz bin Shaik Mydin. 9H
Abdul Majid. 10A, 10E
Abdul Majid, Haji. 9C3
Abdul Malek bin Hassan. 10A
Abdul Rahman bin Ahmad. 9C3
Abdul Rahman Putra Al-Haj, Tunku. 11A
Abdul Rahman, Tunku. 11A
Abdul Rashid bin Ismail. 9H
Abdul Razak bin Dato' Hussein, Tun. 10A, 10B1
Abdul Razak bin Dato' Hussein, Tun Haji. 10A
Abdul Razak bin Hussein, Tun, Haji. 9F
Abdul Tai bin Mahmud. 11A
Abdul-Aziz, Engku. 9B
Abdullah, Dato' Sedia Raja. 9C3, 9E
Abu Bakar bin Pawanchee. 9C3
Acton, C. J. 7E
Adams, Frank D. 10F
Adams, Theodore. 9C3
Addison, G. H., and M. R. Henderson. 7D
Agarwal, M. C. 9I1, 10A, 10B3
Agoes Salim. 10B4
Ahmad bin Mohd, Ibrahim. 9C3
Ahmad bin Yunus. 10B3
Ahmad, Z. A. B. 9C3
Ahmat, Sharom. 6A
Ahpa, T. (pseud. for J. Nield). 4
Ainsworth, Leopold. 4
Aiyer, K. A. N. 9C5
Akasli, Yoji. 6A
Akers, R. L. 7C
Akhurst, C. G., and W. B. Haines. 7E
Akib, S. 10B2
Alatas, Hussein, Syed. 6A, 9C3, 9E, 11A
Al-Attas, Naguib, Syed. 9E
Albuquerque, Afonso. 6A
Alexander, J. B. 7A, 7C, 7E, 9I1
Alexander, Patrick. 9E
Alfred, Eric R. 2, 7D, 10D
Al-Hadi, Alwi, Syed. 9C3

Alisjahbana, S. Takdir. 9C3, 9D
Alisjahbana, S. Takdir, Xavier S. Thani Nayagam, and Wang Gung-Wu, eds. 6A
All Malaya Council of Joint Action. 11A
Allan, F. H., and E. J. H. Berwick. 10B3
Allard, Elizabeth. 9E
Allee, Ralph H., and Clifton R. Wharton. 10B1
Allen, Betty Molesworth. 7D, 10E
Allen, D. F. 10I
Allen, E. F. 10B1, 10B3, 10B4
Allen, E. F., and D. W. M. Haynes. 10B3
Allen, E. F., and J. R. Milburn. 10B3
Allen, G. C., and A. G. Donnithorne. 10A
Allen, G. F. 10B7
Allen, J. De Vere. 6A
Allen, James de V. 11A
Allen, Richard. 5, 6A, 11A
Alliance Party of Malaya. 9I1
Allouard, P., and P. Sallenave. 10E
Al-Rashid. 9B
Alunan, Rafael R. 10B1
Alwi bin Alhady. 9C3
Ambikapath Rai. 9C5
American University, Washington, D.C., Foreign Areas Studies Division. 5
Aminuddin bin Baki. 9C3
Anderson, J. 9C2
Anderson, J. A. R. 7D
Anderson, John. 6A
Anderson, P. 4
Andrews, C. F. 9D
Andrews, Isobel. 2
Andy, J. R. 9I1
Annandale, N., J. Coggin Brown, and F. H. Cravely. 9B
Annandale, Nelson. 8, 9, 9A, 9C1, 9E
Annandale, Nelson, and Herbert C. Robinson. 9A, 9C1, 9C2, 9C3
Anonymous. 9C1
Anuar, Hedwig. 2
Arasaratnam, S. 6A, 9C5
Ardizzone, Michael. 11A
Armstrong, D. S. 10B6
Arnot, David Blair, and J. S. Smith. 10B1
Arnott, G. W. 7E, 10B5
Arnott, G. W., and H. K. Lim. 10C
Arun, K. C., and G. D. Ness. 9H
Aschaimbault, Charles. 9F
Ashby, J. K. 10B3
Asimont, W. F. C. 10B4
Asmah Binte Haji Omar. 5

Cook, John Angus Bethune. 6B
Cooke, D. F. 9H
Cooke, E. M. 10B3
Cooke, F. C. 10B5
Coope, A. E. 9E
Coope, A. E., tr. 6A, 9C3
Cooper, Eunice. 9F, 9I2
Cooper, J. M. 9C2
Co-operatives. 10A
Coote, P. 9C3
Cope, Captain. 6A
Copithorne, T. 6A
Copley, J. 9H
Corbet, A. Steven. 7E
Corbett, A. S., and H. M.
  Pendlebury. 7D
Corbett, G. H. 10B5
Corbett, G. H., and C. Dover. 10B1
Corden, W. M. 10A
Cordier, Henri. 2
Corner, E. J. H. 7D
Cornish, Vaughan. 12
Corry, W. C. S. 9I1, 11A
Coulson, N. 10B2
Coulter, J. K. 7D, 7E, 10B5, 10E
Coulter, J. K., A. R. McWalter, and
  G. W. Arnott. 7E
Coupland, Reginald. 6B
Courtenay, C. E. 10B6
Courtenay, P. P. 8, 10B1, 10F, 10I
Courtier, D. B. 7C
Cousens, J. E. 10E
Cowan, C. D. 6A
Cowan, C. D., ed. 6A
Cowgill, J. V. 9C4, 10B2
Crabb, C. H. 5
Craig, J. A. 10B1
Cramer, P. J. S. 10B4
Crandall, J. R. 9C3, 9F
Crawford, John. 5
Crawford, Oliver. 4
Crawfurd, John. 6A, 9B, 9C3, 9E
Creagh, C. V. 9E
Creech-Jones, A. 11B
Crockett, Anthony. 4
Croix, J. E. de la. 9C2
Crookewit, H. 10F
Cross, B. 9G
Cross, John. 4
Crosson, Pierre R. 10A
Crotty, Raymond. 10C
Cubitt, G. E. S. 10E
Cuisinier, Jeanne. 9C3, 9E
Cullin, E. G., and W. F. Zehnder.
  6A
Cumming, C. M. 10B4
Curle, Richard. 4
Curtis, William E. 5
Da Silva Rego. 6A
Dale, W. L. 7B
D'Almeida, W. Barrington. 8
Dalton, Clive (pseud.). 6A

Dalton, H. G. 4
Dalton, H. Goring. 10I
Daly, D. D. 7C
Dammermann, K. W. 7D
Danaraj, A. G. S. 9E
Daniel, Padma, comp. 2
Danjou, Andre. 12
Danwar, H. I. S. 11B
Darbishire, C. W., et al. 10A
Daroesman, R. 9I2
Daroesman, Ruth. 10A
Dartford, Gerald. 11B
Dartford, Gerald P. 11A
Dartford, Gerald Percy. 6A
Das, S. K. 10B2, 11A
Davidson, L. R. 10B4
Davidson, L. R., and Mohd. Rouse
  bin Mohd. Amin. 10B4
Davies, D. 9I2
Dawson, S. R. 9I1
Dawson, T. R. P. 9C4
Deasy, George F. 10B5
Degani, Amina H. 9I1
Degani, Amina Hatim. 10B1
Deistel, H. 4
Denis, J. 4
Dennery, Etienne. 9F
Dennett, J. H. 7E
Dennett, J. H., and W. N. C.
  Belgrave. 7E
Dennys, N. B. 2
Dennys, Nicholas B. 5
Dentan, Robert Knox. 9C2
Department of Agriculture, Negeri
  Sembilan. 10A
Department of Economics, University
  of Malaya. 3
Department of History, University
  of Malaya. 3
Department of History, University
  of Singapore. 3
Desch, H. E. 10E
Desch, H. E., and A. V. Thomas.
  10E
Deshmukh, G. B. 10B1
Devahuti, D. 6A
Devendra, C. 10C
Dew, A. T. 10D
Dewar, K. G. B. 12
Dijkman, M. J. 10B4
Dinkar, Desai. SC5
Division of Orientalia, Library of
  Congress. 2
Djamour, J. 9F
Djamour, Judith. 9C3
Dobby, E. H. G. 7B, 8, 9I1, 10B1,
  10B2, 10B3, 12
Dobby, E. H. G. (pseud., Guy
  Roberts). 11A
Dobby, E. H. G., et al. 10B3
Dodd, E. E. 5, 11A
Dodd, Joseph W. 10A

381

London, University, School of
Oriental and African Studies. 2
Long, E. E. 9C3
Long, George. 11B
Loofs, H. H. E. 9B
Lopez, C. 9C3
Lord, L. 7D
Low, F. A. 10A
Low, J. 6A, 7E, 9C2
Low, James. 9B
Lowe, B. A. 10B1
Lowe, John. 11A
Lowinger, Victor A. 10F
Lu, Steve. 9C4
Lucas, C. P. 6A
Lyall and Evatt, Singapore. 10A
Lyttelton, Oliver. 11B
Ma, Ibrahim T'ien-ying. 9E
Ma, Ronald. 10A
Ma, Ronald, and Poh-seng You. 10A
Ma, Ronald, ed. 10A
MacAndrew, W. R. 10B1
Macdonald, M. 9I2
MacDonald, S. 7C
Macey, Paul. 9C2
MacFadyean, A. 10B4
MacFadyen, Eric. 11A
Macgowan, D. J. 9C3
MacKeen, A. M. M. 11A
Mackenzie, K. E. 10A
Mackenzie, R. D. 9F
Macleish, Kenneth. 12
Maclusky, D. S. 9H
MacMichael, Harold A. 11A
Mactier, R. S. 10I
Madoc, G. C. 7D
Maeda, K. 9C4
Mahajani, Usha. 9C5
Mahmood bin Yaacob, Haji. 10B8
Mahmud bin Mat. 10B2
Mair, Lucy Philip. 9G
Majid, Haji Abdul. 9E
Majilis Amanah Ra'ayat Malaysia. 3
Majumdar, Bimal Kanti. 9C5
Majumdar, R. C. 6A, 9C3, 9C5
Makepeace, W., R. St. J. Braddell,
and G. E. Brooke. 12
Malan, L. N. 12
Malaya. 2, 3, 10A, 10B1, 10B3,
10B4, 10B7, 10D, 10E, 10I
Malaya (Federation) Department of
Information. 5
Malaya (Federation), Department of
Statistics. 10B1
Malaya, Central Electricity Board.
10H
Malaya, Chief Registration Office.
9G
Malaya, Department of Agriculture.
2, 3
Malaya, Department of Agriculture
and Co-operatives. 10B1

Malaya, Department of Drainage and
Irrigation. 7E, 7C, 10A
Malaya, Department of Information.
11B
Malaya, Department of Information,
Public Relations Office. 11B
Malaya, Department of Labour.
10B5, 10B7, 10D
Malaya, Department of Labour and
Industrial Relations. 10G
Malaya, Department of Mines. 3,
10F
Malaya, Department of Statistics.
9F
Malaya, Department of the Adviser
on Aborigines. 9C2
Malaya, Federal Land Development
Authority. 9I1
Malaya, Federal Legislative
Council. 9I1
Malaya, Federal Ports Committee.
10I
Malaya, Federation of. 10B3, 10B4,
10B6
Malaya, Forest Department. 3
Malaya, Forest Department. Forest
Research Institute, Kepong. 3
Malaya, Forest Service. 10E
Malaya, Geological Survey,
Alexander, J. B. 7C
Malaya, Government Offices. 9I1
Malaya, Government Printing
Department. 2
Malaya, Information Department. 3
Malaya, Institute for Medical
Research. 9G
Malaya, Laws, statutes, etc. 10A
Malaya, Legislature. 11B
Malaya, Malaria Advisory Board. 9G
Malaya, Meteorological Service. 7B
Malaya, Ministry of Agriculture and
Co-operatives. 2, 10B3
Malaya, Museums Department. 6A
Malaya, National Electricity Board
of the States of Malaya. 10H
Malaya, Pineapple Industry. 10B6
Malaya, Prime Minister's
Department, Economic Planning
Unit. 10I
Malaya, Public Relations
Department. 11B
Malaya, Registry of Trade Unions.
10G
Malaya, Rice Committee. 10B3
Malaya, Rice Production Committee.
10B3
Malaya, Rubber Research Institute
of. 10B4
Malaya, South Indian Labour Fund
Board. 10G
Malayan Christian Council. 9I1
Malayan Collieries, Ltd. 10A

384

Tauern, O. D. 9C2
Taunton, H. 4
Tay, T.-H., Wee Y.-C., and Chong
    W.-S. 10B6
Taylor, A. P. 2
Taylor, E. N. 9C3
Taylor, J. C. 11A
Technical Association of Malaysia.
    3
Teeling, William. 4
Teeuw, A. 6A
Teh, Cheang-wan. 9I2
Teilhard de Chardin, P. 9B
Tempany, H. 7E
Tempany, Harold A. 10B3
Temple, Richard. 6A
Templer, Gerald. 11A
Tenison-Woods, Julian E. 7D
Tham, Ah-kow. 7A, 10D
Thio, Eunice. 6A, 11A
Thomas, A. V. 10E
Thomas, K. C. 12
Thomas, P. O. 10B4
Thomas, P. O., and A. Fong Chu-
    chai. 10B4
Thompson, A. 10E7
Thompson, A. M. 10A
Thompson, A., and A. Johnston. 7D
Thompson, Edmund R. 8
Thompson, Elizabeth M. 11B
Thompson, Sir Robert Grainger Ker.
    11B
Thompson, V. 10E3
Thompson, Virginia. 5, 10G, 10I
Thompson, Virginia, and Richard
    Adloff. 10G, 11A
Thomson, A. G. 10F
Thomson, A. M. 10B3
Thomson, Florence A. 9G
Thomson, Florence A., E. Ruiz, and
    M. Bakar. 9G
Thomson, G. G. 12
Thomson, John. 4
Thomson, John Turnbull. 9C2
Thomson, R. K. 10B6
Thong, Yaw-hong. 10A
Thürk, Harry. 4
Tibbetts, G. R. 2
Tiele, P. A. 6A
Tilman, Robert O. 2, 11A
Tilman, Robert O., ed. 11A
Tilman, Robert Oliver. 11A
Tiltman, H. H. 12
Tinker, Irene. 11A
Tippetts, Abbett, McCarthy, and
    Stratton. 10B2
Tisdall, C. E. G. 9C3
Tjoa, Soei-hock. 10A
Tomlinson, H. M. 4
Tomlinson, Henry M. 4
Topley, Marjorie. 9C4, 9E
Tregonning, K. 11A

Tregonning, K. G. 5, 6A, 8, 10A,
    10I, 12
Tregonning, K. G., ed. 6A
Trevor, J. C., and D. R. Brothwell.
    9B
Trimer, George. 10I
Trimmer, G. W. G. 12
Tsou, Pao-chun. 9I2
Tsuji, Masanobu. 12
Tufo, M. V. del. 9F, 10A
Turnbull, C. M. 2, 6A, 11A
Turnbull, Mary. 6A
Turner, G. E. 9C5
Turner, G. E. A. 10G
Turner, P. D. 10B5
Turner, P. D., and R. A. Bull.
    10B5
Turner, P. D., ed. 10B5
Turner, W. 9A
Tweedie, M. W. F. 6A, 7D, 10D
Tweedie, M. W. F., and J. L.
    Harrison. 7D
Tweedie, Michael William Forbes.
    9B
Tylor, E. B. 9C3
Uhle, Max. 9C3
Uhlig, Harald. 8, 9F
Ullman, Edward L. 9I2
Unger, Leonard. 9C4
United Nations. 10A
United Nations Tin Conference. 10F
United Nations, ECAFE. 7B
United Nations, Economic Commission
    for Asia and the Far East. 10A
United Planting Association of
    Malaya. 3
United States Army Command and
    General Staff College. 11B
United States Board on Geographic
    Names. 5
United States Weather Bureau. 7B
United States, Department of State.
    11A
United States, Embassy, Kuala
    Lumpur. 10A
United States, Interdepartmental
    Committee on Nutrition for
    National Defence. 9G
University of Malaya. 3
University of Malaya, Agricultural
    Society. 3
Uno. 9E
Vacher, Henry. 4
Valkenburg, S. van. 8, 10B1
Van der Velde, Edward J. 9C5
Van Loon, F. H. G. 9C3
Van, T. K. 10B3
Vandenbosch, Amry. 9C4
Vanter, Warner. 10B7
Vaughan, J. D. 9C3, 9C4
Veldhuis, J. 10E5

Venkatarangaiya, M. 11A
Verhoeven, F. R. J. 6A, 8, 9C5
Vermont, J. M. B. 9C5
Vickers, W. J., and J. H. Strahan.
  9G
Villa, E. M. de. 10F
Vine, J. M. 9H
Vlieland, C. A. 9F
Volz, Wilhelm. 9C1
Von der Mehden, Fred R. 11A
Vonk, H. 10B4
Voon, Phin-keong. 10B4
Vreede, A. G. 10G
Wah, Francis Chan-wong. 10B4
Waide, Bevan. 10A
Wake, Christopher H. 6A
Wales, Dorothy C., and H. G.
  Quaritch Wales. 9B
Wales, H. G. Quaritch. 9B
Wales, Horace G. Q. 11A
Walker, D. 7C
Walker, T. M. 10B5
Wallace, A. R. 9A
Wallace, Alfred Russel. 4
Wallace, W. A. 9B
Walton, A. B. 10E
Walton, A. B., R. C. Barnard, and
  J. Wyatt-Smith. 10E
Wan, Ming-sing. 9C4
Wang, Gung-wu. 6A, 9B, 9C4, 11A
Wang, Gung-wu, ed. 5
Ward, Marion W. 10A, 10I
Ward, Marion Wybourn. 8
Ward-Jackson, C. 10B4
Warner, Denis. 11A
Warrington Smyth, H. 10I
Warsfold, William B. 12
Watherston, D. C. 10A
Watson, G. A. 10B4
Watson, J. G. 7D, 10E
Watson, Malcolm. 9G
Watson, R. G. 10B2
Watts, I. E. M. 7B
Wavell, Stewart. 4
Weatherford, W. D. 9I1
Weaver, George L. P. 10G
Webb, B. E. 10E
Webber, M. L. 9I1, 10E
Wee, Y.-C., and Ng J.-C. 10B6
Wehl, David. 9C3
Weld, Frederick A. 4
Weller, George A. 12
Wells, Carveth. 4
Wells, Marian. 9C3
Wen, Chung-chi. 9C4
West, A. J. F., and J. Rose. 8
West, Henry W. 10A
Westlake, E. 9C3
Westorp, A. R. 10B4
Wharton, C. R., Jr. 10A
Wharton, Clifton R. 10B1
Wharton, Clifton R., Jr. 9G

Wheatley, J. J. L. 7B
Wheatley, P. 2, 6A
Wheatley, Paul. 6A, 10B1
Wheeler, L. Richmond. 9D, 9E
Wheeler, Leonard Richmond. 9C3
Wheelwright, E. L. 10A
White, Bruce. 10I
White, W. G. 9C2
Whitehead, C. 10B7
Whitford, H. N. 10B4
Whitney, Caspar. 4
Whittingham-Jones, Barbara. 11A
Whittlesey, Charles R. 10B4
Wicki, Josef. D. 6A
Wickizier, Vernon D., and M. K.
  Bennett. 10B3
Wiersbitzky, Kurt. 11A
Wignesan, T., ed. 4
Wijeyewardene, Gehan, ed. 11A
Wijeysingha, Eugene. 9H
Wikkramatileke, R. 8, 9F, 9I1
Wilcox, Clair. 10A
Wild Life Commission of Malaya. 7D
Wilder, William. 9C3
Wilken, G. A. 9C3
Wilkinson, Berkeley, and Robinson.
  10D
Wilkinson, Hugh. 4
Wilkinson, R. J. 6A, 9B, 9C2, 9C3,
  9E, 12
Wilkinson, Richard J., ed. 9C3
Willbourn, E. S. 7C, 10F
Williams, C. N. 10B1
Williams, G. C. Griffith. 9C3
Williams, W. J. 10A
Williams-Hunt, P. D. R. 9B, 9C1,
  9C2, 9C3, 9E
Williams-Hunt, P. D. R., and E. F.
  S. Buxton. 2
Willis, Granville Pratt. 4
Willis, J. C. 10B1
Willmot, R. B. 10A
Wilshaw, R. G. H. 10B3
Wilson, J. N. 7C, 10B1
Wilson, Joan. 10A
Wilson, M. C. 4
Wilson, Peter J. 9C3, 9I1
Wilson, T. B. 10B2, 10B3, 10B5
Winks, Robin W. 11A
Winstedt, R. O. 6A, 7B, 9B, 9C2,
  9E, 11A
Winstedt, R. O., ed. 6A
Winstedt, Richard. 5
Winstedt, Richard O. 9D, 9H
Winstedt, Richard Olof. 9C3
Winstedt, Richard Olof, and G. E.
  Shaw. 9C3
Winstedt, Richard Olof, and P. E.
  de Josselin de Jong. 9C3
Winstedt, Sir Richard O. 4
Wint, Guy. 6A